D1612960

SPINNING FOR LABOUR: TRADE UNIONS AND THE NEW MEDIA ENVIRONMENT

For Winnie with Love

Spinning for Labour: Trade Unions and the New Media Environment

PAUL MANNING
Department of Sociology
De Montfort University

Ashgate
Aldershot • Brookfield USA • Singapore • Sydney

Published by
Ashgate Publishing Limited
Gower House
Croft Road
Aldershot
Hants GU11 3HR
England

Ashgate Publishing Company
Old Post Road
Brookfield
Vermont 05036
USA

British Library Cataloguing in Publication Data
Manning, Paul
   Spinning for labour: trade unions and the new media
   environment
   1.Trade-unions - Great Britain
   I.Title
   331.8'8'0941

Library of Congress Catalog Card Number: 97-078314

ISBN 1 84014 339 8

Printed in Great Britain by The Ipswich Book Company, Suffolk.

Contents

Figures and Tables

Preface

This book has taken rather a long time to produce. The initial idea first came to mind during the 1984-85 Coal Strike; a research proposal was formulated in 1987, field work started in 1991 but the conclusions, in the form of a doctoral thesis, did not emerge from this elongated process until 1995. The 'extended longitudinal' nature of this project was a cause of frustration not only to the author but, no doubt, to his colleagues, supervisors, and family, too. It is, however, a reflection of the contemporary problems shared by academics up and down the country who try to combine heavy teaching and administrative loads with a sustained research effort. During this protracted time, some of the most important aspects of the themes of the research project have undergone almost unprecedented processes of rapid change.

This is one reason for referring to a 'new media environment'. The 'newness' of the media environment can be understood in two senses. Firstly there is, of course, a huge recent expansion in the number of national and local news outlets and very few organisations with a political orientation can now escape the consequences of their immersion in this dynamic news media environment. But secondly, for most trade unions the decision to devise formal strategies to engage with this media environment is, itself, a new development. The arrival of the press officer and spin doctor in the offices of trade unions and labour movement organisations is largely a phenomenon of the last ten years.

The profile of trade unions has changed in ways which simply could not have been anticipated two decades ago and were still accelerating as the research began. Membership has declined significantly for most unions but the bastion of the labour movement is now to be found amongst workers in education, health and white collar sectors rather than the shipbuilding yards, mines and factories of earlier decades. If at the very beginning of this project the National Union of Miners was engaged in a bitter struggle to defend the interests of over 100,000 members (itself, a small fraction of earlier memberships) and their communities, the coal industry is now close to extinction. The labour movement of the mid-1980s, in the early days of this project, remained distinctly 'old labour'; Michael Foot had only just resigned as leader of the Labour Party, Neil Kinnock had yet to embark upon the programme of modernisation which has culminated in the marketing of Tony Blair's New Labour.

However, not only trade unionists but also news journalists have experienced recent and dramatic processes of change. The research commenced in the year Rupert Murdock moved News International to Wapping and subsequently news journalists have undergone not only geographical re-location but, older journalists often believe, social dislocation, too. Traditional journalists' networks have declined along with the 'watering holes' which sustained them; the possibilities of new communication technologies interacting with the growing sensitivity of news organisations to the 'bottom line' have meant that journalists are likely to feel rather more desk-bound in the 1990s. Much of the routine of news journalism can be undertaken by journalists sitting in front of their desk top PCs and next to a telephone. While the field work for this book was undertaken before the full impact of the introduction of electronic news gathering systems could be detected in the news room, such systems were already on the horizon. And as described in subsequent chapters, the traditional specialist news hierarchies were already dissolving and being reconstructed, as the fortunes of industrial journalism waned and news editors turned towards financial news, education and other specialisms.

To what extent do such profound developments in areas central to the concerns of this book undermine its value? I hope the answer is not at all and the reasons for this are partly to do with the nature of the questions the book pursues. Given the ever increasing centrality of the news media in democratic politics, it remains vitally important to assess the extent to which a diverse *range* of voices can secure access to the arenas of the news media. While we may now be familiar with the kinds of techniques the spin doctor employs on behalf of official sources and powerful institutions, it remains a matter of important debate as to whether or not less powerful or non-official organisations can successfully employ news media or communication strategies. Yet, this is a vital question if one accepts that communicative rights should be included in a comprehensive understanding of modern citizenship. Why choose trade unions as examples of non-official sources? One of the fundamental structured inequalities in Britain can still be found in the relationship between capital and labour and despite the best efforts of recent governments trade unions still represent one of the few ways in which ordinary employees can articulate their interests and their perspectives in relation to the politics of the workplace. Trade unions still speak for several million workers occupying subordinate positions in the labour process.

One anxiety an author is likely to have in researching a theme over an extended period of time is that the study may be overtaken by events. In the course of conducting the field work, labour correspondents I had arranged to meet in a Soho pub began to discuss rumours of a book then being written which included references to the penetration of labour and industrial journalism by MI5[1]. This was a proposition which I had hardly considered up to that point and the prospect of employing qualitative field work to smoke out the spooks amongst the journalists I was studying seemed daunting. However, while this study does not address the issue of relations between journalists and the security services, there are sound reasons for believing that the central conclusions it draws remain valid. Similarly, I am confident that these conclusions stand despite the potential of electronic news gathering systems only now beginning to be fully exploited by news organisations. The study suggests that to understand relations between news sources such as trade unions and news media organisations, it is necessary to locate a delicate network of exchange relationships between journalists and news sources, each party seeking to control flows of 'contextual information', in a wider political economic environment which constrains but does not always determine the precise nature of such reciprocal 'bargains'. This, the study contends, lies at the heart of the process through which labour and industrial journalism is produced. The arrival of new communication technologies do not, in themselves, alter these arrangements. Rather, their application will be profoundly shaped by the various interests within the political economic environment and by the nature of the reciprocal relations between news sources and journalists. Similarly, the presence or absence of spooks amongst professional groupings of journalists does not detract from the central importance of such relations, as I hope this book demonstrates.

I hope it is also the case that in some ways the study has been strengthened by being conducted at a time of rapid transition. Certainly, there are difficulties in studying organisations and people in the midst of significant change - eight out of the eleven unions originally selected as subjects merged with other unions, were 'taken over' or changed their names in corporate re-branding exercises during the course of the research, as described in appendix one. Nevertheless, I am convinced that these difficulties are out-weighed by the benefits. After all, the central theme of the study is precisely to do with the organisational attempts of trade unions to adapt to change, particularly in their political and media environments and the interviews with journalists have been lent an additional significance because labour correspondents, too, have been forced to adapt to significant change during this period.

While much of the energy in communication and media studies in recent years has been directed along the theoretical dimension, it remains true that an empirically grounded sociology of the news media still has a great deal to offer. I hope that this study provides one example of the way in which such a sociology can be deployed to address themes which run to the heart of our concerns about the relationship between the news media, structured inequalities and the workings of democratic societies.

Paul Manning

Bedford, October 1997

1. This, it transpired, was Seumas Milne's 'The Enemy Within' (1994).

Acknowledgements

Many people have greatly assisted in the research and writing of this book. Thanks must go firstly to Peter Golding who was always a patient and inspirational supervisor, combining critical rigour, invaluable experience and indefatigable enthusiasm in equal measure. The arguments, conclusions and deficiencies of this book, however, are my responsibility alone. I also owe an enormous debt to the many trade union officers and journalists who were so helpful and patient in allowing me to waste their time. It would take too long to identify each one here but their names are listed in appendix two and I am grateful to each one. Thanks must go also to my colleagues in the Sociology Department, particularly Bob Blanchard and Phil Brown, to De Montfort University for granting me study leave for one semester, and to the staff within the Polhill campus library.

I am grateful to Tim Jones and *Times* Newspapers Limited for permission to quote from 'Overtime Ban May Hit 999 Calls' ©*Times* Newspapers 1989, the *Sun* newspaper for permission to quote from 'Troops on Standby as Mercy Men Turn the Screw' and other reports (© The *Sun*), Mirror Syndication International for permission to quote from '999 Men Overtime Ban Goes Ahead' and other news reports (©*Daily Mirror* 1989), Express Newspapers PLC for permission to use quotes from 'What Price the Lifesavers?' and other *Daily Express* reports (© Express Newspapers 1989), The Independent newspaper for permission to include copyright material, and Keith Harper, Angella Johnson and Guardian Newspapers Limited for permission to quote from 'Emergency Cover As Overtime Ban Begins' and other news reports(*The Guardian*©). I am grateful to the editors of Media Culture Society and Sage Publications Limited for permission to reproduce some of the interview transcripts.

Finally, thanks are due to Winnie, Daniel, Peter and Michael for stimulating such vigorous debates around the kitchen table.

Abbreviations

ACTT	Association of Cinematographic, Television and Allied Technicians
AFL-CIO	American Federation of Labor - Congress of Industrial Organisations
APEX	Association of Professional, Executive, Clerical and Computer Staff
ASTMS	Association of Scientific, Technical and Managerial Staff
AUE	Amalgamated Union of Engineering Workers
AUEE	Amalgamated Union of Engineering and Electrical Workers
CPSA	Civil and Public Services Association
COHSE	Confederation of Health Service Employees
EETPU	Electrical, Electronic, Telecommunication and Plumbing Union
GMB	National Union of General and Municipal Workers
IPMS	Institute of Professional and Managerial Staff
LIPA	Labor Institute of Public Affairs
MSF	Manufacturing, Services and Finance Union
NALGO	National Association of Local Government Officers
NEDDY	National Economic Development Council
NGA	National Graphical Association
NUCPS	National Union of Civil and Public Servants
NUHKW	National Union of Hosiery and Knitwear Workers
NUKFA	National Union of Knitwear, Footwear and Apparel Trades
NUM	National Union of Miners
NUPE	National Union of Public Employees
NUS	National Union of Students
NUT	National Union of Teachers
NUTGW	National Union of Tailors and Garment Workers
POEU	Post Office Engineering Union
TASS	Transport and Salaried Staff Association
TGWU	Transport and General Workers Union
TUC	Trade Union Congress
UCW	Union of Communication Workers
WIRS	Workplace Industrial Relations Survey

1 Introduction: Trade Unions and their 'Enemies Front Line Troops'

Why study the relationship between trade unions and the mass media, yet again? After all, the question of how trade unions were represented in the news media was all but fully exhausted almost twenty years ago. Since then, unions have hardly acquired greater political significance, as their membership bases have haemorrhaged and they have been bounced off the political centre stage by a government determined to re-cast workplace relations in ways which afford trade unions only a 'supporting' role at best. They are regarded by journalists, particularly those who cut their professional teeth during the height of Mrs Thatcher's 'reign', as relics from an earlier and quite different historical period. And now, as a consequence of the huge erosion in membership, even the TUC, itself, is having to implement major cut backs in resourcing and impose a cost-saving re-organisation of its departmental structure. There is no better symbolic representation of the TUC's recent history than the changes which have occurred at its London headquarters, Congress House, where the TUC's own administrative apparatus has shrunk from four floors to two and rooms along empty corridors are now rented out to commercial companies.

At first glance, then, there seems little justification for rehearsing old arguments and exploring dated material. However, while the status of union elites as 'political insiders' in the past might be questioned, there seems little doubt that unions now must be regarded as 'outsiders'.[1] There remains quite a lot that media sociology has yet to explore concerning the nature of the relationship between the news media and politically marginalised groups. How do such groups seek access to the news production process and how successful can they hope to be? Two related developments now make this question even more pertinent. Since the 1970s, when trade union relations with news media last enjoyed sustained academic attention, there has been a significant growth in the range of news media both at national and local level. In this sense, trade unions now inhabit a rather more complex or 'new' news media environment. And secondly, as shall be discussed further in chapter two, trade unions have been encouraged by authoritative political voices within and outside the labour movement to embrace the new techniques of communication strategies and news media management. Trade unions now confront an environment in which there is both an increase in the sheer quantity of news discourse - something from which they do not necessarily benefit - and a world in which there is heightened sensitivity to the contours and quality of news coverage. News coverage, in itself, is now an important political issue for any large organisation.

At an even more fundamental level these questions point to issues which should always be of concern to sociologists and those interested in how societies reproduce and disseminate ideas. Seventeen years ago Golding and Murdock complained that, too often, a sociology of the mass media was severed from wider questions regarding stratification and power (1977:2-13). It remains as true today that,

> Groups can remain dominant only if they have the resources to reproduce their dominance. This is not only true economically, but also socially, culturally, and especially ideologically. (Van Dijk,1991:32).

The mass media in general and the news media in particular, will inevitably reflect the most important relations of domination and subordination in society and will play an important part in their reproduction. As such relations change, so such changes will be reflected in the politics and practices of news production. An interest in the ways in which subordinate groups mobilise symbolic, communicative and material resources to intervene in the news production process should be a perennial preoccupation not only for media sociologists but for all those concerned with the ways in which power is reproduced.

Relations between capital and labour remain not the only but one of the most crucial patterns of domination and subordination in late capitalist societies, such as Britain, and continue to be characterised by both material and symbolic conflict. Trade unions have long played an important part in defending the interests of labour against capital but they have also played a part as ideological agencies in the continued reproduction of such patterns of subordination. Although Engels described unions in England as 'schools of war', according to Hyman they should be regarded as 'at one and the same time, part of the problem and part of the solution, a form of resistance to capitalism and a form of integration within capitalism' (Hyman 1985:123). Of course, the view that trade unions help to incorporate oppositional sections in the workforce, as well as articulate their demands, is hardly a new theme. A variety of writers have sought to describe the politically contradictory position that unions may find themselves in, both at the structural level (for example, Anderson,1967; Coates and Topham,1980; Milliband,1991: ch3) and in terms of the micro-politics of the workplace (for example, Lane and Roberts,1971; Nichols and Benyon,1977). As the political relationships of the post-war settlement crystallised, so the contradictory position of trade unions was thrown into sharper relief, prompting theorists of corporatism to describe formal union organisations in terms of an integrative politics (for example, Middlemas,1979) and writers further to the left, to describe unions as 'the brokers between labour and the state' (Milliband,1982:56).

So in the past, formal union organisations have often generated contradictory political impulses, expressed both in terms of the mobilisation of material and symbolic resources. However, relations of domination and subordination are never static and over the last fifteen years, both formal and unofficial union organisations have been subjected to a ferocious political assault directed from the centre of government which has, paradoxically, delineated more clearly the traditional political role of unions in defending the interests of labour.

Given the role of the mass media in both reflecting and reproducing the most important patterns of domination and subordination, the heightened tensions and shifts in the balance of forces between capital and labour will find expression in the work of the news media. If such conflicts are of both a material and symbolic nature then it is likely that the news media, themselves, will be identified as an arena through which material and symbolic resources will be mobilised by the groups engaged in conflict. This is not to suggest that the news media can be conceived as neutral arenas or 'level playing fields', - particular news media will be characterised by particular ideological configurations which present specific difficulties and opportunities for those seeking access to the process of news production. Neither is it to suggest that such processes are new. The reverberations of the conflicts between capital and labour are always likely to surface through the practice and output of the news media. However, in times of exacerbated conflict such reverberations are louder and the strategic political importance of the news is revealed all the more clearly for those groups engaged in conflict.

This is why the issue of news communication is always likely to be identified by both trade unionists and the representatives of capital as of particular importance during periods of heightened industrial tension as in, for example, the 1890s (Harrison, 1974: chs 8 and 9) or 1926 (Curran and Seaton, 1985:67-68) and why, as will be discussed below, during the late 1970s and 1980s, the issue of news communication became a sharper political issue within the workplace, itself.

In the period after 1979, the trade union movement experienced more rapid rates of change in the political and economic landscape. These changes were important not only for the ways in which they refashioned the political environment for trade unions and posed particular problems of communication and ideological construction, externally, but also because they prompted important questions concerning the values and commitments which formed the internal ideological framework of the labour movement. During this most recent period, then, trade unions have been compelled to address issues of communication and the deployment of symbolic and material resources in communicative activity in terms of both external and internal environments.In terms of the external environment, for example, we find a number union journals attempting to reconstruct the language and vocabulary of trade unionism in response to the ideological legacy of the 1979 'Winter of Discontent' and the accumulation of negative imagery deposited by the news media over several decades.[2] In the work of the union press officers (chapters three and four) we find a concious and explicit attempt to counter this imagery through the application of particular 'news work' skills in the course of their work in presenting their unions to the outside world . As we shall see, the communications strategy employed by the ambulance workers unions, during the 1989 dispute, to secure more favourable external communication treatment was regarded as sufficiently important to shape the industrial tactics employed (chapter eight).

On the other hand, the crisis brought about by economic structural change and hostile political intervention also triggered internal conflicts within the labour movement and these, too, found expression in symbolic as well as material form. For example, the conflicts generated by the rise of 'new realism' in the 1980s were articulated partly through the journals and media work of the unions involved. As some prominent unions sought to establish a position of hegemony within the labour movement so, too, the associated   political   struggles   found   expression   through   union communication work.[3] Changes in the economic structural position of unions, their relation to the state, and in their place in the relations of domination and subordination between capital and labour, have compelled unions to re-think and revise their approaches to issues of communication (chapter two).

There is, though, another compelling set of reasons why not only media sociologists but also those interested in the workings of power and democracy should take more than a passing interest in the attempts made by trade unionists to come to terms with an era of 'media saturation'.

Trade Unions, the news media and the public sphere

In his earliest formulation of the concept, Habermas suggests that the public sphere, 'may be conceived above all as the sphere of private people come together as a public...'(1989:27).That is to say, through the productive energies unleashed by seventeenth and eighteenth century capitalism in Europe (economic relations orientated towards the market rather than the household, the emergence of printing and publishing industries, and the creation of new forums for the exchange of ideas including the salon, the coffee house and the theatre) a new space located between the 'private realm' of market transactions and bourgeois family life, on the one hand, and the 'sphere of public authority' (the state and the monarchy) on the other, emerges in which for the first time not only 'the general rules governing...commodity exchange and social labour', but the very authority of the state to regulate public discourse become the subject of *public* debate (1989:27). For Habermas, while these developments are inextricably bound up with the development of a political consciousness and the implicit delineation of political interests, nonetheless the nature of such debate was characterised by both a rationality (in the sense that ultimate authority was assumed to rest not upon a doctrine of absolutism but rather reasoned argument) and a commitment to the principle of universality in terms of participation (1989:53).

The criticisms of Habermas' early formulation are familiar and, indeed, now partly acknowledged by the author (Habermas, 1994). It rests upon an idealised vision of 'a golden age' which underestimates the extent to which bourgeois class interests were successfully represented as a public interest and the extent to which voices other than those of the male bourgeoisie were excluded (Garnham,1986:44). Similarly, it may exaggerate the degree to which debate within the early 'public sphere' was characterised either by reasoned debate or a commitment to the principle of universalism (Dahlgren,1991:5). Certainly, the omission of any sustained discussion of the forums in which alternative class interests might be articulated leaves the historical account incomplete (Curran:1991:40). This is curious given Habermas' acknowledgement of the existence of a 'plebeian public sphere' and the work of the Chartist Movement in the preface to 'The Structural Transformation of the Public Sphere' (1989:xviii). Habermas makes it clear at the outset that he is concerned only with the 'bourgeois public sphere'; the 'plebeian public sphere' he argues, made only a brief historical appearance before being suppressed. And yet, given his view of the 'public sphere' as a forum through which 'private people come together as a public'; that is as a mechanism for harnessing the power of a multitude of individuals each contributing to rational but critical debate, it is surprising that the role of trade unions in the late nineteenth and twentieth centuries, together with other communicative activities within the 'plebeian public sphere', are not accorded a greater recognition.

For Habermas, by the end of the nineteenth century (at the time that trade unions in Britain were discovering a political voice), the energies within European capitalism responsible for promoting and expanding the 'public sphere' were now contributing to its terminal decline, as new and reinvigorated market energies (the growing importance of advertising, and the expansion of commercial markets in the nineteenth century; twentieth century tendencies towards concentration and conglomeration in media ownership) 'invaded' the public sphere and placed new limitations upon the circulation of ideas and the possibility for rational debate. Most importantly, the growing dominance of public relations as part of both commercial and state activity brought about a 'refeudalisation' of the public sphere, as authority bestowed by reasoned argument was supplanted by a return to forms of authority secured through rituals of representation (1989:195).

To the critics, just as Habermas idealises the public sphere of the eighteenth century, by the same measure he underestimates the vitality and diversity of public spheres to be found in societies of advanced and late capitalism (Curran,1991). While the pressures and constraints imposed by the dominance of private capital and commercial energies upon the mass media should not be underestimated, it is still possible to point to 'micro-spheres' within the bourgeois public sphere and to 'alternative public realms' (Downing,1992), where reasoned debate can be extended beyond the boundaries defined by political and commercial public relations. In this context, trade unions have, potentially, an important part to play. Not only have they historically provided a 'plebeian public sphere' in which private working people 'came together as a public'. Trade unions also provided one channel through which the debates and concerns of the 'plebeian public sphere' could be presented to the bourgeois or mainstream 'public sphere'. In this sense, the question of the position of trade unions in relation to the news media is also a question of citizenship and enfranchisement.

Despite the weaknesses in Habermas' early formulation, the concept of the public sphere remains an important analytic category, not to be abandoned (Garnham,1986). For the purposes of this study, it reminds us that a sociology of news sources presents a series of important questions for the study of mainstream politics and the democratic process. Trade unions continue to represent the main channel through which the aspirations and interests of those located in the workplace can be presented in the public domain and directed towards the formal political system. They continue to represent thirty-six per cent of the working population (Central Statistical Office, 1995:74). Beyond this, they have an important role to play in the marshalling of arguments in current debates concerning the future of public institutions and public services,- arguments which properly should be made if such institutions and services are not to fall victim to the advocates of radical marketisation by default. In the contemporary political climate, one of the most prominent features of a healthy 'public sphere' should be a sustained debate regarding the future of public provision of services and facilities, involving a wide and diverse range of voices, not merely those 'loud' voices with a predatory interest in privatisation. The extent to which trade unions can secure the coherent presentation of their agendas and an effective representation of their perspectives is one indicator of the health of the mainstream public sphere and, of course, the news media have a crucial role to play in this respect.

This is particularly important given the decline of the 'plebeian public sphere' with the loss of the Daily Herald and the difficulties in sustaining an alternative, left wing press. In the experience of trade unions in Britain in recent years there are grounds to support the pessimism of Habermas' picture of the public sphere in the twentieth century. National broadcasting has offered only infrequent opportunities for trade unions to construct coherent presentations of their arguments. Despite considerable lobbying effort being expended by the TUC, Channel Four scrapped 'Union World' in the late 1980s and live coverage of the TUC conference continued to diminish throughout the same period. Popular national newspapers take less interest in labour news; some no longer employ industrial correspondents and broadsheet papers devote less space to the reporting of industrial affairs. Yet, in terms of national news coverage, it is only the broadsheet papers, with their comparatively low circulations, which unions can depend upon as channels of access to the public sphere.

The historic paradox for trade unions is that their new found interest in communication strategies, news media work and the arts of presentation has arrived just at the point when their access to the public sphere is diminishing both for the specific reasons noted above and as a result of the broader threats to the public sphere arising from deregulation of media markets, increasing commercial pressures and the frailty of public sector broadcasting, - the patterns Habermas anticipated in his account of the 're-feudalisation' of the public sphere. It is now fashionable to present a picture of the media and media practices as disconnected from their material context. Such an idealist account has been encouraged both by certain developments in social theory (the growing influence of postmodernism) and by the enormous expansion in the 'public relations industry', which in promoting itself, highlights the 'skills of PR' whilst masking the question of the distribution of resources, - economic and political, as well as symbolic, - which is both likely to determine the success of any communications strategy and which acts to disadvantage and exclude particular social groups and communities. To the extent that a few trade unions have embraced the philosophy of corporate public relations, they have accepted a 'postmodern prescription' for their ills.

In contrast, Habermas formulates the question of access to the public sphere in essentially material terms and, consequently highlights, 'the need to consider the future of democratic politics, and of the institutions and practices of public communication...in terms of the allocation of scarce resources' (Garnham,1986:43). Habermas' formulation directs our attention to questions of how economic, political and symbolic resources can be deployed in the attempt to secure access to the public sphere, and to the nature of the social practices involved in such processes. And yet, as Garnham argues, a weakness of Habermas' account is that he, himself, is reluctant to formulate questions in these terms. There is little consideration of the process of political mediation (Garnham,1986:44), through which particular sources of information or knowledge secure privileged positions in relation to the public sphere, effectively acting as 'knowledge brokers'.

In seeking to describe the attempts of trade unions to come to terms with the news media this study may contribute towards a critical assessment of the value of 'the postmodern prescription' or corporate public relations diagnosis for trade union ills. More importantly, it will seek to describe the concrete, material practices through which a still important representational group seeks to secure access to the public sphere. The nature of the obstacles and constraints which impede such attempts will provide some guide, at least, as to the degree to which the pattern of relations between the news media, political institutions and representational or pressure groups can sustain an inclusive, universalistic and open public sphere, regarded as desirable in a democracy.

Trade Unions and their 'front line enemies'

The original plan for this research was prompted by events during the Coal Strike of 1984-85 and a series of exchanges which appeared in the *Guardian* between journalists and Nell Myers, assistant to the President of the NUM and the official responsible for the union's press and media work. Patrick Wintour (*The Guardian* 20th May 1985) took the view that the public relations performance of the NUM had been ineffective and that with the application of more efficient techniques for dealing with the news media the union would have been able to secure more favourable news coverage. Greater attention to press and media work; more briefings, a greater willingness to respond to journalists' enquiries, a recognition of the appetites of news organisations for daily supplies of fresh information would all have helped to reverse the tide of hostile or ill-informed coverage. This view was later endorsed by other industrial correspondents (Torrode, 1985; Adeney and Lloyd, 1986; Jones, N, 1986). Nell Myers argued, however, that there was little to be gained for the NUM in investing greater effort or resources in media work. The representation of the dispute through the national news media had to be placed in the context of dominant political and economic structures and the distribution of power in a capitalist society:

> The industrial correspondents, along with broadcasting technicians are basically our enemies' front line troops. They are used as canon fodder by editors and proprietors who throughout the strike were in regular consultation with Cabinet Ministers and Coal Board chiefs. (Nell Myers, The Guardian 3rd June 1985).

No amount of energetic media work, careful presentation, briefing of industrial correspondents, or investment in corporate communication strategies would alter the 'inevitable' ideological representation of the union, given the location of the news media in relation to the main centres of economic and political power.

This debate touched upon a number of enduring sociological issues relating to the nature of power, the effectivity of structure and the role of the news media. It also prompted questions about the importance of pressure groups, trade unions and similar organisations as sources of news. In the late 1980s there remained an absence of much empirical research on the relationship between organisations as news sources and journalists, - a gap only just beginning to be filled through the work of Deacon (1996), Tumber and Schlesinger (1995), Anderson (1991 and 1993), Schlesinger et al. (1991), Ericson et al. (1989). And yet, it was widely recognised by academics employing a variety of perspectives that the news media were becoming increasingly important as a central arena of political activity (Newton, 1988). In other words, groups organised around particular clusters of interests might invest significant energy and resources in seeking access to the process of news production as a primary objective. Lobbying might involve lobbying the news media as well as the government. And yet, as Nell Myers' response above suggests, there are good grounds for doubting the effectivity of such strategies for groups positioned politically on the margins of conventional Westminster party politics. For many, the ideological and structural position of news media institutions; their dependence upon the 'primary definers' of the state, their restricted lists of 'accredited witnesses' and the integration of many news organisations within formidable structures of private economic ownership, would imply the 'inevitable' futility of attempts, however fashionable, to make public relations work for the groups and organisations of the left.

The present research represents an attempt to explore empirically, on a small scale, these 'big' issues. Although there is now a huge literature on the sociology of journalism and news production, little has been written on the strategies employed by non-official sources to overcome the obstacles of structure, ideology and organisation which confront them in the routine practice of the news media. The 'media work' of environmental pressure groups, voluntary organisations and outsider groups in the sphere of crime and penal policy is now beginning to be reported but despite the obvious interest, given the ideological and political positioning of trade unions, in exploring the effectivity of union news media strategies, not much progress has been made in the last twenty years beyond the first tentative steps taken in the preliminary work of the Glasgow University Media Group (1976:ch 6; Philo and Hewitt, 1976). The whole question of the representation of the labour process in the news media has been out of academic fashion, of course, for most of this period and is only now beginning to re-awaken the interest of media researchers (Puette,1993; Philo,1990; Douglas,1986). For the first time in a number of years academic and political interests have coincided to focus upon the relationship between trade unions and the news media[4] but the specific question of the role of trade unions as sources and, in particular, the work of trade union press and media officers, remains neglected.

In some ways, this is rather surprising because there has been an explosion in both the public relations industry and in the voluminous literature on 'do-it yourself' public relations for non-commercial organisations. The huge growth in state sponsored public relations over the last two decades has been noted by Golding (1992:507) and Altheide and Johnson (1980); a comparable tendency in local government charted by Franklin (1986). In tandem with the familiar growth in corporate and financial public relations (*The Economist*,1989; Newman,1984), it is now common place for all manner of occupational groups and voluntary organisations to engage in public relations work. Thus, there is a literature on how best to 'handle the media' for groups who may feel exposed by the harsher ideological winds of the right blowing through much of the news media in recent years, including social workers (Walder,1991; Dossett-Davies,1987; Eastman,1987), probation officers (Smyth,1990), voluntary organisations (Jones,1984), 'workers and community activists' (MacShane,1983), health authorities (Hyde,1987), scientists (Jerome,1986), and even sociologists (Gans,1989). The literature extends beyond the ideologically vulnerable to those groups who may normally feel quite comfortable when subjected to the gaze of the news media,- including prison officers (Deas,1988) and the police (Fry,1991; Hyder,1989; Hodges,1987).

The problem, of course, with the majority of 'do-it-yourself' public relations guides is that they are rarely theoretically informed and frequently grounded in only the most insubstantial, anecdotal empirical material. The result is, too often, a discussion characterised by a naive account of the process of political communication in which the problems ideologically marginalised groups experience are judged to be the result of a failure to communicate rather than the consequence of the institutionalised practices of news production or the structural positioning of news sources and news organisations. For example, a recent handbook on public relations for the 'human services' tells us that:

> Many of the barriers that exist to the achievement of positive media treatment of human service topics are primarily psychological in nature. (Brawley,1983:13).

Gloomy social workers, too often on the defensive, have underestimated the extent to which the mass media can represent an opportunity rather than a threat, the handbook insists. The task must be to break down the 'barriers to communication' - the 'professional insulation' of social workers and their unhelpful reluctance to discuss their work in terms of simple news friendly propositions (Brawley,1983:34-35). While the popular news values of news organisations are recognised as a problem for which an appropriate public relations strategy must be devised, the aim must be to project a 'clearer image' of social work in order to alter the stereotyped image of the profession (1983:27-35). Why and where from these stereotypes have arisen is not discussed. In order to answer these questions, it would be necessary to apply a theoretical lens which permitted discussion of the political context and ideological structures governing the social representation of welfare provision at specific historical moments (Golding and Middleton, 1982). After all, according to Franklin and Parton, for much of the news media social workers have become "a metaphor for the entire public sector, personifying the 'evil' which the political new right presumes to be inherent therein" (1991:9). This is not to dismiss, out of hand, the techniques advocated in such textbooks,- one of the central themes in this study is to consider their effectivity in the context of union communications. However, an approach which fails to empirically explore the politics of source and news media interaction or to place such interaction in the wider context of power distribution, organisational structure and ideology, will be unable to grasp the complexity of the news communication process.

It is common to find empirically unsubstantiated assumptions about the effectivity of public relations work in even the more theoretically sophisticated accounts of how marginal and ideologically vulnerable groups may engage with the news media. To take the example of social work briefly once more, Franklin and Parton note that voluntary and private sector social work enjoys 'a much more positive media representation...' which they attribute to 'the much more proactive public relations strategies...', that organisations, such as the NSPCC and the Save the Children Fund have adopted in contrast to the statutory sector (1991:44). Little hard empirical evidence is offered to support this explanation. Later, however, in the same chapter they appear much less confident regarding the effectivity of proactive public relations, suggesting that media coverage of social work reflects 'circumstances of political, economic and ideological change...' and that only:

> ...structural changes in the nature of social work, or in the political economy and the new welfare consensus , might radically shift media presentations of the profession. But such reasoning smacks of determinism and recourse to a media strategy of passive fatalism. A proactive media relations policy may be able to achieve only limited objectives, but these are extremely valuable and there appear to be few alternatives. (Franklin and Parton,1991:52).

This encapsulates precisely the question which requires empirical exploration. Between the 'doomsday' scenario of Nell Myers and the gung-ho naivety of the public relations textbooks, lies the middle ground reality of structural and political limitation, on the one hand, and the impact of agency and skilled intervention, on the other. The ambivalence in Franklin and Parton's final conclusion arises from the uncertainty of concrete, empirical circumstances. Much has been written on the ways in which we should describe, theoretically, the relationship between the news media and their political and economic environments. We know a great deal now about the routine practices of news journalists. We know much less about the effectivity of the techniques and strategies marginal or unofficial news sources may use to negotiate the various structural, political and ideological barriers which may obstruct their attempts to offer alternative perspectives and agendas through the news media.

This chapter will now briefly consider what bodies of theoretical literature are available to assist in the analysis of the relationship between news sources, such as trade unions, and the national news media. The conclusion to be drawn is that this area has been, until very recently, neglected both empirically and theoretically.

Trade union communications: a gap in the literature

In beginning to consider the relationship between unions and news sources we might anticipate relevant concepts and insights to be offered by three research traditions:
i)   Conventional pressure group theory
ii) The sociology of industrial relations
iii) The sociology of journalism and news production.

Conventional Pressure Group Theory

If, as Schlesinger suggests (1990), one of the problems with much of the sociology of journalism is its 'media-centrism', then equally the problem with a great deal of the work on pressure groups is its 'state-centrism'. A common assumption running through much of the conventional pressure group literature is that the primary objective of any pressure group, sectional or promotional, insider or outsider, is to secure influence within the central or local state. Thus, in the early post war 'classic' accounts we find Finer defining pressure groups in terms of their attempts 'to influence the policy of public bodies in their own chosen direction' (1966:3), while Eckstein even more emphatically insists that,

> Basically, it is always the interplay of government structures, activities and attitudes which determines the form of pressure group politics.in a given society. (1960:17).

There seems little scope for the exploration of source media relations in these early approaches. More recently Richardson and Jordan insist that organisations only count as pressure groups if their main aim is to attempt to persuade 'the authorities in the political system or sub-system' [that they] 'should make an authoritative allocation' (1985:16) and even more recent pressure group textbooks retain similarly narrow definitions (see for example, Smith,1993:2).

Such state or government-centric definitions almost preclude the possibility of theoretically constituting the mass media as an additional arena for lobbying activity. And yet, there are very good grounds for developing just such a theoretical model. Some political organisations appear to have much wider ambitions than simply winning influence within government or amending particular legislative paragraphs. The 'new social movements', for example, have much broader agendas concerned with encouraging wider changes in values and lifestyle (Roche,1995; Scott,1990) and the mass media are often identified as playing an important part in this process. Even on a less ambitious scale, a number of groups who are ultimately concerned with securing influence within the state, identify the mass media (rightly or wrongly) as offering an important tool in cultivating an appropriate climate of opinion as a pre-condition for more focused lobbying of the state. The National Union of Communication Workers, for example, has recently been identified by political correspondents as the organisation behind a successful lobbying campaign to obstruct government plans to privatise the Post Office. The *Daily Telegraph* was targeted as a key news medium because it was likely to be read by large numbers of voters living in the constituencies of back bench Conservative MPs.

Beyond this, there are a number of lobbying groups which have at times explicitly identified mass media organisations rather than the policy making institutions as their prime targets for political activity including, for example, groups campaigning against sexism and racism in the media or against the misrepresentation of unions or other groups (Manning,1991). Broader definitions of pressure groups and more flexible approaches to the study of the lobbying process in the pressure group literature would allow a deeper and more fruitful investigation of the relationship between such political organisations and the mass media. The typologies conventionally used to classify pressure groups also tend to deflect rather than concentrate theoretical attention upon the mass media. Simple dichotomies between 'promotional' and 'sectional' (Potter,1961:25) or between non-economic and economic interest groups (Moran,1989:123; Marsh,1983) focus attention upon the values and ambitions of members in relation to state policy, not the strategies employed. In turn, the various relationships which may exist between pressure groups and the mass media are frequently entirely overlooked.

Yet, these relationships in their own right can be crucial in determining the options open to particular groups. Golding and Middleton show that journalists frequently distinguished between the 'reliable' and the 'unreliable' political axe-grinding groups (1982:119). A 'legitimacy' on the pages, particularly, of the broad sheet press is likely to be of assistance in achieving legitimacy in the eyes of ministers and officials within state departments, too. We know, for example, that the CPAG, Shelter and some other groups in the 'poverty lobby' were able to accumulate political capital through the shrewd use of media campaigning in their early years during the 1960s and early 1970s.[5] Both Shelter and the CPAG ensured that their headquarters were located in very close proximity to Fleet Street, despite the very high office rents, because as Des Wilson explained, '...it would cost us a lot more if were not there. Shelter has been built by, and around, the communication world, and it owes a lot to its close proximity to the media' (Wilson,1970:158).

In recent years an alternative way of classifying groups in terms of their proximity to the departments of state has become widely accepted. Grant (1990 and 1985) distinguishes between 'insider groups' who enjoy regular access to government departments and 'outsiders' who are denied such privileged access. However, he further subdivides insider groups into 'prisoners', dependent upon government for a variety of reasons and 'low profile' or 'high profile' groups. 'Low profile groups' opt for behind the scenes negotiation with government officials while 'high profile' groups seek to exploit the mass media to strengthen their position. 'Outsiders' are also sub-divided into 'potential insiders', 'outside groups by necessity' (these groups lack the required skills or resources to win insider status though this may simply mean formulating politically 'unrealistic' demands) and 'ideological outsiders' who prefer to remain on the outside, rather than embrace the 'rules of the game' which govern relations between government and 'insider groups'. What is important about Grant's typology is that it directs attention towards questions of ideology and legitimacy as well as access. If, as Grant implies, those groups who project 'radical' values and objectives, are less likely to enjoy 'insider' status, this suggests that the mass media may play a crucial part in 'constructing' the ideological and political status of such groups. We know, for example, that both the CPAG and Shelter were careful to publicly distance themselves from the more militant wing of the poverty lobby (Whitely and Winyard, 1984:35-36; Seyd 1975:426).

Although the insider-outsider typology is suggestive and prompts further questions regarding the 'politics' of source-media interaction, these are rarely explored in the conventional pressure group literature. The insider-outside model might usefully be applied to news media organisations, themselves. Journalists frequently distinguish between sources whose track record of 'reliability' and 'usefulness' normally ensures that they can secure a correspondents attention and those 'axe-grinding' groups who lack sufficient political credibility to command the attention of news journalists and consequently, remain on the 'outside'. To secure media attention these groups have to work harder, organise publicity stunts and generate high profile 'celebrity' status (Gitlin, 1980:ch 5) though the danger is that such strategies can further reinforce an ideological marginality (Greenberg, 1985).

What is required is a model of the political process which describes the dynamic inter-play between the political standing of groups in the eyes of government, their status in the eyes of the news media and the skills and strategies (the 'political and cultural capital') which particular groups can draw upon. Beyond this level, of course, deeper questions of power and structure have to be addressed. Unfortunately, the roots of conventional pressure group theory in pluralism have, in the past, tended to encourage a narrow focus upon the empirically measurable process of decision making and away from the broader questions of power (broadly defined), ideological legitimacy and the work of the news media.[6] As has been frequently pointed out, a narrow focus on decision making and political outcomes is likely to ignore the dimension of non-decision making and agenda setting (Crenson, 1971).

Even where the role of the news media is included in a model of the decision making process, the methodology of pressure group theory is unlikely to capture either the processes through which the news media might impact upon the state or the 'media work' undertaken by pressure groups in the process. Kingdon, for example, simply asked the U.S. government officials involved in his case studies of transport and health policy, whether or not they had been consciously influenced by media coverage to which the majority, not surprisingly, replied in the negative (Kingdon, 1984). Grant, himself, has studied those pressure groups broadly representing the interests of capital (1987;1983 and 1977) and yet without including a sustained empirical investigation of the ways in which the significant command over resources, enjoyed by these groups, can be deployed in media work or the 'cultivation of opinion' preceding decision making (or non-decision making). Noting the dissatisfaction of the Chemical Industries Association with news coverage of industrial issues is not an adequate investigation of the ideological 'pull' which capital may exert over the processes through which news is represented and nor is it sufficient to refute the main thrust of the Glasgow University Media Group's work (Grant, 1987:31-35). Too many questions are left begging. Infrequency of coverage of particular sections of capital or of other powerful groups does not, in itself, prove a lack of influence. This is precisely the point Crenson (1971) seeks to establish in his 'classic' study of 'silent' agenda setting; a large steel corporation can exert influence over the public sphere, including the news agenda, by simply having a presence in a local community. It may not have to lift a finger.

At the same time, however, the conventional pressure group literature frequently pictures the mass media as 'channels of last resort'. The 'state centrism', characteristic of conventional pressure group theory, leads writers to conclude that resort to 'high profile' media campaigning is an indication that an 'insider' group's influence is on the wane (Grant 1990:ch 1; 1985). Far better to be on the 'inside' enjoying quiet dialogue with government. Only groups lacking real influence in government will go public.This common assumption can be found in much of the writing on pressure groups dating back to the early post war 'classic' texts (Rose, 1974:252; Finer, 1966:83; Eckstein,1960:73). However, just as a low media profile may not indicate either a lack of ideological 'gravitational pull' or, indeed, confirm a powerful influence in government, so the application of 'high profile' media techniques may not automatically imply that the doors of the state are shut. We have already noted that in the pre-Thatcher era, the poverty lobby used carefully calibrated news media campaigning to accumulate political capital and establish credentials in the eyes of relevant state departments. Far from representing the channels of last resort, the news media may offer one set of routes through which power can be consolidated. This may be even more true in the contemporary political environment in which public relations techniques and spin doctoring now represent central processes at the heart of government (Golding, 1992).

To summarise, for the purposes of this study, the weakness of conventional pressure group theory lies in its privileging of state orientated political activity above all other forms and its consequent failure to recognise the central importance of the news media as an arena for political work, independent of, but related to the state. Indeed, the news media represent not one but several distinct arenas (Cracknell, 1993). It is for this reason, that important empirical questions concerning the nature and effectivity of media strategies and interventions into the news production process by pressure groups and sources are rarely posed.

Industrial Relations Theory

Demanding of researchers and theorists in the field of industrial relations that they should have anticipated the growing importance of communications might be compared to condemning modern European historians for not anticipating the fall of the Berlin Wall. It might be argued that there was very little in the routine of British industrial relations in the first two decades after the Second World War to suggest the dramatic growth in commercial and corporate public relations in the 1980s. It is clearly the case that most representatives of both sides of industry continued to largely ignore the issue of communication for a very a long time. As far as journalists were concerned, managers and the representatives of capital were habitually much worse at public relations than their trade union counterparts (Adeney, 1983). And although we know that large corporations were beginning to study the example of corporate America in the use of public relations campaigns to, for example, ward off the threat of nationalisation, as early as the early 1950s (Finer, 1966), these strategies tended not to touch the routine working lives of most managers or union representatives.

Thus, there was little in the empirical nature of the field to prompt a sustained interest in either trade unions or business organisations as sources of news. And the central thrust of the dominant theoretical influences within the field also directed attention away from questions of communication and the mass media. Nevertheless, the growth of white collar unionism, which was noted and identified as of major significance, was crucially assisted by the use of public relations techniques, as pioneered by certain white collar unions including the NUT, NALGO and, of course, Clive Jenkins at the ASTMS (the history of union communication strategies is discussed further in the next chapter). The absence of sustained interest in issues of communication in the early post-war literature is more difficult to understand in the light of the development of white collar unionism.

The direction of enquiry was determined by a number of theoretical traditions, each of which implicitly prompted some attention to communication, but rarely privileged communication issues, over other 'determinant' variables which appeared to loom much larger in the processes of bargaining and the eruption of industrial conflict. Limitations of space prevent more than a brief identification of each. On the one hand, human relations theory, in presenting an alternative to the economic and technical determinism of much pre-war industrial relations theory, implicitly offered an agenda for the exploration of industrial communication issues but from within the enterprise, rather than through external relations, and certainly not in terms of union concerns. Thus, the propensity for strikes to erupt might be described as a function of 'work place community integration' (Kerr and Siegal, 1954) but the immersion of employees in a wider symbolic and ideological environment ignored. The alternative major early influence is to be found in various versions of structural and systems theory. In the consensual version, an emphasis upon the capacity of the normative order within the industrial relations environment to regulate interation between managements and unions (Dunlop,1958; Flanders,1968) encouraged a search for the mechanisms through which equilibrium was maintained within the workplace. As Eldridge comments (1968:20), Dunlop's systems model invites connections to be made with the external environment and for questions to be posed regarding the relationship between industrial actors, the internal normative order within the enterprise and ideological structures in society. However, these themes are not developed and the opportunity to formulate specific questions about industrial communication strategies not taken. As Banks notes, such models rarely explore the connections between industrial relations systems and wider structures of political power and economic ownership in society (Banks 1974:18), let alone power in relation to symbolic representation and communication.

An alternative theoretical tradition which does acknowledge the importance of wider structures of political and economic power, identifies conflict as an essential feature of the industrial relations system (Allen,1971; Hyman,1984). However, conflict is normally defined in industrial rather than ideological terms. The movement away from theories of system and structure represented an attempt to avoid the dangers of socio-economic or technical determinism and to place in the foreground the dimension of social action. Batstone et al. (1978), for example, argued that while 'structural and general theories', might 'point to the conditions under which strikes occur...strikes involve groups of workers making common decisions...' (Batstone et al. 1978:223). It was to this level of social action, involving group dynamics and the exchange of meaning to which theories of industrial relations should address themselves. Again, a focus upon the meanings and definitions which shape patterns of action within the workplace might prompt questions relating to workplace internal communications and the possible contribution of the external symbolic and ideological environment to the definitions which workers employed. After all, Batstone et al. spend considerable time exploring the vocabularies and rationales used by participants to make sense of industrial action (1978: 54-55). Even when employing the social action perspective to explain the rise of white collar unionism, theorists were reluctant to privilege communication or high profile recruitment strategies over the familiar neo-Weberian concepts of work situation and economic situation. As Bain comments, for example, the former are, 'most of very secondary importance' (Bain 1970:120).

So, much of the literature of the period between 1950 and 1980 rested upon theoretical frameworks which prompted potentially illuminating questions about trade unions and issues of communication. However, the empirical absence of much formal public relations work in the field together with the traditional uses to which these theoretical frameworks were put, led researchers to attach little importance to the issue of communication strategies or relations with the mass media. Only theorists influenced by conventional pressure group theory were prompted, through the case study methodology, to make a start in examining these questions. Coates, for example, in a study of the teaching unions describes, in passing, their external communication strategies and the internal organisational arrangements for press and publicity work. Most of the teaching unions recognised the need to employ publicity along two dimensions; to exert short term pressure upon government but also 'in order to generate a more long term climate of opinion favourable to educational expansion' (Coates 1972:17). The NUT, for example, upgraded its press bureau to departmental status in 1959 before launching the innovative 'Campaign for Education' which made some impact upon the agenda of the 1964 general election. The other two main case study approaches to trade union organisation drawing upon pressure group theory, produced during this decade (May, 1975; Moran, 1974) , similarly explored issues of communication in only the most tentative way. Moran, for example, spent little time in considering external communication in a study of the Union of Post Office Workers and was primarily concerned with the techniques the union employed to secure 'the compliance of membership' (1974:1) which directed research inwards to the problem of internal politics and communication between leadership and 'ordinary' members.

While in these studies, the theoretical framework does prompt a consideration of the relations between unions and their ideological and symbolic environments, the analysis is left, at best, at the stage of a communications audit. The structure of the relevant departments and their responsibilities are noted but more fundamental issues are left unexplored. What is the nature of the relationship *between* unions, as organisations, and news organisations? What processes of interaction occur between union officials and journalists on the labour beat? Given the ideological and political map of the news media, how might trade union officials 'target' particular news or publicity outlets? Above and beyond these dimensions, the issue of news source activity has to be placed in a broader structural context. How do the ideological, political and economic structures which impinge upon news production offer up or limit opportunities for unions to communicate their agendas?

A decade later, as the growing use of public relations techniques and communication technologies in many aspects of organisational life grew more and more common, the 'empirical significance' of internal and external communications for unions compelled a critical response. Writers such as Jones (1986) and Sherman (1986) began to address these issues but without the benefit of the insights to be gained from the application of sociological or media theory. Conventional pressure group theory and industrial relations approaches, then, have offered insights but little empirical research or sustained theorising. With the exception of the preliminary Glasgow University Media Group research (Philo and Hewitt, 1976), surprisingly as we shall see next, the sociology of news sources and news production is little more helpful.

The Sociology of News Sources and News Production

Blumler commented fourteen years ago that we should...

...expand the range of actors whom we are prepared regularly to take into account when conducting research into mass communication as a social process. That is, we should increasingly be treating mass communication as a 'three-legged stool', involving not only journalists and audiences but also all those political and other interest groups that strive to reach audiences by developing strategies for influencing journalists. So a more full and rounded version of agenda setting still awaits in the wings to be called onto the research stage. (Blumler, 1980:373).

A sociology, informed by a theoretical awareness of the nature of power and control over symbolic resources, but capable of empirically exploring the strategies through which potential news sources sought to negotiate and influence journalists, was a timely suggestion. Surprisingly, it has taken almost a further decade for researchers within the sociology of journalism to turn Blumler's 'three-legged stool' into a research agenda. Of course, there are a number of distinct theoretical traditions which inform the field, each of which offers a particular vantage point. Golding and Middleton usefully distinguish 'biographical' accounts which stress, in an overly-simplistic way the overt bias and ideological predisposition of individual journalists; 'organisational' explanations which point to the routine rhythms and dynamics of news organisations and finally, 'ideological' explanations which may incorporate a number of elements identified in the first two explanatory types but which seek to subsume these within broader accounts of the part the news media play in lending 'form and authority' to 'dominant values in British society' (Golding and Middleton,1982:113). A similar 'map' is provided more recently by Schudson (1989) who adds a 'political economy of news' to the 'social organisation of news work' tradition and 'culturological approaches', broadly Golding and Middleton's 'organisational' and 'ideological' explanations respectively.

The earliest 'gatekeeper' models of news production did focus exclusively upon the selection criteria of particular journalists (for example,White 1950) and they find their parallel in some of the more naive contemporary public relations textbooks. As Elliott and Golding comment with an appropriate aphorism; '...the obvious weakness of this explanation is that news changes very little when the individuals who produce it are changed' (1979:207). A 'political economy' approach, on the other hand, in emphasising the way in which news production and communication generally is 'shaped at every level by the structured asymmetries in social relations' (Golding and Murdock, 1991:18), insists upon the need to place the activity both of individual journalists and the social relationships through which they produce news in a wider social and economic context. In Schudson's critical review, it is recognised that 'the more sophisticated versions [of political economy] not only add to but are essential to an understanding of the generation of news' (1989:267).

However, Schudson also notes a number of 'possibilities' which the 'political economy' approach, he believes, is inclined to overlook. One is the, perhaps, increasing frequency of occasions when the news media 'turn upon' governments and institutionalised authority in ways allegedly inconsistent with the interests of the economically powerful. Critical coverage of Watergate and the Vietnam war are offered as examples. This criticism conflates the instrumental and structural dimensions of the political economy approach, condemning both with the 'sins' of the cruder versions of the former. But perhaps, more importantly , it misses one of the essential points of the political economy of news production,- a market driven system of news production is most unlikely to weave a seamless ideological web. There will be frequent occasions when the imperative to compete in ever sharper circulation and ratings battles generates corrosive news values which override the more conservative inclinations of editors and proprietors, as the British Royal Family and successive Conservative cabinet ministers have recently discovered to their cost. And some of the other 'omissions' Schudson notes; little discussion of either the characteristic dependence upon official sources or the predilection for 'news bite' formats, are not unrelated to such pressures either.

Nevertheless, for Schudson 'the failure' of political economy to pursue enquiries into the news room is a significant weakness. It thwarts a sustained investigation of the possibility of 'ideological contestation' and the 'institutional mechanisms', 'cultural traditions', and 'contradictions of power' which 'provide room for debate and revision' (Schudson,1989:270). In other words, there are always possibilities and opportunities for those, outside the sphere of the dominant political and ideological elites, to make interventions within the news production process and to present alternative political agendas but for Schudson these are only accessible through an analysis of 'the social organisation of news work'. While Schudson recognises the importance of the processes political economy seeks to describe, he fails to do justice to the subtlety of a sophisticated political economic analysis. For Golding and Murdock, we should 'think of the economic dynamics as defining key features of the general environment within which communicative activity takes place, but not as a complete explanation of the nature of that activity' (1991:19). There is plenty of scope, then, for exploring the social relationships of news journalism, the organisational dynamics of news production and the politics of journalist-source interaction within such a framework. At the broadest level, this is 'the picture' of the place of the news media within society which is assumed at the beginning of this book. The task is to trace the possibilities for 'ideological contestation', 'debate and revision' as they emerge through the politics of labour journalism and within the constraints of the political economic environment.

The role of the state, too, is often highlighted in political economic accounts of media production. In this project, also, the state is found to play an important part. The fortunes of the labour correspondents as an occupational group were strongly associated with the growing and then diminishing political potency of trade unions, on the one hand, and changes in the political composition of government, on the other. And, of course, government had a lot to do with the fortunes of trade unions, in the first place. In turn, the media work of trade unions in seeking to gain access to the news media, is inextricably bound up with the fortunes of labour and industrial journalism. So at both instrumental and structural levels, the presence of the state cannot be ignored.

The 'ideological' or 'culturological' approach identified above 'emphasises the constraining force of broad cultural symbol systems regardless of the details of organisational and occupational routines', according to Schudson (1989:266). Some of the examples selected by Schudson are a little unrepresentative here, too. While Stuart Hall, for example, has been associated with debates over the nature of 'dominant ideologies' and the role of the media in their reproduction, the importance of the concrete, material and organisational context is frequently acknowledged (Hall et al., 1978). However, it is the case that there are difficulties in seeking to 'read off' or make inferences about the politics and social relations of news production on the basis of the analysis of ideology as it 'appears' in media content (Elliot, 1981; Cottle, 1993:9). For the purposes of this study, the importance of journalists' 'inferential frameworks' is recognised as, for example, they relate to trade unionism and industrial relations, but these are placed within the context of the politics and day to day routines of labour and industrial reporting. Undoubtedly, the significance of generalised values and ideological perspectives in shaping the practice of news journalism has to be acknowledged but there is a danger in beginning an analysis at this level. From this starting point, it is easy to slip towards an account of ideological reproduction which pictures ideology as an enveloping blanket and overlooks the tensions, conflicts and struggles involved in all communicative activity, including union media work and labour journalism.

This is the source of difficulty with the concept of 'primary definers', a concept deduced from 'reading' the ideological nature of media texts, rather than through empirical investigation of the concrete practice of sources and journalists. In the work of Hall et al. (1978), it is assumed that the state and its associated agencies will act as 'primary definers' of events and agendas in the news, given their privileged, strategic ideological position. A sociology of news sources, however, is likely to reveal that in particular circumstances, it is possible for non-official sources to exploit opportunities to intervene in the news production process and to counter 'official' definitions of events, as in the case of environmental politics (Anderson 1993:53; 1991). As Schlesinger comments, too often in employing the concept of 'primary definers' research reveals a disappointing lack of curiosity about the nature and effectivity of source strategies (1990 :68).

Further to this, as Schlesinger argues (1990:62-69), models based upon the concept of 'primary definition' are by implication 'uni-directional' with the flow of 'definitions' travelling always outwards from the state to the media and little allowance being made for the possibility, however rare, that media coverage may impact upon the state and its 'accredited witnesses'. It is also possible to find plenty of instances when 'primary definers' are not wholly satisfied with the 'definitions' communicated as in the case, for example, of social policy coverage (Golding and Middleton,1982: 114-117).

The concept also tends to over-emphasise the cohesion of the state as a structure. As this study explores through a brief history of labour and industrial correspondents, some of the most valuable source material for journalists is produced through the tensions between departments of state and the contradictory 'definitions' which may emerge, on and off the record. Recent work on the 'representation' of the 'poll tax', vividly illustrates how things can go wrong from the point of view of the government as a 'primary definer', if tensions 'within the power structure' (Deacon and Golding,1994:202) begin to generate a critical discourse which undermines the primary definition of policy or events. As Deacon and Golding demonstrate, the 'seeds of dissent' regarding the poll tax, 'were sown by other elite sources' (1994:202), including from within the Conservative Party, and subsequently reported by the news media.

There are difficulties in drawing up the boundaries between those agencies regarded as 'primary definers' and those on the outside, and use of the concept without historical context will fail to capture the processes of political change through which organisations may lose or gain media authority. In this study, for example, it becomes clear that the TUC and contacts within the larger trade unions were integrated into the labour beat from the very earliest days of pre-war labour journalism. Where, then, should trade unions be located in terms of the distinction between 'primary' and 'secondary definers'? Reflecting both the corporatist tendencies in British politics two decades ago and the theoretical influence of Althusser's approach to the state, Hall et al have no hesitation in identifying trade unions within the category of 'primary definers' (Hall et al, 1978:58). Now, of course, the picture looks rather different. Two questions have to be asked. Where even during the height of the 'beer and sandwiches at Number Ten' era, was the distinction between 'primary' and 'secondary definers' to be drawn *within* the trade union movement? If senior trade union figures enjoyed 'media authority', such accredited status was certainly not extended to all shop floor activists or 'ordinary' trade union members. Secondly, if the elite within the labour movement no longer enjoys a 'primary' authority how has this come about and how were the changes in relationships between journalists and members of the union elites managed?

Schlesinger recognises that 'the way in which journalistic practice is organised *generally* promotes the interest of authoritative sources, especially within the apparatus of government and the state' (1990:69) but the task must be to explore how both this occurs and how, at the same time, it is possible for alternative definitions to be promoted by sources outside this sphere, through an empirically constituted sociology of journalism and news sources.[7] As Deacon and Golding emphasise, the capacity of primary definers to establish a favoured interpretative framework (agenda), does not necessarily mean that the dominance of such an interpretative framework is maintained beyond the 'generative' or initial phases of news coverage, or that within a particular interpretative framework, the evaluation of issues will reflect their perspectives (1994:202). It is one thing to successfully place one set of issues on the news agenda, it is quite another to influence how those issues are assessed. Primary definition, according to Deacon and Golding, involves a continuing interpretative and evaluative contest between news sources.

This brings the discussion back to Schudson's third approach, the study of the 'social organisation of news work'. One of the difficulties here, of course, is that within this broad category, there a number of quite distinct theoretical orientations including phenomenological and ethnomethodological investigations into the social processes through which journalists 'construct' meaning in interaction with sources (for example, Tuchman,1972; Molotoch and Lester,1974; Chibnall,1977; Fishman,1980); dramaturgical perspectives which frame journalist and source relations in terms of elaborate front stage/ back stage impression management (Altheide and Johnson,1980; Ericson et al,1989); organisational perspectives which place interaction with sources in the context of the organisational imperatives of news production (for example,Tunstall 1971; Schlesinger,1978; Cottle,1993; Negrine,1993), not to mention research which draws upon political perspectives (mainly varieties of pluralism) to explore the role of political elites in news production (for example, Seymour-Ure,1968; Gerbner,1969; Tunstall,1970; Sigal,1973; Cockerall et al 1984; Cracknell,1993). Space precludes an extended discussion of each.

However, it is important to note that each implies a particular view of the balance of power between source and journalist. Schlesinger has criticised the 'media-centric' nature of most research in the area of media-source relations (Schlesinger et al 1989; Schlesinger,1990). In the main, the research focus has been from the perspective of journalists and news organisations, rather than the sources themselves (Ericson et al 1989:24). The strategies and techniques journalists employ to re-work and 'make sense' of source material are described; the ways in which the organisational imperatives of news production imprint themselves upon journalist and source interaction are observed. From these perspectives, the frequent conclusion drawn is that ultimately official sources are in the driving seat and that the nature of journalism as an occupation encourages official source dependency (for example, Altheide and Johnson 1980; Fishman 1980; Sigal 1973; Chibnall, 1977). For Fishman, journalists spend quite a lot of time actually 'repairing' official and bureaucratic accounts, as part of their 'account constructing work' (1980:135). Cottle stresses the restrictions of resources, staffing and time which encourage official source dependency (though he also stresses the variety of communications which emerge from this) (1993:50-52); Altheide and Johnson argue the time and space limitations imposed by most news media formats prevent the emergence of critical contextualising analysis in coverage of official 'propaganda' (1980:75). For Chibnall, if crime correspondents established 'exchange' relationships with official sources, their exclusive dependence upon the police for information was always likely to lead to subcultural 'assimilation' and ultimately 'manipulation' (Chibnall,1977:225).

And yet, there is plenty of evidence to suggest that the nature of the conditions in which specialist journalism in some fields is practised means that the balance of power does not without interruption favour the interests of the powerful and ideologically privileged. Tunstall argued that while journalists working in specialisms directly related to revenue goals might be disadvantaged in their dealings with key sources, correspondents working in specialisms relatively insulated from revenue goal pressures, were less vulnerable to the dangers of source-dependence (Tunstall, 1971:ch 5). In the area of social policy correspondents may turn to non-official sources in order to frame stories in terms of 'balance' and 'diversity' of perspective (Golding and Middleton, 1982:114-124). Even Molotoch and Lester's concept of 'parallel needs' implies an interdependency between the 'producers, promoters and assemblers' of news (1974:106).

Most recently, in employing a consciously anti-mediacentric research perspective which seeks to explicitly adopt the perspective of social control agencies as sources of news, Ericson et al find that these agencies feel themselves to be at the mercy of the news media, having to work within their 'frames' and accept their format constraints (Ericson et al 1989:378). For Ericson et al, a great deal depends upon the concrete circumstances in particular news communication contexts:

> There is considerable variation in who controls the process, depending upon the context, the type of sources involved, and what is at issue. (1989:378).

What is required is an approach which addresses this empirical activity and variation within the structural constraints of economy and polity described above. As Schlesinger argues, 'there is the potential for opening up a distinctive problematic: that of the social organisation of non-official sources and the ways in which they achieve (or fail to achieve) their impact' (1990:71). Some work has already begun along these lines in the area of environmental news coverage where the source strategies of environmental pressure groups have been recently examined (Anderson,1993; 1991) and greater weight attached to the influence of non-official sources (Dunwoody and Griffin,1993) and green 'issue entrepreneurs' (Cracknell,1993) in the communication of environmental news. Anderson (1993), for example, argues that where official sources are slow to react to news events and where there is sufficient weight of public opinion, it is possible for non-official sources, such as Greenpeace, to establish an agenda on their terms. The degree to which such successes can be maintained over an extended period of time is another matter.

However, considerably more work is required in exploring the range and effectivity of the strategies employed by news sources outside the sphere of state, parliamentary party and institutionalised power. If access to the news media is 'structured' (Schlesinger 1990:75), how do sources negotiate these structures and what resources, material and symbolic, are most useful in assisting them? How much difference do inequalities in the distribution of symbolic and material communication resources make for groups seeking access? How do journalists respond in particular circumstances to the strategies employed by groups engaged in media politics? How do the broad structures of political and economic power impact upon these processes? To pursue one theme in a little more detail, how do groups experiencing political and ideological marginalisation attempt to counter this process,- a question particularly pertinent for trade unions?

Access to the news media is partly governed by 'political credibility', a resource not necessarily monopolised by the agencies Hall describes as 'primary definers'. According to Molotoch and Lester (1974), the only device which may open up access for groups without 'sufficient political credibility' is the mounting of 'disruptive events' and yet as Greenberg (1985) and Gitlin (1980: ch 5) note, cultivated notoriety is a double-edged sword,- it may purchase short term access to the media at the long-term price of even greater political marginalisaton. Is the choice for marginal groups quite so bleak? Some work has been conducted into the relationships between marginal groups such as Friends of the Earth,- before the sudden success of green parties in Europe in the late 1980s (Greenberg,1985), 'resource poor' community groups (Goldenberg,1975) and civil rights and political reform groups (Paletz and Entman,1981), and the news media.

One point to emerge is that marginal groups will vary 'in their capacity and ability to exploit the mass media's interests and practices' (Paletz and Entman,1981:124). In other words, the agendas of such groups may or may not lend themselves to presentation in terms of the conventional news values and frameworks employed in the news media. By 'individualising' and 'personalising' key issues, the poverty lobby, for example, has achieved some media success in Britain but other marginal groups will experience greater difficulty in translating their concerns into appropriate news frames. Secondly, the extent to which marginal groups can offer knowledge, information or recognised expertise will determine the level of interest specialist correspondents will take in their communicative work (Greenberg,1985; Goldenberg,1975:ch 4). A research department which enjoys credibility and can respond to the needs of journalists is an important resource but this is not a realistic option for many marginal groups. Goldenberg, however, argues that while, 'status, officiality, knowledge and money' are 'in short supply for most resource-poor groups', other relevant resources, such as 'size, legitimacy and credibility' may be more abundant and all will assist in allowing 'group leaders' to gain access to the media (Goldenberg,1975:47).

Questions are begged here concerning how 'legitimacy' and 'credibility' are achieved; which institutions have the power to confer such status positions and what interests are served in the process? Nevertheless, Goldenberg's research is particularly useful in distinguishing between types of newspaper. He examines four 'resource poor' groups and three metropolitan newspapers in Boston, two of which were conservative in editorial outlook but one of which (*The Globe*) had an unusually liberal approach in hiring radical staff and encouraging 'advocacy journalism'. Goldenberg's analysis attaches appropriate weight to the inequalities in communication resources between the 'resource-poor' and more powerful conventional sources; he charts the ways in which revenue goals and advertising imperatives shape editorial policy, particularly in the case of the conservative papers and he explores the ways in which the beat system, the organisation of journalistic specialisms and the organisational requirements of daily newspaper journalism work against the attempts of 'resource poor' groups to gain access. But, at the same time, Goldenberg finds there are some limited opportunities, particularly for groups establishing contact with journalists at *The Globe*. Whilst acknowledging the importance of the commercial and organisational environments, Goldenberg pays particular attention to the disposition of key journalists and specialist correspondents because...

> ...certain properties of reporters affect the likelihood that resource-poor groups can gain access to them and through them to their newspapers. In spite of the constraints placed upon reporters by their newspaper organisations, they still have considerable leeway and discretion. (1975:109).

The 'reporter is the key media person for resource poor groups, the major filter in the access process' (1975:145). Goldenberg argues that gaining access to the press once was easily achieved. The problem for 'resource poor' groups was in 'regularizing' contacts with the press and in securing 'continuing access'. 'Resource-rich' groups enjoyed considerable advantages in initiating and then sustaining press and media contacts because they possessed greater amounts of the political, symbolic and material resources identified above. Given four 'resource poor' groups and three daily newspapers in Goldenberg's study, only three out of the possible twelve 'interactions' became 'regularized' (1975:137). In some cases, the 'resource poor' groups lacked even the resources required to begin to identify who the sympathetic journalists on particular newspapers might be. Where sustained 'regularized' contact was established, this was often on the basis of 'bargains' being struck between sources and reporters (1975:36) in which sources could provide exclusive information or privileged interviews with leaders and a guarantee of accuracy. In return, reporters would submit stories in ways which acknowledged the source perspective and agenda.

The value in Goldenberg's study is that it acknowledges the importance of the political and economic context and the organisational environment of newspaper production, whilst seeking to explore empirically the strategies which are available for marginal groups in seeking access. Two parts of the story, however, are left unexplored. More needs to be said about the processes through which groups can secure important resources like 'legitimacy' and 'credibility' before they seek access to the news media at any particular moment. Schlesinger, for example, suggests the concept of 'cultural capital' as a way of describing the distribution of authority and legitimacy (1990:81) in society which in turn implies reference to fundamental structures of power. In their study of political reform groups, Palentz and Entman point to the importance of visible contacts with political elites in securing legitimacy in the eyes of correspondents (1981:141). In focusing empirically upon the media work in which sources engage with journalists, it is important not to lose sight of the wider picture of political interconnections which may privilege or disadvantage particular groups in terms of direct influence and symbolic capital. While it may be possible for non-official sources to secure some 'media work' successes, they frequently remain disadvantaged by virtue of their politically subordinate positions. The 'power to create and distribute meaning still resides with centres of material and political power' (Deacon and Golding, 1994: 203). Given such centres of power, it remains the case that non-official sources must struggle harder and make more concessions in the effort to win credibility in the eyes of journalists. As Anderson (1993), for example, illustrates in the arena of environmental politics and media work, green pressure groups continue to be identified as 'axe grinders', or 'advocates' in Deacon and Golding's terms, rather than authoritative sources, despite occasional successes in promoting particular news frames. 'Axe grinders' are unlikely to exercise sufficient authority or credibility to significantly shift dominant news agendas.

Secondly, Goldenberg's study tells us little about how sources may modify their agendas, - the content they seek to present to the news media,- according to their understanding of 'what is possible' and how their agendas relate to the distribution of legitimacy or 'cultural capital'. Gitlin (1980:ch 5) and Palentz and Entman (1981:130-131) have explored the ways in which media coverage may have an impact upon the strategy of marginal groups. Essentially, marginal groups face a crucial dilemma in seeking access to the media precisely because of their ideologically marginal status. Seeking *regular* access to the news media will inevitably involve compromise in terms of political strategy and the message communicated. An uncompromising radical stance may generate transitory initial coverage, as Goldenberg notes, but after a process whereby the radical is 'appropriated as spectacular entertainment' (Palentz and Entman,1981:131) the radical group is consigned to the ideological waste lands. On the other hand, accommodation to the news criteria, news frames and inferential structures of the news media also presents dangers. Typically, news frames limit the discussion of 'social process' and the dimension of power (Elliott and Golding,1979:209) ; news is rarely historically informed in anything other than a superficial manner which may render the action of radical groups 'incoherent' or 'irrational' (Hartmann 1975; Glasgow University Media Group 1976; Downing 1980, etc).[8] Even within the news media, a commercial logic drives news selection criteria towards entertainment and a concentration upon the atypical which, through the relatively constant flow of news, comes to appear as the 'typical' (Golding and Middleton,1982:128-129). Radical or marginal groups have to consider the extent to which they 'format' their messages to suit these patterns in coverage or attempt to undermine them. Too great a resistance to conventional news formats and formulae is likely to result in failure, too great an accommodation to the 'needs of the news media' may result in 'incorporation'.

To take one example, from a recent article advocating the use of modern public relations techniques to assist the media work of one ideologically beleaguered group of public agencies, local authority social service departments. Walder claims that is possible to modify potential dominant story lines selected by the press and provides as an example a 'story' she handled in Bradford as press officer for Bradford social services. Following comments made by a local politician, local media developed the theme of Bradford as the 'child sex capital of Europe'. National tabloid and broadcasting journalists picked the story up but through a process of 'negotiation' with the media, Walder was successful in persuading them to drop the 'child sex capital of Europe' headline, in return for some documented cases and an interview with the director of social services (Walder,1991:211). The headline may have been amended but the original news agenda and frame remained unmodified and legitimacy given to the story through the case studies and interview with the director of social services. This could be regarded as a public relations success but equally it involves a process of 'media incorporation' in which news values and journalists' inferential structures are allowed to 'frame' the main elements of the communicative work undertaken by the sources.

Further to this, a 'holistic' perspective is needed which places the media strategies of source organisations in the context of their overall objectives and broader political strategies. What impact, for example, does anticipation of the likely news frames and interpretations have upon broader strategy and practice? There is evidence in the areas of social policy (Seyd, 1975 and 1976; Whitely and Winyard,1983 and 1984), crime and criminal justice (Schlesinger et al., 1991) and environmental politics (Cracknell,1993) that anticipation of media responses can shape and constrain the political strategy of source groups in significant ways. Is it the case that media incorporation can go hand in hand with political incorporation? Possible incorporation along either political or media dimensions has been given relatively little explicit attention in either the developing empirical work on source media interaction (Goldenberg,1975; Anderson,1993) or the theoretical manifestos for future research (Schlesinger,1990).

This section has described how the theoretical framework for a sociology of sources and news work has emerged in recent years and the extent to which empirical research has illuminated our understanding of the social practices of news sources in their contact with the news media. It has pointed to some of the ways in which this work may be related to the broader structures of political and economic power in which such source-media interaction takes place. Schlesinger suggests that the work of 'internalist' researchers, those engaged in exploring the accounts of journalists, editors and those directly engaged in the production of news, needs to be supplemented with an 'external' account, a thorough going analysis of the strategic and tactical action of sources in relation to the media' (1990:72). The intention of this book is to employ both 'internal' and 'external' perspectives in exploring the relation between unions as sources and journalists working for the daily press.

Researching Trade Unions as News Sources

The present research grew out of these theoretical and empirical concerns. In the complaints expressed by Nell Myers in her battle with the NUM's 'front line troops', many of the difficulties of a non-official source with limited symbolic or cultural capital were being expressed. An important task appeared to be to consider the position of trade unions as news sources; determine their preferred news agendas and assess the problems they experienced in offering these agendas to the news media. What strategies could secure access to news media coverage or to what extent was the 'structural pessimism' of Nell Myers warranted? In turn, this involved tracing the nature of the relationships established between union press officers, officials and journalists on the labour beat, whilst at the same time, in the light of the theoretical discussion above, not losing sight of the political and economic context in which news media work occurs.

Further information on the selection of unions for the panel and the research methodology is supplied in appendices one and two. As Schlesinger implies, a purely quantitative research design based upon measures of source 'input' and media 'output' is unlikely to do justice to the complexity of the social relationships - and the possibilities and constraints which these entail-involved in source-media interaction.

> As for applying cost-benefit analysis, despite its heuristic value, we would be well advised to be cautious. The reason for this is the difficulty of establishing unambiguous criteria of success in the realisation of communicative goals, and indeed, in ranking such goals themselves. (1990:80).

The study, then, is broadly qualitative in nature though quantitative evidence is used in appropriate places.[9] It is assumed that neither the processes of negotiation through which union press officers and labour correspondents exchanged information, nor the evidence of the success or failure of union news strategies can be captured through exclusively quantitative measures. The focus of the research is upon the use made by trade union personnel of material and symbolic resources and strategies in their efforts to gain access to national daily newspapers;[10] the response of journalists, particularly labour and industrial correspondents to these interventions; aspects of the political and economic environment as they impinge upon these processes through the history of the organisation of labour journalism as a specialism, and a final evaluation of the effectivity of union news media strategies in a case study of newspaper coverage, the 1989 Ambulance Dispute which involved four of the unions selected in the panel.[11] A formal list of research questions for this study is as follows:

1. As politically marginalised, non-official news sources what strategies are employed by trade unions in the attempt to present elements of their preferred agendas to the national newspapers and to secure more favourable coverage?

2. Are there differences in the nature of the strategies employed by unions? To what extent do differences in material, political and symbolic resources advantage or disadvantage particular trade unions in these attempts?

3. What is the nature of the relationship between those at the 'interface' between trade unions and national newspapers, - in other words, those positioned strategically in relation to the flow of information generated by trade unions and received by national newspapers? This involves examining the nature of the relationship between trade union press officers and specialist correspondents, particularly those working the labour and industrial beats.

4. Given that access to the news media is structured, what difficulties do trade unions face in employing strategies to present their agendas to national newspapers and in seeking to secure favourable coverage? Are these difficulties related to the political and economic environment in which labour and industrial news is produced and in what ways? Have historical changes in the nature of the political and economic environment impacted upon relationships between trade union personnel and newspaper correspondents?

5. What costs (material, political or ideological) do trade unions incur in seeking to employ news media strategies?

6. What can an assessment of newspaper content tell us about the effectivity of news media strategies as employed by trade unions?

The organisation of the chapters is self-explanatory and follows the evolution of each research stage. Chapter two completes the introduction to the study by considering the recent history of British trade unions' growing interest in communication and news media work. In section two, Chapter three deals with the unions' preferred agenda while beginning to explore the practice of trade union press officers within their union organisations. Chapter four examines the practice of trade union press officers in their dealings with the external environment and in particular the nature of their relationships with labour and other specialist correspondents. Section three focuses upon the history of labour journalism in the context of the changing political and economic environment in which labour news is produced. Chapters five and six develop a historical dimension to trace the development and contraction of labour and industrial journalism as a national newspaper specialism. Chapter seven examines contemporary union-newspaper relations from the point of view of labour and other specialist correspondents. Section four draws the various threads of this study together with two final chapters. Firstly, chapter eight deals with the representation of labour through the news media,focusing particularly upon newspaper coverage of the 1989 Ambulance Dispute as a 'case study'. The news media strategies of five unions is assessed in the context of what we know of the general patterns of labour and industrial news coverage. Finally, chapter nine attempts to provide more general answers to the questions posed in this introduction.

Notes

1.   This draws upon Grant's distinction between insider and outsider pressure groups (Grant,1990).

2.   This is discussed further in chapter nine. See also, Manning (1996:ch 3).

3.   This is illustrated in the content of certain union journals (Manning, 1996: ch. 3) and in the news work of particular leading unions (discussed in chapters three and four).

4.   The 'Unions 93 Conference' sponsored by the *New Statesman and Society* and New Times, included two academic papers on union communication work. See Riley (1993). A recent issue of *Free Press*, the journal of the Campaign for Press and Broadcasting Freedom, was also devoted to academic and activist perspectives on 'Trade Unions and the Media', Number 75, July/August 1993.

5.   See, for example, Seyd (1975 and 1976) on the origins of Shelter and the Child Poverty Action Group. Also Whitley and Winyard (1983 and 1984), McCarthy (1986) and Banting (1979). It is clear that both Shelter and the CPAG were essentially media orientated lobbying organisations in their early years, though the CPAG sought to draw upon the scholarly skills of its academic

supporters whilst Shelter relied more upon the media 'barnstorming' skills of its first director, Des Wilson. See Wilson (1970 and 1984).

6. This is not to condemn pluralist accounts out of hand. As Paul Hirst has demonstrated in his rehabilitation of Dahl, it is possible to think through these wider questions within a pluralist framework (Hirst, 1987).

7. For Schlesinger, this route offers the means to transcend 'the grand debates' between Marxism and Pluralism, structuralism and action theory, economic or cultural determinism (1989:305-6). This study does not necessarily have such grand ambitions but it is assumed that both theoretical traditions are helpful in describing the various aspects of the concrete practice of journalist-source interaction, the process of news production and political-economic environment in which these processes occur.

8. This point anticipates a fuller discussion of debates over the nature of political and industrial news coverage in chapter 8.

9. A survey of trade union communication resources was conducted as a preliminary step in undertaking this research and is briefly described in the appendices. In addition, an extensive quantitative content analysis of trade union journals was also conducted. Discussion of this has been omitted for reasons of space but can be found in Manning (1996).

10. National newspapers rather than broadcasting outlets were prioritised both because resource limitations precluded the use of video monitoring equipment and because broadsheet newspapers represented the most favourable *national* media terrain for union press officers. If they failed to secure significant successes within this arena of the public sphere, it was unlikely that they would do so in terms of national broadcasting. It is acknowledged that union communication staff are increasingly considering the potential offered by *local* broadcasting outlets.

11. The GMB was added to the original panel of trade unions for reasons detailed in appendix one.

2 Trade Unions: Structure, Power, Ideology and Communications

Trade unions must inevitably find new ways of speaking to their members and their potential members. Twenty years ago you could probably recruit a hundred people by standing outside the factory gates at 5.30am and handing out a few leaflets saying, 'That person in there is a bastard, you need us.' There are smaller units now, it is far more difficult trying to recruit two or three people working in a small office in Beaconsfield than it used to be to recruit two or three hundred at Camel Laird. Industry has changed and trade unions have to change with it, which means that your communication techniques have to change. More and more people get their information from television, radio, papers and magazines, and that means that there are becoming more and more important ways to communicate with any potential recruitment audience. (Adrian Long, Media Officer at the GMB).

A union is not a marketing operation. i.e. we are often reacting to an agenda not set by the union itself. A union can't be sold like a commodity. Press enquiries reflect what's going on in the real world. (Eddie Barrett, Press Officer at the TGWU).

British Unions in a changing environment

For many observers it is the Thatcher administration of the 1980s which is primarily responsible for the most remarkable changes in the political and economic environment within which British trade unions now find themselves. Certainly, the most *visible* political factor shaping the social and economic landscape during the 1980s was Thatcherism. A number of writers have taken this as their starting point in attempting to understand political and economic developments within Britain during this period (Kavanagh, 1990; Jones, 1989; Riddell, 1983 and 1989) while some have pointed to the social and economic forces underpinning Thatcherism but, nonetheless, have still emphasised the particular political potency of Thatcherism as an ideological force in its own right (for example, Hall and Jacques,1983). The implication of this approach is that we must understand the fortunes of trade unions and patterns of industrial relations in the 1980s as being shaped primarily by the policies and intentions, or the political project of the Thatcher Government. It is certainly the case that the Government identified industrial relations and a weakening of trade union power as a primary objective in its economic strategy.

However, other theorists place a greater emphasis upon less visible but, perhaps, more permanent developments in the nature of capitalist production; the impact of the introduction of new technologies to the workplace, and the re-structuring of labour markets. After all, a number of crucial structural patterns (decline in manufacturing employment, growth in unorganised service sector work, feminisation of specific labour markets, etc) are features to be found appearing in many advanced and late capitalist societies and early signs of their emergence can be traced back to the 1960s and before (Edwards et al,1986:5). Indeed, in its early days the new Labour administration, under Tony Blair, shows little inclination to attempt to reverse the 'flexibilities' in labour markets embraced and encouraged by previous Conservative administrations. For some analysts, then, much of the political and economic change experienced by British trade unions requires an explanation which moves beyond the style and policies of particular governments and directs attention towards changes in the nature of production, specifically from Taylorist-Fordist to Post-Fordist organisation. The effects and future implications of these changes are traced outwards, in terms of patterns of employment, industrial relations, consumption patterns, and so on (Aglietta,1982; Offe, 1985; Lash and Urry, 1987; Hall and Jacques, 1989 and Murray 1989).[1] These writers have devoted a considerable amount of time to discussing the implications of a shift towards post-Fordist production and the structures of late 'disorganised' capitalism for trade unions and workplace social relations. Most agree that such shifts bring with them an enhanced capacity on the part of employers to control workplace relationships and limit union influence. It is suggested that this, in turn, is likely to herald the collapse of traditional unionism and labourism, forcing upon trade unions the inevitability of re-thinking their roles and strategies (for example, Lash and Urry,1987:ch 8; Brown,1986, or Foster and Woolfson,1989).

Another point of departure for the analysis of recent change is with the structure of labour markets, themselves. Goldthorpe, for example, argues that a tendency towards 'dualism' is now characteristic of most late capitalist economies where private capital and the state may respond to the power of organised interest groups representing sections of labour, not by directly confronting such power but by taking steps to encourage the expansion of secondary labour markets, characterised by the exclusion of workers from the rights and rewards of those located in primary markets, including the protection afforded by union membership (Goldthorpe, 1984). While the government in the hands of Mrs Thatcher did, at times, appear to relish the prospect of directly confronting and weakening the power of organised labour, there is some evidence that a number of large employers in the private sector were not so combative in their treatment of unions and did, indeed, choose rather to encourage the development of such 'dual' labour markets rather than exploit the new legislative arsenal provided for them by the government (Rubery,1986:108; Ferner and Hyman,1992: pxxvii).

Whether the starting point is with changes in the organisation of capitalist production or with the re-structuring of labour markets, strikingly similar conclusions are drawn regarding the political future for trade unions in late capitalist societies. For writers such as Goldthorpe (1984) and Cameron (1984), the segmentation of labour markets and the emergence of 'dualism' as a feature of capitalist economies are likely to spell the decline of corporatist political arrangements and with this, an end to trade union influence at the centre of government. This is because trade unions are no longer able to 'deliver' workers in the growing and largely unorganised secondary sectors whilst the state may seek to loosen their grip upon organised workers in the primary sector.

Although employing rather different theoretical frameworks, Offe (1985: ch 6) and Lash and Urry (1987), for example, draw very similar conclusions concerning the collapse of corporatism but are tempted to extrapolate further than 'dualist theory' in relation to patterns of culture, consumption and associated political movements. Given the complexity of the ways in which a 'disorganised capitalism' draws upon sections of labour, Offe argues that it is no longer possible for trade unions to represent a 'unified' working class in their dealings with the state. The interests of 'core' workers enjoying relatively affluent, consumer orientated lifestyles associated with well rewarded positions in primary labour markets, may be quite distinct from casualised workers in other secondary labour markets, who may only enjoy a tenuous grip upon formal employment. Similarly, Lash and Urry identify 'a decline in the collective identity of the working class' (1987:234) as a result of growing differences between private and public sector labour markets, the feminisation of occupations and increasing diversity in consumption patterns. As unemployment rises there may be increasingly sharp conflicts *between* groups of workers, as 'core' employees defend their interests against those in weaker positions (migrant workers, younger workers and older workers, women in non-unionised sectors, etc.).

Offe envisages several dangers for trade unions at this point. Certainly, corporatist politics are no longer viable if unions are no longer able to represent to the state the 'universal' interests of an organised working class. But further to this, there is a danger that unions will find themselves defending the interests of privileged 'core' workers against the marginalised (1985:160). In turn, given the high rates of unemployment and the casualised, sporadic experience of work for many sections of the labour force, a more fundamental problem arises, Offe argues, because wage labour grows less and less important in shaping the values and lifestyles of potential union recruits. For Offe, unions must both adjust their own agendas to reflect these broader concerns (quality of life issues, environmental politics and the problems of industrialism) and devise strategies which will offer ways of re-integrating marginal groups into the core (campaigns over the quality of work, campaigns for flexible and job sharing arrangements, etc) (Offe, 1985:162-169). There are some indications that these issues are beginning to emerge in the concerns of trade union journals (Manning, 1996). Offe's attempt to trace the implications of his analysis into the spheres of culture, identity and lifestyle find a parallel, of course, in the writings of the proponents of the 'New Times' perspective (Hall and Jacques,1989; and also Laclau and Mouffe,1985), where it is assumed that movements towards 'decentralisation' in the organisation of work, decline in large scale Fordist mass production and the consequent differentiation of social classes will produce a decline in traditional class based politics and a new preoccupation with a diverse politics of identity and lifestyle. Again, there is some limited evidence that some unions are developing an awareness of these issues in the content of their journals and communication work (Manning, 1996).

However, it is worth pausing for a moment to consider the empirical breadth and theoretical significance of the changes described above and the durability of the abstract models which have been constructed to describe them. The value of 'dualist' models in describing political and industrial change in Britain has been questioned by Longstreth (1988), while the 'post-Fordist/disorganised capitalism' account has been challenged from several quarters (Rustin,1989; Hirst,1989; Sayer,1989; Hyman,1991; Crompton, 1993). A common theme to be found in the critiques of both the dualist and disorganised capitalism theses is a questioning of the extent to which the structural changes described can provide the basis either for a generalised analysis of the present or for an extrapolation of future trends. Longstreth, for example, argues that while there is compelling evidence for a 'dualization of the workforce', it remains unclear whether these patterns are the product of a long term, permanent structural process characteristic of late capitalist economies, as suggested by dualist theory, or simply the conjuncturally specific product of a particular government's policy and pragmatic adaptation by employers in certain but not every employment sector (Longstreth,1988: 430-431).

Similar objections are levelled against the more ambitious claims of Offe, Lash and Urry and the proponents of the 'New Times' account. There are dangers in over-stating the case in two senses. Sayer (1989) and Hyman (1991) question the extent to which a shift towards post-Fordist production relations has really occurred throughout the main sectors of the British economy; they take the view that the movement towards post-Fordism is uneven and that there are good reasons why capital may retain traditional forms of production and employment patterns in particular areas. Secondly, there are enormous dangers in over-simplifying the historical account. The reluctance of the British working class to mobilise in mass political action has long been the subject of debate during 'old times', let alone new. There is plenty of evidence to confirm a working class preoccupation with 'pleasure', 'lifestyle' and 'consumption' in late Victorian, as well as late twentieth century Britain (Crompton,1993:88). The 'post-Fordist/disorganised capitalism' account, then, too frequently rests upon a stark polarisation between two 'ideal types' and, implicitly, a rather mechanistic model of the relationship between the sphere of production and the polity and civil society (Ferner and Hyman,1992: xix). After all, it is possible for a society such as Japan to combine a high degree advancement towards post-Fordist production arrangements in a number of economic sectors, with extremely conservative patterns in the spheres of family life and cultural identity (Hirst,1989: 325).

For critics such as Rustin and Hyman, it is important to recognise the diversity in forms of capitalist production and in related political arrangements. Post-Fordist production relations should be regarded as one variant but even within one society there may co-exist a variety of forms of production, depending upon the formulation of particular accumulation strategies on the part of capital and the nature of the 'balance of forces' at a local level (Rustin,1989:308-9).

A similar point can be made in relation to the development of political structures. According to the 'post-Fordist/disorganised capitalism' account, corporate political structures are strongly associated with the era of capitalist mass production and Keynesian economic management. Accordingly, corporate state structures wither as capitalism develops new 'post-Fordist' forms of production. Even critics such as Longstreth and Crouch (1986) concur with the view that one of the distinctive features of recent years has been the level of sustained political pressure exerted by the central state against corporatist arrangements and the legitimacy of trade unions in both political and industrial arenas. However, a 'de-corporatised' state is not necessarily a weak or de-centralised state, as the Thatcher years in Britain have illustrated. Once again, for Ruskin and Hyman, one of the sets of considerations central to an understanding of political-economic developments are the strategies and interests of capital. There is no necessary contradiction between a growing centralisation of many state powers and a decentralisation of particular processes in production and consumption (Rustin,1989:309). There is a danger, then, in underestimating the importance of political strategy in the response of capital to the crises of accumulation which characterised the experience of advanced capitalism in the first three decades after the war and in stressing, to too greater a degree, the impact of structural change in production relations. Hyman (1986), for example, argues that it is the crisis of accumulation and the consequent fiscal crisis of the state in late capitalist societies which renders the concessions to labour secured through corporate 'post-war settlements' no longer sustainable. This kind of analysis places more emphasis upon the factors which prompt capital to politically confront organised labour, rather than the longer term structural processes which may fragment and undermine working class organisation. Viewed in this light, it is possible to point to an important continuity in the underlying economic and political rhythms of capitalism.

Three conclusions can be drawn at this stage. Firstly, there is a general agreement that unions must now undertake the development of a political strategy which does not assume a return to the politics of coporatism in the near future. The growing trade union interest in media and communication work is one consequence of this recognition, although union strategies and tactics still often suggest a reluctance to abandon the politics of the centralised state, too. Secondly, while there may well be quite an advanced movement towards the de-centralisation of industrial relations and enforced labour 'flexibility' in certain sectors of the British economy (Ferner and Hyman,1992:xx) , this movement is uneven and there remain very sizeable sectors based around traditional patterns of production and employment. Thirdly, and following from this, it is likely that while some unions may display, in their journals and in their wider recruitment and communication strategies a recognition of these changes and an attempt to articulate new forms of politics and new patterns of consumption, this is unlikely to be a universal feature of trade union responses to the events of the post-1979 era. In terms of political strategy, for example, on the basis of experience in organising and representing particular employment sectors, unions may be more or less sympathetic to the interpretation which stresses political intervention, rather than change in class structure and sources of class identification. A great deal depends upon the positioning of particular unions in terms of industries, labour markets and exposure to the effects of government policy.

As Ferner and Hyman note, the changes British trade unions have experienced in recent years are likely to be partly conjunctural in nature, the product of recession and particularly hostile government policy, but there are, also, more fundamental structural processes at work, stimulated by international competition and the globalisation of large-scale capital (Ferner and Hyman,1992:xxiii). The dramatic decline in manufacturing, a drop from eight million jobs to five million between 1971 and 1988 and the growth in service sector employment from 11.6 million to 15.2 million in the corresponding period (Crompton,1993:82) has had a significant impact upon union membership and the landscape of the labour movement. Three positions can be identified which appear to imply continuing, long term difficulties for British trade unions. There are those writers, including Offe (1985) and Lash and Urry (1987), who emphasise structural change in the class structure and the composition of segmented labour, concluding that the traditional basis for collectivist organisation is being eroded. Although employing a distinct theoretical framework, Goldthorpe (1984) can be included here. There are those arguments, specific to the British experience, which assume that Thatcherism was successful in securing a permanent purchase upon employees, fostering a more individualised workplace outlook (Hall and Jacques,1983;Hall,1988) and those who remain sceptical of the view that a new form of capitalism is emerging but who, nonetheless, believe that there are good reasons why capital should mount a sustained attempt to claw back the ground lost to labour through the 'post-war settlement' (Hyman,1991; Coates,1989;Hyman and Elgar,1981).

However, it is by no means certain that structural or 'compositional' changes (changes in the nature of the class structure and/or changes in the ideological orientation of employees) will 'inevitably' produce a decline in the vitality of trade unionism. There are good grounds for treating the 'compositional' analysis with some caution (Kelly,1990). A number of the socio-economic changes identified by theorists such as Offe, Scott and Lash, and Hall (1988) pre-date Thatcherism and can be found in periods of union growth as well as decline; while many late capitalist societies display the structural features and patterns of change identified in the compositional argument, there is enormous variation in the ways in which trade union movements have responded (some with significant success), empirical attitudinal survey data fails to support the argument for permanent ideological change, and even within the economic sectors most likely to display features of new 'post-Fordist', non-unionised workplace relations, such as electronics, there is considerable evidence to suggest that it is the 'business cycle' and the accompanying political climate rather than deeper, permanent structural change which has brought a harsher climate for unions (Kelly,1990:33-34).

One of the most acute problems for the labour movement as a whole is to distinguish between the permanent feature and the conjuncturally specific. As discussed below, the debate between those stressing structural or compositional change and those suggesting that a decline in unionism is a less permanent product of the business cycle, is of vital significance for unions in considering questions such as the effectivity of recruitment drives (Mason and Bain,1993) and of course, political and communication strategies.

Practical implications: the concrete experience of unions since 1979

Though Thatcherism may have left collective bargaining structures relatively unscathed at a local level, nonetheless, its impact upon the national political environment for trade unions was dramatic. Step by step legislation which place very significant restraints upon the mechanisms used traditionally by trade unions to defend their members' interests was enacted. Secondary action and closed shops were, in effect, banished; individual members rights of employment protection severely weakened, and long-standing immunities protecting industrial action withdrawn (McIlroy,1989). In addition, legislation now overrides internal union constitutions in a manner not paralleled elsewhere in civil society, so that all senior positions and the executive committees of all unions have to be filled by compulsory secret ballot (Edwards et al,1992:14-15).

As a number of commentators have remarked, many of these measures were not entirely new in their own right. What was new in the last decade was the combination of civil and criminal law (Hyslop,1988:78) in conjunction with a cheerful toleration of mass unemployment, an extensive programme of privatisation, other measures designed to 'free up' the labour market (abolition of wages councils, training schemes designed to depress wage rates for the young, abandonment of the Fair Wage doctrine in the public sector), a dismantling of tripartite corparatism, and the sheer political will behind the whole process (McLroy,1989:103; Rubery,1986:108; Longstreth,1988:415). The sequestration of union funds, effectively paralysing the NUM and NGA during disputes and successfully cowing the NUS, seemed in the mid Eighties to symbolise the triumph of the government in taming trade unions but, as McIlroy (1989:102) points out, the defeat of the miners was secured by encouraging 'working miners' to employ existing common law, rather than the new legislative arsenal.

Doubts regarding the impact of the new legislative framework were expressed during the mid and late 1980s. Rubery (1986), MacInnes (1987 a and b), Mitchell (1987) and Longstreth (1988) all pointed to evidence of continuity, as well as some change, in industrial relations at a local level. Once local collective bargaining structures are established, it is difficult to eradicate them (Rubery,1986:83) and the Workplace Industrial Relations Surveys (cited in Rubery and Longstreth), conducted during the early 1980s, suggested that unions were generally being successful in preserving local recognition agreements. Indeed, according to the W.I.R.S., the gradual extension of formal, local agreements in the workplace continued into the first half of the 1980s (Longstreth,1988:420), with the number of establishments drawing up agreements at least covering pay and conditions, discipline and dismissal, increasing from 85% to 94% between 1980 and 1984. For these writers, the pace of change at a local level was much slower than might be suggested by the government's legislative project and the rhetoric of ministers.

However, in the first half of the new decade a rather different picture emerges. It remains the case that employers have often been reluctant to exploit the full potential of the new legislative framework to confront unions in the workplace. Relatively few have simply terminated existing agreements, preferring instead to marginalise their influence through more subtle 'partial exclusion policies' (Smith and Morton,1993:97) including, for example, greater emphasis upon direct communication with employees, by-passing union channels of communication, fragmentation of bargaining and the introduction of performance related pay (Smith and Morton,1993). Nevertheless, there is evidence of a growing rate of de-recognition.[2] The most significant impact is in the case of 'greenfield' sites and new enterprises where employers appear now to be much more willing to resist unionisation in the first place and exploit the greater discretionary power afforded by the new legislative framework (Smith and Mason,1993). Given the decline in traditional, usually organised, manufacturing and the growing dominance of the new service sector activity, this is a particularly sharp problem for unions seeking to bolster membership levels through recruitment in new areas.

The evidence does not all point in one direction. Unions have enjoyed some success in securing new recognition agreements. One hundred and three new agreements were signed between 1988 and 1993, covering 60,000 employees.[3] Nevertheless, according to the Department of Employment, the proportion of workers covered by collective pay agreements has dropped from 55% of all full-time employees in 1975 to just 34% in 1993.[4] Similarly, there has been a decline in the number of members organised in closed shops, from 5.2 million in 1978 to 2.6 million in 1989 (Edwards et al,1992:15). Overall, the pattern seems to be that while employee rights have clearly been weakened in significant but specific ways, 'the basic system of individual employment rights [has been] left largely intact', and indeed, in some ways has been strengthened, through the application of European community law and the rulings of the European Court of Justice (Edwards et al, 1992:15). Even rising rates of unemployment do not, in themselves, necessarily imply a weakening of trade unions. Given increasing labour market segmentation, union organisation in 'core' skilled markets may remain relatively strong despite very high levels of unemployment in other segments (Ferner and Hyman,1992:xxvii).

The 'law of unintended consequences' has also, to an extent, worked in favour of trade unionism. If the government implicitly assumed that the 1984 Trade Union Act would deny trade union funds to the Labour Party and effectively impede most trade unions' own political campaigning, the consequences of the Act in practice have been quite different. In being compelled to actively campaign amongst their memberships to secure a vote in favour of a political fund, unions have been spurred to devise new internal communication techniques, compile accurate centralised membership lists, consider sometimes for the first time the nature of the target audiences within their memberships, and think through the relation between communication strategies and political objectives.[5] Perhaps, most important was the evidence which suggested clearly to union leaderships that communication was a crucial factor. Opinion poll data demonstrated that a majority of unions would have failed to secure a 'yes' vote from their memberships if ballots had been held before each campaign got underway (Blackwell and Terry,1987:639). While one view is sceptical regarding the more extravagant claims of union leaderships in relation to the mass participation of ordinary members in these campaigns (Blackwell and Terry,1987:640), there is no doubt that the success of every union, including even those which had never previously considered the option, in securing support for the establishment of political funds, was a tremendous success which pushed communication work much higher up each union agenda. Very much the same effect was produced by the 1988 Employment Act. If the hidden agenda behind this Act, which required unions to hold postal ballots for all senior posts and national executive committees, was to alter the political balance within union leaderships in favour of 'moderation', once again, the consequences were quite different. In almost every case, on turn-outs significantly lower than for comparable workplace elections, the union status quo prevailed. However, the 1988 Act also acted as an important spur to unions in the development of internal communication and campaigning work.[6]

A great deal depends upon the orientation of management. There is evidence that not only unions but managements are frequently uncertain as to how best to adapt to a new environment in which unions are weaker and the labour market more de-regulated (Streeck,1987). There is certainly evidence of a greater insistence on the part of managers upon 'flexibility' and 'flexibile specialisation' (Hirst, 1989) in the labour process (the application of specialised skills but without the demarcations which afforded skilled workers considerable control over their experience of work in earlier decades). Managements are more likely now to encourage a shift away from collectivised employee relations towards individualised arrangements in terms of pay and performance but there is little evidence that managements have sought to impose full-blown 'human resource management' techniques on a large scale (Edwards et al, 1992:27). Ironically, it has been in the public, rather the private sector where new 'hawkish' management styles have provided the context for the more determined application of human resource management approaches.

At the same time, the various indicators of industrial conflict all suggest a decline in overt workplace resistance. The annual number of officially recorded strikes fell throughout the 1980s to just 354 in 1991 (compared to an annual average of 2,885 between 1970 and 1974), and the number of days lost through strike activity fell from 11,964 in 1980 to 759 in 1991 (Edwards et al,1992:55). The effect of recession and unemployment in dampening strike activity is difficult to untangle from the additional obstacles to strike action created through the legislation of the last decade and the 'deterrent effect' of the high profile union defeats of the 1980s (Kelly, 1990). Nevertheless, while there are significantly fewer stoppages, unions have generally been successful in retaining the potential for strike action as a weapon in their armouries.[7] In the 1970s, the tendency was for there to be a large number of short strikes, involving relatively few workers. While the total number of strikes dramatically declined in the 1980s, the number of long strikes involving greater numbers of workers, actually increased.[8]

Evidence on earnings also suggests that within the organised primary sector of the labour market, unions have had some degree of success in maintaining the strength of collective bargaining in a very hostile climate. Those workers in traditionally strong positions have often managed to consolidate their positions, though there has been some relative decline in two key areas, manufacturing and the public sector (Rubery,1986:94). Of course, as MacInnes stresses, the success of certain groups in preserving or improving their earnings has not been through sustained economic growth during the last decade but because the labour policies of the Government have allowed such groups to enhance their positions at the expense of weaker groups in secondary labour markets, unorganised industries, and the young, the old, and the unemployed (MacInnes,1987: pxiv), - very much the danger anticipated by Offe (1985). Polarization between those in prosperous primary sector positions and the low paid, between the private and public sectors, between the prosperous regions and the depressed, and between occupations within companies, is clearly increasing (Edwards,1986:7; Longstreth,1988:420-422; MacInnes,1987: preface; Rubery,1986:94-95). The evidence suggests, then, an uneven picture with certain groups of workers insulated, to a degree, from the impact of labour market deregulation whilst others suffer a significant deterioration in their market positions.

A similar situation exists regarding multi-skilling and job controls. There clearly has been widespread change in working practices and procedures for the use of new technologies in many occupations during the 1980s. Some theorists have interpreted these as part of an employers offensive to loosen the control of unions over the labour process (Hyman and Elgar,1981). While many employers have probably sought to develop such strategies, evidence of their success is, once again, patchy. Changes in working practices have often been introduced within the framework of existing agreements rather than by abandoning them and unions have been quite successful in retaining controls and safeguards over the pace of work (Rubery,1986: 96-98). Often management try to introduce changes to working practices as part of a pragmatic and piecemeal response to changes in market conditions rather than as part of a 'grand strategy' (Edwards,1992:60). On the other hand, many of the industries in which unions were sufficiently organised to secure job controls are now declining and new areas of employment are developing without any tradition of agreement over working practices or the nature of jobs. In introducing computerised technology, employers have often side-stepped the craft unions by recruiting white collar staff (Rubery 1986:97-98; Longstreth 1988:425). Once again, the evidence suggests an uneven picture in which some groups of workers successfully employ strategies to preserve gains they have made over the years or to accomodate change within acceptable frameworks while other groups are more fully exposed to the impact of political and economic macro trends. Attempts by management to secure higher levels of productivity from workers through changes to shift arrangements, new working practices and the utilisation of new technologies are not necessarily opposed by union members but neither are they welcomed, as one might expect if employees were fully embracing a new ideology of individualised industrial relations. Rather, it seems that the response of workers is characterised by a fatalistic and grudging acceptance of their 'inevitablity' (Kelly,1990).

The Union response

One point to emerge immediately is that given the uneven and complex nature of the impacts of the political economic environment upon unions in recent decades, unions are unlikely to produce a common response. Rather, particular unions will respond in distinct ways, according to their perceptions of their positions in relation to certain segments of the labour market, the extent to which they can shield themselves from the more severe consequences of the new legislative climate and each union's own traditions and organisational culture.

Overshadowing the strategic thinking of every union is the aggregate decline in union membership. From the historic peak of 13.3 million affiliated members in 1979, membership of the TUC had dropped to little more than 10 million in 1988 (Bird et al,1989) and continued to fall towards 7 million by 1993 (Mason and Bain,1993; Hutton,1993). Perhaps more worrying for unions is the evidence regarding union density. On all the various measures of density, the data suggests a declining union profile but the accelerating decline in the proportion of union members to those in full-time employment in the late 1980s, indicates that unions were failing to make significant in-roads into the new employment sectors which began to expand (Edwards,1992:32). According to Mason and Bain (1993), opportunities do exist for unions to increase recruitment amongst the estimated three to four million non-unionised employees to be found in workplaces where recognition agreements remain intact and in 1989, they point out, 27 out of the 78 TUC affiliates did actually increase their membership totals. However, as described above, debate continues regarding the extent to which unions can exert influence over the fundamental forces shaping the ebb and flow of unionisation, with some academics, the 'structural determinists', taking the view that 'exogeneous' factors (the business cycle, government policy and employer strategy) are decisive, whilst others, the 'union interventionists', more recently taking the view that union leadership, strategy and organisation have an effectivity,- they can 'make a difference' in assisting unions to expand in hostile environments (Mason and Bain,1993). In particular, Kelly (1990:41) argues that there are good grounds for believing that under-investment in recruitment campaigns and the provision of services for members is partly responsible for declining membership.

In practice, the exogeneous 'structural' environment is likely to provide the context within which the effectivity of union strategy and leadership is tested; appropriate union intervention 'making a difference' but within the limitations and constraints imposed by labour market conditions, the practice of employers and the orientation of the state. The example of the effectiveness of the recruitment strategies of white collar unions, such as ASTMS in the 1960s and 1970s, and white collar union leaders, such as Clive Jenkins, are often cited by supporters of the 'interventionist' account but, of course, the particular structural conditions of many white collar and professional employees, especially in the public sector, have clearly also favoured unionisation. The complex position now regarding the success of unions in mounting recruitment strategies reflects the segmentation of labour markets and the uneven impact of 'exogenous' factors described above. For example, decline in overall union density masks some areas of considerable strength and union success, although these are hardly the examples one might have anticipated during the 1960s and 1970s. Manual workers are still more likely to be in unions than white collar workers, as a whole, but according to the 1991 Labour Force Survey union density was highest amongst professional occupations (52%), accounted for largely by the very high rates of unionisation in teaching, lecturing and other 'public sector' professions.[9] More recent evidence confirms this pattern (Central Statistical Office, 1995:74). Kelly identifies 23 unions successful in increasing their membership levels between 1979 and 1988; 17 of these are wholly or mainly public sector or organising within sectors only very recently privatised (Kelly,1990:32). The employment areas which provided fertile ground for recruitment during the 1980s are very much removed from the heavy industrial manual heartlands. While the unions organising in traditional manual sectors have suffered membership decline, it is sectors including media and entertainment, telecommunication, education, banking, health and other public sector work, where unions have actually expanded (Kelly,1990:32).

Contrary to some views, it is 'de-professionalisation' which triggers unionisation, rather than vice-versa (Raelin,1989). The public sector in Britain, as in many European countries (Ferner and Hyman,1992:pxxviii), has seen sustained state pressure to depress pay and secure increased productivity through a combination of cut backs in staffing and pressure to agree new 'flexible' working conditions. However, in Britain this has also been accompanied by reforms and re-organisaton designed to introduce market disciplines to the delivery of public services and new market oriented management perspectives. The combination of growing job insecurity, deteriorating rewards, and in the case of public sector professional occupations, decreasing professional autonomy, has created a fertile climate for the public sector unions.

But there are other areas of opportunity for unions. Although union density is, historically, much lower amongst part-time employees, it has remained stable and, indeed, has actually slightly increased while full-time union density has declined.[10] As almost a quarter of the workforce is now part-time this is of some significance. Similarly, there are some indications that unionisation amongst female employees has remained more buoyant while male rates of union density have continued to decline.[11] A large number of part-time jobs are now taken by school leavers and young workers. In the past unions have invested little time targeting 'young people' as potential recruits; the complacent assumption that union values will somehow be automatically transmitted to the next generation can no longer be made, given the destruction of the apprentice system and the concentration of young people in part-time, casualised and 'super-exploited' segments of labour markets (Kossof,1988b). The process of segmentation not only reflects patterns of gender and age differentiation but, of course, race as well (Ohri and Faruqi,1988). It is clear that some of the largest unions which traditionally recruited in largely masculine manual employment sectors are now turning to these other segments of the labour market. The T and G and the GMB, for example, have begun to recruit significantly more young people, part-time female workers, and temporary workers (Haque,1990) though the T and G lost almost forty percent of its membership between 1979 and 1990.[12]

A fundamental challenge, then, for unions in the present decade is to respond to the increasing segmentation of labour markets with appropriate recruitment strategies. As many of these segments consist of 'unorganised' employees with little previous experience of unions and little daily contact with union activists, a central element in such strategies must be communication. However, this process must involve more than just finding an appropriate symbolic formula with which to communicate union values; it is likely that structural and organisational reform of existing union power structures will be a prerequisite for really effective work in these unorganised or under-organised segments. Often the reasons for particular social groups not joining unions in large numbers are complex, not merely that the union message has so far failed to reach them. This issue has grown sharper as the feminisation of important segments of labour markets has accelerated and the traditional patriarchal nature of many union structures, thrown into sharp relief (Briskin and McDermot, 1993). Even in the late 1980s, the higher echelons of most unions remained in male hands, although a minority of female salaried officials were making some progress.[13]

Some unions have recognised the need to respond to the changing nature of labour markets through reform of their organisational structures as well as their approaches to communication. As we shall see in the next chapter, there is evidence that some unions are trying to formulate communication strategies employing new vocabularies and imagery with, free from the traditional masculine symbolism which used to characterise much union communication - the example of pictures of rows of male delegates in shirt sleeves at conference is often cited. The content of certain union journals certainly indicates this (Manning, 1996). UNISON, the product of a merger between NALGO, COHSE and NUPE, has attempted to extend the process of reform beyond communicative work and has created a constitution which formally requires the establishment of organisational structures reflecting the dimensions of race, gender and disability (Collinson,1994). Other unions have not moved so far as to build a recognition of new potential membership profiles into their constitutions but there is a growing awareness of the need to make union membership more attractive and more meaningful for groups traditionally neglected by unions but which are likely to become increasingly important union constituencies as labour market segmentation progresses. Thus, a number of unions, including the CPSA, USDAW, and MSF, are seeking new ways of 'reaching' young workers (Kossof,1988a; Labour Research, September 1990b). The CPSA has recently adopted a 'Charter for Youth'. Other unions are adopting strategies designed to weaken existing mechanisms of male control, particularly at branch level, where 'progressive' strategies supported by female activists and, often, salaried officials are sometimes resisted by male members (Cunnison and Stageman, 1993).

However, pressures for change do not inevitably produce evolutionary refinement. As discussed further below, the TUC has sought to define a new strategic role for itself as a recruitment agency for the labour movement as a whole. In response to the dramatic decline in union membership through the 1980s, a TUC Special Review Group was established in 1987 to draw up a plan for union survival. One product of this review was the suggestion that the TUC should take responsibility for recruitment drives targeted at 'greenfield sites' and employment sectors with low union densities. In 1990 the TUC targeted Trafford Industrial Park in Manchester and Docklands in London, both areas with new industrial and commercial enterprises; jobs in services, white collar work and information technology, and a significant amount of associated part-time and casual employment. However, in both cases the results were unimpressive and the costs in terms of publicity materials and advertising high (Harper,1990). The reasons for the failure of these initiatives are complex but one of the factors undermining the projects was the half-hearted support of the largest unions, still conscious of the competitive nature of union recruitment, particularly around unorganised and greenfield sites in an era of single union deals. In fact, there is evidence to suggest that some unions, including the largest, are inclined to seek the 'line of least resistance' by competing for a larger share of existing organised memberships, rather than undertaking the fundamentally more difficult task of recruiting in new unorganised sectors (Willman, 1989).

Similarly, another defensive response to membership decline is merger and the late 1980s saw a wave of merger activity. By 1990 twenty of the major TUC affiliates were engaged in merger discussions of some kind.[14] Thus, the three public sector unions, NUPE, NALGO and COHSE merged to form UNISON, now the largest TUC affiliate; the two biggest unions for skilled engineering workers, the EETPU and the AUE, merged to form the AUEE; two major technical and white collar unions, APEX and the ASTMS combined to extend their activities throughout the professional service and financial sector in the form of MSF; and the GMB has expanded through a series of effective 'take-overs'. Only four from the original panel of eleven unions selected for the present research have not been affected by merger or take-over in the last six years. As discussed below, merger activity is likely to have important implications for communication work because potential union suitors will seek to construct appropriate public images.

Some writers believe, however, that an even more fundamental re-orientation is occurring arising from the pressure to sustain memberships and the new cultural ethos of the 1980s. For example, Bassett and Cave (1993), Field (1988),Wickens (1987:ch 9), Bassett (1986), Sherman (1986), all share the view that to survive unions must re-fashion their primary purpose, place far less emphasis upon the protection of collective rights, spend more time in exploring the ways in which they can assist individual employees in negotiating with employers and develop the range of services they supply to members as individual 'consumers'. For Bassett, the series of 'strike free' and 'single union' deals negotiated from the early 1980s onwards at plants, such as Sanyo, Nissan, Hitachi, Toshiba and Silentnight, signal the way forward. Such deals are the necessary price unions must pay for recognition in the new sectors of economic growth which do not have the traditions of manual unionisation and collective representation (Bassett,1986:chs 8 and 9) In these circumstances, unions must find new ways of meeting the needs of their members through the provision of services customised more finely to suit the requirements of individual employees. This may involve the development of financial services (Wickens,1987), welfare provision (Field,1988), 'off the peg' contract clauses to facilitate individualised employee bargaining (Bassett and Cave,1993) or a rolling programme of market research and improved internal communication (Sherman,1986). No longer will unions be able to recruit simply on the basis of the collective protection they afford through the possession of industrial muscle.

A number of these writers, including Bassett and Cave, Sherman and Foster and Wolfson (1989) are inclined to regard the rise of 'business unionism', as these developments are sometimes described, as the first indications of a more general pattern which is emerging as a consequence of the changes in the class structure, the shift in production towards post-Fordist arrangements, and the hegemonic effect of Thatcherism. In this sense, such union initiatives are 'read' as structurally determined responses and are regarded in some way as 'inevitable'. However, there are some who question the extent to which such evidence does provide an indication of a more generalised pattern yet to emerge. MacInnes (1987:151) and Edwards (1992:28) point out that 'new style' agreements relating to industrial behaviour, pendulum arbitration, flexible working, and other concessions made through 'business unionism', still only involve a small proportion of workers. In fact, only one union has shown a consistent appetite for single union deals. Between 1988 and 1993, eighty-one such deals have been negotiated and fifty-three have involved the AEEU.[15] It is entirely possible, then, to read the concessions made by some unions towards 'business unionism' in recent years as pragmatic responses to a hostile environment, rather than a permanent and structurally inspired re-orientation.

Nevertheless, it is true that unions have had to review and, in some cases, re-think the basis of the relationships they have constructed with their memberships. Whether or not particular unions are seeking to organise in sectors directly affected by technological innovation, or new management techniques, or changes in the composition of the working class, as we have seen, all unions have had to fight harder to retain members and find new ones. This has led to a steady growth in the provision of financial, legal, leisure and other services by unions for members[16] and greater effort being invested in market research techniques and communication work. Heery and Kelly (1994) believe that the 'servicing relationship' between trade unions and their members can be understood as having passed through three phases in post-war Britain. While they concede that by no means all unions have conformed to this typological history, they argue that immediately after the war many unions were characterised by 'professionalism unionism' through which 'a cadre of professional representatives' negotiated on behalf of 'a largely passive membership' (1994:3). This type of servicing relationship was undermined in the late 1960s and 1970s as full time union officials had to accommodate new claims for greater power and involvement at shop floor level with the growing influence of shop stewards in many industries. This period is described by Heery and Kelly as a period of 'participative unionism' but this, in turn, has been broken up by 'the sharp decline in aggregate union membership since 1979 which 'has prompted the emergence of a new servicing relationship' (1994:7). This third form of 'servicing relationship' is characterised by Heery and Kelly as 'managerial unionism' and is based upon a new perception of union members as 'discerning and calculating consumers who must be deliberately attracted into the union fold' (1994:7). Hence, the increased investment of time and resources in researching and monitoring employee needs, and in designing and promoting union services in ways calculated to appeal to particular sections of the labour market. In short, union membership is regarded as a product to be marketed.

There are important implications for union communication work in these developments. By no means all unions have fully embraced a new understanding of 'servicing relationships' but there is evidence in both union journals and in the work of union press officers that a number of unions now attach more importance to communication work because they can no longer assume that the workplace environment will continue to offer up a continuous flow of membership applications. If unions do seek to present themselves to employees in new ways, this has to be communicated and, given the increasing inclination of employers to seek ways of 'directly communicating ' with employees themselves, it is ever more important for unions that their communication strategies are effective.

Summary

Union communication work has to be understood in the context of a changing political and economic environment. As Ferner and Hyman (1992) suggest it is quite possible that capital will seek to organise labour through a variety of new and traditional production relations depending upon its particular needs in different sectors of the economy. And yet it is possible that the advantages of 'flexibility' and 'efficiency' in the new forms of production represent a compelling logic which employers will seek to apply and extend. On balance, while much of the new industrial landscape may be more permanent than the supporters of the 'business cycle' model assume, it seems probable that union intervention in terms of recruitment strategy, political campaigning and communication work does 'make a difference'.

Union leaderships certainly assume this to be case and have responded to the changes in the political-economic environment in a number of ways. The exclusion of the union elite from the centre of government in the period since 1979 has compelled trade union leaderships to think more about the nature of political communication. Only 'insider groups' can afford the luxury of ignoring media and political communication work. Beyond this, the new harsher legislative environment has forced unions to re-consider the importance of communication and public relations in the industrial context. The collapse in the traditional membership bases in manual and manufacturing industries, combined with the increasingly complex segmentation of labour markets, has necessitated a more sophisticated targeting of existing and potential members, particularly part-time and casualised employees, women working in un-organised sectors, young workers, black and Asian workers. The distinct experience of employees in the public and private sectors and the pressure towards de-professionalisation in the caring occupations has generated a number of politically important agendas which unions have had to address in their communication work. Just as Offe (1985: ch 6) recommends, some unions have sought to attract new members in the public sector caring occupations through re-asserting the professional status of such work but, at the same time, other public sector unions have interpreted the new assault on public sector pay and conditions as an opportunity to re-assert traditional collective union values. As we shall see, this can produce certain ambiguities in the discourse and symbolism employed by unions in their communication work.

Union communication strategies

Before tracing the slow development of trade union communication work it is important to consider the range of possibilities from which British trade unions have selected their strategies. Clearly, as with all aspects of political strategy, choice and decision making regarding communication work are bounded by the constraints and circumstances of the period. Nevertheless, even though in earlier periods communication technology was both cruder and relatively more expensive, there were choices to be made. Comparison with the experience of trade unions in the USA illustrates this point, though it also suggests that trade unions are likely to confront a set of common obstacles to effective communication work, whether they organise in Britain or the USA (there is little substantial comparative material on trade union communication work in Europe). A great deal depends upon the assumptions which are made regarding the possibilities of working 'within' or 'without' the organisations of news production and agencies of communication.

(i) *Radical Critique and Structural Reform*

There are those, of course, within the labour movement who hold a view of politics and of the structural position of the mass media which leads to a scepticism regarding, not only public relations techniques but any communications strategy which does not address the need for fundamental structural reform. In other words, the problem has to be addressed from without, through the application of measures external to the news media and communication systems. In relation to newspaper publishing, for example, it has been frequently argued by trade unionists and others (Basnett and Goodman,1977) that the tendency towards concentration of ownership in the hands of powerful proprietors and companies hostile to the objectives of the labour movement, makes the task of presenting a diverse range of political perspectives, including a trade union agenda extremely problematic. Only an elaborate regulatory framework or interventionist mechanism, enforced through state legislation, will begin to open up opportunities for trade unions to develop a coherent news agenda. Those who question the neutrality of the state doubt whether even this approach will succeed given the advantages which wealth and the possession of resources confer upon those resorting to law (Foot,1984).

A great deal depends upon the model which is used to describe and analyse the news media and communication agencies. Albert Zack, director of public relations for the AFL-CIO in the U.S. (1958-1980), insisted that anti-union bias in news coverage was a product of reporter ignorance rather than a reflection of dominant political and economic structures. The remedy, therefore, lay in ever greater 'accommodative' efforts to brief journalists and provide them with appropriate news materials amongst other conventional public relations techniques. However, this approach was attacked by several different unions, particularly during the 1970s, who argued that strategies were required which did address the problem of the structural positioning of the news media, including media education for trade unionists (in order to give them the critical skills to decode ideological content) and campaigns to publicly highlight the inter-locking corporate media structure of American capitalism (Douglas,1986:46-48 and 239-256).

Only, perhaps, during the period in which News International became the focus of public attention during the 1987 Wapping dispute, have British unions adopted a similar strategy of corporate 'outing'. However, some British trade unions have supported campaigns for structural reform and state intervention in news publishing. The TUC and some individual unions submitted evidence to the last Royal Commission on the Press (MacGregor) during the mid-1970s and, more recently, several unions have helped to fund the Campaign for Press and Broadcasting Freedom, which campaigns for a number of regulatory reforms to increase diversity of political perspective within the news media. The TUC has also taken an active role in submitting evidence and proposals to the government during the preparation of the 1988 Broadcasting White Paper and 1990 Act.

The underlying logic of the strategy here assumes that while institutional and structural forces may shape the nature of news and cultural production in ways which disadvantage subordinate groups like ordinary workers and trade unionists, nonetheless, it is possible to employ the power of the state, as an external pressure, to modify these patterns of representation and open up opportunities for the expression of subordinate perspectives. The obvious difficulty with these strategies in Britain is the absence, in the last sixteen years or longer, of a political administration likely to seriously consider such proposals. The record of progress of privately sponsored 'right of reply' proposals in the House of Commons is not encouraging.

(ii) *Advertising and Independent Channels of Communication*

As in Britain, at the root of the communication problem for unions in the USA has been a suspicion of the daily national newspapers which have a history of hostile labour coverage (Douglas 1986:18). Just as in Britain, the structure of the newspaper market has worked against the survival of newspapers sympathetic to the goals of the labour movement but unions in the USA moved much earlier towards developing comprehensive independent communication strategies. For American unions too, the dilemma has been whether to choose to work through the dominant communication and media systems with all the difficulties which arise from the political and economic structures which underpin them, or to seek to develop alternative and independent channels of communication which afford greater control over the nature of the message constructed but which have major implications in terms of resources and access to capital.

Attempts were made to develop union supported alternative daily papers in the first two decades of the twentieth century but as these floundered American unions turned to explore the possibilities of pioneering of trade union radio. The first AFL funded station began broadcasting in Chicago in 1926 and individual unions also established local FM stations in the 1940s (Douglas,1986:chs 2 and 3). As the costs of FM broadcasting mounted in the post war period unions made greater use of free public service slots on radio and on a more limited scale television, too (Pomper,1959). However, with gradual de-regulation, the 'public sphere' supported by the public service slots also began to shrink and in order to avoid dependence upon newspapers as the main channel of communication with existing members or the general public a number of unions in the US have turned to advertising despite the costs.

Given the high costs involved, advertising is only likely to become a more attractive option as the political and ideological environments grow harsher. American unions turned to advertising in the 1950s as the costs of running FM radio grew prohibitive; the public service slots on networked broadcasting began to shrink and public opinion grew alarmed at the prospect of the merger of the CIO and AFL in 1955 (Pomper,1959:483). In the 1960s, American unions turned to advertising in response to the perception that the hostility of newspaper coverage was growing more intense (Douglas,1986:38). Most recently, unions in the US have resorted to advertising in recognition of the weakening of their industrial muscle and the toughening of corporate management attitudes during disputes (Riley,1993). Of course, advertising is not free from institutional, political and economic constraints but it does allow even union clients greater control over the construction of the message than attempts to disseminate information through mainstream news organisations.

Larger memberships, greater incomes and a more diverse media environment have encouraged American unions to be more ambitious than their British counterparts. However, their communication goals have been characterised by a similar defensiveness and commitment to a 'labourist agenda'. Perhaps reflecting the experience of organising during the McCarthy years, a common theme in much communication work has been the part American organised labour contributes to the 'American way of life'. American manufacturing unions in textiles and car production, for example, have regularly organised 'label' campaigns aiming to persuade consumers to buy goods produced by American organised labour. They have chosen not to develop more radical themes which place issues of workplace power and control on the political agenda, except in one respect. American unions have pioneered in the last decade a technique termed 'corporate campaigning' in which the public image of particular companies is highlighted and attacked in order to weaken their bargaining position, using a variety of media opportunities from advertising to briefing journalists, with a focus upon the poor records of such companies in terms of the treatment of employees, their environmental record, and even the inter locking directorships of the management teams (Riley 1993; Douglas 1986:239-256).

The institutional and regulatory arrangements for broadcasting in Britain have not provided British unions with either opportunities to establish their own broadcasting institutions or regular public access slots on mainstream broadcasting channels, although the TUC is now planning to utilise the BBC television's night time education schedule. British unions have also been much slower to consider the possibilities of advertising through mainstream media though white collar unions have occasionally invested in advertising since the 1960s for the purposes of recruitment or more recently in campaigns against public expenditure cuts and the privatisation of public utilities. Though advertising affords greater client control over the nature of the message constructed, the costs involved combined with the labour movement's historic suspicion of commercial advertising and, perhaps, a scepticism regarding its effectiveness, have caused unions to distance themselves from the world of professional advertising until the 1980s. Related to this is a view of the cultural and the industrial as quite distinct spheres of social activity, which was shared by much of the British labour movement until relatively recently. Unlike many European labour movements and even the USA, where unions have sponsored and even participated in plays, films and broadway musicals (Douglas,1986:ch3), British unions have been reluctant to stray too far into the sphere of cultural production. Once again, it is only in the recent past and through the initiatives of mainly white collar unions, that a labour movement perspective has been presented in terms of union sponsored drama and film.

(iii) *Media Pressure Politics*

While unions may lack the material and symbolic resources to develop alternative channels of communication or advertising, given certain prerequisites, considerable political energy can be harnessed through a lobbying and complaints strategy directed at the news media. This involves the identification of the media as a target for lobbying in much the same way as conventional pressure group politics positions the state. The underlying assumption here is that there exist within the news media, institutional forces which act as a barrier to the encoding of a union perspective. The Glasgow University Media Group argue that so entrenched are the 'inferential structures' or taken for granted assumptions of news journalists that use of public relations techniques or communication strategies are unlikely to alter the 'culturally skewed' nature of news reporting. According to their own sample of television news, the more energetic generation of 'publicity inputs' by white collar unions in the 1970s failed to achieve very significant 'improvements' in the quality of coverage, even if interventionist media strategies sometimes increased the quantity of media coverage (1976:235-243). The familiar news values which might, for example, prioritise the personality of an established 'high profile' union leader over coverage of a wider union agenda were resistant to union interventions.

The logic of this analysis led the Glasgow team to favour a complaints strategy over the investment of more resources in conventional public relations (Philo et al,1977). A strategy of complaint concerning particular examples of coverage, supported by evidence derived from content research would have the merit of focusing upon 'the overall framework within which industrial activities are reported' (1977: 136). In other words, the aim would be to expose in the public arena the inferential frameworks shaping mainstream news coverage through documented examples and research. The Glasgow team commend the work of the ACTT in producing the pioneering 'One Week' report on television coverage in 1971 and the work of unions like NALGO in gathering evidence to submit to the 1975 Royal Commission on the Press and the Annan Committee on broadcasting.

A complaints strategy is one way of exerting pressure upon news organisations to review and modify editorial policy. By the 1990s we have become much more familiar with 'media pressure politics', from the establishment of a 'media monitoring unit' at Conservative Central Office, under the chairmanship of Norman Tebbit, to the demonstrations outside Thames Television by the disabled in protest against the passive images of disability conjured by 'telephon' charity events, and the invasion of Fleet Street newsrooms by activists from the women's movement. Any attempt to raise public awareness of issues of selection and news values in the organisation of media production can be regarded as part of the process of 'media pressure politics' and could include anything from organising a day conference to the more spectacular examples above.

The work of the ACTT and NALGO in gathering evidence on patterns of news coverage was followed by the TUC's own analysis of the coverage of the 1979 'Winter of Discontent' (TUC, 1979a) and the union supported work of the Campaign for Press and Broadcasting Freedom in producing an early critical discussion of news media coverage of the 1984-85 Coal Strike (Jones et al,1985). In the USA, as in Britain, monitoring and complaints strategies rose to the top of the union agenda as immediate responses to particularly hostile dispute coverage, where political and industrial conflict had intensified but where there remained a strong ideological commitment to a labour movement agenda. It was in these conditions, for example, that the International Association of Machinists and Aerospace Workers published the first union sponsored research on television images of trade unionism in 1980 (Parenti,1986: ch. 5) in the USA and the same pressures led to the eventual creation of the Labour Institute for Public Affairs, funded by the AFL-CIO in 1982 (Douglas,1986:ch 2), with a brief to develop comprehensive communication strategies for unions, including monitoring research.

The strategies discussed so far have all involved the positioning of unions as external to the news media and main agencies of communication. The final strategy involves the attempt to work with and within the news media. In the cases above, unions seek to modify the communicative practice of media and communications agencies, by pressure exerted through the state and legislature or self initiated 'pressure politics'. Alternatively, unions may seek to exert control over the message communicated, by buying the agency of communication (a radio station) or buying access to the channel of communication (an advertisement or a union funded public access programme). The final strategy, however, requires trade unions to expend resources in the modification of their own organisational arrangements and to modify their cultural practice in order to accommodate the 'needs' of the news media.

(iv) Accommodative News Media Strategies

For the reasons outlined above, through the 1980s a number of leading trade unions have attached more importance to exploring the ways in which they can accommodate their communication goals within the parameters determined by the routine workings of news organisations. In a sense, there has been a movement towards strategies which attempt to work within the existing 'system' of news gathering and production, rather than exert pressure from the outside. In a preliminary survey of trade union communication arrangements in preparation for this study, conducted in 1988, only seven unions with memberships over 45,000 employed one or more full time press officers (see appendix one). The remaining 31 TUC affiliates allocated the duties of a press officer to a member of staff with other administrative responsibilities and frequently without experience as a journalist. Partly as a result of the wave of mergers which created a smaller number of much larger organisations, it has become the norm rather than the exception for unions to employ at least one member of staff with a full time responsibility for press and news media work.

This is one feature of a broader process in which a number of unions have invested significant resources in developing organisational structures geared to internal and external communication work. A movement towards 'working with' news organisations; attaching more importance to making information available to journalists, providing other types of assistance to the news media, and anticipating the work of journalists by 'pre framing' information in terms of mainstream news values, implies a rather different model of the news media to those which underpin the strategies outlined above.

Implicit in this strategy is the view that news production is not wholly shaped by the structural position of news organisations or by the levers of instrumental power available to the enemies of trade unionism. It implies that the 'inferential frameworks' shaping the approaches of journalists still allow some opportunities and possibilities for union press and media work to be effective. A criticism often levelled at the work of the Glasgow University Media Group, for example, is that they paid insufficient attention to studying the process of news production in the field (Elliott,1981;Cottle,1993:9). A theme to be developed in this study is that, not withstanding the political and structural context within which news production occurs, the politics of engagement between union officials and journalists cannot be ignored if we are to fully understand the process of encoding labour and industrial news. In the course of dealing with industrial and labour correspondents, the skills of an effective union press officer and a thoughtful approach to news agendas can 'make a difference', albeit within parameters determined by the logic of national daily news production.

Amongst trade unionists suspicions of the dangers which a hostile press may present have not disappeared. Many within the labour movement, including those at a senior trade union level, retain an analysis of media organisations which places them in the context of the class and power relations of capitalism. Nonetheless, 'accommodative strategies' are now more common; more senior officials appear to believe that resources can be invested to exploit what communication opportunities may arise and insure damage limitation exercises are conducted with expertise. Some union leaderships are more optimistic and have committed their unions to 'proactive' and highly interventionist strategies. Nevertheless, British unions have been notably slower to embrace strategies of accommodation and the politics of news media work associated with them, than their American counterparts.

In the USA, it was a crisis in the coverage of labour relations in mainstream news media, following a wave of strikes (Douglas,1986:25) immediately after World War Two, which prompted a public relations firm to be hired jointly by the AFL and CIO in 1948 (prior to the merger of the two organisations in 1955). The aim was to tackle the problem of apparent declining public esteem after years of growing popularity in the pre-war period. Since then 'in-house' public relations departments have become a common feature of most large American unions and a number of the smaller ones (Douglas,1986:111).Larger memberships, greater incomes and a more diverse media environment have encouraged American unions to be more ambitious than their British counterparts in terms of all communication strategies. The Labor Institute for Public Affairs (LIPA) was established with funding from the AFL-CIO and individual unions in 1982. LIPA's primary aim has been to develop comprehensive communication strategies in the USA and to explore the ways in which new communication technologies can be exploited including video and cable television (Douglas,1986:38-43). This may mean that in the future American unions will begin to place less emphasis upon accommodative work with news journalists but at present such work remains a central part of many union communication strategies in the United States.

American union communication goals, then, have often been characterised by a similar defensiveness and commitment to a 'labourist' agenda - with the exception of 'corporate campaigning' - to their British counterparts. The absence of a sustained discussion of workplace relations and issues of power, for example, is a notable feature of British union journals (Manning, 1996; Grace, 1985; Selvin, 1963). The greater the tendency to rely upon accommodative strategies, the more likely it is that union agendas will reflect the caution of labourism and articulate even quite conservative themes because of the need to mobilise dominant media news values.

The slow emergence of trade union communication strategies

For some writers, 1979 marks the point at which trade unions begin to take communication issues seriously (Seaton,1982; Verzuh,1990). It is in 1979 that the unions suddenly find themselves dramatically cast out from their 'insider' relations with government, with the arrival of Mrs Thatcher in office, and according to conventional pressure group theory organisations enjoying only 'outsider' status quickly come to see media work as the main weapon in their armouries (Grant,1990). And, of course, it is from 1979 onwards that, for the multiplicity of reasons discussed above, the need for effective communication work grows ever more pressing. However, this view is an over-simplification in both theoretical and empirical terms. To begin with, as argued in the first chapter, the conventional insider/outsider model is state-centric and underestimates the importance of the news media as foci for lobbying activity on the part of both 'insider' and 'outsider' groups. Secondly, in terms of the historical record, it is clear that some unions, particularly but not only white collar unions, have prioritised communication work for considerably longer and that the issue of news media representation of trade unionism was a matter of sharp concern shared by trade unionists at various intervals throughout the history of the labour movement but especially during the decade before, as well as after, 1979.

A labour and industrial beat for newspaper correspondents emerged in the 1930s (Evans,1953) and this will be discussed at length in chapters five and six. However, in the period before the Second World War, while journalists attended a large number of union conferences and developed informal contacts with many union officials, very few unions assigned specific press and publicity duties to particular staff. The TUC established a press bureau during the 1930s but the official view of the appropriate function of this department was information dissemination rather than a more proactive role (Tracey,1953). During the war, Walter Citrine, TUC General Secretary (1926-1946) showed an interest in the possibilities of radio broadcasting as an educative tool for trade unionists and discussed his ideas with the BBC but in the main, trade union attitudes towards news media coverage were characterised by a 'fatalistic attitude' (Seaton,1982: 273). While the view of radio and newspaper coverage might have been critical, there were few sustained discussions amongst trade union leaders as to what could be done about it and, indeed, not all trade unionists regarded the mass media as their enemy. The NUR executive actually passed a motion thanking the press for its coverage after one dispute in the late 1950s (Wigham,1961:169).

Only some white collar unions and staff associations, presumably because they lacked the certainty of recruitment afforded by the closed shop agreements common in manual industries, demonstrated a willingness to invest resources in the appointment of press officers or the development of publicity campaigns. By the beginning of the post war period the civil service unions, USDAW and NALGO employed staff with these specific responsibilities (Wigham,1961:166) and the NUT appointed a full time press officer in 1956 (Gerbner,1969:219) but as Wigham points out, the customary salaries of union officials in this period were unlikely to attract staff with experience in journalism and, in any case, union etiquette required that union members rather than the general public should be the first to hear of significant developments in union affairs. On the whole, blue collar unions ignored the potential of communication technology and expertise although the NUTGW, in one of the more bizarre union communication initiatives, released a promotional gramophone record in the late 1950s (Wigham, 1961:180).

In its submission to the Donovan Commission, the TUC indicated that it saw little need for an expensive public relations campaign (Seaton 1982: 273). And yet as Eric Wigham, the Times labour correspondent during the 1950s and 1960s, argued this indifference regarding news media coverage flew in the face of evidence of a sinking public standing and a continuing failure to communicate the essential arguments to support the organisation of workers in the workplace (1961:ch 9). This was in marked contrast to trade unions in the United States where ambitious projects to support first newspapers and later radio programmes and even whole radio stations were devised in both the pre and post war periods (Douglas,1986). In the United States, of course, most large employers already used a range of sophisticated public relations techniques, sometimes directed against labour. In Britain, during the 1950s, although some political communication and public relations work was undertaken by large companies, such as ICI, and trade associations including, for example the Iron and Steel Federation and the Road Haulage Association, in response to the threat of nationalisation (Finer,1966:ch7), frequently companies matched trade unions in their reluctance to exploit communication techniques (Wigham,1961:ch 10). In this sense, there was little incentive for unions to invest in media work.

A decade later, Wigham still considered that most trade unions had made little progress in developing appropriate responses to 'the fierce newspaper campaigns' frequently directed against them (1969:172). Several well publicised incidents of ballot rigging and the application of draconian disciplinary measures had provided hostile sections of the press with plenty of ammunition and yet a majority of blue collar unions continued to deplore their portrayal in much news media coverage whilst continuing to regard it as part and parcel of the industrial environment (Philo and Hewitt,1976). However, by the late 1960s Clive Jenkins, general secretary of the newly formed ASTMS, had started to integrate recruitment and publicity campaigns within one systematic strategy. ASTMS planned to recruit in previously unorganised white collar employment sectors and the mass media offered an initial channel of communication between union and potential recruits. Jenkins expended considerable effort in developing a network of contacts, not only with journalists on the labour beat but also science, technology and even education correspondents.[17] It was ASTMS who had the audacity to first take out a newspaper advertisement in the 'top people's paper', The Times, in 1968 and also began to invest in the development of a large publicity and communications department (Jenkins and Sherman,1979:55). It seems that a number of white collar unions began to explore the possibilities of more elaborate communication strategies by the end of the 1960s but blue collar unions, in the main, insulated by their relative strength in terms of recognition agreements and union density, remained more passive in their external communication (Philo and Hewitt,1976) and unimaginative in their development of internal communications (Selvin,1963).

Union Communication Work in the 1970s: the Unions Look Outwards

Certainly, as Seaton (1982) and Verzuh (1990) suggest, the news media coverage of the 1979 Winter of Discontent was generally hostile and did further encourage unions to attach more importance to media and communication work. However, this is better understood as the culmination of a process which had its origins in the growing political and industrial polarisation which began in the late 1960s and quickened in pace throughout the 1970s. There is considerable documentary evidence to confirm that much earlier in the decade an anxiety about the damage hostile news media coverage might do was widespread throughout the union and labour movement. By October 1975 64% of the general public and even 56% of trade unionists in a MORI poll agreed with the proposition that 'most trade unions are controlled by extremists and militants' and 75% of the public and 65% of trade unionists sampled believed that 'trade unions have too much power'.[18] In this decade, though, union membership continued to grow and the size and influence of the TUC continued to expand. Union confidence was high and political prospects appeared fair. Against this background there was less pressure to consider issues of internal communication with memberships and, with some exceptions, trade unions defined the problem of communication as an external one, concerning the representation of trade unions by broadcasting organisations and the press. Rather than accommodate the 'needs' of the news media, encouraged by the political confidence of the left and the radicalism of the shop stewards movement, many trade unionists looked outwards, developing a critique of the work of the news media, themselves. Consideration of how union practice and organisation might be best reformed to accommodate the rhythms of news organisations only began to emerge as an issue towards the end of the decade. As early as 1971, the ACTT conducted a limited content analysis of television content in an attempt to demonstrate 'bias' in coverage.[19] By 1977, concern regarding media treatment, expressed particularly forcefully through a series of resolutions to successive TUC annual conferences, had prompted the TUC to organise a one-day conference on 'Trade Unions and the Media' and establish the TUC Media Working Group.[20] Other union officials and activists were already developing substantial critiques of news media coverage several years before 1979 and beginning to contemplate what communication policies might be necessary to address the problems identified.[21]

If the TUC's approach, as set out in its submission to the Donovan Commission, betrayed a certain complacency in the 1970s, this changed as pressure within the labour movement grew. A two-pronged TUC approach emerged which combined a monitoring and complaints strategy with a later recognition that some development of 'accommodative skills' was necessary. In combination with several individual unions, such as NALGO, the TUC submitted critical evidence on news media coverage of industrial relations both to the MacGregor Royal Commission on the Press (1974-77) and the Annan Committee on broadcasting (1977-79). The TUC Media Working Group also began towards the end of this period to produce a series of practical guides, some of which were intended to encourage the acquisition of 'accommodative skills' on the part of union activists and grass roots members. In 1979 'How to Handle the Media: a guide for trade unionists' (TUC, 1979b) was published with a description of the routine processes of news production and advice on how best to write and distribute press releases, hold press conferences and handle inquiries. This was followed by a more specialised briefing on the use of local radio (TUC Campaign Bulletin,1980) and detailed advice on making formal complaints (TUC,1983).

There are several reasons why the TUC and individual unions began to adopt more active and critical approaches. Firstly, the shop stewards movement of the early 1970s, which both responded to and encouraged a devolution of negotiating power from the national forum to the level of the plant, had a radicalising effect as more rank and file union members found that daily union politics touched their working lives (Heery and Kelly,1994). It is likely that in gaining more first hand experience of industrial relations processes, a number of ordinary employees were provided with a more substantial 'benchmark' with which to assess news media representations of industrial relations. Secondly, in a number of ways the political and cultural circumstances of this period encouraged a more radical and critical perspective to be applied to 'establishment' institutions including television and daily newspaper organisations. Opposition to the Heath government's 1971 Industrial Relations Act, the coal strikes of 1972 and 1974 which culminated in the collapse of the government, the growing industrial and political opposition to the Social Contract and the imposition of 'IMF' cuts in 1976 by a Labour government, all helped to foster a radical and critical perspective amongst a number of trade unionists making them more sensitive to the ideological contours of news coverage. Resolutions denouncing news media coverage of trade unions and industrial relations were submitted by local union branches almost every year to the Annual Trade Union Congress during this period, - a pattern which significantly tails off in the 1980s.[22]

Thirdly, the influence of academic interventions should not be underestimated at this point either. As discussed further in chapter eight, a number of British academics had begun the task of describing and analysing the nature of the ways in which trade unions were represented through the news media and this work added an additional authority to the critical perspectives already developed by trade unionists (Hall,1973; Hartmann, 1975; Morely,1976; Glasgow University Media Group,1976 and 1980; Edwards, 1979; Downing,1980). Much of this work was funded by organisational sources with significant public legitimacy including Unesco and the Leverhulme Trust which lent further weight to the critique being developed from within the labour movement. In turn, once the MacGregor Royal Commission of the Press was established, it became clear that it, too, would seek to gather evidence on the subject of press coverage of industrial relations (McQuail,1977) which signalled the state's endorsement, at least of the legitimacy of the question as to whether or not industrial relations coverage was 'biased'. This, incidentally, may partly explain the ferocity of the response from the broadcasting organisations and some other journalists to the publication of the Glasgow work (Skirrow,1980). Some trade unions including the ASTMS entered into a dialogue with academic researchers (Sapper,1977 and 1983) and others, such as NALGO, began to make use of academic expertise in designing media training programmes for members (Philo and Hewitt,1976; Philo, Beharrell and Hewitt,1977).

If part of the trade union complaint was that, too often, there was a failure in the news media to recognise the rationale for particular union policies or strategies, this was in part a reflection of the decline in the labour and left daily press, a process with roots in a history which stretched back long before the 1970s (Curran and Seaton,1985). Not only were there, by the late 1970s, far fewer newspapers with even a lukewarm sympathy for the labour movement, there was also a gradual and almost imperceptible erosion of the space within all popular newspapers devoted to serious political commentary. This shrinking of the public sphere provided by popular newspapers was a feature of the process of tabloidisation as competition in Fleet Street intensified. Competition at the popular end of the newspaper market had always been fierce but by the late 1970s and early 1980s, a number of critics began to voice fears about the erosion of formal political content in popular daily papers. For Ron Todd of the T and G, this amounted to the disenfranchisement of working people; popular newspapers no longer supplied ordinary trade unionists with the information necessary to make informed choices or participate in a meaningful way in democratic decision making (Sparks,1992).[23] For some unions, this too was an additional spur to consider more seriously communication policies and alternatives to the popular press for the purposes both of presenting a public case and in terms of internal communication with their own members. The process of tabloidisation rapidly gained momentum in the 1980s and was exacerbated, from the labour movement's point of view, by the unqualified enthusiasm for the new Conservative government which characterised the right wing popular papers in the early 1980s.

Finally, not only labour but sections of capital began to explore more systematically the possibilities of communication work and this, even in the mid to late 1970s, placed more pressure upon trade unions. As noted above, British employers, in contrast to their American counterparts, had been slow to utilise public relations techniques in the first two decades after the Second World War and had been content, in the main, to allow workplace trade union structures to function as the main means of internal communication between management and employees (Cayford,1985:1; Jones,1986:ch2). However, in the late 1970s aggressive new management styles were already emerging in companies including British Leyland under Michael Edwards, United Biscuits, IBM(UK), Cadbury Ltd, Talbot Motor Co., Continental, and Kellogs (UK) (Cayford,1985; Wickens,1987:140-142). It was clear that there was a new determination on the part of some managements to by-pass the traditional lines of company union communication and appeal directly to employees over the heads of shop stewards and union officials. Trade unions were compelled to begin to consider more seriously their own internal communication strategies. Some white collar unions had long records of substantial resource investment in internal communications but by the late

1970s, some blue collar unions began to move in similar directions. Sid Weighell became general secretary of the NUR, for example, in 1975 and immediately introduced a programme to develop the NUR's communication systems with a re-launched union journal, a series of newsletters to members and a new 'open' policy with industrial correspondents (Weighell,1983:106- 107).

At the end of the 1970s, then, the issue of media coverage and the representation of unions was already widely perceived as an important *political* issue within the labour movement. A number of unions had already invested time and resources in sharpening their critical understanding of news media processes and coverage; some, mainly but not exclusively white collar unions, had taken steps to re-structure their internal communication systems, and some of the now familiar 'do-it-yourself' guides for dealing with the news media were already being produced both by the TUC and individual unions.[24] What happened in the following decade was that the pressures producing these responses grew in intensity but were also exacerbated by the changes in the political and economic environment discussed earlier in the chapter.

The 1980s: the Rise of Accommodative Communication Work

If it is an over-simplification to suggest that it was the events of 1979 which prompted unions to take media work seriously, nonetheless, it is true that intensity of the hostility of sections of the press during the 'Winter of Discontent' in 1979 shocked many union officials, a mood reflected in the TUC's pamphlet, 'A Cause for Concern' (TUC 1979), published just after the election of Mrs Thatcher. The period following 1979 is best understood as one in which developing but underlying structural changes intermesh with the conjuncturally specific, to force both internal and external communication work to the top of the labour movement agenda. These are the political-economic changes discussed at length earlier in the chapter. If, in the 1970s, the security of the unions' membership bases encouraged unions to become preoccupied with the external political context of communication,- the issues of 'bias' and 'balance' in the news - the structural forces of change, reinforced by the policies of the incoming Conservative administration in 1979, provided powerful stimuli for unions to develop more comprehensive internal and external communication strategies in the 1980s. The emergence of new forms of production, new employer strategies for organising labour and new patterns of segmentation in the labour market represent the backdrop to contemporary union communication policy.

As we have seen, the collapse of the manufacturing base, the rapid decline of heavy industry in both public and private ownership and the privatisation of the public utilities all contributed to the dramatic decline in union membership levels. Half way through the 1980s, it was clear to many unions that there was a desperate need to respond to the growing complexity and segmentation of labour markets in order to find ways of compensating for the loss of members in traditional sectors. This required a sustained review of communication work, both internal and external and an attempt to find new forms of discourse, new vocabularies and symbolic systems with which to express union values and appeal to the new target groups, amongst young workers, the growing feminised and unorganised work forces, black and Asian workers, the part-time and the casualised (Kossof,1988 (a) and (b); Cunnison and Stageman,1993; Heery and Kelly,1994).[25] As we have seen, unions did not consistently take up the challenge of attempting to organise in virgin territory and frequently mergers with other unions or intensified competition within already organised sectors[26] appeared more attractive options but each of these also implied the need to develop more fully elaborated communication strategies. In developing merger plans, for example, unions found that it might be advantageous not only to invest in the production of appropriate communication materials such as, promotional literature, videos, and union journal articles but also to engage in news media work. The more frequent the appearance of a union on the inside pages of the quality newspapers taken by senior union officials and the labour movement elite, particularly in the context of stories about modernisation or innovation, the stronger the position of a trade union as a merger suitor.

The impact of the increasingly severe political and legislative environment was also double-edged. If it seemed as if the series of employment measures and trade union reforms enacted by the government throughout the 1980s and early 1990s aimed implicitly to legislate the emasculation of the labour movement, the unintended consequence was to provide unions with an additional spur to develop effective communication strategies as a response and the 'success' of the campaigns to secure membership support for political funds confirmed that investment in communications work could be justified in terms of concrete results. The imposition of compulsory secret ballots for industrial action and the requirement to run postal elections for senior posts had similar consequences, compelling unions to develop more adequate infrastructures to support internal communication, computerised membership lists with home addresses, mail shot software and the appropriate organisation of staff at head offices. In short, while the legislation was unwelcome, it did have the effect of forcing many unions to significantly improve their communication systems.

If the tougher managements had already begun to develop aggressive communication strategies in the 1970s, the trend spread as the impact of the government's legislation and the change in political climate began to tip the balance of power within the workplace against organised labour. Techniques first tried at British Leyland were applied at British Steel to 'soften up' the workforce in anticipation of the large scale redundancy programme (Cayford,1985) of the early 1980s. British Rail applied the 'new' communication techniques in the dispute with the NUR in 1983 over flexible rostering, employing a direct mail shot to the homes of employees and a 'personal' letter from the chairman; a telephone call line and a series of advertisements (Jones,1986 ch 2; Parker,1989 ch 10). In the financial year 1983-84, British Rail spent £19 million on corporate communication and £0.5 million simply on corporate advertising aimed at 'opinion formers' (Parker 1989:268). At the same time, despite Sid Weighell's determination to introduce an innovatory approach to union communication, the NUR executive suffered a humiliating defeat when the membership refused to back industrial action in a postal ballot and this appeared to underline the success of BR management in communicating 'over the heads' of union officials. Three years later the strategy of the NUM during the 1984/85 Coal Strike was criticised for a failure to invest in sustained communication work to match that of the Coal Board and government (Jones,1986; Adeney and Lloyd,1986). Management use of 'new' communication technology then, as part of a strategy to side-line trade unions and foster individual employee identification with corporate goals, rather than collective union ambitions (Smith and Morton,1993), provided an additional pressure upon unions in the 1980s to 'fight fire with fire'. In an era in which an increasing number of professional organisations and, indeed, even the government itself (Jones,1986; Golding,1992), were beginning to invest significant resources in communication and public relations work, unions would ignore communication issues at their peril. The expansion of the symbolic environment (though not necessarily the public sphere) through the growth in local broadcasting and day time national television only reinforced this point.

If unions were compelled by the new political and legislative environments of the 1980s to think in more imaginative ways about communication issues, the lowering cost of communication technology began to make more ambitious plans realistic. By the mid 1980s many unions, including the CPSA, UCW, TGWU, NALGO, NUPE , EETPU, were either producing in house or commissioning their own recruitment or training videos (Cayford,1985; Peers and Richards,1986). Even relatively small unions like the Tailors and Garment Workers chose to invest in a recruitment video. A few began to exploit video technology in developing more sharply focused political campaigns over issues like the political funds (Peers and Richards,1986). By the end of the decade a small number of unions developed much more ambitious projects such as the in house television production studio built by the AEU and named 'Hamlet Television' after president Bill Jordan's fondness for Shakespeare.[27]

At the same time, a new willingness could be detected within sections of the labour movement to consider the opportunities provided by communication technology (Landry et al, 1985). The example of the success of the GLC anti abolition campaign which had apparently won a notable success in terms of public opinion if not a political victory, appeared to suggest that well targeted communication strategies could succeed in popularising a left agenda. Under Neil Kinnock, the 'shadow communication agency' and other 'modernisers' within the Labour Party gained increasing influence in calling for the left to place communication and presentation at the centre of political strategy. As Ken Livingstone said, 'It's a TV age...Three minutes on the box with Janet Street Porter is worth hundreds of public meetings'.[28] The suspicion with which much of the labour movement traditionally viewed the institutions of mass communication had not disappeared. However, a new interest in the opportunities presented by communication systems found an influential intellectual support amongst the advocates of the 'New Times' perspective (Hall and Jacques,1989) where a new politics of consumption, identity and lifestyle appeared to imply that the left should engage in a project of 'niche' campaigning to reach an increasingly divergent and segmented set of constituencies.

Indeed, according to Heery and Kelly (1994), the organisational culture within trade unions was not immune to change. Some union journals during this decade reveal a new emphasis upon the services which unions can provide for 'individual' members, with articles and news items outlining, legal and financial services, support for the negotiation of 'customised' or individual employee contracts and union provision in the spheres of health, leisure and tourism (Manning, 1996). Several union press officers interviewed for this study indicated that one of their objectives was to raise the profile of union work in these areas. This is consistent with Heery and

Kelly's view that the 'servicing relationship' between unions and their members has passed through three phases in the post war period. In the immediate period after the war, 'the servicing relationship' between unions and members could be typified as 'professional', where full-time salaried union officials played the major role in representing the interests of members to employers and in securing collective agreements. In the late 1960s and 1970s, with the rise of the shop stewards movement and more radical shop floor politics, a new pattern characterised by 'participative unionism' emerged, reflecting a suspicion of the familiarity of relations between full time officials and managements, and based upon the principle of 'self activity' whereby ordinary members exercised greater influence in collective negotiations (1994:5). However, recently Heery and Kelly suggest, a third 'servicing relationship' has emerged, characterised as 'managerial unionism' based upon '...a perception of union members as discerning and calculating consumers', 'primarily instrumental in their orientation' who 'must be deliberately attracted into the union fold' (1994:7). As a consequence union bureaucracy must become more managerial in its functioning, researching and monitoring employee needs, designing and promoting union services to match and planning the organisation, training and deployment of its own human resources to support service delivery (Heery and Kelly,1994:7).

So pressure to develop communication work and formulate more coherent communications strategies came from both without and within during the period after 1979. Once union members began to be constituted as 'consumers' or 'market segments' to be serviced, the identification of particular 'target audiences' and work on improving and widening the range of communication techniques was bound to follow.

Communications, the TUC and the Wider Labour Movememt in the 1980s

It is 1985 which marks the more fundamental departure in which accommodative work is given the highest priority.The TUC Media Working Group, established in 1977 in response to growing rank and file and elite concern about media coverage, had a brief to develop strategies which could be recommended to individual TUC affiliates and to take a lead in encouraging the labour movement to develop communication work, so its publications can be regarded as examples of officially endorsed best practice and as indications of the political assumptions underpinning the communication strategy of the union elite. The work of monitoring news media output, started by scholars and individual unions, was continued and broadened to include the general representation of women in the media. The TUC Media Working Group published a series of pamphlets concerning the dominant themes and imagery of the media (TUC 1979a; TUC 1980; TUC 1985) and sought to extend the lobbying and complaints strategy by involving rank and file union members, at a local level (TUC 1981; TUC 1983). The critique of media coverage continued to reflect the legacy of the sharper, more radical politics of the labour movement in the 1970s. In terms of the options set out above, the emphasis was upon exerting pressure from without or by establishing independent means of communication rather than working 'within' the news gathering system through accommodative news work. The use of the legislative force of the state to establish mechanisms to redress the balance in union and political coverage was first formally endorsed by the TUC Media Working Group in 1983 (TUC 1983) and, at first, as TUC policy began to evolve and consider new possibilities, attention turned to the strategies which afforded the most control over the construction of the message including advertising (TUC 1985), independent video production (1986a) and the commissioning of market research (1986b).

As we have seen, some individual unions had already begun to invest in accommodative media work before the start of the 1980s but this was hardly common practice. The TUC Media Working Group did not dismiss accommodative work and the TUC published its own 'do-it yourself' manuals (TUC, 1977; TUC, 1979b; TUC, 1980) on dealing with journalists and the news media but up to the mid-1980s, there was little consideration of substantial investment or fundamental organisational reform with regard to accommodative work.

It is at this point that the TUC's orientation towards communication issues appears to shift. For one thing, the routine supply of angry resolutions to conference condemning news media coverage began to dwindle. Coverage of the 1984- 85 Coal Strike briefly revived the old debates but by the end of the decade reports of annual conference contain little evidence of the deep-seated antagonism towards the news media characteristic of conferences in the 1970s.[29] A thorough examination of the reasons for this is beyond the brief of this investigation but is likely to be, in part, a reflection of the influence of the 'soft left' and 'modernisers' within both unions and the Labour Party and also the product of a feeling that the complaint and critique strategy had somehow been exhausted. 'Bias', 'distortion' and 'cultural skew' had been documented dozens of times and yet few clear gains appeared to have been secured. The changes in the orientation of unions towards their members- 'the servicing relationship' described by Heery and Kelly (1994) -

was already prompting a re-consideration of the role of communication work and encouraging unions to focus more upon the symbolism and language through which they could represent themselves, rather than the dominant 'frames' imposed by the news media. And, of course, following the defeat of the miners, the crushing 1983 general election defeat of the Labour Party, and the other set backs experienced by the labour movement in the first half of the 1980s, the political confidence which had underpinned the left-critique during the 1970s had all but disappeared.

This is the background to the shift in the TUC's own approach to media and communication work. In 1984, the TUC began to consider more fundamental questions concerning the organisation of union structures in relation to communication and this marks the development of a more sustained attempt to accommodate the imperatives of news organisations, as part of a broader re-orientation towards the mass media in general. The mass media began to be regarded less as hostile sources of ideological conflict. Rather, accommodative media work was to be treated with sufficient priority to warrant significant additional allocations of resources and even structural re-organisation. In March 1984, the TUC General Council produced a consultative document on strategy for the coming decade which included a long section on communications.[30] It provides a good example of the ambivalence which was to characterise many union approaches as they embraced accommodative media strategies during the next few years. On the one hand, the document rehearsed the familiar criticisms of 'anti union bias' in the news media and yet also noted that:

> The opportunities and demands for unions to put across their points of view through the media will increase and this in turn will place more pressure on unions to deal with the media in a professional way in order to ensure that the best use is made of the opportunities.[31]

The document reviewed the work of the TUC Media Working Group, noting the publication of practical guides and the forthcoming advice on use of advertising, video and market research. However, it moved beyond these by placing in the context of communication work, a need for organisational reform, the role of full time officers, and union training programmes. Following the circulation of this consultative document amongst TUC Regional Councils and County Associations, the TUC Standing Conference of Principal Union Officers held a conference to review responses in January

1985. The document produced for consideration at this conference set the tone:

> Trade unions cannot ignore the message of June 1983 - that even after four years of economic failure, public service cutbacks, public asset stripping, and the scandal of rampant unemployment, so many trade unionists and others were unconvinced by our presentation of the alternative.[32]

The first section of the document reviewed the internal communication systems which unions employed to reach their own memberships and dwelt mainly upon the development of union journals. The second section reviewed the external communication systems employed by unions and considered:

> the scope for enhancing the use made by unions of printed and broadcasting avenues of communication which, for all the justifiable suspicion of them which exists, remain the most immediate link between working men and women and the organisations which represent them.[33]

Once again, the ambivalence of trade unions towards mainstream news media surfaced. One the hand, the political analysis developed by many trade unionists and the assumptions regarding structures of power and control suggested that the news media were always likely to prove hostile territory and yet, on the other hand, their importance in the lives of most ordinary trade unionists, and the public at large, pointed to the political imperative to acknowledge and anticipate their work in 'producing news'.The document explicitly notes a number of the changes in the political and economic environment noted above,- the appeal of Thatcherism even amongst trade unionists, the threat of recent legislation   and the proposed compulsory ballots for political funds, the use by employers of new communication techniques,[34] and the expansion of the news media environment in the early 1980s.[35] The efforts of unions in working with local broadcasting media were acknowledged but "union communication experts generally recognised that British unions do not do as much to initiate publicity and influence opinion as, for instance, unions in France and Sweden where 'communications' attract a far greater share of resources".[36] The paper summarised the results of a survey of the union arrangements to support media work undertaken in preparation for the conference. Significantly, although the conference paper rapidly passes over this point without elaboration, very few unions employed full time press officers at this stage. Most either relied upon the media skills of their general secretaries or employed staff to combine the role of press officer with other duties such as research or producing union publications.[37]

The provision for media training also appeared very uneven with some unions investing very little time or resources in developing appropriate skills for staff and even the TUC, itself, only at the stage of piloting new 'Communication Skills' courses at its national education centre. The important position of industrial correspondents as points of contact for most unions was acknowledged in the document and yet curiously, in the light of the reservations regarding the 'anti-union bias' of the news media expressed in the introduction, the discussion moved on without any consideration of the politics of union-journalist interaction or the techniques which might advantage union press officers within these politics. Instead, there was some limited discussion of the new terrain where unions had found some opportunities for developing media work including local radio and the specialist press and a call was made for greater attention to be paid to the ethnic minority press.[38]

The document signalled an important shift in the thinking of the TUC towards accommodative media work. In reviewing the staffing and resourcing of media work within trade unions and in calling for further survey work to be undertaken, the document pointed to the possibility of institutional re-organisation and significant investment in media work orientated towards news organisations for the first time. Of course, other communication strategies were not simply abandoned and the document noted the enthusiasm a number of unions expressed for the advertising campaigns particular unions had employed in their opposition to the privatisation of British Telecom and the water industry. Nevertheless, the document was notable for the absence of any discussion of the more combative strategies, such as monitoring and complaint or structural intervention. Of course, there remained plenty of support for such strategies within the labour movement but they were no longer being placed in the foreground in the official policy discussions of the TUC.

One practical outcome of the January 1985 conference was the establishment of an ad hoc group of Union Communication Officers to meet regularly. The brief of this group was to review further the use of communication technology, marketing and advertising services; consider the role of the TUC in terms of union communication strategy, and provide a way of pooling expertise and appropriate resources for dealing with the news media. In the following year, the ad hoc group met four times and helped to draw up the TUC guidelines on use of advertising and video, in conjunction with the TUC Media Working Group.[39] Given that the latter was comprised mainly of general secretaries and senior officials from the print, media and other relevant unions but without the knowledge of media practice to be found amongst the union press and communication officers in the ad hoc group, it is likely that the ad hoc group was able to exert considerable influence in terms of practical policy. This was all the more likely because the Media Working Group became preoccupied with the dangers implicit in the government's review of broadcasting policy through the establishment of the Peacock Committee and the later green and white papers on the future of broadcasting.[40]

The ad hoc group continued to meet sporadically over the next two years. It reviewed the work of trade union press officers, the role of trade union journals, and collated information on a variety of specialist media services, including even the repair of union banners.[41] Its main significance was, perhaps, as an opportunity lost. For the first time a forum existed in which union press officers could meet and discuss common problems but which also offered the possibility of more structured co-ordination of union press and media work, along the lines of the arrangements established by the media and press officers of the various environmental pressure groups (Anderson,1993:61). In addition, representatives from the Labor Institute of Public affairs (LIPA) had been invited by the Media Working Group to brief the TUC on the ways in which a variety of media techniques could be integrated within one strategy.[42] However, these opportunities were not seized and the ad hoc group ceased to meet regularly in 1988. This was partly a consequence of the unambitious brief given to the ad hoc group in the first place but it was also because the work of the group was overtaken by events. Firstly, the policy of the state towards broadcasting and the dissemination of information had been thrown into sharp relief by the crisis of the Spycatcher case, the treatment of union members at G.C.H.Q. Cheltenham, plans to reform the Official Secrets Act, new restrictions placed upon access to information generated by the former public utilities, and the broadcasting white paper. Secondly, the TUC had become increasingly alarmed by the steady haemorrhaging of union members through the decade and the dramatic fall in revenue, to the point at which it was decided in 1987 to establish a Special Review Body to examine the whole future strategy and direction of the TUC itself.[43]

Inevitably, the issue of communication work was subsumed within this broader review, in an atmosphere of perceived crisis, as the impact of the developments in the political and economic environment discussed above, became sharper and ever more visible. The Special Review Group drew up, amongst other things, plans for the TUC co-ordinated recruitment drives (the 'Union-Yes' campaign) to reach under-organised and green field employment sectors, which were pioneered at Trafford Park, Manchester and Docklands in 1990.[44] As the TUC lost profile and presence in so many employment sectors, so the importance of communication opportunities, for projects such as 'Union-Yes', continued to be underlined. Yet, as Annual Congress noted with alarm, policies of media de-regulation, the growing centralised control of the state over information and increasing concentration of ownership in media markets all meant that the 'public sphere' which afforded such opportunities was actually shrinking.[45] For example, the Media Working Group expended considerable energy in trying to persuade, with only limited success, both BBC and ITV not to drastically cut back staff and broadcasting time allocated to labour and industrial affairs[46] in response to a new political and commercial climate, hostile to traditional public service broadcasting values.

By the late 1980s, it is possible to detect a further re-focusing in TUC communication strategy. In fact, the focus widens, once again, to take account of the generalised threat presented by these changes in the communications environment. The importance of accommodative media work had been 'flagged up' by the ad hoc group but this now became part of a more generalised concern about the nature of the symbolic environment and communicative activity. However, in very different political circumstances to the 1970s, in the wake of the ravages of the 1980s and without the buoyancy afforded by the shop floor radicalism of the 1970s, the tone of debate was both more defensive and less ambitious. There is no return to the combative 'monitoring and complaints strategy' of the mid-1970s, though continuity can be detected in some elements of policy. The 1988 Annual Congress passed resolutions on the dangers of concentration in press ownership, calling for legal obligations to be placed upon wholesalers to distribute a diverse range of newspapers and a statutory of right of reply.[47] The Media Working Group were given the task of formulating a general policy statement on the mass media and a conference, 'The Role of the Media in a Democracy' was held in March 1988 with speakers including representatives from the Campaign for Press and Broadcasting Freedom and industrial corespondent, Philip Bassett, closely associated with the politics of 'new realism'.[48] A 'shopping list' of desirable legislative reforms emerged which expanded the resolutions of Congress and included repeal of the Official Secrets Act, a freedom of information act, and the establishment of one regulatory 'Communications

Council' to embrace all media sectors.[49] In practical terms, it was agreed to continue the fight to preserve public service broadcasting, partly through co-operation with European unions facing similar threats.[50]

The 1980s can be characterised, then, as a decade in which the deteriorating political and economic environment forced the TUC and the labour movement on to the defensive. Paradoxically, one consequence of this was the development of a more comprehensive communications policy which involved a period in the mid-80s in which the issue of the necessary infrastructure for accommodative media work was placed in the foreground by the TUC. By the late 1980s, the changes in the communications environment, the threat posed to the 'public sphere' and the growing profile of the state in both controlling and sponsoring information flows,[51] had prompted a more generalised concern about communication policy at the macro level. Nevertheless, an awareness of the issues and necessary investments involved in micro communication work had emerged and was now to be found in the policy of individual unions, as well as the TUC. The irony is that the TUC moved to a position where it could formulate a comprehensive strategy for communications, including both accommodative work and approaches offering more autonomy, just at the moment when it became increasingly difficult to resource and sustain such work. By the early 1990s, the crisis of funding through declining membership had reached a point at which severe retrenchment had to occur. In 1990, all the work of the various TUC committees was suspended as the full implications of the financial deficit were revealed (Harper,1990). The TUC announced a re-organisation and 'modernisation' of its press and publicity departments in 1992[52] with the rationale that the TUC had to find a new role as a research and lobbying organisation but the evidence of drastic cutbacks in other departments suggested that the motive was as much to do with cost as reform. Inevitably, there are now severe limits on what communications initiatives, the TUC can undertake. The 'TUC Bulletin', the TUC's own newspaper for union members, launched in 1986 , was axed in 1991 as a cost cutting measure.[53] New promotional campaigns, such as 'Towards 2,000', launched in 1991, are less ambitious than 'Unions Yes' and involve less resourcing in terms of advertising and staffing. Against this background the TUC Media Working Group was wound down and finally subsumed by the Finance and General Purposes Committee, also in 1991.[54]

Some media initiatives continue. The 1992 conference, 'Making the Most of Local Radio', which included presentations by Geoffrey Goodman (former *Daily Mirror* industrial editor and LBC industrial correspondent) and

Nicholas Jones (formerly BBC radio industrial correspondent) represented an attempt by the TUC to encourage more flexible media work by individual unions in areas where it was perceived that there were possibilities to articulate a reasoned union case[55] but the flow of pamphlets and guides on communication work has ceased and there is little discussion of the exploitation of new communication technologies by the TUC, itself. Chapter six discusses the recent decline in the number of labour correspondents and changes in the geography of the labour beat. The TUC is no longer, as it was for almost forty years, a part of the daily round for labour correspondents and indeed, even the press conferences which follow the monthly meetings of the TUC council are no longer well attended by journalists. There is less momentum in the TUC's communication work and fewer opportunities for its development.

This is not the case, however, with individual unions. A view of accommodative media work as offering significant potential and more than just exercises in 'damage limitation' began to gain ground amongst individual unions, as well as the TUC itself, in the second half of the 1980s. Several reasons can be suggested. As we have seen, a number of unions, had already begun to consider accommodative techniques and had published guides or 'DIY manuals' to foster better 'media handling' at branch level.[56] The factors which pushed unions to develop these approaches to the point where it was considered necessary to invest centrally in accommodative work probably included both 'positive' and 'negative' impulses. In the case of the former, the influence of 'modernisers' within the Labour Party and the labour movement was already strong by the mid-1980s. In the light of the example of the Greater London Council, where a hostile press had been 'turned around' by a policy of selective media engagement, and the advice provided by the Labour Party's 'shadow communication team' (a group of advertising and media practitioners close to the Labour Party leadership), there was much more support for the view that the media generated a symbolic environment which had to be acknowledged in political terms.

A number of unions, particularly those who saw themselves as politically close to the Labour Party leadership, began to travel in the same 'modernising' direction. Hence, the decision of the General Municipal and Boilermakers' Union to embrace the world of design consultants and 'corporate imaging' in re-launching itself as the 'GMB', complete with new logo and a new 'high-tech', 'post-modern' headquarters in Wimbledon.[57] As Heery and Kelly (1994) suggest, there was a general movement to be found in a number of unions to re-fashion the 'servicing relationship' between union and membership in the 1980s and this involved placing much more emphasis upon communication with individual members, rather than collectively with branches. However, as the 1985 TUC survey of communications noted, union journals and publications normally worked to a monthly cycle.[58] If unions wished to communicate more speedily with individual members the daily press and broadcasting channels offered the only route. Given the pressures to reach new potential members in more diverse segments of the labour market and consolidate the support of existing ones, this became increasingly important.

In terms of negative impulses, the collapse of the *News on Sunday* project ended the hopes of some unions that it would prove possible to sustain a commercially viable newspaper of the labour movement to replace the old *Daily Herald*. A number of unions had invested in this project and its collapse in 1987 meant the end of attempts to establish an independent channel of news communication.[59] This reinforced the trade unions' dependence upon the mainstream news media. Towards the end of the 1980s a number of unions took steps to re-organise and invest in accommodative media work, often as part of more comprehensive communication strategies. The survey conducted by the TUC for the Conference of Standing Officers Conference on communications in 1985 found that 'only a few of the largest unions have one or more staff whose time is spent exclusively on media relations'.[60] The preparatory work for this study revealed that out of the thirty-seven trade unions with membership levels above 45,000 in December 1987 only, seven employed a press officer with a full-time commitment to press and media work. Twenty-three unions employed staff who combined press work with other duties including, for example, research or editing the union journal.[61] The remaining unions left press work to the general secretary or an equivalent senior official.

Today, the picture is quite different. Partly arising from the recent series of large mergers which have allowed unions to pool resources to produce economies of scale, it is now the norm for large unions to employ at least one full-time press and media officer. Accommodative media work receives a significantly greater investment and is often supported by organisational structures designed to improve communication work. In the case of the 1988/89 Ambulance Dispute, the unions involved took a conscious decision to integrate industrial and communications strategy, so that the requirements for effective accommodative media work largely determined the pattern of industrial action adopted by the union leadership. The role of those primarily involved in accommodative union work is explored in further depth in chapters four and five and the example of the Ambulance Dispute is examined in chapter eight. The possibilities, constraints and dangers of accommodative media work for trade unions is the main focus of this book.

Conclusion

As the balance of power between unions and employers shifted in the period after 1979, unions experienced changes not only in their external ideological orientation to the outside world but also in terms of the values and commitments which formed the internal ideological framework for the labour movement. This is hardly surprising. If unions are positioned in a crucial way to express and transmit conflicts between the powerful and the subordinate in workplace relations, then tensions will appear through the mobilisation of symbolic as well as material resources.

The crisis brought about by structural change and political assault inevitably triggered conflicts within the labour movement, too. These, also, are bound to be expressed in symbolic as well as material form. The EETPU journal 'Contact', offered, for example, a particular way of 'representing' the conflicts within the labour movement during the late 1980s (Manning, 1996) over the union's aggressive recruitment practices and the union's final expulsion from the TUC (in itself a theatrical piece of stage management for the news media with the general secretary and delegates striding from the TUC conference hall). In the same period, the GMB sought to underline its political interventions through accommodative media work, seeking to highlight its distinctive political position as both a 'modernising force' but also an opponent of 'new realism', through the 'proactive' briefing of selected correspondents working for the key newspapers read by the labour movement elite.

All forms of political and industrial communication can be understood as both expressions of conflict and means for the articulation of conflict. Each of the possibilities for media and communication work discussed above implies particular positions in terms of degrees of combativeness or defensiveness. The 'proactive' targeting of particular news media and briefing of correspondents is often understood as quite an aggressive, interventionist pattern of communicative work. However, as an accommodative strategy it involves embracing or, at the very least, making compromises with the dominant news values and criteria of mainstream news journalism. In this respect, it is actually a defensive strategy, often requiring concessions to be made and with the danger of 'incorporation' a possibility. The extent to which union staff and press officers, in particular, are required to make concessions in their accommodative media work and the extent to which they can engage in a politics of symbolic representation and source activity to secure advantage is a major concern of this book.

We have seen, then, that union communication strategies are shaped without and within. The changes in the structural positioning of unions with regard to labour markets , in their relationship to the state, and in their role in the relations of domination and subordination between capital and labour have all prompted changes in the ways in which they seek to exercise control in the processes of communication and symbolic representation. At the same time, though, decisions about communication strategy and media work are not merely responses to external pressure but also reflect the nature and internal politics of particular unions, as organisations. the next chapter, for example, discusses the crucial importance of the relationship between media workers and union leadership in supporting effective accommodative work. The case of the NUM during the 1984/85 strike casts a shadow across the whole study. As we shall see, not only many journalists but a number of union press officers were critical of the uncompromising stand taken by the union with regard to communication. There were few concessions made by the NUM to the needs of accommodative work with the news media. Arguably, the ambulance unions achieved more in terms of news coverage through a strategy which required not only union organisation but industrial strategy to be geared to media work. And yet, as chapter eight describes, there are costs and dangers here, too.

Notes

1. Hall and Jacques distinguished their more recent work which stresses the importance of changes occuring throughout late capitalist societies from their earlier work which did allocate to Thatcherism a unique potency (Hall and Jacques, 1989: 15).

2. See, 'New Wave of Union Busting', Labour Research (1988), April vol 77, pages 13 -15, and 'The Union Derecognition Bandwagon', Labour Research, (1992), November, vol 81, pp 6-8.

3. See 'Union Not Beyond all Recognition', Labour Research (1993), vol 82, pp 4-5.

4. Data supplied in the Department of Employment Gazette, September 1993, and summarised in the The Guardian, 13th September 1993.

5. 'Political Fund Ballots: a multiple victory', Labour Research (1986), May vol 75, pp 4-5.

6. Labour Research (1990), May vol 79, pp 11-12.

7.   Labour Research (1992), July vol 81, pp 13-14.
8.   'New workers Retain the Strike Weapon', Labour Research (1992), June vol 81, p 13.
9.   'Where Union Membership is Best', Labour Research (1992), June vol 81, pp 11-12.
10. Ibid.
11. Ibid.
12. 'A New Era for the TGWU', Labour Research (1991), July vol 80, pp 9-10.
13. 'Are Unions Outside the Woman's Realm?', Labour Research (1988), August vol 77, pp 13-14.
14. Labour Research (1990), June vol 79, pp 9-11.
15. Labour research (1993), September 1993, op cit.
16. See, for example, 'Legal Services: a safety net for union members', Labour Research (1990), January vol 79, p 18.
17. Author's interview with Clare Dover, formerly science correspondent on *Daily Telegraph* and later medical correspondent on the *Daily Express*, 9th June 1993.
18. Data supplied to the author by MORI.
19. 'One week', ACTT Television Commission, 1971. See also Sapper (1977).
20. See appendix one in Beharrell and Philo (eds.) (1977).
21. See, for example, Sapper (1983) and the contributions by Marshall, Sapper, Beckett and Griffiths in Beharrell and Philo (eds.) (1977).
22. See The Reports of the Annual Trade Union Congress, TUC, London, between 1974 (106th Congress) and 1993 (125th Congress).
23. Writers such as Fiske (1992) and Connell (1991) argue that critics apply too narrow a definition of the political; that an alternative wider definition allows the critic to recognise the value of work undertaken by the popular press in introducing readers to 'political' issues of relevance in a broader sense and also in pointing to the role television plays as a main source of information for most people in their daily lives. Sparks (1992), however, insists that it is unhealthy in a democracy for there to be an absence of much discussion of the formal political process (the exercise of state power) in popular papers. However, the implication of accepting a wide definition of the political is that a wider range of media (popular magazines, consumer programmes on television and radio) should be targeted by union communication officers in response to the shrinking of the public political sphere. As we shall see, there is some evidence that this is, indeed, happening.
24. See, for example, 'Trade Councils and the Media: notes for officers of Trade Councils and County Associations', London TUC, 1977; 'Press and Public Relations', NATFHE, London 1978; 'Getting Your Message Across', NCU, London, 1985. See also the material produced by the TUC Media Working Group (TUC 1979, 1980, 1983 and 1984).
25. See, also 'Are Unions Outside the Womans' Realm', Labour Research (1988), op cit. See also, Labour Research (1990A), September vol 79, pp 7-8, on the strategies employed by some unions including, MSF, CPSA, and USDAW, to recruit new young members. The

CPSA has launched a 'Charter for Youth'.

26.   Mason and Bain (1993) estimate that between three and four million workers in organised sectors are yet to be recruited.

27.   AEU Journal, April 1988.

28.   Labour Party News, No 1, 1987.

29.   See The Reports of the 117th Annual Trade Union Congress (1985) through to the 125th Annual Trade Union Congress (1993), London, TUC.

30.   'TUC Strategy', TUC Consultative Document, unpublished, TUC March 1984 (held at the TUC Library).

31.   Ibid, p 30.

32.   'TUC Strategy: Union Communications', Standing Conference of Union Principal Officers, 24th January 1985, unpublished, TUC London. (held in TUC Library).

33.   Ibid, p 4.

34.   Ibid, pp 1-4.

35.   Ibid, p 17.

36.   Ibid, p 19.

37.   Ibid, pp 19-20.

38.   Ibid, pp 19-21.

39.   Report of the 118th Annual Trade Union Congress,1986, p 385. London, TUC.

40.   Ibid, p 385. See also, Report of the 119th Annual Trade Union Congress, 1987, pp 328-332, TUC, London.

41.   See Reports of the 118th and 119th Annual Trade Union Congresses, op cit. See also, Report of the 120th annual Trade Union Congress, 1988, p 323, TUC London.

42.   Report of the 119th annual Trade Union Congress, op cit.

43.   See the Reports of the 119th, 120th and 121st Annual Trade Union Congresses, op cit.

44.   See, the Report of the 122nd Annual Trade Union Congress, 1990,p 236.London, TUC.

45.   See the Report of the 121st annual Trade Union Congress, 1989, op cit.

46.   The TUC Media Working Group protested to Channel Four about the axeing of 'Union World'. Channel Four offered as a 'sop' the chance to participate in the making of a series about the work of unions by an independent production company. See Report of the 121st Annual Congress, 1989, p 282, op cit. In 1987, the Media Working Group had lobbied and written to the BBC regarding reductions in specialist labour correspondents and in the amount of coverage devoted to industrial issues, including coverage of TUC Annual Congress, itself. See, Report of the 119th Annual Congress, 1987, p 332, op cit.

47.   Report of the 120th Annual Trade Union Congress, 1988, p 285, op cit. Also, Report of the 121st Annual Trade Union Congress, 1989, p 284, op cit.

48.   Report of the 121st Annual Trade Union Congress, 1989, p 285, op cit.

49.   Ibid, p 286.

50.   Ibid, p 287.

51.   The concern over government use of advertising and public relations for 'political' purposes was first noted at the 121st Annual Congress (1989).

See p 288, op cit.

52.   See Report of the 124th Annual Trade Union Congress (1992), p 171.
      London, TUC.

53.   See the Report of the 123rd Anual Trade Union Congress (1991), p 200.
      London, TUC.

54.   Ibid.

55.   See the Report of the 125th Anual Trade Union Congress (1993), p 186.
      London,TUC.

56.   See NATFHE (1978), NUT (1980), NCU (1985).

57.   Labour Party News, no 4, July/August 1987.

58.   'TUC Strategy: Union Communications', Standing Conference of Union
      Principal Officers, op cit.

59.   Report of the 118th Annual Trade Union Congress, 1986, p 385, op cit.

60.   'TUC Strategy: Union Communications', Standing Conference of Union
      Principal Officers, 1985, op cit.

61.   See appendix one.

3 Briefing for the Union: the Practice of Trade Union Press Officers and their Internal Union Environment

This chapter begins to consider the work of union press officers in the context of the theoretical themes set out in chapter one. If communication and symbolic work express the central relations of domination and subordination in society, and given the position of trade unions within those relations, how best can unions organise their media and symbolic work in ways which acknowledge the structures of material and ideological power? The first step is to focus upon the central organisation of the trade union; upon the question of access to the decision making process and upon the allocation of resources for media work. In short, the union press officer's internal environment. In the following chapter, the external environment is considered through the relationships press officers develop with journalists and the range of external factors which constrain their work.

Responsibilities and working conditions

The working conditions for the trade union officers visited in this study varied enormously and not only in accordance with the size of the union that employed them. Frequently the officers working for the smaller unions in the study inhabited small, sometimes dingy offices, with cramped conditions and papers piled high over desks and filing cabinets. However, it was notable that conditions were not much better for officers representing some of the largest unions in the country. Only the GMB had appeared to have embraced the modern world of corporate office design with a new purpose built headquarters reflecting the union's emphasis upon 'corporate branding',-

building up an association in the public's mind between the GMB and modern, progressive trade unionism. A brand new post-modern architecture, the GMB logo mounted on the public face of the building; bright, open plan offices, bristling with information technology and coded security zoning requiring employees to tap in their 'PIN's to move from one section to another, all provided a sharp contrast with other union environments. The 'Communications Directorate' for the GMB occupies one entire floor of open plan, modern office furniture and television monitors. NALGO, too, allocated an entire floor to its Publicity Department. Indeed, it was so large that a map of the seventh floor was helpfully provided for visitors when they alighted in the lift.

So working conditions vary widely. More detailed descriptions of the resources allocated to each press officer will be provided in a section comparing union by union below. The duties and responsibilities of press officers also vary widely. Here, the size of union is a better guide to circumstances. The bigger trade unions were all able to allocate at least one officer to press and media work, more or less full time. Sometimes these officers would take on additional tasks but this was out of choice, to facilitate their press and media work or to enrich their jobs. For example, Charlotte Atkins of COHSE acted as a 'Political Officer', engaging in lobbying work at Westminster and some background research but this was not at the expense of press and media work. It arose from the coincidence of her background and interests, on the one hand, and the strategy of the union, on the other, in moving away from public rallies towards 'quieter' forms of political communication, at Westminster. The variety of duties is reflected in the range of official titles for posts. Adrian Long acted as Media Officer in the Communications Directorate at the GMB, John Lloyd was Head of Communications at the EETPU, Ken Jones of the NUCPS was officially Head of the Research Department, while Mr Lomans was Assistant to the General Secretary at NUHKW. Few of those interviewed were known simply as press officers.

The position within each union

As we shall see, staffing or 'time' as a resource is often an important point of differentiation between large and small unions and is likely to determine the degree of proactivity in media work. In addition, the degree of access media or press officers have to the higher levels of decision making within the union (the national executive committee or equivalent) is likely to be important, for reasons discussed further below, and the level of resourcing in terms of budget and facilities - the technology of media work. Precise information on levels of funding, specifically allocated to press or media work, is extremely difficult to obtain. At the time the research was conducted very few unions cost-centred such work with a specified budget. Usually, the cost of media and press work was subsumed within broader budget headings ('publicity', 'administration', even 'education') and to make matters even more complicated, campaigning work which might include press and media activity was often supported from the legally distinct political fund, as well as the main budget lines. Information derived from the accounts registered with the Certification Officer is included in appendix four, though only one union, the NUCPS, included a specific figure for 'press and media work'. Most press officers could only provide estimates of the figures involved in specifically supporting press and media work, as distinct from broader publicity functions and journal production. Would, for example, the costs involved in entertaining journalists, be funded from an administrative budget line or the political fund or both?[1] As Charlie Whelan (formerly AEU press officer) asked, 'what is press work?'[2] For many press officers, the distinction in practice was artificial. Proactive campaigns might be funded jointly by Publicity, Industrial, Publications or even Education departments.[3]

This makes it very difficult to isolate specific figures for the resources involved in supporting specifically press and media work, but where press officers were able to supply a detailed breakdown of their costs and budget allocation these have been included in the following discussion of resources. Set out below is a set of brief summaries of the conditions for press and media work within each union. Details of union budgets and membership levels for the year 1992 are set out in appendix four.

Larger Unions

The AEU

One officer (Charlie Whelan) worked exclusively upon press and media work, with access to typing and administrative support from a pool. He had a position on the editorial board of the union journal but was not involved in day to day editorial decisions. Involvement in editorial work was limited to the planning of a small number of campaigns developed through the journal, media work and publicity materials. Though running a relatively small department and without any formal experience in journalism, Charlie Whelan had an extremely high reputation amongst journalists and other press officers. He proved the 'exception to the rule' in that he did not have formal access to the national executive committee of the AEU, an important advantage in helping to acquire the kind of inside information valued by journalists, but he did have a very close working relationship with the general secretary, to whom he was formally responsible, and it was this which was valued by journalists. He has subsequently joined the staff of the present Labour Party leader with responsibility for communication work.

In 1992/93, the total AEU budget for publicity, including the publication of the 'AEU Journal', was £835,000, a figure which placed the AEU above the media oriented GMB in the spending league but still significantly below NALGO's budget of over £2 million. Little of this money appeared to be invested in the press office, the only obvious items of expenditure being a primitive personal computer, a fax machine and the P.A. (Press Association) link, which Charlie Whelan used 'sparingly' once each mid-morning to monitor emerging news stories.

COHSE

One officer (Charlotte Atkins) worked exclusively upon press and media work, though she was developing her role in political communication and lobbying activity. She had the 'luxury', however, of being able to devote her time fully to media work whenever necessary. In contrast to the AEU, as press officer Charlotte Atkins worked closely with the team of three involved in producing the journal and could call upon their help for additional support for her press work when required. In the past, press work and journal production had not been co-ordinated, being located in separate buildings,- 'it was a crazy situation, we might be working on the same story but in separate buildings'[4]. However, COHSE moved all communication staff into one office, in order to integrate the work and now all staff worked as one 'team'. Charlotte Atkins enjoyed card carrying status as a full member of the union, rather than merely an employee, and on this basis was allowed to attend national executive meetings.

An annual income £11,117,874 in 1992 made COHSE one of the richer unions in the study and around 78% of this was spent on administration, including publicity (the journal alone cost £60,000 per issue to produce). In contrast to the AEU, where Charlie Whelan battled against the imposition of strict budget lines, the COHSE budget was, according to Charlotte Atkins, one of the most tightly controlled amongst large unions. A video camera, for example, could only be purchased by wiring money from a media monitoring account. Approximately £20,000 was allocated to media and press work each year, excluding salaries,[5] although additional support was provided from the publicity department (the production of leaflets, etc) and the journal budget. The press and media budget paid for, amongst other things, a P.A. link to receive news up dates and circulate copy, and a subscription to the '2/10 Universal News Service' (UNS) which allowed the circulation of a fixed number of press releases each year. The budget also included a press clippings service and a contract with 'Telemonitors', a company which provided transcripts of television output. In common with a number of press officers, Charlotte Atkins was beginning to question the value of media monitoring and 'Universal News Services', at the time of the study, a theme to be explored further below. Following the merger of COHSE, NUPE and NALGO, Charlotte Atkins has become a full-time political officer.

EETPU

John Lloyd as Head of Communication was the only officer of the larger unions in the sample to combine press and media work with editing the union journal. The Communication Department was responsible for all media, press, and publicity functions. John Lloyd had a full time assistant with design and layout skills, acquired through working in magazine journalism, to support journal production and could call upon further clerical and administrative support from other sections. However, in comparison to the large publicity or communication departments at unions such as NALGO or the GMB, the EETPU's was relatively small. Even COHSE, with a membership half the size of the EETPU, supported a larger publicity department. However, as appendix four indicates, despite a lower membership, COHSE enjoyed an annual income more than twice that of the EETPU. Although staffing levels were relatively low, there was a considerable investment in communication technology. The department used Apple PC's with sophisticated desk top publishing and printing facilities, - 'the best in-house business communication system in South East England',[6] - to produce all its own communication materials, including leaflets, newsletters, and press releases. The journal was edited on the same system but printed externally. Rather than subscribe to UNS, or the P.A., John Lloyd used an 'intelligent' fax machine to distribute press releases to key journalists. Although without a formal training in journalism, John Lloyd recognised the importance of 'speaking with authority', in the eyes of journalists, and was given full access to EETPU Executive Council meetings.

GMB

Next to NALGO, the GMB probably had the biggest communications department, amongst British unions. Adrian Long had the official title of Media Officer in the Communications Directorate. He worked under the Director of Communication, Nicholas Woolas, a former current affairs television journalist. Two staff, including Adrian Long, worked full-time on 'media related activity', out of a total staff of nine within the department. Nicholas Woolas lent additional support in meeting and briefing journalists but Adrian was able to devote himself 'almost totally' to press and media work. All media and communication work, including journal production and press work, was integrated through an annual strategic plan produced by the Communications Directorate. This plan was, in turn, informed by the broader strategic thinking of the union leadership and the senior staff within the Communications Directorate, including Adrian Long, had access to all national executive meetings. With an annual income of £39,136,000 in 1992, the GMB was the third most prosperous union in the sample and £726,000 was spent upon 'publicity'. Adrian Long estimated that direct costs (staffing, facilities, PA and UNS services, mobile phones, and media monitoring) for media and press work amounted to approximately £55,000 and indirect costs (PR stunts, commissioning of external research, etc) a further £30,000.[7] A total of approximately £85,000 in 1992/93 would have made the press and media work of the GMB some of the most well resourced in union circles, matched only by NALGO.

NALGO

NALGO's Publicity Department, occupying an entire floor of the union's headquarters, was the biggest developed by any union at the time of the study. The Press Office was located within this department with a staff of three full-timers, headed by Mary McGuire. She worked closely with the editor of the NALGO journal, 'Public Service' but was not involved in day to day editorial work, though particular campaigns were developed through both the journal and media work. Once again, Mary McGuire had full access to national executive and senior political circles within the union, a policy pioneered by NALGO many years before other unions recognised the importance of allowing those who spoke publicly on their behalf a full understanding of the political context in which they worked.NALGO's income in 1992 was the highest of the unions in this study and the Publicity Department enjoyed, what was in union terms, a huge budget of over £2 million, excluding staffing costs (see appendix four). The bulk of this was spent upon the production of the union journals and other publicity materials. During the research period over £300,000 was invested in a new desk top publishing system (compared to £20,000 spent by IPMS). However, in 1992/93 NALGO allocated £103,200 to the Press Office, which was spent on staff salaries, media monitoring (£14,600), 'campaigns' (£5,000) and newspapers/magazines (£3,700). NALGO had recently terminated its UNS contract.

The TGWU

Although the largest union, at the time this research was undertaken, with the second highest income (see appendix four), unlike other large unions in the study, the TGWU operated with a straight forward press office, without the ramifications of publicity or broader communications functions. The journal, 'T and G Record', was produced quite independently, the only link being the inclusion of the journal editor on the mailing list for press office press releases. The head of the press office, Eddie Barrett and his 'number two', Andrew Murray were both professional journalists with experience on national newspapers. Despite the size and resources of the T and G, the press office provided a sharp contrast to the relative 'media opulence' of the GMB and NALGO. Without a specific budget, Andrew Murray said it was impossible to calculate the cost of press work, 'too many imponderables'[8] but major items of expenditure had to be approved by the national executive. Other than two PC's and a FAX machine, the press office displayed none of the investment in media technology which confronted the visitor to, for example, the GMB headquarters.

Unlike NALGO, COHSE and several other large unions, the tradition and organisational culture of the TGWU did not permit its press officers routine access to the highest levels of decision making. In contrast to Charlotte Atkins (COHSE), Eddie Barrett and Andrew Murray were not TGWU members; they retained their NUJ memberships and saw themselves as employees and 'professional journalists'. They were not given access to the national executive, although they did enjoy a close relationship with the general secretary, to whom they were directly responsible. Nevertheless, while many journalists gave a positive assessment of the TGWU press office, others and a number of union press officers, referred to the 'secretive' culture of the union.

Smaller Unions

IPMS

A team of two media officers with three support staff handled all press and media work but also produced the union journal and publicity materials. The Head of the Communications Department (Charles Harvey) devoted most of his time to editing the journal, leaving press and media work to Sarah Goodall, his assistant. However, the degree of inter-changeability in terms of staff and functions was probably greater at IPMS and NATFHE than in the other unions in this study. At the time of the field work, IPMS had just invested £20,000 in a new Desk Top Publishing system which was eventually going to permit the integration of all media work, including the journal and press work. Although a relatively small union in terms of membership, IPMS still generated an income seven times greater than that of the NUM in 1992. The total budget for the Publicity Department was £459,000 in 1993, a sum equivalent to other unions of a similar size, such as NATFHE and the NUR. However, despite this budget allocation, IPMS had not invested in either a PA link or UNS and this, according to Charles Harvey, was as much a matter of policy as resource limitation. A sceptical view of UNS was common amongst press officers and will be discussed further below. As in the case of the TGWU, the staff within the IPMS publicity department regarded themselves as employees, rather than union members. Formerly, the department was accountable to the general secretary and staff did not enjoy routine access to the IPMS General Council, although this met only infrequently anyway.

NATFHE

Two officers within a Communications Department, Paula Lanning and Midge Purcell, took responsibility for press and media work and combined this with editing two union journals (a magazine and a tabloid), and responsibility for the production of all publicity materials. Both officers provided in-house media training courses. Thus, NATFHE tried to do with two staff what IPMS achieved with five, the GMB with nine and NALGO with a staff, perhaps, six times larger. From an annual income of around £5.5 million each year, NATFHE allocated £400,800 in 1993 for all publicity work. Although, 'exceptionally',[9] £56,000 had recently been spent upon re-launching the union, including £6000 on the design of a new logo, in the main the resourcing of NATFHE's media work was modest. £1,700 was spent upon a press cuttings service; £2,700 set aside for a '2/10 Communications' (UNS) contract, though less than half of that was eventually spent and Midge Purcell estimated that, perhaps, a further £500 was spent specifically upon press and media work.[10] Both Paula Lanning and Midge Purcell had the opportunity to attend national executive meetings and they had 'pretty good access to the general secretary'.[11]

NUCPS

At the time the field work was conducted, Ken Jones acted as press officer almost by default. Press work was directed to his office by virtue of his role as Head of the Research Department. In this sense, NUCPS provided an example of how unions used to organise their media work before the recent prioritisation of communications. Since the field work for the present study was completed, a full-time press officer has been appointed and the media and communication work reorganised within the union headquarters. Ken Jones was not involved in the editing of the journal, - 'quite a different style of writing',[12] though he did provide background research for articles on occasions. Six research officers worked under Ken Jones and he often referred press enquiries to the appropriate research officer or, indeed, to staff in other departments. An annual income in 1992 of £10,548,029 made the NUCPS fifth most prosperous union in the study, with a very large proportion being spent upon 'administration' (almost 97%) and according to the accounts, £19,384 being spent upon 'press and media work'. This, of course, appears a relatively small sum compared to NALGO or the GMB but is probably comparable to other unions of an equivalent size. One difference may lie in how that budget was spent. At the time of the field work, the NUCPS spent significantly more on their UNS account than other unions,- 'four to five thousand pounds',[13] compared to less than one thousand at NATFHE and less at NALGO. The higher expenditure on UNS was, in fact, a substitute for a more proactive press and media strategy. Ken Jones had access to national executive committee meetings and regular meetings with the general secretary but necessarily as a press officer, rather than as Head of Research.

NUM

Nell Myers was appointed as an Assistant to the President and General Secretary. In this role she combined the work of the NUM'S press officer with a number of other duties, including some media training. She had recently edited 'The Miner' in the absence of Mervyn Jones, the paper's editor, though there was not a formal integration of journal and media functions. Like the NUCPS, the NUM did not possess a press or publicity department and indeed, Nell Myers conducted much of her work from her home in East London, while the union's headquarters was based in Sheffield. Although the union recorded a membership of 93,684 in 1992, its income was lower even than that of the NUKFA (NUHKW), at only £1,331,943. The accounts give little indication of how resources were allocated to publicity or campaigning work, although £65,758 was spent during the 'Campaign Against Pit Closures', a modest sum given the importance of the issues at stake. Overall, it appears that press and media work was relatively poorly resourced, Nell Myers having at her disposal one PC and a FAX machine. Nell Myers was able to 'sit in' on national executive meetings but it was clear that she regarded herself as 'someone first and foremost who works for the President'.[14] As we shall see later, this very sharply defined understanding of line management had important consequences for the pattern of relations between the NUM and labour correspondents. The position was made more complicated by the federal structure of the union which meant that 'constitutionally' Nell Myers was unable to speak for each NUM Area. A common complaint amongst journalists was that it was very difficult to get either an 'on' or 'off record' comment from the union.

NUHKW

In his post as Assistant General Secretary, Mr Lomans combined press and media work (a surprisingly high volume for a small union rooted mainly in the East Midlands) with the formal role of journal editor. In practice, although he supplied many of the ideas, much of the day to day work for the journal was farmed out to a local free-lance journalist. Similarly, many press and media enquiries were referred to shop stewards and local officers who might be directly involved in disputes or closures. Mr Lomans also took formal responsibility for the production of publicity materials with free-lance support. A total administrative budget of only £2,980,816 placed severe limitations upon the resourcing of media work (even press releases were posted rather than faxed), though factory closures and the 'sweatshop' image of the textile industry generated regular media interest. Investment in media work amounted to little more than an annual advertisement in the Leicester Mercury, to contribute to the 'hosiery and knitwear special edition', hospitality for local journalists at the annual conference and occasional coach trips to Westminster for the purposes of lobbying local MPs and briefing journalists, en route.

There is considerable variation, then, in terms of the resourcing of media work, the organisational arrangements through which press and media work is related to the decision making process within each union, and the extent to which media work is integrated within a broader communications strategy. Regarding the latter point, it was clear that the unions which did not regularly synchronise their journal publication with media work (TGWU, NUCPS, NUM and AEU), were also unions with less commitment to the general concepts of communication strategy and proactive campaigning. Press and media work were more narrowly defined as simply that, - working with the news media, rather than contributing to broader communications campaigns. This, in turn, often reflected the organisational culture within particular unions, - there remained a widespread suspicion of journalists and 'media folk' in many unions, - and, sometimes, a professional scepticism on the part of union press officers regarding 'proactiveness'. It was often the case that in these unions the membership and general public were defined as quite distinct 'target audiences' and the point made frequently was that journal publication worked to a monthly cycle which made it an unsuitable vehicle for immediate communication purposes. The question of resources for media work and the crucial question of how news media work was related to the organisational hierarchy within unions are now discussed in further detail below.

The press officer and the chains of command

Trade unions retain essentially bureaucratic structures. Each official has a precise set of duties and must relate in quite specific ways to other officials and departments. In addition, most trade unions are typically organised on a principle of democratic accountability. Each officer or official is made accountable to the membership of the union through the role of the General Secretary. Officers are subordinate to the General Secretary, the General Secretary supervises their work and, in turn, is answerable to the national membership for the performance of the overall organisation. A few trade unions such as the NUM are organised on more de-centralised federal lines.

Trade union press officers face a potential problem because these structures are not tuned to the rhythms and demands of the national news media. Media enquiries seek to solicit almost instant responses from spokespersons and press officers because of the value placed upon 'immediacy' in the selection of news (Chibnall,1977:23), the pressure of news deadlines (Elliott and Golding,1978:ch 5; Schlesinger,1978: ch 4; Cottle, 1993: ch 2) and competition not only between rival news organisations but between journalists within particular organisations. Industrial correspondents were by no means assured of getting their copy into print, particularly by the late 1980s (the 'decline' of labour and industrial journalism is discussed further in chapters five and six). The formal structures of many trade unions are cumbersome and inflexible when viewed from the perspective of journalism. If every media enquiry had to be referred upwards to the General Secretary trade union press officers would face an impossible task in trying to cater for the needs of correspondents.

In the majority of unions in this study it was clear that a normative framework has evolved to circumvent this problem without undermining the formal principles of accountability. Firstly, many press officers indicated that it was essential to develop a set of ground rules to structure the relationship between press officer and general secretary. These ground rules had to include a large measure of trust on the part of the general secretary to allow press officers sufficient independence to respond to 'routine' media enquiries without continually referring upwards. In return, press officers had to accept certain boundaries. Most press officers emphasised that their work was delimited by the agreed policies of their union; making policy on the hoof as they responded to journalists was a real danger. This means that it was essential to have a thorough working knowledge of the policies of the union as agreed by the union conference and national executive. Secondly, a number acknowledged that there were certain issues of particular political sensitivity which had to be handled with greater care and caution. Here, referral upwards might be required by general secretaries and senior officers. This was likely to occur most frequently in those unions experiencing sharp internal political conflicts or with those closely associated with the politics of the Labour Party. However, all trade union press officers had to exercise considerable political judgement in assessing the nature and implications of news stories and media enquiries.

If a set of ground rules can be agreed between press officer and general secretary, then a system of what might be called 'delegated quotation' can be employed. When speed of response was essential trade union press officers often constructed a comment or statement themselves, hastily had it 'agreed' by the general secretary and then issued it. In certain circumstances the quote might have been simply constructed, issued to the press with the general secretary being told what he or she had officially said later on. Of course, this required considerable faith in the judgement of the press officer but the possession of such 'authority' was regarded as an important attribute by journalists.

> Mostly I will be doing the instigating and then I'll say, "Look I need a quote for this" or something...but sometimes if I'm desperate I'll make something up like on the Royal Ordnance story, if it has to go out quickly.[15]

In some circumstances the principle of 'delegated quotation' can be dramatically extended. When I visited one large union, the Head of Communications, had just finished constructing an entire interview with the General Secretary, to be published as a preview to the union conference on the front page of the journal. The opening paragraph began:

> This is the conference that decides the direction of the Union's main policy commitment for the next two years. So [name of journal] went along to [general secretary's name] office at [location], the union's H.Q. to talk to the General Secretary. The day we were there, [...] was joined by the Conference Chairman, [...], President of the Union. We were in luck. We could get both of them to let us know what they were expecting from conference. 'What', we asked, 'are the key industrial issues for the [name of union] in Blackpool this year?'

There then followed an extensive interview in which the journal quizzed an absent General secretary and President about their views on conference issues. 'Delegated quotation' on such an elaborate scale is, perhaps, rare but use of the device allows press officers much greater flexibility in making media interventions speedily.

There are clearly differences in practice between unions. The degree of rigidity in the union organisational structure and the nature of the relationship between General Secretary and press officer are likely to be important factors. For some press officers, like Charlie Whelan formerly of the AEU, his licence to employ delegated quotation varied depending upon the issue.

For some, like John Lloyd of the EEPTU 'delegated quotation' could be used in good measure but in certain unions press officers enjoyed far less freedom to exploit the flexibility and speed of response offered by the device. Ken Jones of the NUCPS did have the authority 'according to custom and practice' to issue press statements independently but only did so in 'exceptional circumstances'.[16] Normally, all press releases were produced after consultation upwards. At NATFHE, the General Secretary 'likes to have pretty much of a hands-on approach to press and publicity materials', according to Midge Purcell (one of NATFHE's two press and publicity officers) which, again, limited the scope for 'delegated quotation'.[17]

The union organisation and the 'Inside Track'

Most press officers will say that they enjoy a cordial working relationship with their general secretaries but there clearly are differences in the degree of access to the highest levels of decision making enjoyed by different press officers, and differences in the smoothness of the relationships they enjoy with their senior officials. As noted above, considerable political judgement has to be exercised by press officers in anticipating the political implications of particular issues or enquiries from the news media. They are likely to be much more confident in making such judgements if they are fully briefed about policy making, the strategic thinking of the national executive and the internal politics of the union. As described above, not all press officers, for example, are given access to national executive committee meetings. Eight of the trade unions in this study did give access but in three cases (the T and G, IPMS, and the AEU) press officers had to work without being privy to formal national executive deliberations.

The diagram (figure one) sets out two 'ideal type' union structures. The 'type A' structure reflects the 'civil service' organisational culture within some unions. A rigid distinction is drawn between elected officers and salaried employees; the former exercising the formal task of decision making, the latter undertaking the administrative tasks of implementation. The press office is formally accountable to the general secretary; the role for staff within being defined as the execution of union policy as determined hierarchically by the executive committee and directed by the general secretary. In organisational terms, the press office might be isolated both from the political process at executive level and the day to day practice of other departments within the union, including publicity and journal publication. The 'type B' structure suggests a higher degree of integration

Figure 3.1   The Position of the Press and Media Officer within the Union Organisation: two contrasting ideal types

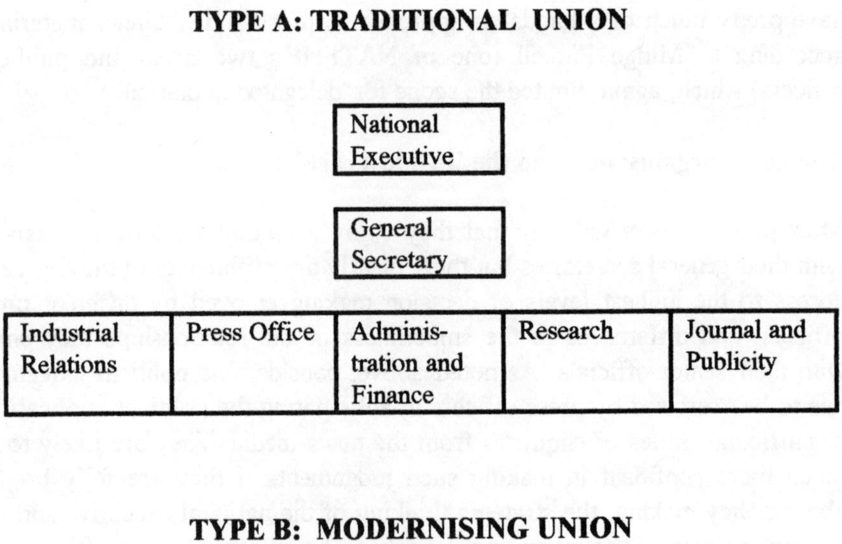

TYPE A: TRADITIONAL UNION

National Executive

General Secretary

Industrial Relations	Press Office	Administration and Finance	Research	Journal and Publicity

TYPE B: MODERNISING UNION

General Secretary and National Executive

Press and Media Journals Publicity In-house PR	Industrial Relations	Research	Finance and Administration

← Annual Communication Strategy →

with a 'press office' being located within a broader communications department and formal access to executive meetings being granted to communications staff. It is tempting to predict that journalists would indicate greater satisfaction with the performance of press and media officers working for 'type B' unions. However, the informal relationships and culture within a union also have to be taken into account. At the AEU, for example, Charlie Whelan compensated for a lack of formal access to executive meetings by developing valuable informal, 'corridor contacts', in addition to regular informal access to the general secretary. In a union with a divided and 'leaky' executive, it was still possible to gather 'intelligence', despite the more closed and less integrated formal structure.

Enjoying the confidence of senior officials and access to the higher formal arenas of decision making are not only important in allowing press officers to meet journalists' requirements in terms of speed of response. As we shall see in chapter seven, the ability to provide 'intelligence' is valued, perhaps, above all other qualities by labour correspondents. A good union press officer, in the eyes of these journalists, is one who has the ear of his or her general secretary and can provide accurate briefings on likely developments within unions; or can indicate how the political balance of an executive might determine future policy, or whether or not an executive is likely to accept an employers final offer. And a good union press officer will exploit this appetite for intelligence by granting particular journalists a position 'on the inside track'.

Achieving access to the decision making process within organisations, characterised by highly sensitive political cultures, is by no means a problem pertinent only to union press officers (Franklin,1986; Walder,1991). None of the press officers I interviewed indicated that lack of access or a poor relationship with their general secretary actually impeded their work. At the same time, several press officers argued that access to the highest decision making forums in a union was essential for effective media performance. Mary MacGuire of NALGO, for example, believed that press and media officers must have access to all key committees ,'so that they know the ins and outs of union policy'. John Lloyd of the EEPTU agreed that was essential to be 'on the inside track'.[18] At the GMB, the Media Officer, Adrian Long, and the Head of the Communications Directorate, Nicholas Woolas, developed the annual strategic plan for communications work jointly with the General Secretary (John Edmunds) and worked 'very closely' with the General Secretary and senior officials on a daily basis.

> That's not only because we expect it but because in our General Secretary you have someone who thinks the union's public face is a very important part in fulfilling his project which is to make the GMB the biggest union in Britain.[19]

Although few press officers would acknowledge the point in public, some remain on tracks nearer the outside than the inside and this is related to the structure and organisational culture of different trade unions. As noted above, a common perception of the TGWU, shared by many but not all journalists, was that the organisational culture of the union was an impediment to the work of its press officers, sometimes placing them in a position in which journalists appeared better informed about developments than they. The interviews conducted for this study at both the NUCPS and IPMS suggested that officers worked within similar cultures. Charles Harvey, Head of Communications at IPMS, sometimes had to 'use his common-sense' because IPMS General Council met infrequently and the General Secretary was sometimes unavailable but he regarded his job as strictly that of implementing IPMS policy. He had no desire or brief to 'push a political line' and was not normally involved in strategic decision making.[20] A similar situation existed at the NUCPS. Ken Jones, Head of the Research Department was given access to executive committee meetings and enjoyed 'a close relationship with senior officers' but he added:

> ...having said that, I do perceive myself as a civil servant. I don't get involved in politics or political currents. I tend to shelter behind the scenes. I let them get on with it.[21]

While none of the press officers in this study believed that it was appropriate for them to be actively involved in the political process, an organisational culture which strictly reinforces the 'civil service model' may inhibit the ability of press officers to gather the contextual political information which confers their position on 'the inside track'. Certainly, journalists regarded with more credibility those press officers who they believed 'spoke with authority'.

In some unions the distinction between officers and salaried officials is not so sharply drawn. Indeed, Charlotte Atkins, press officer at COHSE, was a card carrying member of COHSE with full officer status. This meant that, if necessary, she had the authority to give an interview and be quoted in her own name as a senior officer of the union. Although, 'normally' she attributed a comment or a statement to the general secretary, 'if it's only local radio, I'll do it in my own name'. There were differences of opinion between press officers about the advisability of raising one's own profile. Some believed that press officers should never be quoted as representatives of their union but the advantage of Charlotte Atkins' position at COHSE was that it permitted a rapid response to media enquiries but also ensured that she played a full part in the development of the union's policy and strategy which, in turn, placed her in a position of confidence in explaining the detail of union views to the news media. At NALGO and the GMB those representing each union to the media had a greater role in actively shaping union strategy than the 'civil servant model' might permit. Mary MaGuire at NALGO was formally accountable to the Publicity Committee but in practice the Committee usually went 'along with my recommendations on budget and strategy. It's rare for the Committee to order me to do something different.'[22] As noted above, Mary MacGuire had access to all the key committees and decision making forums at NALGO, while at the GMB communications was a central element in the overall political strategy of the union, developed jointly by the General Secretary, senior officers and the Communications Directorate.

The Press Officer and the General Secretary

While the formal structure and the organisational culture of a trade union are important factors in the working environment of a press officer, the personal relationship between press officer and general secretary must also be taken into account. Some senior union officers relish a high media profile while others have to be bullied into developing relationships with the media. Some take considerable interest in media work while others still have to be persuaded that press and media work is worth more than cursory consideration.

There is no doubt that a telegenic General Secretary is a considerable asset to a trade union press officer. The media performance of Jimmy Knapp, gruff 'plain speaking' general secretary of the NUR was identified as a crucial element in the success of the NUR's public relations work during the 1989 rail dispute by Laurie Harris, the NUR's press officer. Roger Poole, a NUPE senior official, became the very effective public face of the health unions during the 1990 ambulance dispute, discussed further in chapter eight. A similar strategy was used by NALGO which targeted 'Question Time' and similar television shows as platforms for its general secretary. However, by no means are all general secretaries 'telegenic' or eager for a high media profile. Some remain media shy and others continue to discount the value of media work. The EETPU always had difficulty in persuading one former general secretary to contribute, particularly to the prestigious Radio Four

'Today' programme, because it involved getting up too early in the morning. Other general secretaries only acquire a taste for media work after being thrust into the media spotlight during high profile disputes. Officers face a difficulty here. Enthusiasm is to be encouraged but there is a danger that an over-developed appetite can create difficulties for the press officer. Some senior officers may have such an enthusiastic 'hands on' approach that the work of the press officer is actually impeded. And Mr Lomans of the NUHKW noted wryly that the interest of officers in media work and particularly in appearances in the union journal always seemed to intensify in periods leading up to union elections. Press officers also have to tread wearily. One aspect of the normative framework which regulates their relationship with senior officials dictates that the latter be afforded, at least, 'first choice' of media opportunities. Mary MaGuire, at NALGO, 'has been very tempted' to do national television interviews when opportunities arise but the General Secretary is not immediately available. However, on each occasion she has resisted the temptation. Mr Lomans of the NUHKW recognised that 'most General Secretaries and Presidents will feel a bit peeved' if television opportunities are not passed up to them. Charlotte Atkins (COHSE) confirmed that national, as distinct from local, broadcasting media had to be reserved for the senior officers.

In damage limitation or 'fire fighting' situations, the union press officer will face a dilemma which may involve reconciling the interest of the organisation in limiting the flow of information to external agencies, with the need to preserve credibility in the eyes of journalists, - particularly as silence is often interpreted as an indication that the union has 'something to hide'. At best, a set of informal rules can be agreed on how to deal with such awkward situations which incorporate some kind of compromise between the interests of the union, on the one hand, and the need to nurture relationships with journalists, on the other. Eddie Barrett, of the T and G, commented:

> We have a rare but useful understanding with the General Secretary (at that time Ron Todd). We don't tell anyone lies. Nobody asks us to say anything that isn't true because if that happens your whole credibility is blown...but there may be times when we say nothing...so journalists know what they *do* get from us is reliable.[23]

Press officers, resources, and technology

One central question for any study of media and press work concerns the impact of resources and the 'technology of news work'. Is it the case that a higher level of communication resources advantages the wealthy and powerful? This has certainly been the assumption in much of the 'classic' writing in the field of pressure group theory (Finer,1966) and more recently, in some of the accounts of the eventual 'triumph' of the Coal Board over the NUM, in 1985 (Adeney and Lloyd,1986; Winterton and Winterton,1989). However, the evidence from the present study strongly suggests that while it is the case that the possession of wealth and resources can be translated into public relations power, a great deal depends upon the kind of resources employed, - human or technical, - and how they are exploited organisationally.

Even in the relatively short duration of this study, the technology of media work has changed significantly. When I first began making enquiries about media resourcing only a minority of the unions in the original sample used FAX machines.[24] The arrival of cheap FAX machines has produced an 'equalising effect' between unions because they can be used as a cheap, and probably more effective alternative to UNS. 'Two-Ten Communications', owners of the UNS newswire, offered several different types of contracts dependent upon the number of news rooms clients wished their press releases to reach, using the Press Association lines. For a press release to reach 170 news rooms, 'Two-Ten Communications' would charge £215 per three hundred words.[25] Not only was this prohibitively expensive for many unions but rather like a 'buckshot' approach to media work, it distributed press releases to too wide a range of targets. Except in exceptional circumstances (during for example, national disputes) most press officers might wish to target a far smaller number of correspondents, working for perhaps twenty national news organisations. Unions with UNS accounts tended to allocate between one and two thousand pounds per year, although NUCPS spent between four and five thousand pounds.[26] Many unions simply could not afford to allocate what amounted to, for the smaller unions, up to approximately ten per cent of their press budgets. Not only was the fax machine a cheaper alternative but combined with an 'intelligent' dialling system, it offered an equally efficient and more finely honed mechanism, delivering press releases not simply to the news room but to particular news desks or even individual correspondents within news organisations.

It is hardly surprising, then, that the value of UNS was being increasingly questioned by trade union press officers but this was not only because of the arrival of FAX. There was considerable scepticism about the value of press releases in the first place. While all trade union officers dealing with the news media issued press releases, few believed that this was sufficient. Almost all those interviewed said that if a story was important they would attempt to make personal contact with key journalists by telephone. The general view was that technology was no substitute for the development of personal relationships with journalists. An unselective issuing of press releases was likely to do more harm than good as busy journalists, overwhelmed by the sheer volume of pieces of paper arriving on their desks, were inclined to 'bin' most and resent those they read, unless they were also briefed about their significance. The UNS account represented about a quarter of the COHSE press and media budget and on the basis that 'it was rarely used', following a review, the contract was not renewed. Similarly, even at NALGO, the union with probably the most generous allocation of resources to media work, UNS was eventually dropped. Mary MaGuire renewed the UNS subscription when she had just taken over as Head of Press and Publicity but:

> I think I have used it about five times. Frankly if a story holds up it will be used by the P.A. (Press Association) and the nationals. If it doesn't it's a waste of time. Journalists don't look at it (UNS copy). I've been looking at the content,- it's all company news but it costs a third of a press officer.[27]

Eddie Barrett of the T and G dismissed UNS as 'a waste of time'. On the other hand, there may be other reasons for subscribing. The NUCPS, one of the smaller unions in the study, spent far more than any other union on UNS during the study (four to five thousand pounds per year). One officer justified the expense on the grounds that while journalists regarded UNS as a public relations vehicle,

> ...it is a very easy mechanism if you haven't a lot of time to phone up journalists. You don't necessarily get them interested in the story but you do make sure that every journalist has a copy of the information. It's like using a fax, it saves individual faxes.... . If you're short of time and you just want to satisfy your bosses that you've put out the information on people's desks, it's useful.[28]

There is the suggestion here that technology was being used precisely as a substitute for effective personal contact.

Though also expensive and beyond the means of most small unions, a P.A. [Press Association] link allows press officers to monitor the development of national news stories. In this study the AEU, COHSE, NALGO, and the GMB all used this P.A. service. It not only allows press officers to keep up with the daily national news agenda but also to intervene in the news encoding process when an appropriate story breaks. This opportunistic strategy implies a willingness to commit a significant amount of time and energy to watching and waiting. For example, Charlie Whelan of the AEU always checked the P.A. copy at around 11.30 am each day. Even the AEU could not afford to use the P.A. service continuously throughout the day. However, by mid-morning most of the stories to be used by the broadcasting media, evening papers and following day's nationals were developing.

> ...you can see what's on the news and something might come up that everyone else is doing and you think 'Fuck ...we've got no quote from the union on that.' So I ring up and I say, 'there's a quote from Gavin Laird on that story and nine times out of ten they'll add it in.[29]

This illustrates, again, the importance of having the authority to use the practice of 'delegated quotation' when necessary. In contrast to the AEU's sparing use of the P.A. link, Adrian Long at the GMB, with the luxury of probably the second largest union budget for media work, did have a P.A. monitor working over his desk almost continuously through the working day and a modem system which allowed the union's communication directorate to be connected to the Press Association and Profile, a media data base, via electronic mail. Charlie Whelan believed press officers suffered 'a serious handicap' without the P.A. service. However, even here the importance of the human dimension is underlined. Charlie Whelan made the P.A. service effective because he used it as part of a considered strategy of intervention. In contrast, the NUCPS spent significantly more on UNS for probably less effect because the investment in technology was not matched by a comparable investment of time, combined with tactical thinking.

Media monitoring services were used by some unions. NATFHE still employed a press cuttings service; the GMB invested in the 'high tech' Profile system but COHSE decided to cancel its contract with 'Telemonitors', during the course of the field work. None of the press officers in this study regarded media monitoring as an essential tool, despite the blandishments of the commercial companies. Desk top publishing was becoming much more common though. Of the larger unions, the GMB, NALGO, and the EEPTU all invested in expensive DTP systems which allowed them to produce glossy, professional quality materials in-house. Of the smaller unions, only the IPMS bought a DTP system which was used, at that time, only for the production of the union journal but had the capacity to handle publicity and media materials as well. The problem of DTP for the less well resourced unions is that such systems tend to generate work rather than save labour costs. As word gets around within an organisation about what a DTP system can do, more departments develop new projects to exploit its potential. And DTP systems usually require at least one member of staff to be allocated more or less full time to their operation. It is unlikely that a DTP finished press release had any more chance of being read by journalists than a conventionally typed one. However, press officers sometimes need to produce more elaborate briefing materials for journalists and here the speed and quality of DTP systems may be of significant value. Once again, it was not the technology in itself but the way in which it was combined with 'staff time' as a resource which was most important.

Another significant use of resources available more to the larger unions than the smaller ones was to, in effect, buy news worthiness through the practice of commissioning surveys of public attitudes or economic trends.In other words, to supply 'information subsidies' (Gandy,1982). An important theme prioritised by the union can then be wrapped around the publication of the results of the survey, at a time likely to maximise media interest. The AEU used this technique very successfully on a regular basis, through the publication of survey data on unemployment prospects in manufacturing industry released to coincide with the monthly publication of official government economic statistics and the health unions have began to exploit it. It will be discussed further in the sections below dealing with inequalities between unions. However, professionally conducted surveys are expensive and cannot be used on a regular basis by the smaller unions.

Time as a key resource

Generally, the larger unions have more of the 'technology of media work' at their disposal, though as the case of the NUCPS illustrates, smaller unions may be willing to spend considerable amounts of money on technology as a substitute for human labour. However, what emerged as an important theme in the field work for this study was the importance of time as a resource, in itself. A very common comment amongst press officers working for the smaller unions was that they simply did not have enough time to move towards proactive rather than reactive media work. A proactive strategy requires time in planning and preparation, time invested in targeting key journalists and time in actually working with those journalists. Given the limited staffing and range of duties from journal editing to research, publicity and administration, undertaken by some press officers in smaller unions, it is sometimes difficult for them to move off the backfoot. A long term media strategy requires careful discussion, planning, an element of additional 'creativity' or 'flair' and the necessary time invested in targeting particular journalists or media outlets. Midge Purcell of NATFHE, for example, would have liked to reach a wider broadcasting arena beyond news and current affairs. With the necessary research and planning, NATFHE views concerning women and education or training could have been presented through radio programmes like 'Womans Hour' or the consumer programme 'Punters' on Radio Four:

> There's a lot more that we could do if we had the time. We could think creatively about how to get issues across. It does take time and a certain amount of creativity. If we targeted Woman's Hour we would have to think what angle they might be interested in, what is topical but hasn't been done before... .[30]

What made this situation even more frustrating was that a former senior officer at NATFHE had just moved across to the Education Department at the BBC. Midge Purcell, therefore, had a ready made contact but was unable to invest the time required to exploit the opportunity. To move off the backfoot; to become 'proactive', trade union press officers must construct agendas or messages which combine appropriate thematic elements, or news values, with mechanisms which exploit the symbolic resources, political capital, or just straight forward 'newsworthyness' which unions may possess.

Not all union press officer concurred with the view that staffing and associated allocations of 'time' was a significant factor. Charles Harvey, for example, believed that the smallness of the IPMS Communications Department was an advantage, allowing a cohesive and more flexible response in comparison to their main 'opponents', Civil Service press officers locked into 'a slow and cumbersome bureaucracy'.[31] Similarly, Laurie Harris believed that as he was the only press officer at the NUR, he could move more rapidly to 'outflank' the unwieldy public relations department at British Rail.[32] However, neither Charles Harvey nor Laurie Harris approached press and media work with such elaborate strategic thinking as, for example, the GMB Communication Directorate; each being a little sceptical of the more extravagant claims made by some supporters of 'proactivity'. With horizons more limited to the day to day skirmishes of media work, the issue of staffing and time was, perhaps, felt less acutely.

Nevertheless, it is time which largely determines the quality of the social relationships developed by press officers with journalists and it is time which allows a press officer to apply the skills of his or her craft in exploiting both material and symbolic resources:

> Our job would be more difficult without some of the new technology but it wouldn't be impossible. If you've got a good story and you know how to present it and how to handle the story then it doesn't matter whether you've got two or three FAX machines...A FAX machine cannot put a spin on a story ...it can't give you nuances, the political or industrial feel of a story.[33]

Of course, this view can be read as an example of a professional ideology at work, legitimating the skills of a particular occupation, and on one level that is precisely what it is. However, it is the case that the most fundamental inequalities between organisations seeking access to the news media are not those related to the distribution of communication technology. The distribution of advantage and disadvantage in the struggle to achieve access to news media is shaped by forces largely beyond the capacity of the press officer to influence, a point to be discussed further in the next chapter, but in terms of the factors controlled within their internal environment, staff time and the skills involved in mobilising both symbolic and material resources are of most importance. As illustrated in the case of the NUCPS at the time of the field work, investment in communication technology is no substitute for time invested in developing contacts with journalists and assessing the symbolic and material resources to be deployed. UNS distributed press releases were likely to be ignored; a measured and judicious use of the telephone, as practised by, for example, Charlie Whelan was likely to be more effective.

Inevitably, then, we are forced to consider what is meant by 'effective press and media work'. Discussions with journalists and labour correspondents confirmed that Charlie Whelan was almost universally regarded as one of the best union press officers. 'Quick', 'sharp', 'professional', 'an eye for a good story' were some of the phrases invoked by both journalists and other press officers in support of this view. Jim Fookes, a press officer at NALGO, believed that Charlie Whelan was being groomed[34] and, indeed, after the field work was completed he joined the Labour Party leaderships' communications team, and now works for Chancellor Gordon Brown. It is notable, then, how the professional perspectives of many press officers coincided with those of journalists. Both journalists and press officers stressed the importance of being able to spot 'a good story' and the importance of 'getting the right angle'. Both cited 'professionalism' as the criterion upon which to assess performance and some press officers referred to the 'obligation of objectivity' in much the same way as some journalists. Although frequently critical of the nature of the news media as a whole, particularly tabloid newspapers, a majority of the press officers in the study shared a common modus operandi with journalists; to be 'effective' they had to acknowledge the news values of daily national journalism and its rhythms and routines. Hence, the need for chains of command within unions which allowed press officers to respond quickly to inquiries and have a 'delegated quote' from the general secretary to hand; hence the commitment to embed union communication in the news values of national journalism and the elevation of 'professional skills' above the power of the technology of news communication.

Press officers: background, career and professional style

Most press officers arrive in their positions through one of two routes; professional journalism or trade union administration. Of the press officers in this study, only Eddie Barrett and Andrew Murray at the TGWU had worked extensively on national newspapers. However, Charles Harvey, at the IPMS, had worked for regional newspapers in the Midlands and developed an interest in trade union communication through experience as an NUJ activist. His assistant at IPMS, Sarah Goodall, had worked in the trade press. Midge Purcell, at NATFHE, held an American degree in journalism, but had also worked for a number of community and campaign groups in the USA before coming to Britain. In contrast five of the press officers in this study had arrived in their current positions through promotion within trade union administration. John Lloyd almost fell into his position as Head of Communications at the EEPTU. After joining the EEPTU as a research officer in the early 1970s he got to know most of the industrial correspondents through his work in supporting EEPTU negotiating sessions.

'I used to make the tea for the industrial correspondents'. However, in the mid 1980s he was asked to write the official history of the union, 'Light and Power', and his appointment was made on the strength of that book's light and entertaining style. Charlotte Atkins first started as a political and research officer at TASS before moving into a post at UCATT which 'grew' into press and media work. She took up her post at COHSE on the basis of the media experience acquired there. Charlie Whelan was 'spotted' whilst working as a local AEU organiser at Fords, Dagenham, whilst Ken Jones at NUCPS had been involved in trade union research throughout his career.

The one exception to this pattern was Adrian Long at the GMB who first made his mark as President of the National Union of Students, then moved to a small communications consultancy, 'Gould Mattinson Associates' and worked closely with the 'shadow communications team', supporting the Labour Party's new media strategies. His particular brief was to support the British Labour Group in Europe before the European Parliamentary elections.

Table 3.1 Backgrounds of Union Press Officers in the Study

Journalism	Union Administration	Other
Eddie Barrett TGWU	John Lloyd EEPTU	Adrian Long GMB
Charles Harvey IPMS	Ken Jones NUCPS	Nell Myers NUM
Mary Maguire NALGO	Charlie Whelan AEU	
Midge Purcell NATFHE	Charlotte Atkins COHSE	
	Mr. Lomans NUHKW	

The difference in background and experience produced differences in emphasis and priority but it was notable that most of the press officers without formal training in journalism still shared a common modus operandi with labour correspondents. Eddie Barrett argued that his twenty six years experience in journalism meant that:

> We understand what national journalists want because that's our background and we're in a position to angle our material for them (journalists).[35]

Similarly, Charles Harvey (IPMS) talked of the importance of a sense for news values and the skills involved in writing a good news story while Mary Maguire (NALGO) emphasised the need for 'a professional approach', - an awareness of which stories 'will stand up'.

> I don't just release any old story because somebody wants me to. I will judge what is the story that's going to be used, if its going to be used we go ... and ninety nine times out of one hundred I'm right.[36]

Those press officers from non-journalistic backgrounds might expand or qualify the list of essential attributes but not reject the common framework of shared assumptions. According to Adrian Long (GMB), for example, a political awareness was vitally important, particularly in a trade union with a national political presence close to the Labour Party and a significant 'political responsibility' inside the TUC.

> It would be virtually impossible for a journalist, no matter how well trained, to come in and understand some of the political subtleties of what we're trying to do , unless they had a background in politics as well.[37]

Yet, at the same time, he added, a combination of trade union political experience and the 'approach and feel' of professional communicators was required...

> ...to cut through the way trade unions sometimes speak. Trade union speak is a language all of it's own, and part of our job is to make sure its turned into a language people understand when they're eating their tea in front of the telly. Some of us don't have the twenty years experience but what we do have are the skills to make that twenty years mean something.[38]

Not all union press officers were convinced by these sorts of arguments. Charlie Whelan, for example, nine months into the job, took a more irreverent view but, nonetheless, still embraced the dominance of mainstream news values:

> Its easy. My old granny could do it! I just write pieces as I would like to read them in the newspaper![39]

There were differences in temperament and style between press officers, ranging from the up beat 'corporate professionalism' of Adrian Long, the iconoclastic but energetic and opportunistic 'shop floor' or 'union corridor wisdom' of Charlie Whelan, the rather dogged professionalism of Eddie Barrett, Andrew Murray and Mary McGuire, to the more fatalistic outlook of Ken Jones and Nell Myers. Ken Jones (NUCPS) and Adrian Long (GMB) provided marked contrasts in terms of time and thought invested in the preparation of media work. Adrian Long belonged very much to the new breed of union officer, drawing concepts and vocabulary from the world of commercial marketing and corporate communications. He identified three target audiences for media work, - existing GMB members, potential GMB members, and 'opinion formers' (political and media elites). Distinct strategies were devised to reach each of these groups, through particular media (one politician may be known to read a particular paper, for example) and all this was done in accordance with the communications plan drawn up on an annual basis. In contrast:

Interviewer: 'Are there any tricks of the trade which can be applied ?'

> Ken Jones (NUCPS):'...(long silence)...not really...other than the professional points...get releases out early, don't issue releases on a Friday. We do all the normal things but we don't do the proactive bit...digging up stories which can be packaged for the press. We don't have much contact with the press.   Normally, its just statements and summaries of negotiations.

Ken Jones was pessimistic regarding opportunities for much more than 'damage limitation work' with most papers, other than, perhaps one or two of the more sympathetic broadsheets. He identified low pay as the key issue the NUCPS would like to insert into a preferred news media agenda but he added...

> Getting that across to the media is a thankless task. Middle grade civil servants are not high up most people's league tables of deserving causes.[41]

While broadsheet papers might carry something, with the rest of the papers, 'you might as well forget it'. Too often papers simply reinforced a stereotyped image of civil servants as 'a privileged, parasitic group'.

For rather different reasons, Nell Myers, of the NUM, was equally pessimistic. She could see no evidence of 'the public relations way of dealing with media', prevalent in a number of unions, 'actually protecting the interests of members, winning disputes, or building the strength of those unions in areas of massive exploitation'. For her, 'the aims, intentions, and purposes of the media are not only completely different to those of the NUM but often in utter contradiction and completely hostile'.[42]

Other press officers in the study recognised the political role of the news media but drew finer distinctions between types of media and the interests of particular groups of journalists. It was common to find union press officers apportioning blame for hostile coverage, not to individual correspondents but to proprietorial influence or editorial decision making at a higher level within news organisations. Most still believed that it was possible to secure successes, at least with broadcasting media and broadsheet papers. As one union press officer argued:

> You haven't asked me how important public opinion is. Presumably, its crucial. I mean if Scargill wasn't such a crackpot the Miner's wouldn't have lost. Look at the ambulance workers...public opinion was crucial there...absolutely crucial...when you've got no clout, its all you've got.[43]

Other press officers were also able to offer anecdotal evidence for the effectivity of media work. At the T and G, for example, Eddie Barrett recalled a dispute over the sacking of a British Airways cabin crew for alleged stealing. The 'key themes', - the high handedness of management, the innocence of the crew, inconvenience to the pubic, - were identified in terms of popular news criteria and the strategy worked quite effectively. A large amount of publicity was generated, the crew was reinstated and eventually the newly appointed B.A. Director of Human Resources was sacked. Here, then, is an example of the way in which mainstream news values can be harnessed to communicate trade union themes. Only Nell Myers (NUM) appeared to take an uncompromising line on the issue of news criteria and union agendas. The other press officers in the study were all more or less engaged in a common enterprise to identify mainstream news pegs around which to hang themes drawn from unions' agendas or to defensively invoke mainstream news values in the presentation of their unions' positions, a technique known as 'fire fighting' and discussed further in the following chapter.

Summary

This chapter has looked within the union organisation at the press officer's internal environment. It has considered the ways in which the inevitably bureaucratic nature of organisations which acknowledge a formal accountability to mass memberships, constrains the nature of press and media work, and at the techniques which press officers can employ to overcome such problems. Surfacing again and again throughout this chapter is evidence, too, of the tensions inherent in the role of trade union press officer. Whether they are recruited from within the ranks of the union or whether they are appointed on the strength of their experience in professional journalism, trade union press officers must 'speak for the union'; their primary function is to represent the perspectives and interests of their union to the outside world. There are frequent occasions when this function is not easily reconciled with the interests and needs of professional news journalists. And yet, at the same time, a majority of union press officers in this study acknowledged the importance of 'professionalism' and the need to accommodate the requirements of professional journalists. In this context, union press officers are required to act both as trade unionists or 'advocates' of clearly defined political interests *and* as more dispassionate 'professionals' involved in the assessment and dissemination of information. The tensions inherent in the role of trade union press officer will be explored further in the following chapter.

    The chapter has also considered the extent to which an unequal distribution of material resources disadvantages those 'resource poor' trade unions seeking access to the news media. Goldenberg's study of the attempts by 'resource poor' community groups to secure favourable news coverage in Boston offers a comparable approach (1975). Inequalities of wealth and political power do, indeed, skew the distribution of access to the news media but, as Goldenberg concluded, 'resource poor' groups may still secure some successes in the struggle to win favourable news coverage, providing they can mobilise particular kinds of material and symbolic resources (1975:47). 'Contactability', according to Goldenberg, was valued by journalists and this has implications in terms of staffing. Credibility, too, in terms of the provision of information or research data in a digestible form, which journalists could rely upon and 'process' was also important. Above all else, the quality of relationships established with journalists and the extent to which these were informed by a common understanding of news values and the beat system, allowed such groups to make some headway (1975:140-141).

In the same way, those unions in which press officers enjoyed sufficient authority to respond quickly and in ways regarded as credible by journalists, were more likely to report successes in securing favourable coverage. Press officers who possessed sufficient expertise in particular areas, or who could quickly supply answers to inquiries by drawing upon the expertise of other departments in the union (industrial, research, etc), were highly valued by journalists. The absence of the 'technology of communication' was not, in itself, a disadvantage. What counted was the ability to mobilise symbolic and material resources to maximum effect and this depended more upon the capacity of press officers to construct their preferred themes using the vocabulary and symbolism of dominant news values.

The danger of this discussion is to lose sight of the structural constraints within which press officers work,- political and ideological, as well as economic, - and to produce an account which describes the *action* of press officers in naively volunteristic terms. The following chapter begins to anticipate this danger by considering the union press officers' external environment and includes a section which examines the ways in which the best laid proactive plans may be blown off course. Subsequent chapters add to the description of the external environment; they describe the 'exchange' relationships between press officers and labour correspondents and the ways in which structural developments impact upon the opportunities and constraints for the actors involved in the production of labour and industrial news. In focusing upon the ways in which actors negotiate organisational impediments and develop patterns of stable interaction, there is always a danger that one loses sight of the 'big picture'. After all, as Laurie Harris of the NUR commented, good publicity has hardly improved the pay of nurses. Even Charlotte Atkins of COHSE conceded that while the health unions won the publicity battle during the ambulance dispute, the war ended in stalemate. For the moment, however, whilst noting the importance of the structural context, the focus will remain upon the *activity* of the actors involved in forming some of the social relationships which underpin news encoding.

Notes

1. Example provided by Midge Purcell (NATFHE), interviewed 16.7.93.
2. Interview with author, 12.7.93.

3.   Midge Purcell, ibid. Also, interview with Andrew Murray (TGWU) 13.7.93.
4.   Interview with Charlotte Atkins (COHSE), 16.7.91.
5.   Ibid.
6.   Interview with John Lloyd (EETPU), 24.5.91.
7.   Correspondence with the author, 26.8.93.
8.   Interview with the author, 13.7.93.
9.   Interview with Midge Purcell, 9.7.93.
10.   Interview with Midge Purcell, 16.7.93.
11.   Ibid.
12.   Interview with Ken Jones (NUCPS), 7.6.91.
13   Ibid.
14.   Interview with Nell Myers (NUM), 20.9.91.
15.   Interview with a highly respected press officer working for one of the
        larger unions.
16.   Interview with Ken Jones, op cit.
17.   Interview with Midge Purcell, 21.6.91.
18.   Interviews with Mary McGuire (NALGO), 31.7.90. and John Lloyd, op cit.
19.   Interview with Adrian Long (GMB), 21.6.91.
20.   Interview with Charles Harvey (IPMS), 21.6.91.
21.   Interview with Ken Jones, op cit.
22.   Interview with Mary McGuire, op cit.
23.   Interview with Eddie Barrett (TGWU), 6.3.91.
24.   A preliminary survey of media resourcing conducted by telephone was
        conducted in 1988. All unions with a membership over 45,000 were contacted
        a selected few with memberships below this.
25.   At 1992/93 prices. See, 'UK Services and Price List' (January 1993),
        Two Ten Communications, 210 Old Street, London EC1V 9UN.
26.   Interview with Ken Jones, op cit.
27.   Interview with Mary McGuire, op cit.
28.   Interview with senior officer within the NUCPS, summer 1991.
29.   Interview with Charlie Whelan (AEU), 6.6.91.
30.   Interview with Midge Purcell, op cit.
31.   Interview with Charles Harvey, op cit.
32.   Interview with Laurie Harris (NUR), 25.8.1989.
33.   Interview with Adrian Long, op cit.
34.   Interview with Jim Fookes (NALGO), 10.6.93.
35.   Interview with Eddie Barrett, op cit.
36.   Interview with Mary McGuire, op cit.
37.   Interview with Adrian Long, op cit.
38.   Ibid.
39.   Interview with Charlie Whelan, 12.7.93.
40.   Interview with Ken Jones, op cit.
41.   Ibid.
42.   Interview with Nell Myers, op cit.
43.   Interview conducted with a union press officer during the summer of 1991.

4 Press Officers, Correspondents and the 'Inside Track'

The study now turns to examine the nature of the relationships which pattern the interaction between union press officers and their external environment. Chapter three suggested that it was not the possession of material resources as such, but the ways in which those resources could be invested to support and direct interaction between the representatives of source organisations and journalists which was of particular significance in the practice of press and media work. This chapter explores the relationship between union press officer and journalist in greater depth; it describes the nature of the 'bargain' through which many union press officers and correspondents direct their relations, but also begins to consider the intrusion of 'external' forces which disrupt and re-order such relations.

Changing relationships

As chapter five describes in more detail, there was some truth in the old picture of labour correspondents. There certainly used to be a common pub conveniently sited around the corner from most leading union headquarters (perhaps two, if the union executive was politically split as in the case of the AEU) where labour correspondents and union officers would meet, drink and forge a beverage inspired esprit de corps.

However, whatever the importance of the pub as an arena for social contact in the past, relationships between press officers and journalists rarely follow the pattern of Private Eye's Lunchtime O'Booze, today. Only Eddie Barrett of the T and G and John Lloyd of the EETPU appeared to invest much time in the traditional form of intercourse between sources and journalists. John Lloyd, only recently appointed Head of Communications, spent four months meeting journalists socially in order to establish a framework of connections. 'Only the other week', he had spent the afternoon in the pub with the chair of the Industrial Correspondents' Group, 'gossiping about unions and football'. One union press officer, a former journalist now working for one of the largest unions still mixed socially with journalists and the location of his union in the centre of London, allowed regular meetings 'around the watering holes of Westminster'. He met journalists 'frequently socially':

> ...if someone calls us and asks us if anything's happening...we'll suggest popping around for a drink and a chat to see how things are going. It's not dishonest but its a way of making people think they are on the inside track.[1]

The importance of making contacts think they are on 'the inside track' was one of the tricks of the trade employed by a number of press officers. It recognised the labour correspondents' appetite for 'intelligence', or information which allowed 'informed judgements' to be made about future developments and likely scenarios, and it depended upon the cultivation of a 'shared intimacy', through which off-record material and snippets of information could be exchanged. The nature of such 'exchanges' and the importance of the inside track will be developed below. In the past, such relationships may have been cultivated around the pubs of Fleet Street and Westminster, or seaside hotel bars during 'conference season'. The cash registers in such venues may still ring with deposits made by some labour correspondents and their contacts within unions but much less frequently. The era of such frequent personal contacts has gone; in its place a new pattern of 'telephonic interaction' is now the norm. The irony is that as unions in recent years have taken steps to make themselves more accessible to journalists, through the appointment of full-time press officers, so changes in the nature and organisation of daily news journalism have compelled journalists to retreat from the networks of personal contacts which used to sustain their 'intelligence' gathering. Of course, these patterns, - the re-location and rationalisation of national newspaper journalism, the increasing use of electronic information gathering, the changing geography correspondent's beats and the decline of particular news specialisms, - are not unrelated or isolated developments but more visible manifestations of a process of fundamental change through which commercial news organisations have sought to exploit new technologies and organisational structures to respond to ever fiercer competition in news markets.

The history of industrial journalism; the recent decline in the fortunes of the Labour and Industrial Correspondents Group and recent changes in the nature of the labour beat are described more fully in chapters five and six. Briefly, both media organisations and many trade union headquarters have re-located away from the centre of London. Further to this, the nature of work for national news journalists has changed as news organisations have sought to rationalise and improve productivity. Few journalists now have the time to indulge in the extended lunch breaks of previous decades. The result of these trends is a change in nature of relationships between journalists and union officers and a decline in the frequency of their face to face contact. Many of the most significant exchanges now take place by telephone between the suburbs of London and various points along the south bank of the Thames; between, for example, Banstead in Surrey and Battersea or Bromley in Kent and Blackfriars. According to Charlotte Atkins of COHSE, 'the boozy image of journalists is less and less true'.[2] Adrian Long (GMB) argued that there had been a generational shift in journalistic culture; younger journalists having neither the time nor inclination to spend much of their working lives propping up bars.[3] Both Adrian Long and Phil Woolas (Head of the Communication Directorate at GMB) engaged in regular wining and dining of targeted journalists but this remained a highly structured strategy focused upon a specific goal (for example, a briefing upon a key theme) rather than the development of casual, unfocused pub culture. Most press officers, as Charles Harvey (IPMS) observed, will spend very little time in face to face contact with journalists. For most, the typical day to day contact will be by telephone and Fax machine with much less regular personal contacts at, perhaps, the union annual conference or a special press event to launch a campaign. For Charlie Whelan (formerly at the AEU), it was a point of professional pride never to have to buy a journalist a drink.

> They have to make the effort to see you. I've never taken a journalist out anywhere. I'd feel slighted if I had to go and buy *them* a drink![4]

The diminishing numbers of industrial correspondents has accelerated the decline in regular personal contact. There are fewer specialists around to develop working relationships with. As described further in chapter nine, some newspapers, including *Today*, the *Daily Star* and the *Sun* now only have an intermittent commitment to a labour desk; all other papers have reduced the number of labour and industrial specialists. And yet, most union press officers remained quite sanguine about the long term prospects. Many believed decline was cyclical:

> Interest has fallen off with the perception that unions generate less news but all daily papers with the exception of the *Daily Star* have at least one or two industrial correspondents. We try to play our part in sustaining them with stories of strikes that are happening and so on.[5]

Of course, it is in the interests of union press officers to sustain the work of industrial correspondents because as Charlie Whelan (AEU) says, 'there's nothing worse than dealing with someone who doesn't know what you're talking about'.[6] The value of a shared frame of reference goes beyond a common knowledge of names and organisations. As discussed below, a mutual interest in the comings and goings in the world of industrial relations allows a kind of rapport to develop which helps to foster a mutually beneficial normative regulation. Non-specialist journalists are much less likely to recognise the 'rules of the game' which can regulate the relationship between union press officer and industrial correspondent. Union press officers have grown accustomed to the most hostile 'hatchet jobs' being written by non-specialist general reporters or feature writers (Seaton,1982:280). Journalists outside this normative framework are not bound by a personal and career investment in relationships with union staff.

Which newspapers ?

Ericson found that the Canadian police, as news sources, distinguished between tabloid and broadsheet correspondents, favouring the former, but frequently excluding the latter from an 'inner circle' (1989b:3-4). Most trade union press officers in this study were more likely to be wary of admitting tabloid journalists to their 'inner circle' or 'inside track'. Nevertheless, the approach of many was to regard the disposition of the right wing tabloids, almost as part of the 'natural' condition of the political-media environment. Journalists on these papers were...

> ...just doing their job. If they're working for a right wing newspaper they don't want a load of left wing polemics. So if you're working for the

Morning Star you don't write in the same way as if you're working for the *Sun*.[7]

Nevertheless, a number of press officers distinguished between papers in the way they dealt with enquiries whilst professing sympathy and respect for journalists in general. One union press office distinguished between its 'A' and 'B' service:

> We have an A service and a B service...the B service is what the *Sun* get. They don't contact us to confirm a story, they only contact us to get some kind of quote that will land the union in the shit. They're never looking for positive stories, so we deal with them honestly and give them anything they want, we send them the normal faxes, press releases etc, but we don't give them anything else. I mean we don't phone the *Sun* industrial editor and say 'check that - you might find something in that'.[8]

A number of interesting points are illustrated here. To begin with, apart form the differentiation between the *Sun* and other papers, there is the suggestion that a normative framework can regulate relationships between journalists and press officers. The *Sun* cannot be trusted to play by the rules of the game; quotes may be used simply to confirm a pre-established angle rather than to illustrate the union's perspective. The response to *Sun* enquiries, therefore, is to provide basic 'factual' information, the bare bones of a story (this is a 'fire-fighting technique' employed by a number of press officers) but not involve *Sun* journalists in more elaborate exchange relationships. The nature of such exchange relationships will be discussed below and 'fire fighting techniques' are analysed in a subsequent section.

There was by no means complete unanimity amongst the press officers in this study regarding the trustworthiness of particular journalists or media organisations. Fairly widespread misgivings were expressed regarding relationships with the *Sun*. One press officer commented that she felt she always needed a witness in the room when dealing with *Sun* inquiries because of the danger of 'having words put in your mouth.'[9] And yet, the same press officer felt more comfortable with the tabloid *Daily Mirror*, where she believed *Mirror* journalists were 'on our side'. Indeed, *Mirror* journalists would make helpful suggestions about how best to construct the union perspective in tabloid discourse. Given this kind of collaborative atmosphere she felt comfortable in allowing *Mirror* journalists to take draughts away to be re-worked before going to press.

Suspicion of the *Sun* was not universal. John Lloyd (EEPTU) said he could not remember 'being betrayed' by any journalists (another indication of a normative framework structuring relationships). All journalists respected the distinction between on and off record briefings, for example. Indeed, the *Sun*, perhaps because of the political position of the EETPU, gave the union more coverage than the *Mirror*. John Lloyd regarded the *Mirror* as a 'priority' for further work. In the *Sun*, by contrast, the EEPTU General Secretary, Eric Hammond, was presented as 'Hambo', crusading against left extremism.[10]

On the other hand, Ken Jones (NUCPS) despaired of all tabloid papers. As far as the *Sun*, *Star*, *Mail*, and *Express* went, 'you may as well forget it', while Today had just produced five paragraphs on civil servants as privileged and parasitic, with index linked pensions and more holidays than anyone else. Only the *F.T.*, *Guardian*, *Daily Telegraph*, and *Independent* ('sometimes') could be relied upon to carry a reasonable story without attempting to 'editorialise'.[11] Nell Myers of the NUM was reluctant to distinguish even between tabloid and broadsheet journalists.

Interviewer: It sounds as if you don't distinguish much between media, types of
   paper, t.v. etc,?
Nell Myers: Very little...hardly at all. I do distinguish between some of the
   journalism of the labour movement and the capitalist media. I have a
   different feeling for *Socialist Worker, Newsline, Worker's Press,*
   Morning Star, those in particular, than I do for anybody in the capitalist
   media, press and radio... .[12]

There is a certain ambivalence in the approach of Nell Myers. On the one hand, many of her views suggest a model of society in which structured inequalities of wealth and power might be expected to very significantly constrain what a trade union press officer might hope to achieve. On the other hand, she was reluctant to dismiss mainstream journalists entirely.

There are certain journalists that I have come to have a certain regard for and a certain amount of trust in and a feeling that they are not going to "do" you and are going to be reasonably fair...but conversely there are those for whom its just a waste of time speaking to; that if you get a message on the answer phone saying "call back" you don't bother because its just a waste of time...although I try not to get into that trap because you never know what the query might be.[13]

Not surprisingly, those press officers in the study with the most pessimistic views about the prospects of generating 'fair' or 'positive' coverage were the ones least likely to recognise the value of fostering 'exchange relationships' with correspondents.

Exchange relationships: bargains, 'intelligence' and the Inside Track

The suggestion that journalistic culture is based upon a set of binding consensual norms has been challenged in recent fieldwork (Ericson et al 1987:349-50). The point has been made that while rules may exist, journalists frequently and routinely bend them or manipulate them to their advantage in the course of their relationships with news managers, editors, and external contacts. Similarly, the suggestion, here, is not that a rigid consensual system structures all relationships between press officers and journalists in stable and predictable ways. On the contrary, the relationships described by the union press officers in this study were much less structured. The normative framework operated for some officers in their dealings with some journalists. Goldenberg, in his study of the attempts by 'resource poor groups' to secure access to the news media, found that only a minority of potential source-correspondent interactions crystallised into stable, on-going relations. Nevertheless, he describes those that did as centering around an implicit 'bargain' (Goldenberg,1975:136). Sources provided accurate information, exclusive material and privileged interviews and 'in return', journalists tried to ensure that their copy contained a faithful representation of source views and perspectives. If sources had opportunities to shape patterns of news coverage, such opportunities were generated through the capacity of news sources to provide 'information subsidies' (Gandy,1982).

A similar process could be detected in much of the interaction between correspondents and union press officers. Accurate information, advance 'intelligence' or a position on the 'inside track', and access to senior officials, were the 'bargaining chips' which experienced press officers tried to employ in their 'exchange relations' with correspondents. As discussed further in the following chapters dealing with labour corespondents, a prominent goal for such journalists is the acquisition of information or 'intelligence' which puts them 'ahead of the game', or provides a contextual understanding which permits an informed reading of events. The subcultural values and practices of the Labour and Industrial Correspondents Group reinforced this orientation; status being awarded to those journalists with a reputation for shrewd judgements and inside information; the 'Golden Bollock' trophy being awarded annually for the published copy most wildly inaccurate in its assessment of future developments. In return, for a position on the 'inside track', union press officers   hoped to secure a 'fair' representation of union perspectives in the news copy produced. The rules regulating such exchange relationships were not explicit and rested upon a fragile shared intimacy which could rapidly evaporate as circumstances changed. At best, such rules structured   the union source-journalist relationship only so long as it suited both parties in the relationship for interaction to be patterned in this way.

However, the union press officers in this study, identified a number of expectations which had to be acknowledged in order to foster effective 'exchange relations'. Firstly, most stressed the importance of investing time in dealing with journalists. It was widely believed that journalists discriminated between those press officers seen as helpful, usually available; those willing to put effort in responding to enquiries, and those who appeared less willing to pull out all the stops or who were often difficult to contact. In this sense, it was believed that journalists related to union officers as *individuals*, in terms of personal characteristics, rather than according to their status as representatives of particular organisations (Chibnall,1977:ch 6; Ericson et al,1987:350-351).

As Midge Purcell of NATFHE expressed the point: 'You have to make sure that you are as useful to them as you want them to be useful to you'.[14] This meant taking the trouble in Midge's case to either research the answer to a query herself or find someone in the NATFHE Research Department who could. With an enormous quantity of recent government legislation affecting further and higher education, enquiries, particularly from education correspondents, could be extremely complicated and time consuming. In other cases, making the effort may mean making one's home number available to journalists and being prepared to accept enquiries at virtually any time. Industrial correspondents usually avoided abusing this arrangement but there was always the possibility, during national disputes, of a local radio journalist ringing at 5am in preparation for the breakfast news.[15]

Another obligation for press officers was to ensure that they were worth phoning. In other words, they had to ensure that journalists regarded them as authoritative and credible. They had to be seen as 'speaking for' the union and had to be recognised as being sufficiently close to the centre of decision making within the organisation to be in possession of reliable, if not 'inside' information. As discussed in the previous chapter, the nature of the internal culture of a union and the position of the press officer in relation to the senior officers and the national executive were of considerable importance here. Credibility had to be earnt. John Lloyd (EEPTU) spent three months, as we have seen, establishing his credentials with industrial correspondents, even though as a researcher he was already known to a number. Charlie Whelan, on the other hand, enjoyed an immediate credibility because he had worked for one of the senior figures in the AEU before assuming responsibility for media work. 'They [journalists] knew I knew what I was talking about.'[16]

If the framework for exchange relationships between union officers and journalists rests upon a fostering of *individual* contacts, then a great deal depends upon the nature of the approach employed by press officers. Most press officers in this study believed that it was important to avoid identifying journalists, even those working for right wing tabloids, as agents of hostile forces.

> It takes an awful lot of hard work and not treating journalists like your enemies. Treat someone like your enemy and they'll be your enemy.[17]

The union press officers in this study were inclined to believe that labour correspondents held a personal sympathy for trade unionism. Why else, Laurie Harris (NUR) asked, would they choose to specialise in industrial relations? If this was the case, the best strategy was 'to be willing to make yourself available, talk to them [journalists], be as open as you can,- I don't think we ever said "no comment" [during the 1989 rail dispute].[18] During the rail dispute, Laurie Harris worked 16 to 17 hours each day in the office and took a further three or four calls at home during the evening and at night. The key was to ensure that the NUR always had a reputation for accessibility and a friendly response.

There is a more explicit recognition of the normative framework in certain circumstances. The distinction between on and off the record briefings was acknowledged as one the rules of the game, generally accepted by both sides in the relationship. Similarly, most press officers respected the principle of 'exclusivity' and recognised the importance for journalists in protecting 'exclusives' before publication. For example, details of the spending cuts and job losses at Guys and Lewisham Hospital, were leaked to the *Daily Mirror*. The *Mirror* then contacted COHSE for confirmation and comment on what, in the light of the political controversy over the

Government's NHS reforms, was a very important 'exclusive'. Although the temptation was to circulate the information to other news organisations in order to maximise the political impact, Charlotte Atkins 'sat' on the story in recognition of the importance of 'exclusives' for news organisations in a very competitive sector.

> I thought *Mirror* exclusive...I won't break that exclusive and then ten minutes later I was rung by the *Telegraph*. I thought, "Right, its not an exclusive" and then immediately put out a press release to the P.A. [Press Association] and rang Robin Cook's office [at that time shadow Minister for Health]. It was obviously a massively big story.[19]

This suggests that the norms governing 'exclusivity', at least, can exercise quite a powerful restraint. The Guy's story had tremendous propaganda value for COHSE and yet, Charlotte Atkins held back until she was 'honourably' released from her obligation to the *Mirror*, with evidence from the *Telegraph* that exclusivity had evaporated.

Why should both press officers and journalists accept such a normative framework, however fragile, when it can act as an inconvenient impediment in situations which demand rapid responses? Presumably, because on balance the advantages out-weigh the inconvenience. Indeed, some press officers are in a position to exploit the principle of 'exclusivity' in ways which allow them to insert particular themes in particular news media texts. At the heart of the 'bargain' between union press officer and correspondents is the idea of information or intelligence as a 'coin of exchange' which, in turn, implies the possibility of 'credit'. Press officers sometimes have in their possession information which is either not of direct relevance to the message the union is seeking to communicate or sometimes actually damaging to the image of the union. Assuming the information is not deeply discrediting, some press officers are in a position to make fine calculations about the 'value' of such information to journalists and the 'price' they can extract. The 'price', of course, is the inclusion in the journalist's report of other themes that the press officer has either targeted for a particular news text or wishes to publicise widely. Alternatively, the 'value' of such information may be 'banked' as 'credit' for use at a later date. For example, during my visit to one large union headquarters the union press officer offered a story concerning the number of resolutions from Scottish branches calling for the union to re-affiliate to the TUC, to *The Scotsman*. Evidence of quite significant dissent from the leadership's official line might be regarded as an embarrassment not to be highlighted by the union's own publicity machine. However, the press officer believed that in practice it would do little damage 'as everyone knows Scots branches are calling for re-affiliation'. The story was 'a sweetener' which would help to consolidate his standing with some important journalists.[20]

It would be wrong to overstate the case. Some press officers engage in more or less explicit horse trading but others do not. Some have developed relationships with journalists which are based only upon a vaguer and more generalised sense of co-operation and mutual obligation. Some press officers have not 'fine tuned' their media strategies to the point where they seek to target particular news outlets and, as we have seen, some hold much more pessimistic views about the value of media work and, therefore, are much less likely to make proactive interventions of any kind. However, where press officers are encouraged to develop sophisticated media strategies, involving targeting and proactive intervention, the trading value of information is frequently exploited. Given the importance attached to media work at the GMB, it is not surprising that the union's officers responsible for communications are actively involved in such bargaining on a routine basis.

Interviewer: Do you target particular information for particular journalists?
Adrian Long: Yes absolutely and all the time...you actually get involved at
     times in a process of horse trading. I very desperately wanted a certain
     story placed in a certain newspaper about three weeks ago...that is
     where it *had* to be, to be read by the people we wanted to influence.
     I mean it was a good story anyway so the paper would have taken it but
     I wanted to make sure that only that person [a certain journalist] got it,
     so in order to convince that person that they were getting something
     that was important to them, we provided additional information from
     other areas as well...and we serviced that story very, very thoroughly.
     Now the unwritten rule is that that person will help me with other
     stories as well.[21]

The GMB may be an exception. No other union in this study had developed such finely tuned targeting with distinct strategies for reaching members, potential members or 'opinion leaders' amongst political elite groups. However, this example does illustrate the potential advantages of such normatively regulated, exchange relationships. Of course, practical difficulties sometimes intrude. Charles Harvey (IPMS), for example, obtained 'leaked' information concerning the closure of the naval dockyard at Davenport with a significant loss of jobs. As with the item about spending cuts at Guy's Hospital, this information was of considerable political significance and likely to generate widespread interest amongst the national papers. However, Charles Harvey decided to offer an 'exclusive' to a contact on the Financial Times because this would help to consolidate a particularly valuable relationship. The *F.T.* was one of the few national papers likely to take a consistent interest in IPMS issues. As the union annual conference was under way, the journalist from the *F.T.* was invited to spend a day at the union's hotel and a special room was booked with lunch and additional facilities. On the appointed day, however, Rolls Royce announced that it was sacking and re-hiring, on inferior terms, its entire workforce and every industrial correspondent in the country was diverted to Derby.[22] This illustrates an important theme to be developed below, - the vulnerability of the efforts of union press officers to the impact of counter forces, quite beyond their control. Nevertheless, it also confirms the point that exchange relationships were not the prerogative of the large unions alone. Even Mr Lomans of the NUHKW sometimes 'let certain journalists know that something was about to happen', though being regionally based and almost permanently threatened by the contraction of the textile industry, there were limitations regarding the energy of the union's media work.

Exchange relationships and the balance of power

The existence of a loosely structured normative framework, regulating interaction between press officers and correspondents does not, of course, imply equality between parties in the exchange. There are several reasons why journalists may be placed in a position of advantage but, nevertheless, while all sorts of factors may stack the cards against union officers, an exchange relationship implies at least some bargaining power, albeit on an unequal basis. Mary MaGuire (NALGO) recalls ringing to complain about an item to find the journalist concerned, equally annoyed that his story had been 'subbed' at the *Sunday Times* because...

> ...they're professionals and it damages their relationship with the unions. If their stories appear constantly distorted, they won't get anything else from the unions...It is a sanction I could use and its a sanction I would use if I thought a story was *deliberately* distorted by a journalist...a story that was really bad. [The ultimate deterrent?] Yeah... .[23]

There is, then, a complex relationship in which each side has rights and obligations. Journalists are aware of the 'dangers' of producing overtly biased copy and, indeed, this would transgress their own professional norms (this may apply less to journalists working for some popular papers). Equally, press officers are 'expected' to recognise the needs of journalists; the news criteria for 'good copy', the rights of exclusivity, the routines of the news organisation, and so on.

As discussed in chapter one, the picture of source-journalist relations, provided in academic accounts, has been modified slightly over recent years. Although Tunstall believed that correspondents in specialisms without immediate revenue or advertising goal implications, enjoyed greater opportunities to play one source contact off against another (1971), subsequent accounts rooted in a variety of perspectives over the last two decades have portrayed a picture of official source dominance, ranging from the model of primary definers (Hall et al, 1978), through accounts of explicit news management (Cockerell et al,1985) to analysis of the process of 'exchange, dependence and assimilation' (Chibnall,1977:225). All these accounts suggest that on most occasions, official sources are able to exploit their control over information flows, the legitimacy and authority associated with institutional and state power, and the pressures of the various news beats, to secure the upper hand in their dealings with journalists. By implication, non-official and resource-poor sources are at a disadvantage in their dealings with journalists because they possess less legitimacy and are unlikely to be able to exercise control over information flows. However, as the focus has shifted towards non-official sources in recent years the picture has grown more complex (Goldenberg,1975; Schlesinger et al,1991; Anderson,1993). Anderson, for example, shows that while non-official sources usually do face an up-hill battle against the scepticism of correspondents and the legitimacy of official sources, there are particular circumstances in which opportunities arise for non-official environmental sources to make the running (strong public opinion, a news vacuum caused by the slowness of official sources to react to events, etc.). Similar points have emerged from studies of the origins of the 'poverty lobby' (Whitely and Winyard,1983; McCarthy,1986). At the same time, recent work underlines the point that despite all the advantages official sources enjoy, in certain circumstances, they may be deflected from their media objectives, particularly if the messages of the powerful reflect discord at the top, or if non-official 'advocates' are mistaken for more dispassionate 'arbiters' by journalists (Deacon and Golding,1994).

A complex picture is presented, then, in which the structural and institutional advantages of official sources, the inferential assumptions and organisational practices of journalists, and the resource weaknesses of non-official sources, are all likely to disadvantage the representatives of non-official organisations in their dealings with journalists and yet, these pressures are not wholly determinate. There are opportunities and 'spaces'; circumstances in which non-official sources can open up access. Seaton, in her account of the relationship between unions and the news media believed that unions had 'some real sanctions over journalists'; there was a 'similarity with political reporting' because unions could afford to refuse to talk to particular journalists, 'they can talk to his rivals' (Seaton,1982:278). Of course, Seaton made her observations in an era very different to the contemporary scene, a period in which labour journalism was riding high and there was a pronounced appetite within news organisations for labour and industrial copy. And yet, even then, as chapters six and seven demonstrate, it is doubtful if the relationship between union officials and labour correspondents was comparable to the practice of the Westminster Lobby. Certainly, since then, the balance of power has shifted further away from union sources.

In general, the determinants of the balance of power between union press officers and correspondents can be described in the following terms, whilst recognising that a great deal depends upon specific circumstances (the nature of the news story in question, the nature of union and its previous newsworthiness, etc):

(a) Labour and industrial correspondents still need 'intelligence'. Their ability to assess developments and produce copy characterised by 'informed judgements'; their ability to acquire 'expertise' which is recognised within their organisations and which, therefore, strengthens their own security and organisational standing, depends partly upon what they can acquire from union sources. A 'good' union press officer will try to ensure that labour correspondents come to use them in these terms. The offer of a position on the 'inside track' is probably the best 'bargaining chip', a contemporary union press officer has.

(b) However, two forces are likely to undermine and constrain the cashing in, even of this modest advantage. Firstly, most union organisations are characterised by 'porosity' (Ericson,1989:214); that is information 'leaks' from a variety of sources within the organisation (the national executive, senior officials with their own agendas, etc) and this means that journalists, particularly the older and more experienced labour correspondents, have the opportunity to by-pass union press officers and employ alternative contacts to maintain information flows. This underlines the importance, from the union press officer's point of view, of securing their own position on the 'inside track', with access to executive meetings and through being privy to the mind of the general secretary.

(c) The knowledge associated with each branch of journalism has a 'market value', determined by the current dominant editorial strategies of news organisations. As chapters five and six describe, the fortunes of industrial and labour reporting are on the wane. All daily newspapers have cut back the number of staff assigned to the industrial desk; there is less space allocated to labour and industrial copy, and more former labour specialists now find themselves having to widen their briefs to include, for example, employment and personnel matters, the regulation of public utilities, or even matters wholly unrelated to labour relations. Union press officers now find that their 'bargaining chip' is worth less in the market place. Journalists may want to write about union stories but they are no longer routinely required to by their news organisations.

Recognising these constraints, what techniques are available for union press officers when they seek to 'cash' in their bargaining chips?

Tricks of the trade

Textbook accounts of public relations rehearse a number of familiar points about news deadlines, the writing of press releases and the organisation of press conferences (Macshane,1979; Jefkins,1988,etc). While these details of the mechanics of public relations are not to be dismissed, an adequate analysis has to recognise the importance of the social practices which sustain public relations work. The fieldwork in this study suggests that the quality of social relationships between press officers and journalists and the resources (particularly human) devoted by unions to media work are likely to be more decisive. Indeed, some 'street knowledge' of current developments in the relationship between media and unions and knowledge of the political context (inside and outside trade unions) is as important as a textbook understanding of press release design. Although some public relations consultancies like to measure 'output' in terms of press releases distributed, a parsimonious use of press releases is the mark of an experienced press officer.

> Some of the other unions are sending out two or three press releases a day. I never send out more than one a week because I want them [journalists] to think, "Ah this is the AEU, this will be important, we'll do something here."[24]

Charles Harvey (IPMS) imposed a limit of two per week. Mary Maguire (NALGO) issued press releases only 'infrequently'. It was agreed amongst most union press officers that the value of press releases was quickly eroded. However, they faced a dilemma. Unions operate in increasingly competitive environments. Given the importance of maintaining the 'value' of press releases, press officers sometimes chose to 'sit' on certain stories rather than release them. And yet, this ran the risk of allowing a competitor to break the story first and secure the publicity value for another trade union. Charles Harvey (IPMS) 'held back' on a story regarding job cuts at British Nuclear Fuels only to find 'the story breaking from under me' and a T and G official with a high media profile, appearing on television.

Most of the union officers interviewed regarded personal contact with journalists as much more important than press releases alone. The important work was done over the telephone. NALGO, for example, never issued press releases to the fourteen hundred addresses on its mailing list for routine announcements (executive elections, a planned event, annual conferences, etc). For important issues, particularly if the union found itself having to react quickly to a story which had emerged from another source:

> ...we may just phone them [journalists] up because we have a very good relationship with the Labour Group but even if we FAX we will phone them up as well and say it is on its way.[25]

Follow a Fax release with a call, recommended John Lloyd (EETPU), " 'Did you see the press release today about such and such...?".[26]

> The media have their own agenda,- a lot of the things we do are not automatically stories. You have to make them come alive and you just can't do that by Faxing someone a press release. You have to contact them by phone.[27]

The 1984/85 Coal Strike provides a striking illustration of the same point. Nell Myers (NUM) attempted to match the vastly superior resources at the command of the Coal Board (for example, a team of over twenty press officers) through sheer hard work:

> NCB had far greater human resources but we put out far more press releases and press conferences than they did and it just never got the coverage.[28]

According to Nell Myers, there was a reluctance on the part of the news media generally to represent the NUM case in anything but a critical light. Referring to the evidence supplied in 'Media Hits the Pits' (Jones,D, 1986) she argued, '...the received wisdom was always that of the NCB. The disputed arguments were always those of the NUM'.[29] The inferential frameworks employed by journalists, the perspectives developed at a senior editorial level inside news organisations and, indeed, the exercise of political power through interconnections between the political elite and those controlling news organisations, all played a part in shaping the nature of coverage during the Coal Strike. However, part of the explanation for the absence of a robust NUM perspective in much of the reporting may also lie in the nature of the social practices underpinning the relationship between the NUM and news organisations. Nell Myers lacked the human resources necessary to follow up the issuing of press releases with personal contacts. The frequent issuing of press releases alone was unlikely to help the union's cause, particularly as Nell Myers took an uncompromising position in relation to dominant news values and news media rhythms. Information was not organised in terms of 'news frames'. As described in chapter six, tensions between the union and journalists, including labour correspondents, were exacerbated by the NUM's reluctance to acknowledge the normative framework which loosely regulated much of the interaction between journalists and other union press officers.

Of course, the 'big picture', the nature of control within news organisations and the relations which sensitised news organisations to promptings emanating from government and the political elite, cannot be ignored. Would a more pragmatic news media strategy, directed towards the national labour correspondents, rather than exclusively dependent upon the media skills of the President, have made any difference? One feature of the media experience of the strike was the frequency with which labour and industrial correspondents found their copy altered and sometimes transformed, after it was submitted (Jones,N, 1986). To weigh these factors, on the one hand, and the refusal of the NUM to acknowledge the 'exchange relationships' patterning union-correspondent interaction, on the other, is an impossible task. Put at its simplest, the goodwill which clearly did exist amongst a number of labour correspondents, was not utilised by the NUM and, it seems likely, that as a consequence of this at least some opportunities to present an NUM perspective were lost.

The same conclusions can be drawn about the other elements which make up the formal mechanics of public relations. Just as union officers preferred telephonic or personal contact, to the press release, so few relied very heavily upon press conferences. The T and G Press Office held one formal briefing each week on the business of the Executive Council, but for most unions, press conferences were used sparingly. With the highly regarded Civil Service restaurant a floor above, the IPMS Communications Department sometimes used it as a venue for press briefings, in the confidence that these would be well attended; other unions, including NALGO, NATFHE and the EETPU sometimes used press conferences and drinks parties as forums to promote new initiatives and occasionally, new general secretaries. During the field work for this study, the TGWU Press Office invested a considerable amount of time in setting up a series of regional press conferences to launch the agricultural sector pay claim. On the whole, however, much of the work of union press officers was either reactive or opportunistic and in each case a swift initiative was likely to be most effective. Much of the most important work was simply done on the telephone through networks of 'telecommunal' contacts. When asked if he *ever* used press conferences, Charlie Whelan (AEU) simply answered emphatically 'No!'. The time and effort necessary to be invested in setting up a formal media conference was unlikely to yield a commensurate return in comparison to informal contacts.

The argument in this section has been to suggest that the textbook descriptions of the mechanics of public relations do not accurately capture the reality of the social practices which underpin the work of the press officers in this study. So what are the elements of such social practices and how do they relate to the circumstances of particular unions with specific resources and concerns? Many media interventions discussed by the press officers in this study were the result of a 'media street wisdom' and opportunism demonstrated by some officers but not all. The style of Charlie Whelan (AEU) loitering by the P.A. monitor, mid-morning when 'good stories usually break', ready to intervene to inject an AEU perspective, has already been noted. Several other press officers employed similar techniques designed to 'attach' a union message to already emerging stories. Charlotte Atkins (COHSE) gave the example of by-election coverage. There are usually possibilities to be exploited around the issue of local health services. Cuts made by the local area health authority were strongly highlighted during one recent by-election. At the Monmouth (1990) by-election, a simple FAX release to the Welsh regional papers triggered 'an instant response... as soon as the FAX machine sent it off, the phone started ringing, I thought, "goodness I'd forgotten what issuing a regional PR. was like"'.[30] Similarly, unions like the T and G and NALGO or even smaller unions like the NUCPS will try to ensure a union view is included in coverage of accidents, disasters and other sudden news events.

Two important points are worth emphasising here. Firstly, 'effective' opportunistic press and media work is a product of the combination of particular material resources (i.e. a Press Association monitor) and sufficient human resources. Press officers need the time and space to think opportunistically. Secondly, an opportunistic strategy also implies an understanding of, even a sympathy with, mainstream news values and selection criteria. The art is to weave a union perspective within the structure of a story which stands the test of a critical news editor.

Sometimes a news peg has to be found around which a union theme can be hung. This, in turn, may take considerable time and effort. Charlotte Atkins, for example, spent hours searching through coroners' reports in order to find a particular example to illustrate a general point concerning the dangers of low staffing levels in hospitals.[31] Similarly, Mary Maguire knew that news journalists would only be interested in the issue of sick building syndrome if they were supplied with case studies of individuals to enhance the 'human interest' dimension, preferably linked to forthcoming events (tribunal hearings, etc). The deployment of resources can be of major importance here, too. Charlie Whelan at the AEU used the resources of a large union to, in effect, buy access to the news encoding process. The union would commission large monthly surveys of employment trends in the engineering sector. While the data was of value in its own right, the survey also provided a news peg around which an AEU perspective on unemployment was hung. Charlie Whelan released details of the monthly survey to coincide with the publication of the Department of Employment's own figures to ensure maximum news value. This tactic has worked well producing AEU coverage on radio and television, as well as in national newspapers. On a smaller scale the NUHKW employed the same approach in commissioning a survey of job losses in the East Midlands textile industry twice each year. Results were released to the local media and usually generated local television interest, as well as regional press coverage. A similar, though much cheaper, tactic was used by other unions to open up news opportunities. Charles Harvey (IPMS), for example, released 'open letters', in the name of the general secretary, to the government as the employer of civil servants, which provided a news peg around which IPMS perspectives could be hung. The NUHKW organised regular visits to Parliament with invitations to local M.P.s to accompany the party. Local journalists were provided with all the necessary ingredients for a useful story, - a news event involving local personalities and the opportunity to talk to 'ordinary' union members for 'the human angle.' Money cannot always be used to 'buy' access to the news encoding process. One union press officer persuaded his executive to donate £5,000 to Russian miners suffering hardship, hoping that the contrast between the generosity of the members and the absence of any donation from Arthur Scargill or the NUM would interest journalists. Surprisingly, no paper accepted the bait, not even the *Daily Mirror* which had become 'obsessed' with the alleged financial irregularities of the NUM.[32]

Given the rich rewards of regional media work, COHSE shifted the emphasis away from traditional union campaigning towards regional events designed as much for the photo-opportunity as a means of fostering solidarity:

> we want to go beyond picket lines, we want to go for visual events, balloons, children ...not the traditional image of trade unions...double decker buses, jazz bands. In resource terms this is much more effective than a march in London where you need coaches, time off work...a major lobby of the House of Commons costs us money![33]

The importance of being there

> We know that the press may well go for us because of the image of our members as being town hall, tea swilling bureaucrats. Before we get to the stage of anything being written in the papers, we start the process...We write articles in the specialist journals, encourage branches to write letters to the local papers, we draft a special press release with instructions on how to adapt it for local use and to make sure local branches have someone available for interview, we encourage them to contact their local M.P.'s. We start right from the beginning not in an aggressive way but in a proactive

way but we try to make sure that we get our point of view across very quickly and it works...it worked in the local government dispute last year and it worked in the ambulance dispute.[34]

While there may be disagreements over the issue of proactivity, there was widespread agreement amongst the press officers in this study that the essential elements of good practice were 'professionalism' and 'efficiency'. In short, being available for journalists to contact and having something to say right from the outset. Having a clear message and anticipating what 'snags' might arise in terms of the ways in which events may be presented follow from these:

> So the key to it is professionalism and being there right at the beginning, knowing what you want to say and knowing what snags you may face...what questions journalists may ask, the things the *Sun* may write about, etc.[35]

Here, again, the importance of the position of the press officer within the union organisation is illustrated. Press officers need to know what is going on and have the authority to respond quickly. The ability to translate, often complex arguments, into 'newspaper speak' (Charlotte Atkins) quickly was an essential skill.

Journalists were likely to turn first to those they believed could be relied upon to have information or the raw materials of a story readily available. During the 1989 rail dispute Laurie Harris worked 16 to 17 hours each day and still made himself available for three or four media enquiries at home. The health unions found similar hours were necessary at the height of the ambulance and nursing disputes as well. By contrast, while not working to rigid office hours, Nell Myers was inevitably less available to journalists because she combined media work with many other duties as a personal assistant to the President and Secretary and because she had to commute between the re-located head office of the NUM in Sheffield and her own home in East London. The federal and de-centralised nature of the NUM compounded these difficulties because the NUM headquarters depended upon information being relayed from each NUM area.

Fire fighting: techniques of damage limitation

According to Eddie Barrett, 'fire fighting' as distinct from simply reactive media work, arises when there is simply *nothing* good, from a union perspective, in an emerging story.[36] Perhaps the first rule of 'fire fighting' is, 'never say "no comment"'. Otherwise, said Mr Lomans of the NUHKW, 'you are letting your own members down'. 'No comment' simply shows 'you've got something to hide', remarked Adrian Long (GMB). Journalists regard as legitimate the expectation that they will be given 'something'. Here, then, is another illustration of the importance of the normative framework regulating source journalist interaction. Just as 'being there' is an essential attribute, so having some kind of comment is equally fundamental to achieving a reputation as a 'good press officer', amongst correspondents. However, there is more to 'fire fighting' than this. Adrian Long (GMB) provided a detailed list of 'do's and don'ts'. Be sure of one's case and 'get on top of the facts', as quickly as possible. Once one has a full picture of the events involved in a story, 'move swiftly' to deal with media enquiries. At the same time, never saying 'no comment' does not necessarily mean full disclosure:

> Sometimes one needs not to ignore the national papers but just give them the barest of facts...I mean give them every thing they need but not worry that you're not going to convince them. What we've often found is that you can by-pass the national media and go straight to the local or regional media. People often take their information about disputes from the locals. Find one theme that makes common-sense, one common denominator and repeat it and repeat it and repeat it. You have worked out your line. No matter what attempts are made to deflect you, you just keep repeating it. Now some of that just comes down to personal motivation and stubbornness. You have to be consistent. We prefer even in a difficult situation to try and strike back and if necessary try to change the agenda.[37]

During the course of the field work, a number of press officers referred to examples of fire fighting which provide interesting 'case studies'. How are the principles listed by Adrian Long applied in practice? Perhaps one of the most potentially damaging stories for a union's public standing to emerge in recent years was concerned with the evidence of ballot rigging during the election for a new general secretary of the Transport and General Workers Union in 1990. The evidence of ballot rigging was known to the Executive of the T and G two days before the result was due to be announced. This gave Eddie Barrett two days to plan with the general secretary a strategy for handling the news media. Rather than attempt to suppress the information, a probably impossible exercise given the 'porosity' of the TGWU, the first step was to give 'a selective press briefing' to about 15 journalists 'who felt they were on the inside track' (thus, implicitly, seeking to exploit the relationships of exchange between press officers and journalists). The 'line' stressed was that evidence had come to light but that the union intended to take every possible measure to deal with it rather than conceal it. According to Eddie Barrett, 'this held for about two weeks'.[38] However, the 'porosity' of the TGWU, a union with distinct political factions, meant that the TGWU Press Office was unable to maintain effective control over the supply of information, flowing from inside the organisation. 'Then you got all sorts of outsiders digging around and insiders trying to score political points [by leaking information]'.[39]

In other media contexts, the persona of Ron Todd, a gruff East Ender with a predilection for the bureaucratic discourse of traditional unionism and a lack of media fluency, might work to the disadvantage of the union. However, in a situation where the union presented itself as 'coming clean with the public', these personal qualities could be utilised in the construction of 'Honest Ron', unsophisticated but straight forward and trustworthy.

> The overall impression we gave was that 'Honest Ron' *was* in charge and that helped. 'It's a terrible thing but we're going to sort it out' was the message.[40]

NALGO often found itself in the firing line because of the nature of the occupations it organised. Social workers, in particular, have been a 'target' for media concern (Franklin and Parton,1991).

> Three years ago we had screaming headlines about social workers. Now we've had three court cases this year where I've held a press conference on the day the findings are announced, along with our Social Services Officer and I've taken the press conference, briefed the journalists and put out a press release emphasising the problems, the shortages of social workers, etc, and each time we've had very sympathetic coverage and the tables seem to be turning now but that process has taken a very long time and the tables are only just turning. Journalists from the nationals, even the *Sun* don't automatically say it's the social workers fault now but they phone up and ask what the problems may be. Which is an enormous battle but it's half

way won now - where people are prepared to phone up and discuss what the problems are (Mary McGuire, NALGO).[41]

Perhaps, an acid test for such strategies was provided when the *Sun* obtained a copy of a leaflet published by NALGO as part of its campaign for lesbian and gay rights at work. The leaflet had a satirical tone with headings such as 'What to do if you meet a lesbian?' It might not be anticipated that coverage in the *Sun* would be sensitive to the use of subtle irony. Mary Magure confirmed 'with sinking heart' to a Sun reporter that it was true but:

> The piece was quite good for the *Sun*! they didn't say "Loony left NALGO"...it wasn't bad...three years ago it would have been awful. We have a lot of these damage limitation exercises. There was an example the other week, the *Sun* got hold of a story and we managed to keep NALGO's name out of it.[42]

Through sheer persistence, stressing key themes repeatedly, Mary McGuire was at least able to influence the inferential framework with which *Sun* journalists approached 'NALGO' stories sufficiently, to produce a hesitation in the 'construction' of events, - a recognition that a union perspective might be worth investigating. The problem was to ensure that this kind of discipline was maintained at a local level:

> It is absolutely vital that if someone wants a comment from NALGO NALGO is available. This is what I stress to our branches. Frequently they issue a press release but then there's no one there to comment.[43]

The media work of the local branches is sometimes regarded by the national press officers as their Achilles heel. Mary Maguire recalled a damaging story about South London social workers appearing in the *Sunday Times*. The item drew the readers attention to the fact that NALGO had refused to speak to the newspaper.

> The branch phoned me up saying they wanted to make a complaint to the Press Council and I said you haven't got a cat in hell's chance because you refused to speak to them and they refused to speak to them because it was a Murdock paper. O.K. that's very fine, very principled but you're missing out on your chance to put your point of view...so that's the key to it.[44]

A classic example of the dilemmas facing the ideologically marginalised; whether to remain in the wilderness without a voice or to compromise one's message for the chance to speak. This is a theme to which the chapter returns as the concept of incorporation is placed in the foreground. The response of the NUM when faced with the threat of a potentially discrediting story proves an interesting contrast. Five years after the Coal Strike ended, the *Daily Mirror* published a series of articles alleging the mis-appropriation of union funds by the senior officials, Arthur Scargill and Peter Heathfield - stories which were subsequently proved to be entirely without foundation (Milne, 1994):

> Damage limitation doesn't come into it. All you can do is respond with the truth. It was something we had never experienced before, even during the strike...it was so awful for Arthur and Peter because it began with an allegation of personal corruption but it was the one thing guaranteed to shock them - anything else, money from Libya, money from the USSR, - you can count them and they have, indeed, dispelled all those stories, but the accusation of personal corruption, taking money meant for the union or for families facing hardship was something they didn't expect. It was the one thing they never expected and so there was nothing in our experience to help us deal with it.[45]

Rather like the T and G during the ballot rigging allegations, the first response of the NUM was to try to establish that the issue was being dealt with. It was for this reason that the NUM executive commissioned an external inquiry. However, with the publication of its findings the NUM, once again , was the subject of intense news media interest. At this point, the strategy adopted was in marked contrast to the TGWU Press Office. The NUM directed its communication campaign inwards:

> Following the report Arthur and Peter had two choices. The first was to see if the whole thing blew itself out. The other was to go on the road and campaign *within* (my italics) the union to tackle everything the report alleged and that is what between the end of July and September they did. They just went on the road going anywhere and wherever they were invited, speaking to anybody holding a meeting.[46]

Given the nature of the relationship between much of the news media and the union, a strategy directed inwards to secure the continuing support of members rather than one directed outwards at external target audiences was understandable. It was characteristic of the union that the immediate response was a concern for the health of the relationship between leadership and rank and file, rather than its public standing as constructed through the news media.

Presenting industrial action

Press officers cannot always determine when disputes become the subject of media interest. The work of the Glasgow University Media Group (1976; 1980) has demonstrated that the news media present a far from comprehensive account of industrial disputes. Certain occupational sectors with established news value receive disproportionate coverage while other areas are ignored entirely. Some press officers are quite happy to be ignored in this context. John Lloyd of the EEPTU, for example, cheerfully pointed out that the EEPTU was involved in anything up to twenty disputes at any one time but these rarely received publicity and given the union's desire to woo new employers and unorganised sectors, he was quite content to leave it that way. Only in certain sectors where it was advantageous, did the union seek to publicise disputes. In the electrical supply sector, for example, tradition and history made a little sabre rattling appropriate in order to encourage the employers to talk, and help recruitment (the union being seen to back members). In other areas, however, news of disputes would reinforce stereotyped ideas about trade unions in the eyes of employers and employees that the union desired to 'reach' for marketing purposes.[47]

John Lloyd followed much the same principles as applied by other press officers. Never say 'no comment' and ensure a clear and brief short summary of the union case was available. In certain circumstances this simply involved fending off awkward questioning. For example, the EEPTU was put under intense media pressure to clarify what 'substantial' actually meant in its 1990/91 pay claim. John Lloyd had to convince officials that the union response had to be more than 'no comment', although the issuing of precise information was likely to severely weaken the union's bargaining position. The trick was to release a press statement which supplied sufficient 'working material' for journalists without a specific figure for the claim.

On other occasions the press officer may be required to justify the use of industrial action and to deflect potential media criticism. According to Mary Maguire, the key is to anticipate the nature of the coverage and to plan ahead. Echoing Adrian Long's point regarding the importance of speed, she believed that the union press officer had to put the union point of view across 'very quickly...not in an aggressive way but in an proactive way.' Planning and anticipation of likely news media angles worked in both the local government and ambulance disputes of the late 1980s, - the latter being, 'a marvellous operation'. Charlie Whelan made a similar point regarding the AEU and industrial action. Though involved in few disputes, and even fewer likely to attract national media interest, he always tried to identify one or two key themes to stress in briefing journalists at the onset of industrial action.

> I mean with Fords in advance we try and set the agenda. Firstly, they're foreign, secondly they manufacture in America. We can use this to make people think they're nasty and we're the good guys.[48]

Similarly, the IPMS sought to place the Civil Aviation Dispute in the context of public safety. Air traffic controllers had strong 'news value' and the dispute had direct implications for the public during the holiday period. However, Charles Harvey believed that the IPMS was quite successful in developing an agenda which made connections between pay and conditions, on the one hand, and the interest of the public in safe air traffic control, on the other.

Of course, there is likely to be less need for fire fighting during disputes if a more favourable agenda is established at the beginning but this, in turn, is likely to depend upon planning and organisation. Charlotte Atkins says COHSE learnt a lot from the experience of the 1988 Nurses dispute in planning for the subsequent Ambulance dispute (see chapter eight). In the Nurses dispute the three main health unions found it difficult to co-ordinate media strategies and publicity. Local activists in each union exerted pressure for 'days of action' and demonstrations in rivalry with each other rather than in concert. However, during the Ambulance Dispute three unions were already close in negotiations over merger proposals and the smaller size of the ambulance service made co-ordination much easier.[49] Organisation was based upon a division of labour involving the three main unions in the dispute with the agreement of the other two. All media enquiries were channelled through NUPE's press office while COHSE dealt with political lobbying. This meant that although five unions were involved, one consistent, 'common line' was presented to journalists. Despite attempts by journalists to find them (Woolas,1990), very few cracks appeared in the united front.

> Any conflict was dealt with and thrashed out. The line was decided behind closed doors and we kept to it. It was a classic way of running a dispute... . I think people have learnt a hell of a lot about how to present a union case...there are still your officials who still say 'We have to refer this decision to our Executive' but that stuff has gone now mostly. Everyone is becoming more television oriented and if you become more television oriented then you become more popular press oriented as well.[50]

The relationship between television news agendas and those of the popular press is a complex one involving reciprocal stimulation, - what is defined as significant on television is likely to be picked up by the tabloid press and vice versa. Television coverage, then, is likely to not only provide direct access to millions of homes but an indirect route to the press as well. It is, therefore, an important channel of communication to two target audiences; the public as a whole and union members specifically. However, a greater dependence upon television brings problems as well as advantages. The greater the dependence, the more significant the difficulties when television interest begins to wane and, of course, given the nature of the medium, in protracted disputes this is very likely to happen. When it does, channels to both the public and members are restricted and an important mechanism for obtaining access to the tabloid agenda disappears.

> ...in the ambulance dispute we were using television to communicate and when television stopped life became more difficult...we had to produce a bulletin...we had internal problems and we had to find other ways of communicating with members. We went from a very high media profile at the beginning of the dispute to a lower one towards the end. How do you keep them [the media] going? It's very difficult to keep media interest alive.[51]

COHSE noted the lessons of the Nurses Dispute and ensured that there was effective central co-ordination of local activity during the Ambulance Dispute. In contrast, the federal structure of the NUM made this much more difficult during the Coal Strike. Each area effectively developed its own media strategy. Some appointed press officers for the duration of the dispute (for example, South Wales) but others placed liaison with the media at the bottom of the list of priorities. Information about what was happening at a local level was only fed through to the centre in a haphazard way and sometimes not at all. Paradoxically, it was the structure of the NUM itself which contributed to the concentration upon 'personalities' rather than 'issues' in the media coverage. This was because much of the only information available for Nell Myers to discuss with journalists was about the activity of those at the centre, the President and the General Secretary:

> In those circumstances I could grasp the frustrations of journalists who couldn't get at what was happening...I could only deal with what Scargill and Heathfield were doing and that was disappointing...but then again what difference would it have made given the overall coverage? I'm not insensitive to the frustrations of industrial correspondents trying to cover industrial disputes...I can imagine it...I just think there's more to it than that.[52]

It is possible that more effective lines of communication between the NUM headquarters in Sheffield and the local area officials would have allowed Nell Myers to supply material which correspondents might have used to satisfy the criterion of 'balance' in the construction of stories. Similarly, greater attention to issues of organisation and resourcing may have prevented the NCB from playing 'the numbers game' so effectively. Nell Myers argued that many journalists were well aware of the doubtful validity of much of the NCB evidence on numbers returning to the pits:

> Journalists were saying to us, 'the figures are all over the place', especially in early Autumn. They knew about the dummies in vans, etc. *The Financial Times* and *Daily Telegraph* correspondents were saying 'nobody believes those figures'. It's things like that make me think it's no good slagging off the NUM...the information is there and it isn't up to us to get them to use it, it's down to their own character...all they needed to do was point out the turmoil the Board was in.[53]

For Nell Myers the information was there and the onus was upon journalists to use it. Other press officers with more proactive strategies would, undoubtedly, have sought to devise ways of encouraging the use of that information. The passivity of the NUM stance reflects a more pessimistic analysis which points to the function of the news media in capitalist societies and an understanding of journalists as being generally 'locked into' determinate roles in the process of ideological reproduction. The danger in this analysis is to, too quickly, dismiss opportunities to intervene in the news encoding process. Not withstanding the political agenda of the Tory tabloids, it may have been possible to mount a more sustained challenge to the NCB figures, - an issue of central importance during the strike.

News criteria, news management and the external environment

The danger of an approach which dwells, at length, upon the world of trade union press officers from their perspective, is that their place in the 'big picture', and all the constraints which follow from this, are obscured. What are the factors 'beyond the control' of union press officers? In the dealings of trade unions, particularly those representing civil servants and public sector workers, the power of the state looms large, even if its capacity to secure 'primary definitions' has sometimes been over-stated (Schlesinger,1990; Anderson 1993). The government through the machinery of the state has the capacity to exert a very significant degree of influence over the elements of the political news agenda and the pace at which it unfolds. When the government selects a topic as a 'headline issue' the union's involved have to react swiftly. The Further Education White Paper was 'talked up' by ministers and NATFHE found itself suddenly very busy dealing with requests for 'mainly short reaction pieces'. Midge Purcell (NATFHE) distinguished between this and 'intrinsic interest' (i.e. sustained). When political interest in the Government's selection of training as a central plank in its agenda waned, so the media enquiries dried up. Needless to say, the government through the machinery of the state can also do a great deal to either stimulate or dampen down media discussion of policy initiatives, reports and so on, by careful control of the embargo system, publication dates, and timing of press briefings. Trade union officials may sometimes find themselves in a position in which they are 'expected' to react to Government announcements without the benefit of more than a few hours notice. The journalists they are dealing with may have had the benefit of advance briefings.

The actual pace of policy development is also largely determined by the government. Ken Jones (NUCPS) commented that one the biggest problems was simply keeping up with the pace of innovation, particularly in the case of the civil service unions where, at one time, very significant proposals for changes in the conditions of service of members were being launched, almost at monthly intervals (the Next Steps project, privatisation of public utilities and the issue of GCHQ Cheltenham). Even the larger trade unions lack the resources required to keep abreast of rapid policy launches across a number of state departments.[54]

If the state represents one large feature of the external environment for trade union press officers, the configuration of news values and ideological perspectives which govern the selection process in news production is another major consideration largely beyond the power of press officers to influence. Even a major national dispute involving the best news value ingredients, such as the Ambulance dispute of 1989, failed to retain news media interest throughout. COHSE found the interest of journalists declining after the first few months, something which is confirmed in the discussion of newspaper coverage of the dispute, in chapter eight. At first, the health unions were able to insert many of the key elements of their own agenda in press coverage. However, not only did interest decline but over the duration of the dispute, the news frames shifted away from the union agenda, as employers and government figures intervened more actively.[55]

> We went from a very high media profile at the beginning of the dispute to a lower one towards the end...how do you keep them interested,- it is a problem...I even led a whole group people up Banstead High Street (COHSE headquarters)...even stopped buses you know...it's very difficult towards the end of a dispute to keep media interest alive.[56]

The vagaries of particular news organisations present difficulties, too. While the Guardian, for example, had always been receptive to further and higher education stories, the Independent had recently mounted a challenge to the Guardian's dominance in this corner of the market (a lucrative source of appointment advertising). However, the Independent defined 'education' as school and university rather than technical college and polytechnic, thus proving barren ground for NATFHE despite intensive work on the part. of the two NATFHE press officers. In some instances, the editorial inclinations of particular newspapers may lead to problems of presentation and interpretation rather than lack of interest. Despite the efforts of the NUHKW officers to insist upon the existence of sweatshops in the East Midlands as *the* problem, the Leicester Mercury continued to define the ethnicity of the proprietors as the central theme to be highlighted and was twice referred to the Press Council as a result. This meant that Mr Lomans 'thought twice' before providing evidence to the local media despite its abundance.[57]

The typology for initial selection of unions in the study recognised the probable importance of union size as a significant variable. In the eyes of news journalists size normally equates with news interest. Many of the press officers interviewed here concurred with this view. Eddie Barrett of the T and G cheerfully agreed that the size of the T and G as the biggest union in Britain (at the time the field work was conducted) was an enormous advantage. It meant that journalists were routinely in touch with Eddie Barrett most days of the week. It is not merely size but the dominance of the T and G and the fact that it organises clearly identifiable groups of workers that is important. This partly explains why the officers of the GMB, Britain's second largest union at the time the field work was conducted, placed more emphasis upon active media work.

> There is no doubt that Phil Woolas and Adrian Long have a problem at the GMB because they are not the biggest. I mean it is a big union but not the biggest and therefore, doesn't lend itself to the sort of opening paragraph, 'Britain's biggest union today...'.[58]

Indeed, Adrian Long recognised this himself:

> We find it sometimes quite difficult to establish a distinctive identity for whatever we're saying within a wider industrial issue if we're only the second or third union...that's why we have decided to develop the role of the GMB as a major union in the centre ground of the TUC and the Labour Party... .[59]

While the GMB may be the biggest union in certain employment sectors (cleaning, security, hotels and catering) it has lost members in the occupations forming its traditional base, heavy industry and municipal manual work. While the T and G also needs to diversify, it has managed to retain a distinct identity with particular occupations. In the public mind, the T and G organises dockers and bus drivers. The GMB has felt the need to work harder to forge an alternative public identity and this partly explained why it has positioned itself so prominently in the mainstream of Labour Party politics.

No matter how sophisticated the media strategy, or dominant the union, there are certain random events which may destroy the best laid public relations plans:

> It just depends what else is happening in the world. If there's a Gulf War then you don't get many calls because every industrial correspondent is fighting for about the one page that's left in paper. Of course, if there's a dock strike it works the other way.[60]

Charlotte Atkins of COHSE reported precisely the same experience. The Gulf War obliterated media interest in health issues. COHSE suffered a larger share of random bad luck in preparing media campaigns than most unions. The day COHSE picked, months in advance, for the launch of the ancillary nurses pay campaign happened to be the day Mrs Thatcher resigned. Similarly, Charles Harvey of IPMS went to elaborate lengths to feed an 'exclusive' on the Davenport Dockyard closure to the *Financial Times* only to find that on the day in question Rolls Royce attempted to sack and re-hire, on inferior terms, its entire workforce. Every industrial correspondent in the country was diverted to Derby.[61]

On the other hand, news stories trade unions would prefer to delay sometimes emerge prematurely because unions rarely enjoy sufficiently centralised organisational structures to guarantee perfect synchronisation between head office and local branch. News of 300 redundancies emerged, while those affected were still on holiday, despite the determined efforts of the NUHKW to prevent the story breaking. From a local source, the story eventually appeared on national television. Similarly, the health unions found during the 1988-89 nurses pay campaign that it became increasingly difficult to effectively project a common media message, as local COHSE ,NUPE and NALGO branches all organised independent and uncoordinated publicity exercises and 'days of action'. The later 1989 Ambulance Dispute saw much more determined control exerted from the centre. As noted above, unions are normally characterised by a high degree of 'porosity'; it is extremely difficult for press officers to exercise control over the number of potential information flows which journalists may exploit.

Competition between news sources: politics power and strategy

There are three groups of 'key players' in the arena constituted by labour and industrial news reporting; employers and employers' associations, trade unions and the state. In certain circumstances, the 1984-85 Coal Strike for example, the state and an employer organisation may work closely together (Jones,N., 1986; MacGregor, 1986). Governments through the apparatus of the civil service and the substantial resourcing of official information services, have at their disposal a powerful range of mechanisms for shaping the news encoding process. The rise of 'the public relations state' (Deacon and Golding,1994:5-7) has involved more than a doubling of expenditure on public relations and news management work since the beginning of the

1980s. Information and reports can be published or suppressed, at least temporarily; the timing of press briefings and the amount of advance information released can be regulated to ensure that journalists have the maximum opportunity to write about an issue in detail or the minimum. The blurring of the distinction between civil servant and political advisor in the case of government information officers (Hennessy 1985, Cockerall et al 1984) strengthens this capacity. It was revealed at its sharpest during the Coal Strike but can threaten even the smaller unions.

One example illustrates the point. The 1990 White Paper on Further and Higher Education proposed major changes to the education system, including the removal of further education from local authority control and the abolition of the binary divide in higher education. In contrast to some journalists, NATFHE was only able to obtain a copy of the document at 5.00pm on the day of the official announcement, at the very beginning of the Department of Education's press launch. The union was placed at a distinct disadvantage, unable to brief education correspondents with confidence or supply an alternative, detailed analysis. NATFHE was not only forced onto the back foot but actually wrong footed, issuing a statement indicating cautious approval, only to be followed the next day by a much more critical response once the implications of the new policy initiative had been digested by the research department. By then, of course, the damage had been done and only the weekly education press carried the revised position.[62]

Employers and Power

As discussed in chapter two, employers have increasingly turned to communications work in recent years to secure a variety of objectives from raising their public profile ('corporate branding') or combating hostile take-overs, to by-passing trade union organisations and exerting new patterns of workplace control (Wickens, 1987; Jones,N., 1986; Cayford,1985; Newman,1984). However, unlike the apparatus of the state, employers do not always possess a capacity to translate economic power into media influence. Despite the size of Fords UK, for example, one prominent union press officer bluntly dismissed their public relations department as 'total crap'. Many large companies supplement in-house P.R. with outside consultants but the latter are likely to have very little knowledge of the company in terms of the circumstances at plant or shop floor level. This, according to Charlie Whelan, could give trade unions an advantage in the communications battle. Public relations problems could be as inhibiting to management as union.

> What you've got to remember is that you can't have a company like Fords going round slagging off its workers because those workers have got to go back into the factory to make 'quality' cars. So you can't say anything...you can't say nothing really.[63]

Similarly, local employers are often inexperienced in dealing with the media and reluctant to make any kind of statement. This gave, for example, the NUHKW a number of opportunities to fill the news vacuum.[64] Laurie Harris recalled that during the 1989 rail dispute, British Rail sought to exploit its advantageous command over resources by employing ten additional public relations officers to work with journalists and yet, 'British Rail were so inept they played into our hands'[65] B.R. management even allowed the annual accounts revealing large profits to be published in the week that Laurie Harris had been stressing to journalists the theme that profit was being put before safety. Measures of public opinion indicated considerable sympathy for the rail workers even during the period of maximum disruption to services.

Employers are not infallible and command over superior material resources does not guarantee success. Much depends upon the social relations through which material resources are deployed. As we have seen, the ability to invest in the most elaborate electronic networked news distribution and monitoring systems may not count for much. Nevertheless, over time superior resourcing can be made to tell. In the 1984-85 Coal Strike, despite some notorious public relations gaffs in the early phase of the strike (Jones,N,1986), in the end the ability of the Coal Board to deploy over twenty press officers to ensure that a Coal Board spokesperson was always available, usually with 'the latest figures on numbers returning to work' readily to hand, did make a difference. Wealth, of course, can also be converted into judicial authority. In the present study, one media officer representing one of the larger unions was the subject of an injunction issued by Lord Hanson, following the union's involvement in media coverage of the controversy surrounding the possible take-over of I.C.I. by the Hanson Trust and the danger of asset stripping. The power afforded by the possession of wealth and superior resourcing can be used to intimidate and quieten opposing voices. The union officer in question was 'very aware' of the resources deployed by Hanson, including not only a team of lawyers but five times as many press officers. Interestingly, there was developing co-operation between the union involved and I.C.I. to mount a public relations campaign against the hostile bid.[66]

Employer power can also be used to silence one of the main sources of union information, employees themselves. COHSE found that NHS employees, particularly in the Trust Hospitals were being disciplined for making unauthorised comments to the news media. In addition, 'patient confidentiality clauses' in new NHS Trust contracts were being used by managements as 'gagging' devices. NATFHE has recently established a 'whistle blowers hotline' for academic staff, bound by new 'gagging clauses' in their contracts. During the 1989 rail strike, many NUR members were reluctant to 'go on record' and Laurie Harris had to find a variety of elaborate 'ruses' to allow journalists to talk to railway workers.

Rival trade unions represent a third potential source of competition. Chapter two described the pressures trade unions now face, arising from declining memberships and the increasingly hostile economic and political environments. This chapter also traced the ways in which this pressure and the conflicts engendered by it find expression through communication and media work. This is as true of inter-union rivalry as it is of union - employer conflict, particularly where unions compete for new 'unorganised' markets or where several unions compete for one tightly defined market (e.g. primary and secondary teaching unions, unions organising lower grade civil servants, etc). Thus, IPMS and the TGWU have found themselves competing to develop higher news media profiles with a view to targeting technicians in the Civil Service; both CPSA and NUCPS have sought to highlight the IPMS 'capitulation' during the 1987 Civil Service grading dispute and, perhaps, most notoriously, the EETPU waged a high profile publicity campaigning against rival unions in defence of its 'aggressive' recruitment strategies.

A contrast is provided in the health and public service sector, where the three main unions co-operated in two recent major disputes and eventually merged to form one 'super' union. Similarly, the AEU and the EEPTU merged to form one dominant presence in the engineering sector. Again, during the course of this research, the GMB absorbed the Tailor and Garment Workers. In each of these cases, the management of potential conflict was partly achieved through careful communication and media work.

Summary: the dilemma of incorporation

The problem with the overly mechanical textbook accounts of public relations is that while they may provide detailed descriptions of the techniques involved in writing press releases or organising news conferences, they ignore two fundamental features of press and media work. Press and media work involves not merely techniques but social practices; relationships and patterns of exchange between press officers and journalists which crystallise over time, and yet remain quite fragile, easily fractured by the intrusion of external forces. And this points to a second weakness. There is an absence in the textbooks of any discussion of the material or symbolic environment in which press and media work occurs; the political and economic context, the structures of power which shape and constrain, or the reservoir of symbolism located in the public domain from which the ideological representation of events may be fashioned.

What emerges from this study of the practice of trade union press officers is the extent to which such practice is rooted in social relationships, both within each union and, externally, with journalists. Trade union press officers depend upon particular kinds of relationships with their own senior officials and executive committees, in order to establish 'exchange relationships' with journalists. Tentative, implicit 'bargains' (Goldenberg,1975:136) only emerge between union press officers and labour correspondents, if press officers can establish that they can offer journalists a place on the 'inside track'; access to the kind of 'intelligence' which permits 'informed judgements' and accurate assessments of future scenarios. These 'exchange relationships' are never equitable; journalists are likely to hold most of the cards, most of the time. To secure their own positions within their news organisations and in the eyes of their peers, they need access to such 'intelligence', but given the 'porosity' of most unions, experienced labour correspondents are rarely dependent upon press officers, alone. Unlike, other non-official source organisations, such as the Child Poverty Action Group or Greenpeace, the highly factionalised nature of many unions, makes centralised control of information flows nearly impossible. To further tip the scales against union press officers, the 'market value' of labour and industrial information has been declining as news organisations attach less importance to union and industrial relations issues, and correspondents find they have to accept broader beats with less specialisation.

Nevertheless, this chapter has pointed to a number of examples where 'effective' press work has 'made a difference'; a union perspective has been included in the construction of a news item through the intervention of the press officer, or a damaging news frame has been modified on the basis of a union briefing. This will be examined further in chapter eight which explores how the health unions ran a 'successful' media campaign during the 1989 Ambulance dispute. For the moment, what is of interest is the price which is paid for the development of the 'exchange relationships', upon which such press and media work depends. The price can usefully be described using the concept of incorporation. Union press officers recognise that, as Mary McGuire says, 'in order for journalists to be of use to you, you have to be of use to them'.[67] This means acknowledging the importance of news deadlines and the organisational rhythms which dominate a news journalists' day, and prioritising access and availability over other considerations to answer media enquiries. But it means more than this. It requires union press officers to largely define their agendas in terms of mainstream news values; to formulate their material through the eyes of news journalists. Whether or not union press officers possess formal training in journalism, the 'logic' which organises the exchange relationships between union press officers and journalists is likely to lead to the adoption of this kind of approach. As Charlie Whelan, (a union press officer lacking any formal training or experience but, nonetheless, rated as the best by many of the correspondents interviewed for this study) commented, it was 'easy', he just wrote 'it' as he would like to read it in the papers.[68]

Tension and Symbiosis

The role of union press officer, then, involves two dimensions of inherent and irresolvable tension. Firstly, as discussed in chapter three, union press officers must try to accommodate both the political demands associated with their positions within trade union organisations and their function as 'advocates', and yet, at the same time, they must acknowledge and are frequently committed to the objectives of 'professionalism', as defined by news journalists. It is this underlying tension which produces the oscillation between the contradictory and mutually competing goals of promoting a union perspective, on the one hand, and applying the criteria of 'news interest' and 'journalistic detachment' in the selection of information, on the other.

If this is the first dimension of tension, following the discussion in this chapter, we can identify a second but related dimension which describes the practice of union press officers, as distinct from their goals or objectives. Just as union press officers oscillate between competing goals, so also in their routine practice, they oscillate rather like moths simultaneously attracted to and repelled by an electric light, between attempting to 'distance' themselves from the culture of labour journalism, and embracing the symbiotic relationship which they share with correspondents. Thus, on the one hand, as we have seen, union press officers are likely to explicitly recognise the distinct political interests which separate trade unions both from other suppliers of information or 'knowledge brokers' (Garnham,1986:44) in the public sphere and from journalists. On the other hand, they will acknowledge the importance of accommodating the needs of journalists, understanding the imperatives of news production, and the necessity of admitting correspondents to the 'inside track'.

Incorporation and the Union Press Officer's Agenda

This process of incorporation went beyond simply acknowledging the importance of mainstream news values. 'Successful' union media work, particularly of a proactive kind, meant embracing the underlying assumptions or 'inferential structures' which informed the ways in which journalists organised their material. The rather cautious and conservative nature of the agenda unions presented in their journals has been described elsewhere (Manning, 1996; Grace, 1985; Selvin, 1963). There is often an absence of discussion of issues which might prompt a questioning of the fundamental relations of power and control in the workplace. Even discussion of industrial conflict can be muted and rarely related to issues of structure, or control of the labour process. Similarly, the press officers in this study, with the exception of Nell Myers (NUM), were inclined to take the workplace status quo as a 'given'; none in the study proposed to present themes to the news media which would elaborate a radical analysis of power or relations between captital and labour.

Even in the case of industrial action, while some press officers had the task of representing their unions in disputes, little attention was paid to the fundamental causes of workplace conflict. Rather, attention revolved around the 'bread and butter' concerns of a labourist agenda, pay comparisons and relativities, the rationale behind a particular claim, the status of conditions of service and so on. In some cases, where unions were seeking to market themselves to employers or groups of unorganised workers, there was an inclination to suppress news of industrial action.

This is not to suggest that union press officers are without radical sentiments; a majority displayed a very strong commitment to the values of the labour movement and a deep dislike of the present Conservative government. Nonetheless, they would regard any suggestion that a more radical politics might form the basis of their press and media work as naive. The possibilities but also the constraints which are implied by mainstream news values and the inferential structures of journalists were simply regarded as 'inevitable'. Again, as Charlie Whelan said, 'you don't want a load of left wing polemics if you're writing for the *Sun*'. In short, to establish oneself as a 'good' union press officer, amongst correspondents, one must embrace both the working practices and the working assumptions of news journalism. One must, at least in terms of daily working routines, become 'incorporated'.

This has important consequences for what can and cannot be presented to the news media and the particular symbolic constructions employed. For example, the tendency of the news media to 'individualise' what are essentially collective problems (Cottle, 1993:79) is sometimes encouraged by union press officers who recognise that, in difficult and ideologically hostile conditions, one of the few ways of encoding a union perspective is to 'harness' it to individual case studies, rich in 'human interest'. Thus, for example, the health unions during the Ambulance Strike provided journalists with opportunities to interview 'individual ambulance crews', rather than over-emphasise the widespread, collective problems of low pay and under-resourcing, with empirical data. Similarly, the NUHKW had some success in interesting local reporters, and sometimes current affairs journalists, in individual cases of super-exploitation and sweat shop conditions in textile factories, but in doing this, another perspective is obscured. The view that such examples are not 'isolated or extreme instances' but manifestations of a persistent, collective problem of low pay, structurally rooted in the conditions of textile production in England, was assumed not to be compatible with a news format. Similarly, the GMB gathered material on individual cases of work related illness but rarely sought to place these in a broader structural context for journalists.

In summary, union press officers usually work with an agenda delimited by the 'possible'; themes which do not threaten the inferential structures of journalists and which can be elaborated using the conventional news values of journalism. Typically, the agenda will involve three broad elements.

Firstly, a union press officer may formulate a series of themes which allow the prominence of a union to be raised and the constructive contribution it may make to workplace life emphasised. This, in turn, may be related to the marketing work which a number of unions now direct towards prospective members, merger suitors, or targeted employers. Secondly, an important set of themes common to the press and media work of many unions will involve resource demands of one kind or another. Charlotte Atkins, at COHSE, looked for ways of promoting stories of under-resourcing in the NHS; the NATFHE publicity department sought to interest correspondents in the case for better training and more resources in the post-16 education sector; all union press officers would, usually annually, present a case for improved renumeration packages for their members. And thirdly, a union press officer's agenda might involve defensive work. Strikes or industrial action of another kind might have to be explained and publicly defended. Alternatively, the reputation of members might need to be 'repaired', following stigmatisation. Thus, Mary McGuire (NALGO), accepted as a long term project, the task of improving the public standing of social workers. The Civil Service unions had similar problems with the public perception of their memberships. None of these three broad elements of a union agenda for media work, provoke fundamental questions about the industrial status quo or prompt discussion of the issue of control over the nature of production and the experience of work; all three can be elaborated and presented to journalists using conventional news values and without threatening the inferential structures routinely employed in reporting the workplace.

This is not to suggest that the media work of trade union press officers is without value or is counter productive from the union point of view. Undoubtedly, in a difficult political climate with waning news media interest in union affairs, a number of union press officers have made an important contribution in maintaining a union profile in the public domain and in helping to ensure that union perspectives do surface in the news media representation of events. The alternative to this process of incorporation is bleak; to remain on the outside of the news encoding process, with little influence over the way in which the representation of a union's affairs is constructed, or perhaps worse, to be simply ignored and consigned to the ideological margins. The difficulties Nell Myers experienced in trying to present a coherent NUM case in the form of the union's 'Plan for Coal' during the 1984/85 dispute, without making the concessions necessary to foster 'exchange relationships' (Jones,1986; Adeney and Lloyd,1986), illustrate the point.

To remain on the outside is to risk marginalisation; to move inside is to accept, at least, partial incorporation into the mainstream news production system. And yet, even 'inside', the work of union press officer is constrained and delimited by external forces; the presence of the state, the power of employers, the worsening political and economic conditions for unions and, of course, changes in the ways in which news production is, itself, organised. The next three chapters turn the focus more sharply upon this latter aspect, by first tracing the ways in which the emergence of labour and industrial journalism has been shaped by the historical development of the state, trade unions and employers organisations, and then finally, examining the contemporary practice of journalists.

Notes

1. Interview with senior union press officer, 6.3.91.
2. Interview with Charlotte Atkins (COHSE), 16.7.91.
3. Interview with Adrian Long (GMB), 21.6.91.
4. Interview with Charlie Whelan (AEU), 6.6.91.
5. Interview with Eddie Barrett, op cit.
6. Interview with Charlie Whelan, op cit.
7. Ibid.
8. Interview with a press officer working for one of the largest unions, conducted in the summer of 1991.
9. Interview with a press officer working for a large union in the public sector in the summer 1991.
10. Interview with John Lloyd (EETPU), 24.5.91.
11. Interview with Ken Jones (NUCPS), 24.5.91.
12. Interview with Nell Myers (NUM), 20.9.91.
13. Ibid.
14. Interview with Midge Purcell (NATFHE), 21.6.91.
15. Interview with Charlotte Atkins, op cit.
16. Interview with Laurie Harris (NUR), 25.8.1989.
17. Interview with Mary McGuire (NALGO), 31.7.90.
18. Interview with Laurie Harris (NUR), 25.8.1989.
19. Interview with Charlotte Atkins, op cit.
20. Observations made during the course of a visit to the headquarters of a large private sector union during the summer, 1991.
21. Interview with Adrian Long, op cit.
22. Interview with Charles Harvey, op cit.
23. Interview with Mary McGuire, op cit.

24.   Interview with Charlie Whelan, op cit.
25.   Interview with Mary McGuire, op cit.
26.   Interview with John Lloyd, op cit.
27.   Interview with Adrian Long, op cit.
28.   Interview with Nell Myers, op cit.
29.   Ibid.
30.   Interview with Charlotte Atkins, op cit.
31.   Interview with Charlotte Atkins, op cit.
32.   Interview with a union Press Officer, working for a large union on the right of the labour movement, conducted during the Summer of 1991.
33.   Interview with Charlotte Atkins, op cit.
34.   Interview with Mary McGuire, op cit.
35.   Ibid.
36.   Interview with Eddie Barrett, op cit.
37.   Interview with Adrian Long, op cit.
38.   Interview with Eddie Barrett, op cit.
39.   Ibid.
40.   Ibid.
41.   Interview with Mary McGuire, op cit.
42.   Ibid.
43.   Ibid.
44.   Ibid.
45.   Interview with Nell Myers, op cit.
46.   Ibid.
47.   Interview with John Lloyd, op cit.
48.   Interview with Charlie Whelan, op cit.
49.   Interview with Charlotte Atkins, op cit.
50.   Ibid.
51.   Ibid.
52.   Interview with Nell Myers, op cit.
53.   Ibid.
54.   Interview with Ken Jones, op cit.
55.   Which supports the view of Anderson (1993) in that non-official sources are sometimes able to fill a news vacuum. However, I would add that this is unlikely to be sustained when and, if, official sources begin to concentrate their media resources and energies upon the issue over an extended period.
56.   Interview with Charlotte Atkins, op cit.
57.   Interview with Mr. Lomans (NUHKW), 15.7.91.
58.   Interview with Eddie Barrett, op cit.
59.   Interview with Adrian Long, op cit.
60.   Interview with Eddie Barrett, op cit.
61.   Interview with Charles Harvey, op cit.
62.   Interview with Midge Purcell, op cit.
63.   Interview with Charlie Whelan, op cit.
64.   Interview with Mr. Lomans, op cit.
65.   Interview with Laurie Harris, op cit.

66.   Interview with a press officer working for a large 'progressive' union, conducted during the summer of 1991.
67.   Interview with Mary McGuire, op cit.
68.   Interview with Charlie Whelan, op cit. Quote also appears earlier in the text.

5   The Rise of Labour and Industrial Journalism

The next two chapters concern the history of labour and industrial journalism and the role of the Labour and Industrial Correspondents Group. In doing so, as indicated in the introduction, a start is made in tracing some of the ways in which changes in the broader political-economic environment impact upon the day to day practice of journalists and, in turn, union press officers. As the history of this journalistic specialism unfolds four aspects of the political-economic environment appear to play a prominent part:

- the importance of the state as one of the main influences in shaping the nature of the labour beat and in helping to order the hierarchy of journalistic specialisms, through the political orientation of particular governments and their control over information flows from the political centre,

- the wider political-economic dimension in which changes in both economy and polity shape the landscape of industrial and labour journalism so that, for example, trade unions appear to be a waning political force by the second half of the 1980s, as result both of government policy and more fundamental economic structural change,

- changes in the political economy and social organisation of newspaper production, involving changes in the daily rhythms and routines of journalists, the physical re-location of newspaper offices away from Fleet Street and changes in the way newspapers utilise the labour of journalists,

- recent developments in the vitality of alternative specialisms within journalism, including direct rivals, such as financial, personnel and business journalism.

Of course, each of these four aspects of the political-economic environment is inter-linked. The rationalisation and re-organisation of newspaper production, for example, being stimulated by the weakening of print and media unions and the new labour relations climate fostered by the Thatcher administration. For some journalists, the recent decline in the fortunes of labour journalism and the standing of the Labour and Industrial Correspondents' Group should be regarded as simply a 'down turn' in a cyclical process. However, a more careful reading of the political economy of labour journalism suggests that actually more profound changes are occurring through each of these four aspects. This chapter presents a brief chronological account of the rise of this journalistic specialism to its peak in the period between 1965 and 1979 whilst the next chapter describes its decline since 1979 and considers what relevance such a history has for the understanding of contemporary patterns of 'news work' involving union officials and journalists.

A chronological account

The history of daily labour journalism is, in large part, a history of the Labour and Industrial Correspondents' Group.   Three different types of material have been gathered to produce this account, the memoirs of leading trade unionists, journalists and politicians; interviews conducted with journalists who worked as labour correspondents during the last four decades[1], and the official papers of the Labour and Industrial Correspondents' Group dating from 1980 to the present.[2] It is a great pity that the Group has not retained a record of its affairs since its beginnings in 1937 and this has meant that in the absence of any other source of continuous evidence, the historical account must remain a sketch rather than a comprehensive history. Nevertheless, for the purposes of throwing light upon some important theoretical and empirical concerns of the present research sufficient material is available.

During the 1920s a number newspapers carried reports by 'industrial correspondents' (Negrine 1993) but it is unclear whether these journalists were really specialists or little more than general reporters. However, by the late 1930s a small group of such correspondents had emerged and, contrary to one academic account which dates the beginning of the Labour and Industrial Correspondents' Group to 1965,[3] a formal grouping of labour specialists emerged in 1937 with the beginnings of an institutionalised labour beat. It is not the growing intrinsic news value of labour and industrial copy alone which explains the emergence of a specialist organisation such as the

Labour and Industrial Group. One must include an examination of the changing and expanding architecture of the state, itself. A press liaison officer was attached to the Prime Minister's staff in 1932, a public relations department established within the Post Office in 1933 and by the mid-thirties all the ministries 'in daily contact with the mass of the public' had formed 'information divisions', including the Ministry of Labour (Ogilvy Webb 1965:54). The role of each 'information division' was at first defensive; to liaise with the press and deal with journalists' enquiries - in effect, to shield the ministers and senior officials. Later their role evolved towards a more proactive stance which involved planning publicity campaigns and direct communication with the public.

Trade unions were much slower to begin to allocate formal responsibilities for the dissemination of information although some of the public sector unions, including organisations representing local and central government workers, began to appoint press officers at the same time as the Ministries. Nevertheless, on a less formal basis regularised and routine channels of communication between unions and journalists also developed in this decade. The fortunes of labour and industrial journalism, then, are inextricably bound up with the two main sources of labour and industrial information, trade unions and particular departments of state. The history of the Labour and Industrial Group demonstrates the ways in which the state can both open up and shut down information flows, and the capacity of governments to foster particular ideological climates which may either stimulate or dampen the demand for labour and industrial news.

For these reasons, this discussion of the history of labour and industrial journalism will be organised around the identification of three distinct historical phases, characterised not by the strength of appetite for labour news demonstrated by news editors but by the changes in the political and economic environment of labour journalism . Given this theoretical approach, the following framework can be constructed:

1937 to 1965

In this period the first labour and industrial correspondents, appointed during the thirties by a small number of national newspapers, cohere as a more or less formal group. This is because a 'labour beat' emerges based upon the relevant departments of state, the national headquarters of some trade unions and the union conference season. The state plays an important role in fostering a fertile climate for the growth of a culture of labour journalism.

This is in part because the bureaucratic structure of the state begins to regularise and routinise the flow of relevant information for labour journalists. However, it is also because the state during the Second World War and in subsequent decades seeks to reach an accommodation with organised labour. As the state tentatively embraces organised labour, so the status of labour journalism rises and the power of labour correspondents within news organisations increases.

1964 to 1979

This period can be characterised as 'the golden age' for the Group. The movement towards an accommodation between government and organised labour quickens in pace and it is in this period that the state employs a strategy which more closely approximates to a 'corporate style' than at any other time. Relationships between government, organised labour and industry extend through a number of new forums created by the in-coming Labour administration (1964-1970) and this widens the 'labour beat' for journalists. Of course, this does not mean that such relationships are cordial or free from tension but such tensions and conflicts provide valuable copy for journalists on the beat.

This period is also marked by important interpersonal connections between members of the Labour and Industrial Group and the Government. Friendships between Labour Party politicians and labour correspondents grow in importance as those politicians become Cabinet Ministers. Secondly, several labour correspondents 'move across' to take up positions within the administration and others enjoy enhanced status through appointment to government initiated enquiries, including the Donovan Commission on industrial relations.

Against this background numbers in the Group grow to their peak (approximately seventy) and the procedures of the Group are formalised in a written constitution (1965) which seeks to regulate membership, maintain ethical standards, and promote the influence of the Group. It is in this period that the Group most seriously challenges the position of its arch professional rival, the Westminster Lobby.

1979 to the Present

The current condition of labour journalism is one of decline, in terms of membership, energy, political influence, and professional standing. The precise reason for this is disputed by members and trade union officials alike. The more optimistic believe that the current malaise is nothing more than a temporary phenomenon, a function of the cyclical nature of news values. Others, more pessimistic in outlook regard the Coal Dispute of 1984/85 as the turning point at which the fortunes of the Group began to wane with the final, crushing defeat of the trade union movement. Another view believes that labour journalism has suffered most sharply a destructive process which has blighted all national journalism, namely the relocation of national newspaper publishing away from Fleet Street and with it the death of the old social networks supplying the 'meat and drink' of journalism.

The analytic framework employed here points to a rather different explanation and one which suggests that the process of decline began slightly earlier. An explicit aim of the Thatcher administration was the eradication of 'corporatist' arrangements from government. Accordingly, many of the forums and institutions which had formed important components in the 'labour beat' were deliberately neglected by the new administration and some eventually destroyed. As the new Government politically distanced itself from the representatives of both labour and industry, so the Labour and Industrial Correspondents' Group found itself also being pushed away from the centre of things. Indeed, after one less than cordial meeting during her time as Leader of the Opposition, Mrs Thatcher refused to meet the Group and briefings from Downing Street became extremely rare. The memoirs of incoming Ministers suggest that they had far less contact with labour and industrial correspondents than their counterparts in previous administrations. Labour and industrial journalists, then, lost some of their most important direct channels to Government and those that remained no longer produced a regular flow of information likely to make 'front page copy'. In addition, as the TUC was pushed from the centre of the political stage, journalists found that one of the next most important institutions on 'the labour beat' no longer routinely supplied copy of a quality likely to interest news editors and was no longer likely to supply the kind of 'intelligence' which used to justify a regular lunch time appointment. At the same time, the editorial and ideological perspectives of a number of newspapers encouraged the growth in other 'rival' specialisms, including financial, personnel and business journalism (Negrine 1993; Parsons 1989).

The context for this, of course, was the broader ideological impact of the new Thatcher government on the perceptions of the public or, perhaps, more importantly upon the perceptions of news editors concerning the priorities of the public. Whether or not the Thatcher years represent the relentless unfolding of an ideological blueprint remains a source of debate amongst academics. However, it is clear that the Thatcher government worked hard to construct an ideological vision of a new Britain in which trade unions no longer played a part in most ordinary people's lives. This, too, was likely to influence the editors and managers of national newspapers and to shape the decisions they took in terms of the organisation of specialist journalists. Not only did Labour and Industrial journalists no longer enjoy access to routine sources of 'front page copy' but their very specialism no longer appeared to describe something at the centre of most reader's lives.

The creation and development of the Group: 1937 to 1965

During the most severe days of the pre-war Depression in 1936, King Edward VIII undertook a tour of South Wales and the Rhondda. Shocked by the conditions in the which the people of the Rhondda were forced to live, the King made a spontaneous impromptu speech in which he apparently commented that 'something must be done'. The industrial correspondents accompanying the royal tour were prevented from hearing clearly what the King said as the police held the crowds back but a few heard enough to appreciate the potential newsworthiness of the incident. In a political situation suggesting a striking parallel with contemporary relationships between government and monarchy, evidence of royal support for greater government intervention in welfare and regional policy was a very big story. However, a great deal rested on what precisely the King said and while some journalists were convinced that the King had demanded that 'something must be done', others believed that the royal response had been the politically milder, 'something should be done'. In terms of the political news agenda of the day, 'should' was very different to 'must' and rather less newsworthy. According to Trevor Evans, one of the first correspondents to work an industrial beat, in an effort to resolve the matter and produce a definitive account all journalists following the royal tour were required to a attend a meeting in the evening at one of the local hotels. Evans does not tell us whether this included only those who actually heard the King's comment or whether all journalists expressing an interest were allowed to contribute. Nevertheless, the view of the meeting was that the phrase employed was, indeed, 'must' and a dozen front page stories were filed accordingly (Evans 1953: 39).

Of course, this was not the first time that journalists have gathered to collectively 'construct' definitive accounts of reality. However, the story provides one indication that by the early 1930s a sufficient number of national newspapers employed journalists specialising in industrial news for some form of group consciousness to begin to form. Indeed, there is some evidence to suggest that, perhaps, the first industrial journalists' 'ring' (an arrangement to pool information) involving Trevor Evans (*Daily Express*), Hugh Chevins (*Daily Telegraph*) and Ian McKay (*News Chronicle*) had been in operation from the day Ian McKay was appointed as one of the first industrial correspondents in 1933 (Evans 1953:25). The story also points to the emphasis upon regional industrial developments which preoccupied labour and industrial journalists in the decade before the War.

Few trade unions, with the exception of organisations representing white collar public sector workers,[4] had put in place arrangements which would ensure a daily supply of labour news for correspondents, though during this decade the union conference season began to encourage a seasonal migration away from London. Herbert Tracey was appointed as the first press officer at the TUC in the mid-1930s (Tracey, 1953) and industrial correspondents had begun to foster personal relationships with senior trade union leaders in the largest labour organisations in the same period. It was, however, the state which first stimulated the emergence of industrial specialists when the Ministry of Labour began to organise regional tours to brief journalists on industrial affairs in the mid-1930s (Evans, 1953). It was the organisation of particular departments of state of which provided the infrastructure for the growth of a labour and industrial beat because these departments offered a reliable and routine supply of information. While trade union contacts were recognised from the start as vital sources, few trade union organisations could offer the same volume of information on a daily or weekly basis. By the mid-thirties, tours organised by a number of departments of state had become a routine source of industrial information for correspondents. Though, by the end of the 1930s, many industrial correspondents spent a considerable period in the Spring and Summer away from Fleet Street, attending the larger union conferences, the essential foundations of the labour and industrial specialism rested upon the reliability of the departments of state as providers of routine industrial news.

In the very earliest days of industrial reporting, then, a regional focus was quite prominent and much reporting concerned developments in particular industrial regions or sectors. This would explain the interest of industrial specialists in the royal visit to South Wales. Trade unions were unable to establish regular dialogue with government and mass unemployment brought both a decline in membership and political impotency

(Barnes and Reid,1982). With prompting from the Ministry of Labour and other state departments, then, the attention of correspondents was often turned to industrial affairs broadly defined rather than the more specific issue of trade union politics. By default, the state was able to leave its imprint upon the framework which guided the daily routine for industrial correspondents. Indeed, it was while 'door stepping' outside the Ministry of Labour, awaiting the result of a court of enquiry established to resolve the 1937 'Coronation bus strike', that journalists first proposed a formal Labour and Industrial Correspondents Group.[5] It was not long before the invitations from the Ministry of Labour to join the conducted regional tours were being channelled through the secretary of the Group, thus announcing both official recognition of the legitimacy of the Group and enhancing the importance of membership in the eyes of correspondents. The three founding members were Trevor Evans (*Daily Express*), Hugh Chevins (*Daily Telegraph*), and Ian McKay (*News Chronicle*) (Jones, 1988: 11). The first chairman was John Ratcliffe who had been recently appointed as the first Industrial Correspondent for the Times, followed by Ian McKay who employed his wide range of political and labour movement contacts to further enhance the status of the Group amongst trade union leaders and the political elite (Evans 1953:39-52). McKay had formerly been a Lobby correspondent for the *Western Daily Mail*.

Tunstall has noted the role of the state in stimulating the formal growth of particular branches of journalism (1971:225). Thus, the fortunes of the Education Correspondents' Group, formed in 1962, prospered as the Ministry of Education expanded in the 1960s and as successive Ministers, their standing strengthened as their budgets grew, encouraged close relations with correspondents. Similarly, the status and influence of the Labour and Industrial Group reached a peak as the departments of state concerned with industrial policy and economic intervention expanded under the Labour administration of 1964 to 1970. However, this pattern first developed during the War with the collapse of the Conservative administration and the formation of a coalition government which included both a formal representative of the trade union movement, Ernest Bevin in charge of the Ministry of Labour, and several other Ministers who had very close links with the Labour and Industrial Correspondents' Group, including Herbert Morrison (Ministry of Supply), Hugh Dalton (Ministry of Economic Warfare) and David Grenfell (Minister for Mines) (Evans, 1953:54). Indeed, according to Trevor Evans, as these appointments were announced by the BBC, several of the appointees were listening to the radio whilst enjoying a drink with labour correspondents in a hotel bar during the union conference season. A crucial priority of the Coalition Government was to win the consent of organised labour and to avoid industrial conflict during the period of military crisis at the beginning of the war. It was recognised that the fostering of consent rather than the coercion of labour offered the better prospect of stable industrial relations. Hence, the formal representation of organised labour and the labour movement within the government (Barnes and Reid,1982).[6] The value of contacts with key journalists in securing consent was also recognised. Bevin, for example, made little effort to conceal his determination to utilise the press in his campaign to suppress industrial militancy in the coal fields (Bullock, 1967:300-301).

It was this re-shaping of the state during the war with the creation of state departments with a far greater interventionist role, that hugely expanded the range of sources and the volume of information available to the Group. In addition to the Ministries, a framework to regulate industry was created which anticipated corporate developments in the post-war period. The National Joint Advisory Council, involving both sides of industry through the TUC and the BEC (British Employers Confederation) spawned a Joint Consultative Committee to take responsibility for wages and industrial relations. This committee, in turn, established the National Arbitration Tribunal to resolve industrial disputes. Thus, as the structure of the industrial state grew ever more elaborate so the industrial and labour beat expanded.

The expansion in the number of relevant state departments and regulatory structures was not, in itself, sufficient to increase the volume of information flowing to the Group. The normative framework governing relations between politicians, civil servants and journalists also had to permit more open communication and greater frequency of contact. In other words, the culture within departments of state also had to be one which would encourage the growth of relationships between labour correspondents and the political elite. With the appointment of Ministers such as Bevin, Dalton, Morrison and Grenfell to the Coalition Government, members of the Labour and Industrial Correspondents' Group enjoyed 'insider' status for the first time. Bevin, in particular, appreciated the value of co-operating with journalists who had specialist knowledge of industrial matters and enjoyed close relationships with other trade union leaders. Issues such as conscription, the state regulation of war-time production, the constraints imposed upon trade union activity, and later the management of demobilisation, all required very careful presentation to the public. Under Bevin, members of the Group were provided with a room and telephone facilities inside the Ministry of Labour

(Jones,1988). At this stage during the War, only the No 1 correspondents on each paper were allowed membership of the Group and, thus, even at this early stage the Group was able to strengthen its status through the tried and tested professional strategy of devising mechanisms of exclusion. Bevin had been infuriated by press coverage of the 1937 bus strike which had presented the Transport and General Workers Union as an organisation deliberately setting out to sabotage the Coronation of the new King. In addition, he was suspicious of the Industrial and Labour Group for 'being hand in glove' with the rank and file strike leaders (Evans, 1953:54). In retaliation he had restricted press comment to two formal statements each week and had, at one point, tried to insist that industrial correspondents provide a guarantee that his dictated statements be printed in each paper verbatim. In charge of one of the departments of state, however, he saw the advantage of a more formalised arrangement with the Group, one which provided a stable channel of communication to the news media but one which allowed him some significant measure of control.

As we shall see, conflicts and tensions within the political elite have long been an important factor in accelerating the flow of information outwards to correspondents and labour journalists have been amongst the most grateful beneficiaries over the years. Bevin, locked in feud with Beaverbrook within Cabinet and suspicious of the critical coverage of labour issues in Beaverbrook newspapers, nonetheless fostered a particularly close relationship with Trevor Evans, despite the fact that Evans was employed by Beaverbrook on the *Daily Express* (Bullock,1967:98 and 135). It was to Evans who Bevin first turned when he sought to publicly 'trail' his ambitions for office after the war and it was Evans who wrote the first authorised biography of Bevin. It was also Evans who Bevin invited to attend special regional briefing sessions for the managers of local Labour Exchanges' as Bevin sought to lend a personal touch to the presentation of the ministry's strategy (Bullock 1967: 128).

In the early years of labour and industrial journalism in the decade before the War, it was rare for newspapers to hire more than one specialist for the beat. Without a 'number two' or a 'number three' to cover the less important union conferences, most industrial correspondents spent a great deal of their time in the conference season, which began in April and ended with the Labour Party conference in October, away from Fleet Street in a variety of conference towns (Evans 1953:41). In those days the TUC , itself, selected venues from a list which included not merely Blackpool and Brighton but even Weymouth and Norwich (Tracey, 1953:114). According to Frank

Machin, northern industrial correspondent for the *Daily Herald* in the late 1930s and 1940s, every town had a particular pub or hotel where labour correspondents would congregate, for example, 'the Marble Bar' in Newcastle or 'the Land of Green Ginger' in Hull (Machin,1953). In London, the Cheshire Cheese had already become the 'home' for labour and industrial correspondents (Walker,1953), a role it continues to play today, hosting most of the Group's formal functions and informal gatherings. Although the attraction of seaside and hotel was a powerful one, the daily routine for most industrial correspondents for much of the year would include a briefing at the TUC by the TUC Press Officer, followed by a succession of briefings at the relevant Ministries (Tracey,1953).

In the final decade before the War, then, a labour beat had emerged which displayed the main features which were to characterise it for the next four decades. It was a beat shaped by the imprint of the departmental structure of the State and by a strong connection to the elite of the labour movement. It was centred upon London for much of the year and even when, during the conference season or Ministry sponsored regional tours, labour journalists strayed further afield, the close network of contacts with ministry officials and senior union leaders was retained. A problem which was to be a feature of labour reporting for decades to come, the difficulty in establishing effective contacts with grass roots union activists, can be detected at the outset. The bureaucracies within each Ministry generated almost daily supplies of information. Although few trade union organisations included a press office, it was possible for correspondents to develop regular contacts with senior officials within the mainly London based headquarters. It was much harder for journalists to find opportunities to foster routine contacts with union activists or local officials not attached to the formal, institutional structures which made up the routine beat. The tributes to Ian McKay collected by Trevor Evans (1953) reflect this. Very few of the accounts of life as labour correspondents contain more than a mere mention of rank and file trade unionists or workers. In the course of their daily routine, labour journalists simply did not encounter 'ordinary' trade unionists unless they were covering a dispute. In these circumstances, contacts with those involved at a local level would be sought but journalists would have to start from scratch and they often received little encouragement from senior officials within unions who were frequently suspicious of independent dialogue between activists and reporters. Hence, the fury of Ernest Bevin during the 1937 bus strike (Evans, 1953:54; Jones, 1988:11). Only correspondents working for the *Daily Worker / Morning Star* have over the years, through the network of union contacts developed by the Communist Party, enjoyed regular and routine relations with union rank and file members. Access to these journalists' 'contact books' has always been a much sought after prize within the Group.

In the early years, relationships between the Group and the labour movement elite, were based upon a small number of quite specific personal friendships. The 'triumvirate' of Evans, McKay and Chevins was able to establish cordial relations with senior union officials, as well as leading figures in the Labour Party and the Co-operative Party. According to Evans, Ian McKay 'did more than anyone else to breakdown the barriers between labour leaders and journalists...his capacity for anecdotes and drink was prodigious'(1953:22). After having formed the Anti-Luncheon League to promote the virtue of whisky over solid food at lunch times, McKay would often fail to attend the afternoon sessions at conferences. However, according to Evans, union leaders would regularly report to McKay to keep him abreast of events.

> He was happier in their company than perhaps, in any other, save the companionship of his fellow newspapermen...when they [TUC leaders] relaxed and became their natural selves at the adjournment of Congress, Ian was a welcome addition to their party. (Tracey,1953: 114).

A considerable amount of this 'bridge mending' was required because relations between journalists as an occupational group and organised labour were problematic throughout the two decades preceding the Second World. The rivalry between the two organisations seeking to represent journalists during this period is well documented (Christian,1980). While the Institute of Journalists sought to appeal to journalists as members of a professional association, the National Union of Journalists offered journalists the benefits of collective unionised organisation. However, the tensions arising from this conflict over occupational identity and status surfaced inside the National Union of Journalists, itself, leading to furious internal debates over the question of affiliation to the TUC. The NUJ affiliated in 1920, only to disaffiliate three years later over the requirement of the TUC that all affiliates contribute to a propaganda fund which, in practice, involved primarily a direct subsidy to the Daily Herald (Mansfield,1943: ch XIV). A small majority of NUJ branches considered this violated their professional code. It took eighteen years for the union activists within the NUJ to win the battle for re-affiliation. Tensions with the TUC were further heightened during the 1926 General Strike when the NUJ fudged the question of support for the print unions (Mansfield 1943:ch XVII).

If a single labour and industrial correspondent was a familiar feature of most national and some regional papers by the end of the 1930s, the steady increase in the volume of industrial and labour news in the next decade stimulated a further growth in numbers. For example, Mary Stewart was appointed to act as number two to Ian McKay on the *News Chronicle* in 1945 (Evans, 1953:62) and by the end of the war sufficient pressure had been generated around Fleet Street for the rules governing membership of the Group to be amended to allow news organisations to nominate number two's and three's (Jones, 1988:11) Though the Times refrained from appointing an additional labour correspondent until 1963 (Seaton,1982:278), the political climate in the 1950s provided conditions which continued to stimulate the expansion of labour and industrial reporting on most papers. As Middlemas notes, the pressing need for co-operation between the representatives of labour, capital and the state to ensure national survival during the War, established a 'corporate bias' in the development of state policy which continued through the 1950s. Under both Atlee and successive Conservative administrations (Middlemas,1986:340- 342), a philosophy which promoted an unprecedented degree of economic planning and a central role for the state in securing the co-operation of labour and capital, was embraced by civil servants and ministers alike. The institutional arrangements of the post-war settlement came to represent, 'an organic part of the state' (Middlemas, 1986:342). As these institutional and departmental arrangements unfolded in the decade after the war so the labour and industrial beat expanded further.

Middlemas notes that the political and administrative perspectives which grew out of the experience of the War defined not only an institutional structure for the state but also a set of concepts or rules describing the appropriate orientation of the key actors in the political process, towards one another and the state (Middlemas,1990:2). In short, the ideology underpinning the post war settlement achieved, for almost a decade, a hegemonic influence (Middlemas,1986:342) amongst policy makers and opinion leaders. Inevitably, this influenced the editorial thinking of national newspapers and encouraged a keener editorial interest in labour and industrial news. Thus, not only were industrial correspondents finding in the 1950s that their beats were expanding but that also their copy was in more urgent demand within their news organisations. According to Middlemas, by the end of the decade the tensions between the main interests within the corporate consensus were already undermining its authority. By this stage, it began to be recognised that such a framework of co-operation was likely to benefit the state more than the other players in the game (1986:345). Nonetheless, this did not present an immediate threat to the institutional and departmental structure of the state which underpinned the expanding labour and industrial beat. Indeed, such tensions between the key players within these corporate arrangements were likely to generate even more copy. As we shall see in the following section such tensions and also rivalries within the state itself, between departments, proved to be very significant stimuli to the flows of information useful to industrial journalists.

The dominance of the Conservative Party in office during the next decade after the war did not represent a set back for labour and industrial journalism. Before and during the war the Conservative Party had undergone an intense ideological debate over the extent to which it should draw upon its 'One Nation' traditions and renounce 'Baldwinite' market liberalism, as a way of charting a new post war course. Against the right wing of the party, Butler and Macmillan were successful in winning sufficient support to ensure a stable commitment to the politics of the post war settlement. This was formalised in the proceedings of the 1947 Conservative Party conference where policies setting out an extended role for the state in the regulation of the economy and the development of a industrial strategy were presented by Butler and agreed by conference despite bitter attacks from the Beaverbrook press (Gamble, 1974:ch 3).

Following the decisive defeat in the 1945 general election, it was recognised that to resist the overall framework of the post-war settlement would be nothing short of political suicide for the party (Gamble,1988:64). The new Conservative thinking on industrial strategy and the role of the state was contained in an 'Industrial Charter', presented to the 1947 conference. This had been drafted by Butler and included within it a 'Workers Charter', setting out a framework of workplace rights. This was the subject of vigorous debate between Tory progressives like Butler and Macmillan, on the one hand, and the market liberal wing of the party. This political in-fighting, in itself, generated valuable copy for both political and industrial correspondents but an added twist was given to this process by the political rivalry between Butler and Macmillan. Despite their common ideological position within the party both were extremely keen to be seen leading the movement for progressive reform. As a consequence, both wanted to be primarily associated with the Charter and this rivalry produced a sequence of stories for industrial correspondents in the months running up to the 1947 conference (Howard,1987:158-159). In drafting the Charter, Butler had spent months touring the country, talking to industrialists, party members and also trade unionists. In this process, relationships with journalists had also been strengthened and Butler continued to exploit these as the conflicts over the extent of the Conservative Party's new progressivism continued to be disputed right up to the publication of the final policy document in 1949 (Howard,1987:176).

One of the leading lights inside the research department at Conservative Central Office who was involved in the drafting of the Industrial Charter was Iain Macleod who had experience as a former journalist and still retained a number of contacts   (Fisher,1973:138). Once again, Trevor Evans was regarded as a personal friend but it is clear that Macleod retained links with a number of industrial correspondents. It was Macleod who, in becoming Minister of Labour in 1955, breathed new life into the ideas associated with the Industrial Charter. His predecessor, Walter Moncton, had been a less committed advocate. Under Macleod, the ministry moved more firmly towards the adoption of an arbiter role in the industrial relations process and through the National Joint Advisory Council (the forerunner to NEDDY), Macleod secured support from both sides of industry for the drafting of a code for industrial relations reflecting the philosophy of the Industrial Charter (Fisher,1973:110).

So through the 1950s, despite the electoral dominance of the Conservative Party labour and industrial journalism continued to expand. As the state intervened more in the process of industrial relations, so more labour and industrial stories were 'defined' as important and through ministers such as Macleod, and to a degree Butler, informal channels of communication were established between labour and industrial journalists and the Cabinet. These lines of communication were not as significant as they were to become once the Labour Party arrived in office in 1964 but nonetheless they afforded labour journalists sufficient professional authority to ensure the growing status of their specialism. Further to this, a series of strikes in the car and ship building industries and on London Transport buses in the late 1950s placed industrial news on the front pages and compelled Macleod to establish a string of Courts of Inquiry, each of which became an important temporary feature of the labour beat. The 1957 bus strike generated so much media interest that journalists besieged Maclead at his home in Enfield (Fisher,1973:130).

John Hare became Minister for Labour in 1959 while the government continued to find itself being dragged increasingly frequently into the industrial relations arena as the problem of rising wage demands became ever more acute. Prime Minister Macmillan pushed for a 'Pay Pause' in 1962 and sought to extend corporate decision making through the creation of the National Economic Development Council, together with 'little Neddies' for each industrial sector, as a way of securing greater co-operation from capital and labour (Macmillan,1973:ch 3). This helped to expand the labour and industrial beat and opened up more channels through which labour journalists could obtain copy but appeared to have little impact upon industrial behaviour. At one point in 1962, railway workers, postmen, the lower grades in the Civil Service and even the makers of cricket balls were all on strike (Macmillan,1973:50). Throughout the early 1960s, industrial unrest generated a copious supply of copy for labour correspondents.

It is clear that even when in opposition, correspondents were keen to develop contacts within the Labour Party as well as the government. Often, this occurred naturally as they dealt with officials in particular trade unions. For example, George Brown , later to head the Department of Economic Affairs, a key ministry on the 1960s beat, first came into contact with labour correspondents as a TGWU delegate to the Labour Party conference in 1939. Over the next two decades, as he rose to prominence within the Labour Party he maintained close relationships, particularly with Trevor Evans, Ian McKay and John Anderson, the industrial correspondent of the Guardian throughout the 1950s (Brown,1971:64). Brown blamed his later notoriety and adverse publicity upon the erosion of trust and lack of integrity which he believed characterised journalism in the years after the era of McKay and Evans. With the latter 'off the record' meant 'off the record', but for Brown the younger generation of industrial correspondents were merely 'eavesdroppers and gossip writers' (1971:64).

Once Wilson had been elected as leader of the Labour Party following the death of Gaitskell, he established a practice of briefing not only the Westminster Lobby but the Industrial and Labour Group on a regular basis as well (Jones,1988). Wilson was invited as guest speaker when the Group celebrated its 25th anniversary in 1963 at the Hilton in London and a year later Wilson made a point of ensuring that the press party which accompanied his election campaign was made up of members from the Group as well as the Westminster Lobby. Just as in the 1940s, certain personal relationships between elite figures within the labour movement and members of the Group were to play a pivotal part in ensuring that the Group were accepted, even welcomed, as a familiar part of the labour movement's political landscape. During the War, Trevor Evans and Ian McKay were able to befriend a group of ministers including Bevin, Dalton, Morrison and

Grenfell. These friendships were important in reinforcing the legitimacy of the Group as well as in representing significant sources of information. Similarly, in the 1960s George Brown and Barbara Castle, in particular, enjoyed warm friendships with leading figures from the Group and as both were to occupy positions of great importance in the formulation of industrial and labour policy, the Group as a whole was to benefit from these personal relationships between members of the Labour Party elite and senior industrial correspondents.

A similar process of consolidation occurred during the 1950s in terms of the Group's relationships with the elite representatives within the trade union movement. The TUC and the headquarters of the larger trade unions in London became regular components of the labour beat in the 1950s. Union leaders rarely attached a very high value to public relations and, often, journalists had to work hard in explaining to unions why they should attach more importance to the question of how they dealt with the news media. Eric Wigham, a distinguished labour correspondent for the *Times* between the mid-50s and the late 60s, devoted a chapter in a 1961 Penguin Special, 'What's Wrong With the Unions?' to listing the public relations failings of many of the largest unions (Wigham,1961:ch 9). The list is a familiar one which would be recognised by many journalists working throughout the 1970s and the early 1980s. Very few unions at that stage employed full time press officers, they were slow in responding to requests for comment or information, senior officials were too often unavailable for briefings and when officials did talk to journalists their approach was too often characterised by suspicion and caution (Wigham,1961:ch 9). Nevertheless, there were some unions with more enlightened communication strategies (Wigham points to the approaches of NALGO, the NUR, USDAW and the civil service unions) and, in terms of personal relationships with particular union leaders, the Industrial and Labour Group made significant progress. So much so that by 1961, it was possible for the Group to challenge the elite of the union movement to a game of cricket at the TUC Conference, an event which subsequently became a regular fixture and continues to the present today.

Throughout the early post war years, then, the status and prospects of the Group improved. The post-war state displayed a 'corporate bias' which stimulated the growth of a number of departments concerned with industrial and economic policy. These formed the foundations for a structure of routine sources around which the Group could cluster. The main organisations of the labour movement also came to represent important components of the labour beat and particular personal relationships between leading members of the Group and important figures within the labour movement were established. While the labour movement, as a whole, remained suspicious of the press for many good reasons, it was possible for union leaders and senior figures within the Labour Party to recognise that individual journalists, including many of the Labour and Industrial Group, were personally sympathetic to the values of the Left.

For these reasons, by the beginning of the 1960s most national newspapers included an industrial news desk with at least two and often three specialists. A journalistic hierarchy within the news organisation would be reflected in terms of a division of labour on the beat, itself. Thus, the industrial editor or number one would expect to cover the more important stories, take responsibility for the cultivation of the more prestigious sources on the beat and delegate responsibility for the more routine tasks associated with the desk.[7] By the early 1960s the process of specialisation had advanced to the point where a number of newspapers began to distinguish between industrial and labour specialisms (Tunstall,1971:80-89). While some industrial specialists would deal with economic and industrial policy broadly defined, some labour specialists began to concentrate more upon the unions as sources and the other organisations within the labour movement. In this way they began to focus more sharply upon the political dimension, thereby exacerbating friction between the Group and the Westminister Lobby. The potential for rivalry had always existed because of the tradition, established during the thirties, for industrial correspondents to attend not only the TUC Conference but also the Labour and Co-operative Party conferences. Such tensions were notably heightened with the creation of new economic planning departments under the first Wilson administration, to be discussed in the next section and it is in this 'golden era' that the Group seriously challenges the position of the Westminster Lobby at the top of the specialist tree.

1964 to 1979: 'the golden age' of the Labour and Industrial Correspondents' Group

Few observers would dispute that the 1960s and 1970s represented a period in which the Group reached its peak in terms of professional status and authority.[8] It was in this period that membership of the Group reached its highest total in its entire history; senior members of the Group achieved a new prominence through official recognition of one kind and another (knighthoods, appointments to Royal Commissions and even co-option into government), and the enhanced status of the Group was confirmed by the numbers of young graduates, many from 'Oxbridge', who chose Labour and Industrial reporting in preference to the Lobby. Labour and industrial journalism had become, in this period, the 'fast track' route for young ambitious journalists who wanted to make their mark quickly.

For many journalists, these developments in themselves contain the explanation for the high standing of the Labour and Industrial Group. In terms of this explanation, the Group enjoyed unprecedented professional authority because of the importance attached to labour and industrial news inside the newsrooms.[9] So great was the appetite for copy from the industrial and labour desks that Jim Fookes (number two at the Press Association for much of this period) says, 'we were the peace time war correspondents'. The problem, of course, with this form of explanation is that it rests upon a circular argument. Industrial and labour journalism achieves a high standing because news organisations choose to rank it in this way. The task must be to pose a deeper set of questions in order to provide an analysis which can explain why news organisations attached such a priority to labour and industrial news at this time. Once again, it is necessary to consider the role of the state and the political-economic environment.

There are four ways in which the state can be understood as exercising a vital influence over the fortunes of labour and industrial journalism. Firstly, although Middlemas (1986:ch 11) points to the growing difficulty of securing consent amongst the leading producer groups to corporatist political arrangements by the middle of the 1960s, nevertheless the Wilson administration arrived in office with a programme to expand the departments of state responsible for economic planning and intervene even more directly in industrial policy. The political and ideological importance of this programme for the Labour Party gave it a momentum which was maintained for much of the government's term in office, until economic difficulties and opposition from within the Treasury led to retreat in the final two years before the 1970 general election. Similarly, in the post-Selsdon phase of the Heath administration and in the early years of the next Wilson government, with Tony Benn at the Department of Industry, the state was characterised by an expansion in departments with responsibility for planning and economic intervention. As we have seen expansion in these areas of state activity stimulates growth in the labour and industrial beat with the emergence of new potential sources for the Group. In addition, this period was also characterised by the growing importance of nationalised industries to the economy. Here, too, the Group found regular and reliable sources of information.

Secondly, the Wilson government provided an important service for labour and industrial journalism in reaffirming the value of planning and intervention. Wilson's appeal to technocratic values in the 1964 election campaign and the subsequent presentation of policy within this ideological framework, helped to ensure the continuing 'hegemony' (Middlemas 1986:342) of a neo-Keynesian ideology promoting corporate agreement and rational economic planning amongst policy makers and opinion leaders. Thus, while many news organisations were committed to editorial perspectives hostile to Wilson and the government, a broad consensus existed which accepted the 'inevitability' of corporatist intervention and the importance, therefore, of labour and industrial copy in the hierarchy of news values. However, thirdly, the expansion of the state frequently generated internal tensions, often involving a Treasury jealous of its sphere of influence, and these tensions in turn, produced streams of 'leaks', all of which enhanced the cultivation of the labour beat. While it was in the interests of the Group for the state to continue to embrace the values of rational economic planning, it was also in the interests of the Group for the government to experience serious difficulties in implementing such policies. Political tensions and conflicts, either inwardly or outwardly directed, meant interesting copy.

Finally, and perhaps most importantly, with the triumph of the Labour Party in the 1964 election, the elite figures within the labour movement, with whom the Labour and Industrial Group had cultivated contacts throughout the previous two decades, had finally moved into positions of power. While the Group had always sought to maintain good relations with ministers in Conservative administrations, the culture of the Group and the politics of many of its members produced a stronger affinity with leading figures inside the Labour Party. Similarly, it was with union leaders and those managers in the nationalised industries with centre-left political sympathies, rather than the representatives of business and commerce, with whom most members of the Group were likely to develop an authentic rapport. With Labour in office and with particular individuals in charge of key departments, the Group was able to achieve 'insider status', in that it enjoyed the confidence of a number of leading political figures and frequent informal contact. As the Wilson administration, initially, embraced the trade union elite, co-opting Frank Cousins into the Cabinet, so the Group also found that its network of contacts extended into the centre of government, providing a channel for the communication of political information which was a serious rival to the Westminster Lobby.

Changes in the structure of the departments of state and the composition of the political elite were important factors in producing a rising tide of labour journalism but the strength and consequent political power of organised labour, produced through the application of policies of full-employment for almost two decades, was also a crucial factor. Strong and politically potent trade unions were 'news'.

The remainder of this section will consider the development of the Group in the period between 1964 and 1979 in the light of the framework set out above.

The Structure of the State

The election of the Wilson government in 1964 resulted in an immediate expansion in the number of state departments dealing with economic or industrial policy and an enhanced role for existing departments and state sponsored regulatory institutions. Wilson created a Department of Economic Affairs to develop strategic economic planning and a Ministry of Technology, 'to be a ministry of industry' (Wilson,1971:8), under Frank Cousins, on sabbatical from the Transport and General Workers Union. The Ministries of Labour, Technology, Power, and Transport all enjoyed full Cabinet status. The National Research Development Corporation, established by Atlee in 1948, was expanded as was the role of the National Economic Development Council (Wilson, 1971:8). In an effort to come to terms with one of the enduring political problems of the administration's years in office,- the position of the state in relation to the regulation of incomes-, the National Board on Prices and Incomes was given statutory power in 1965 (Wilson,1971:133). The regulatory boards were regarded as routine sources for number two or three correspondents on the industrial desks of most papers.[10] Not only did the new government expand the framework of industrial and economic regulation, it sought to actively intervene in the arena of industrial relations and this generated a great deal of copy for correspondents. The first Wilson administration took an active interest in the resolution of major national industrial conflicts including two rail disputes (1966 and 1967), the seaman's strike (1966), the dock strike (1967), a dispute at Fords (1969), and the strike in the newspaper industry (1970) amongst others (Wilson,1971). In each case, industrial and political specialisms overlapped as Ministers sought to bring union leaders and employers together. The profile of the State continued to loom large in attempts to regulate industrial relations and steer economic development under Heath and the second Wilson administration. The spectacular unravelling of Heath's industrial relations policy between 1972 and 1974 over-shadowed the continuing growth in the size of the departments of state responsible for industrial policy with, for example, the creation of the Industrial Assistance Board in 1972. While the former ensured that the copy produced by the Group regularly appeared on the front pages, it was the latter which permitted the continuing development of the industrial beat. With the return of Wilson to office, the Industrial Assistance Board assumed a greater importance, representing a central mechanism in the state's attempt to 'pick economic winners' or candidates for state support (Wilson,1979:149). The energy of the state in developing an industrial strategy was, of course, a theme which was promoted with enthusiasm by the press officers within the relevant state departments and the Chief Information Officer (head of the Ministry of Labour's information division) was granted access to the highest level policy making forums, including NEDDY (Ogilvy-Webb,1965: 105).

Througout this period the nationalised industries represented a very important section of the industrial beat. In contrast to the period after 1979, the state permitted many of the senior executives within this sector to be recruited from within. As a result a managerial culture specific to the public sector flourished in the post war period, one which placed considerable importance upon public service and often reflected the values of the post-war settlement in its orientation to labour relations. The concept of a partnership between management and unions in delivering a service to the public on behalf of the state was widely recognised, if not always applied in practice. Several of the most senior executives were sympathetic to social democratic or socialist perspectives, including Derek Ezra at the National Coal Board and, a little later, Sir Peter Parker at British Rail (Parker,1989). This culture was later to prompt the Thatcher administration to conduct a purge by stealth in which such senior managers were replaced by senior executives from the private sector. Common ground, then, was often to be found between journalists within the Labour and Industrial Group and the executives of the nationalised industries. Senior executives from the nationalised industries were frequently invited to speak at the 'do's' arranged by the Group at the Cheshire Cheese in Fleet Street and some of the press officers working for nationalised industries were still regarded as the most helpful on the beat by the Group in the 1980s, according to data collected by MORI. [11]

It is in this period stretching from the middle of the 1960s to the end of the 1970s in which close relationships were forged between the 'leading lights' in the Group and particular managers within the nationalised sector. Geoffrey Goodman, for example, rose to prominence in the 1960s through his close political involvement with the Labour administration but also established important friendships with senior managers at a number of nationalised industries and particularly, Geoff Kirk, Ned Smith (the National Coal Board's director of industrial relations) and even successive chairmen, including Ezra and Siddall (Goodman, 1985:34). Indeed, Goodman commanded sufficient authority to act later as a go between during the 1984 Coal Strike in an effort to re-convene negotiations (Goodman,1985: 98).

It was not necessary for the state to actively promote relationships between the nationalised industries and the Group but merely to tolerate and permit relationships which naturally developed as the 'common sense' of economic planning and industrial intervention became the received wisdom within news rooms as amongst the political elite. The capacity of the State to undermine such relationships and radically alter the structure of the industrial beat is dramatically underlined during the course of the Thatcher years. During the 1950s and, most particularly, during the years of Wilson and Heath the state regarded these relationships without the suspicion characteristic of the 1980s.

It was in the late 1960s that a sharper specialisation began to emerge between labour and industrial correspondents. This could only occur when sufficient journalists were attached to the industrial desk and, in any case, rarely represented a hard and fast occupational division. Nevertheless, towards the end of the 1960s journalists within the Group were likely to regard themselves as either industrial journalists with a labour brief or industrial correspondents with an industrial brief (Tunstall,1971:78-85). The latter's beat would embrace the nationalised industries and the growing number of departments of state concerned with industrial policy while the former focused more precisely upon the organisations and institutions most closely involved in industrial relations. It was here that rivalry with the Westminster Lobby grew most acute (Tunstall,1971:144) because the labour beat was likely to include many of the political institutions which represented important features of the Lobby correspondents territory including, for example, the monthly meeting of the Labour Party national executive and the Labour Party conference, as well as the political institutions responsible for the regulation of industrial relations. While news editors sometimes tried to insist upon a co-operative approach between the groups, the occupational culture within each camp was sufficiently crystallised by the end of the second decade after the War for this to be actively resisted by both sides.[12]

As both the Crossman Diaries and Barbara Castle's memoirs indicate, the Labour government of 1964 to 1970 was so preoccupied with problems of industrial relations and so inclined to establish Courts of Inquiry or Tribunals in an effort to resolve them, that a richly fertile territory was set out to expand the labour beat (see for example, Crossman, 1979:653-654). Inevitably, as this territory was populated by employers, trade unionists, and the government, both labour correspondents and the Westminster Lobby gathered upon it. The Industrial and Labour Group, however, enjoyed the advantage of frequently superior contacts within the union and labour movement and for sometime they were able to exploit these to produce information or 'intelligence' of a quality which could not be matched by the Westminster Lobby. Later, however, as the Group sensed the tide of political events moving against them, its attempts to penetrate to the heart of the Lobby's territory inside Parliament were sharply rebuffed. Requests that press passes be allocated to members of the Group were denied.

The Development of the Group

Against a background of expansion in the extent of the beats and an ideological climate fostered by the state, which encouraged the prioritisation of industrial news, the Labour and Industrial Correspondents' Group reached a point of maturity in the mid-1960s which was signalled by the adoption of a formal constitution in 1965.[13] Seaton (1982) estimates numbers in the Group reaching up to 100 at this point though this may be an over-estimate and former officers of the Group interviewed by the author place the figure at closer to 75.[14] Tunstall identifies 33 correspondents but this refers to the labour rather than the industrial beat. However, he also notes that only the Lobby recruited more specialists and that larger numbers were employed in industrial journalism than, for example, football, crime, or education (1971:294). As the Group has failed to retain any written record of its business or its membership totals before 1982, it is impossible to determine precisely what the total membership at the height of the Group's influence and status actually was. Nevertheless, the decline in membership from a maximum of 75 plus in the period up to 1979, to the present total of just under 50 through the decade of the 1980s is an indication of the changes which the Group experienced in its fortunes as the political climate grew harsher and the state broke with the arrangements of the post-war settlement.

In the period between 1965 and 1979, however, all the evidence suggests that the Group enjoyed unprecedented status and influence. Membership totals rose as more news organisations recruited second and third journalists to staff their industrial desks. Experienced senior industrial correspondents who had developed careers through the 1950s achieved positions of eminence, sometimes confirmed through official recognition of one form or another. Trevor Evans was knighted while Eric Wigham was appointed to the Donovan Commission in 1967. Geoffrey Goodman was recruited by the government itself to advise on the presentation of income and prices policy at the Counter Inflation Unit. Goodman was also a member of the Royal Commission on the Press established during Wilson's second term in office, writing a minority report with David Basnett, leader of the General and Municipal Workers Union, which was published by the Labour Party (Basnett and Goodman,1977). Tunstall's material on specialist correspondents of the 1960s indicates that the average age of an industrial specialist was 37, average age of entry was 30 and that a quarter of industrial specialists had spent over 10 years within the specialism (1971:95). The rapid turnover in specialists, indicative of the decline in status which characterised industrial journalism in the period after 1979, was clearly not present in the sixties. Tunstall also noted that by the 1960s the industrial beat was regarded as a stepping stone for the most ambitious journalists who sought to gain entry to the Lobby.

From the beginning of the 1970s, however, a new generation of university educated journalists, often influenced by the intellectual climate of the 1960s, began to arrive in Fleet Street and for many the industrial desk was a first preference, even above the Lobby.[15] Paul Routledge, Donald MacIntyre, Peter Riddell, Christian Tyler, John Lloyd, Peter Jenkins and Mick Costello, for example, all arrived on the industrial beat from Oxbridge or the older red brick universities in the late sixties or early seventies. Together with David Fenton, Barrie Clement, and Chris Potter, these journalists represented a group, largely graduate trained, who achieved very high reputations within newspaper journalism and accumulated considerable professional authority. A large number eventually moved on to positions of national prominence as political editors or senior executives. A number remained within industrial journalism throughout the seventies and the papers of the Group in the early 1980s confirm their continuing influence, though in this decade journalists with a stronger sympathy for the politics of 'new realism' in the labour movement also began to achieve positions of influence and, in addition, it was those industrial correspondents now regarded as 'the old guard' who were most affected by the traumatic upheavals in the mid-eighties, which triggered the crisis of labour and industrial journalism to be discussed below.

The journalists arriving on the industrial beat in the late sixties and early seventies had, in their turn, supplanted the 'ancien regime' (as one describes it) of Goodman, Wigham, Keith McDowell, and, of course Evans and Chevins, those senior journalists who had established their reputations a decade or more earlier. They also brought with them the political perspectives which dominated university departments in the late sixties and early seventies and a rather more iconoclastic approach to journalism. It was this generation, for example, that introduced the annual 'golden bollock' award for the worst labour or industrial news item of the year, presented at the Group's annual general meeting (the significance of this ritual is explored further in the next chapter). According to some of those involved the Group itself became more politicised with rival factions seeking to secure the officerships (the politics and culture of the Group will also be discussed at greater length below). It was clearly the case, however, that the industrial and labour beat at this time attracted the bright and ambitious in newspaper journalism who recognised the importance attached to industrial and labour news, the connections between the Group and the political elite and the sense of influence which these brought. The intellectual tides of the sixties also frequently brought a sympathy for the labour movement and the politics of the left. In this era it was easier, of course, to reconcile personal politics with professional career interests.

Tunstall found that 7 out of the 9 specialist groups of journalists he interviewed in the 1960s ranked the industrial specialism in the top three of a status hierarchy, though only the industrial group ranked itself at the very top (1971:109). Many in the specialism had moved from other specialisms, regarding this as an enhancement in status. Industrial and labour reporting retained a very high professional standing throughout the 1970s and continued to offer the young, bright and ambitious extremely good career prospects (Seaton 1982:278). It was in the period after 1979 that these measures of status began to suggest a significant decline. Towards the end of the 1980s the turn over in journalists on the labour and industrial beat accelerated. The specialism is no longer regarded as a stepping stone to the Lobby or as a rung on the ladder towards a senior editorial career. Journalists are now much keener to move on to something new which might provide more opportunities. The membership of the Group has declined. Interviews with current and former industrial correspondents confirm the picture of a specialism in decline. Indeed, several articles have been written regarding precisely this (Jones 1988; Bassett 1988; Harper 1991). The reasons for this and the role of the State in this process will be discussed in a subsequent section.

The Group Adopts a Formal Constitution

The confidence and optimism of this period for members of the Labour and Industrial Group is reflected in the arrangements formalised in the written constitution which was adopted in 1965. The constitution lays out a set of rules which will be familiar to students of professionalisation. The objects of the Group were to,

> ...represent the interests of all Labour and Industrial correspondents, improve the facilities and amenities available for the collection of news and to stimulate informal contacts with appropriate departments and organisations.[16]

So the intention made explicit in the constitution was for the Group to act not only as a collective organisation to improve the working conditions for labour and industrial specialists but to act as a mechanism to open up a wider range of formal and informal sources of information. Through the regular events at the Cheshire Cheese in Fleet Street and the Clarence in Whitehall, the Group had always facilitated formal and informal briefings from key sources. This was now confirmed as a formal objective of the Group. At the end of the war membership limits had been increased from one to three correspondents per news organisation. The new constitution formalised an upper limit of three labour correspondents *and* three industrial correspondents per news organisation, thus doubling the upper limit on membership. This reflected the increasing numbers of specialists and the advancing division of labour internal to the specialism between the labour and industrial beats. The constitution indicated that labour and industrial journalists should be listed separately, thus confirming the division in specialisation as each membership list would be supplied to the press offices of key sources to make up separate mailing and invitation lists for news conferences, press events, and press releases. However, from an inspection of the Group's papers it appears that, in practice, the distinction between labour and industrial reporting was rarely employed by the Group's secretaries in compiling lists. It seems likely that given the need to rotate responsibilities in order to cover the desk at weekends and holiday periods, in practice it was found difficult to maintain a rigid division between the two. Negrine has recently argued that in practice specialist demarcations are frequently a matter of organisational convenience rather than a function of the distribution of 'real' expertise (1993).

The constitution also confirms the importance of London as the centre of both the labour and industrial beats. Membership was open only to the:

> London-based Labour and Industrial Correspondents employed by national and provincial UK newspapers and news magazines which are on public sale, the Press Association, the BBC News Division and ITN.[17]

The difficulty for London based correspondents dependent upon a London beat in seeking to develop significant contacts with ordinary union activists away from the metropolis has already been noted and will be discussed further below. For the moment, it is sufficient to note that the adoption of this constitution in the mid-60s confirms both the expansion in numbers occurring at this time and the confidence of the Group in seeking to maintain the mechanism of exclusivity to reinforce professional standing. Membership clearly did open up opportunities to reach particular sources of information and was a convenient way ensuring one's name appeared on the most important mailing lists for industrial and labour sources. And at the same time, however, the constitution made it clear that membership and the associated access was not available to journalists who failed to satisfy the criteria for admission to the Group. Thus, at this time, economic and financial journalists, air correspondents (who overlapped with industry), science and technical writers, and those concerned with personnel management were excluded. It is significant that in a very different climate during the 1980s the papers of the Group confirm that serious thought was being given to proposals to slacken membership restrictions and widen the definition of 'industrial' to include, for example, business and personnel journalism, in an effort to combat the decline in membership.

The Routine of Labour Journalism: Relations with Unions and the Political Elite

What was the routine for labour and industrial correspondents like in the 1960s? According to Tunstall (1971:77) labour and industrial specialists found that they could spend up to three quarters of their time devoted to their specialism. This, in itself, is in marked contrast to the contemporary scene where, with the exception of certain broadsheet papers like the *Guardian* and the *Financial Times*, many labour specialists commented that they either had to double up specialisms (for example, with education on the *Express*) or were required by news editors to became flexible 'jacks of all trades', in the absence of newsworthy labour items. Journalists on both the labour and industrial beats, during the 1960s, reported attending two to three formal press conferences each week (Tunstall 1971: 181). This would suggest that informal contact with key sources represented an important and daily part of the routine. Evidence from Tunstall also reinforces the point that the state played an important role in shaping the terrain of the beats. Labour correspondents reported enjoying excellent relations with the Ministry of Labour. It was, 'even more like a news organisation than most other ministries', (1971:180) with an organisational rhythm and a 'nose' for bad as well as good news. Given the likelihood of most serious regional disputes eventually leading to London-based negotiations, few labour correspondents reported, in Tunstall's study, making more than rare trips away from the capital. The hierarchical ordering of the specialism, however, made a difference here. If a story from the regions had to be covered, then unless it had the potential to be of exceptional importance, the 'number three' would be dispatched from the desk.

Former correspondents remember being sent to cover the less important union conferences throughout each summer which often amounted to twelve or more.[18] The industrial editor or 'number one', however, would insist upon venturing away from the capital for the most prestigious conferences, such as the Transport and General Workers' Union, the National Union of Mineworkers, the TUC itself and the Labour Party. Similarly, the daily beat in London was structured along hierarchical lines. Number three correspondents would handle the smaller stories and be assigned to foster contacts at the less politically significant source organisations. Thus, contacts with members of the political elite would be handled by the 'number one' while routine press conferences were attended by the 'number three'. The 'number one' might spend lunch time dining with senior union elders at the TUC, while the 'number two' would meet officials at the General and Municipal Workers Union and the 'number three' would be dispatched at lunch time to the Marquis of Granby in Smith Square, opposite the headquarters of the Transport and General Workers' Union, where contacts might be established with union officials working at the level of trade group secretariat (for example, docks, buses, etc). The latter was a particularly useful source for informal briefings before the Labour Party moved out of

Transport House to Walworth Road.[19] One former 'number two' remembers attending a routine briefing from the press officer at the TUC in the mid-1970s where a 'number one' after glancing around, in the middle of the briefing, exclaimed, 'Hey, I'm the only number one here, where should I be?'.[20] However, for important stories even 'number one' correspondents were likely to find themselves 'door stepping' outside ACAS or a union headquarters where significant negotiations were underway. Thus, Barrie Clement (former industrial editor on the Times and now the Independent) recalls the 'boozy nights outside ACAS' (Hill, 1993). One former labour correspondent recalls the 'door stepping' process as usually running along the following lines:

> We'd be there at the start as people went in to get some indication of how long they were going to be and then we'd go to the pub. But if you were an agency man [Press Association, etc.] you couldn't afford to miss people coming out with new information. Stories might break. But often people would come out and go to the same pub themselves. There was a distinct pub culture.[21]

The early morning, then, would be spent scanning the rival papers, mid morning two or three times a week might involve a press conference or ministry sponsored news event; lunch times would be devoted to informal meetings with contacts and by mid-afternoon industrial staff would return to the desk to begin to select stories. The working day might end around 8.00pm. It appears that there was relatively little resentment generated by the hierarchical ordering of relations with sources. 'Number two and three' journalists on the industrial desk usually accepted these kinds of arrangements as inevitable in Fleet Street. One 'number three' described his relationship with a very senior industrial editor as 'immaculately fair' and, of course, every one week end out of three and during the holiday season, the number three would take responsibility for all stories emerging, big or small.

As one former journalist says, 'the job was all about building contacts' and it was partly for this reason that a 'number two' or 'three' would be sent to cover most of the union conferences through the summer. While the desk needed to ensure that potential sources of stories were covered, attending the conferences also served as a form of apprenticeship for the labour beat. A new 'number three' would have the opportunity of meeting a large number of potential sources very quickly and would make his face familiar. One number three admits that the 'major object of any relationship with a politician or a union leader was to get a home phone number'. Contact books with key phone numbers were and still are the prize possession of journalists on the beat. The size of the contact book and the political status of the contacts within represented a measure of the professional success of the journalist on the beat. Conference debates were rarely as useful as 'what was happening in the corridors behind the rostrum'[22] where not only union leaders but often representatives of the 'big employers' might be present.

As noted above, the routine for industrial correspondents was based for much of the year upon a London beat. This inevitably restricted the access of labour correspondents to ordinary union members or even shop floor activists. Much of the time away from London was taken up with union conferences, conventions organised by employers federations or events sponsored by state departments or nationalised industries. Only during exceptional, protracted disputes were journalists likely to stray sufficiently far from the routine beat to come into contact with shop stewards or ordinary members. This was not for a lack of inclination but primarily a lack of opportunity. Journalists were likely to welcome contacts at a grass roots level for the additional 'intelligence' they might provide but it was the case that the labour and industrial beats, structured as they were around the political and industrial elites and the institutions they commanded, simply did not permit sustained contacts to develop. It was for this reason that the *Morning Star's* labour correspondent usually commanded a particular authority within the Group. Through the Communist Party connections within the shop stewards movement in the 1960s and 1970s, the industrial desk at the *Morning Star* was the one exception to the dependence of most labour correspondents upon London elite sources. Over the years, several journalists sought to 'tap in' to this network of contacts at a grass roots level. An industrial correspondent for one of the leading quality papers who entered Fleet Street in the early 1970s remembers:

> I formed my own link with the *Morning Star* on the grounds hat they were not competitors and they didn't deal with anybody else but it wasn't on a total swap basis. I'd talk to them because they had access to the stewards. It was very difficult for me as a newcomer, - I was only 27,- to make contacts with unions like the AEU. The Communist Party had this vast network of contacts and information through the shop steward movement.[23]

Correspondents working on the industrial desk in the 1960s confirm the authority which the *Morning Star* team commanded through their rank and file contacts. Significantly, such authority was not conferred upon correspondents from other 'far left' news organisations, such as Newsline. In the 1970s a journalist from the latter paper was only admitted to membership of the Group after heated debate and was never to become a fully integrated member. While the Group reflected a commitment to liberal values which proscribed discrimination against journalists on the grounds of the political orientation of the news organisation which they worked for, at the same time, concerns were voiced about the ability of ministers and other members of the political elite to brief the Group in confidence in the presence of a Trotskyist. There was a danger that the normative framework which regulated interaction between the Group and sources would be undermined. It was also the case that such groups simply did not enjoy the range of contacts within union organisations provided through the Communist Party. There was much dismay within the Group, for example, when George Sinfield, the Morning Star's correspondent credited with introducing soccer to Russia, died in the late 1960s without passing on his 'legendary' contact book to his successor or any other member of the Group.

Accounts of relationships between journalists and union leaders in the period of the 1960s and 1970s suggest a paradox. Many of the leading union officials in this period appear to have attached relatively little importance to formal arrangements for dealing with journalists. Eric Wigham's final book on trade unions written at the end of the 1960s contains much the same list of complaints about the inability of most unions to meet the organisational needs of the news media as the first book he produced in 1961 (Wigham 1961 and 1969). However, the conventional news values of journalism directed labour correspondents towards powerful individuals. The fondness of the news media for stories about 'personalities' has been well documented and in the 1960s and 1970s labour news stories were frequently constructed around the 'personalities' of leading union officials, including Jack Jones, Joe Gormley, Hugh Scanlon, and a little later David Basnett and Alan Fisher. Of course, these individuals appeared to be closely associated with the centre of power in Westminster and while there is no reason to suppose that, in practice, they possessed very different personality traits to their contemporary counterparts, their apparent proximity to the political elite and the industrial muscle which they appeared to command, allowed the news media to lend them the 'charisma' associated with the public representation of power. The inclination now amongst some labour correspondents is to mourn the passing of such 'personalities' (Pattinson,1993). Of course, it is much more likely that such 'personalities' were a product of a historically specific period which was characterised by a close association between the elite of the labour movement and the state.

Nevertheless, given the salience of 'powerful personalities' in terms of dominant news values, news organisations would encourage their labour correspondents to work hard at fostering good contacts with the elite figures of the labour movement. While few union leaders during this period attached great importance to the question of organisational arrangements for dealing with the news media, it was the case that some union leaders did develop quite amicable, even friendly relations, with some members of the Labour and Industrial Group. The hierarchical ordering of the specialism dictated that this invariably involved the labour editors and 'number ones' on the desk. Some of the relationships between union leaders and certain senior members of the Labour and Industrial Group were based upon strong friendship. Barrie Devney, industrial editor of the *Daily Express* became a personal family friend of Joe Gormley, President of the NUM in the 1970s, and his wife. Without a full-time press officer, news media enquiries were normally dealt with at that time by either the President or the General Secretary. A common complaint amongst journalists was the difficulty they experienced in contacting senior officials within unions. Nevertheless, Gormley had a sophisticated understanding of the news gathering process and sought to use the normative framework underpinning the on/off record briefing arrangements to his advantage.

> Of course, I recognise that there's a danger in this. Stories which ought to come out can get suppressed. And I've tried to be careful not to put too many things on a man's conscience, so that he has to keep quiet about them, and perhaps get scooped by someone who got the story from another source. But there are inevitably times when you have to say, 'his is what's what, but don't use just yet because there are still certain things to do and argue about.' It's a double-edged weapon, though, and you have to be careful how you use it, because we, and politicians need the Press just as much as the Press need us. (Gormley,1982:156).

Under Gormley, relationships between the NUM and the Group were good and journalists valued the access the Group enjoyed within the NUM headquarters in London, described by some labour correspondents as an 'open door' in this period and contrasted sharply with the policy under the next President, Arthur Scargill (Adeney and Lloyd,1986:242). Despite working for one of the more ideologically hostile newspapers, Barrie Devney proved a very valuable friend to Gormley, sometimes managing to insert sustained verbatim quotes from Gormley even in front page stories with the most critical headlines and on other occasions choosing not to bring certain information into the public domain (Gormley,1982:139). 'I'm sure the number of stories he's had and not used would get him sacked from the paper' (Gormley,1982:156). In one legendary incident, Devney was dining with Gormley and his wife at a restaurant. Being on 'call' Devney rang the newsroom to check in and was told to immediately follow up a story about the President of the NUM who had been sighted dining that evening with a big, fat man with glasses, suspected of being a Communist (1982:157). Despite the ideological project of the Express newspapers, Devney's close friendship with Joe Gormley was common knowledge amongst staff and appeared to be tolerated by senior editors.[24] Geoffrey Goodman, was another leading member of the Labour and Industrial Group who had particularly close contacts not only with Gormley but several members of the NUM executive which he maintained for most of his career (Goodman 1985: 175).

Gormley, then, had a clear understanding of the competitive pressures on the labour beat, the importance of intelligence or strategic information, and the routines of news production. Certain other union leaders had a similar understanding of news media dynamics. The use made by Clive Jenkins of news media strategies to promote ASTMS in the 1960s have been discussed in chapter two. Representing a white collar, technical union, Jenkins targeted both labour and science correspondents but he grew particularly close to Mike Edwards, who rose to become labour editor of the *Daily Mail* in the 1970s. Jenkins had a talent for devising short and concise sentences with an immediate news value and this made him a popular source on the labour beat.[25] Frank Chapple (EETPU general secretary in the 1970s), too, developed a tradition, which was maintained by his successor Eric Hammond, of fostering good relationships particularly with labour correspondents working for papers which were on the right of the Fleet street spectrum. Chapple was in the habit of providing off record briefings to the Group in his hotel bedroom on the eve of TUC conferences to ensure that an EETPU perspective was an acknowledged part of the political context for the week (Chapple,1984: 127-133).

The period between 1964 and 1979 was characterised by a recognised affinity between members of the elite of the trade union movement and the Labour Group. Though by no means all, a number of union leaders recognised the organisational needs of journalists and though most unions were not yet prepared to invest resources in the construction of formal arrangements for working with the news media, nonetheless, several leading union officials, though often hard to contact, were regarded as 'good sources'. The political perspectives which were dominant in the Group will be discussed further below but a number of union leaders, including Gormley, recognised that many members of the Group shared a sympathy for the values of the labour movement, if not an active commitment to the politics of the Labour Party. In short, there were some strong friendship networks which connected the Group to the union elite and there was a broader set of shared cultural assumptions about the legitimate role of unions in society, the nature of industrial relations, and the involvement of the state in the development of industrial policy. The political culture of the post-war settlement represented a bridge between the two and ensured a sharing of certain assumptions about the nature of the political and economic world. In addition, as Tunstall notes, union officials and journalists were likely to share broadly similar market positions and lifestyles. Journalists were more likely to feel at ease with union officials, willing to share a drink in the pub, than managers and senior executives who enjoyed very much higher salaries and different lifestyles (Tunstall,1971:197).

There were also, of course, some more mercenary connections. With union leaders enjoying high public profiles, there was much demand amongst publishers for autobiographies and authorised biographies. With the appropriate journalistic skills and the necessary contacts, members of the Labour and Industrial Group were well placed to cash in. Thus, Barry Devney acted as 'ghost writer' for Joe Gormley (1982), Robert Taylor (currently industrial editor at the Observer) wrote Sid Weighell's 'autobiography' (Weighell, 1983) and Geoffrey Goodman produced a biography of Frank Cousins (leader of the Transport and General Worker's Union and a Labour Cabinet Minister in this period). Weighell took the advice of the Labour Group in seeking to make the NUR more accessible for journalists following his election as General Secretary in 1975 (Weighell,1983:106-7). One or two of the 'ancien regime' within the Labour Group also moved across in this period to take up positions within the press and publicity departments of trade unions. In the 1960s and 1970s, only the white collar and public sector unions were likely to resource departments with a specific communications and publicity function, though many had union papers or journals. Hugh Chevins, one of the 'founding three' of the Labour Group, spent the final years of his professional career working as a press officer for NALGO. Later Jim Foulkes was to follow in his footsteps from the industrial desk of the Press Association.

Were union leaders able to use their contacts with the Labour Group to exert a systematic influence over the content of industrial news? The relationship between Barry Devney and Joe Gormley might lead one to suspect so, but in practice Devney was subject to the same pressures as other journalists on the beat and there is very little evidence to suggest that other union leaders were able to exert even this degree of influence. Older labour correspondents remember certain stories being handled with a degree of delicacy or being passed to another colleague in order to preserve union contacts in certain rare circumstances.[26] Tony Benn in his diaries reports hearing of pressure being exerted upon the editor of one broadsheet by trade union leaders in the late 1970s (Benn, 1990:80) but with these exceptions it seems that union leaders were rarely able to exploit contacts through the Group to achieve an editorial influence.

It is not difficult to explain why this was the case. As described in chapters three and four trade unions are inherently leaky organisations. Very few unions, including the NUM under Arthur Scargill, have been able to successfully control the flow of information from within and this has always strengthened the hands of journalists in their dealings with officials. The Labour Group has rarely been dependent upon one source within a union even if the perspective of the leading officials represents important strategic intelligence. As with the departments of state, so internal conflicts were always likely to generate flows of information as rival interests sought to exploit communication channels for their own purposes. In terms of formal conflicts, union elections often encouraged contact between union officials and journalists, as contestants tried to achieve vote-winning profiles. At the same time, though, many unions were highly politicised and continually divided between factions. Divisions within the AEU national executive were so fierce at this time that left and right factions routinely retreated to separate pubs after meetings. Journalists on the labour beat would organise a division of labour to receive the counter-briefings from each side in the pubs which were located at opposite ends of the same street near the union's headquarters in Peckham. The third dimension to internal conflict might arise when the union elite sought to exert control over 'difficult' rank and file branches, particularly if an 'unofficial dispute' was frowned upon. This, once more, was likely to generate additional, off the record briefings and quicken the flows of information for journalists to collate. Similarly, if a union leadership was required to consolidate its support at branch level in the face of competition from rival candidates or factions, correspondents would benefit from an increase in the volume of the information flows emerging from union headquarters. As one former labour correspondent remembers:

> You needed to know the General Secretaries and, perhaps, even more importantly their number two and three's [deputy general secretaries] and whether they were keen to make progress. They would feed you information which was sound and tell you where they were making a speech, perhaps, and they would know you would be there to report it. The speech might not be great shakes but if it was timed right it would go out on the P.A. and then his name would appear in the run up to a union election...if you were working for the *F.T.* or the *Times* or the *Telegraph*, then General Secretaries like to see their names on these pages. It wouldn't do any harm with the members or those at Congress House It enhanced political standing.[27]

Labour Correspondents and the Political Elite

With the election of the Wilson administration in 1964 two things changed for the Labour and Industrial Group. As discussed above, as Wilson reconstructed the departments of state, so the labour beat expanded. Secondly, relationships and sometimes friendships which had been formed between senior members of the Labour Party and journalists within the Group now represented potential channels of communication between the Group and the members of the Cabinet. Doors which had only been ajar for the Group now opened fully. To celebrate his election victory Wilson held parties at Number Ten not only for the Westminster Lobby but also for the Labour and Industrial Group. The Group began to receive regular briefings at Number Ten on a basis almost as frequent as the Lobby (Jones ,1988). One former correspondent who was first a member of the Labour Group before becoming a political correspondent describes the opportunities which opened up for labour and industrial correspondents:

> When Labour was in power and trade unions were so important in Labour Party affairs, the Labour Party conference and the national executive meetings were the property of the industrial correspondent which meant we were covering the policy making of the ruling party...I remember going to my first Labour Party conference in 1969 for the *Times*, I had a hotel room so small you could pee in the sink without getting out of bed but the paper made sure I had a direct line installed and I generated a tremendous amount of copy. The Labour Party was 'ours' and the NEC was 'ours'.[28]

The memoirs of ministers in the administrations throughout this period from 1964 to 1979 suggest numerous examples of the reasons why the Labour and Industrial Group often proved of value to the political elite because of its well established connections with senior figures   within the union movement. Barbara Castle was a member of the Cabinet as Minister for Overseas Development at the very beginning of the administration. Through her marriage to Ted Castle, by this time a senior editor on the *Mirror*, she knew many of the Labour Group socially, though the Diaires suggest she only enjoyed personal friendships with a much smaller number. Geoffrey Goodman was regarded as 'a close personal friend' (Castle 1984:115) and the evidence also suggests that Eric Wigham (*The Times*) was regarded as more than simply a contact. Barbara Castle took the trouble to send a note to him thanking him for the *Times'* coverage of a rail dispute   (Castle 1984:501). With Ted Castle, Barbara would sometimes attend social occasions for journalists including New Year parties at the Goodmans and when finally in charge at the Ministry of Labour, she made a point of arranging a regular Christmas party for the Labour and Industrial Group. Through the diaries there is quite frequent mention of particular labour correspondents, including Goodman (*The Sun*), Monty Meth (*The Daily Mail*), Jimmy Margach (*Sunday Times*), John Torode (*The Guardian*), John Elliott (*F.T.*), Eric Wigham (*Times*) and Keith McDowell (*Daily Mail*) (Castle, 1984). One of the former labour correspondents interviewed for the present study remembers:

Interviewer:
> Were industrial correspondents working alongside political correspondents at this stage?

Interviewee:
> Oh very much so and at a very high level. I mean Geoffrey Goodman was on
> very good terms with all the ministers. Ted Castle acted as liaison between
> the political and industrial sides. Barbara used to come to our staff parties.
> It was unlikely that we would come out with a bald attack upon Barbara,
> although Ted never tried to influence what Geoffrey and we wrote.[29]

The Diaries illustrate on a number of occasions the ability of labour and industrial correspondents to provide Barbara Castle with valuable information at an early stage. It was John Torode, for example, who provides a rapid briefing for Barbara Castle on the way in which George Woodcock (General Secretary of the TUC in 1969) had responded to the publication of 'In Place of Strife' (Castle 1984:592) and also Torode who let Castle know informally that Vic Feather (at this time a senior figure within the TUC) was becoming increasingly 'unhappy' with her policies at the Ministry of Labour (Castle 1984: 594). The reaction of union leaders to her policies at the Ministry of Transport were conveyed to her via Goodman and Ted Castle (Castle 1984: 115) and even news of a fundamental restructuring of the departments and the closure of the Department of Economic Affairs was first communicated to her by Ted Castle, through Geoffrey Goodman (25th March 1968). Similarly, a decade later it was Paul Routledge (at this time labour correspondent for the *Times*) who was able to give Tony Benn, then Secretary of State for Energy, advance warning of Terry Duffy's emergence as the new President of the AUEW (Benn 1990: 297). Benn was also close to Geoffrey Goodman who would dine quite regularly with the Benns. The diary comments, 'I like Geoffrey Goodman very much; in many ways I find myself more in sympathy with him than anyone else in Fleet Street' (1990: 231). Goodman and Benn were also drawn together through the common experience of both being subjects of security service surveillance (1990:231 and 383). Benn is given an inside account of the furious reaction of David Bassnett and other union leaders to the failure of Callaghan to call an early general election, by Paul Routledge whilst at dinner (1990: 358). Even Callaghan as Prime Minister relied upon the Labour and Industrial Group to provide an insight into the thinking and likely reactions of the senior union leaders regarding pay restraints in the late 1970s (Callaghan,1987:ch 15). One labour correspondent working for a tabloid paper in the 1960s recalls:

> Quite often because labour correspondents were so close to the TUC, the Number Ten political staff would ask, 'which way will it go, you know more about what's happened at the executive meeting than we do?' An elongated table at the TUC prevented everyone from seeing everything but because of our excellent contacts we knew exactly what had happened within a minute of the executive meeting finishing...we had certain friends we would give names to, such as 'leakworthy', and not just within the TUC but even the Cabinet, including Conservative ones.[30]

Similarly, a labour correspondent who worked for the Times in the 1970s, contrasts the experience of the Group during the two great coal disputes of the 1970s and 1980s. In 1974, he had been told by his editor that the Prime Minister had complimented the paper's labour and industrial team for their coverage of the dispute. The Prime Minister regarded this as the most useful source of information for the purpose of assessing the thinking and possible tactics of the NUM. This correspondent was rewarded at the end of the dispute by his editor with a free two week Thompson holiday in Greece. In 1984, according to this correspondent, it was the frequent experience of the Labour Group to find that their own editors had better information and intelligence than them. This was because a government with a very different orientation and a distinct political agenda sought to exercise far greater influence in the management of industrial news during the dispute and did this by ensuring that strong channels of communication were established between ministers and key members of the senior management team at British Coal, on the one hand, and senior editorial staff and political correspondents, rather than labour correspondents, on the other. This will be discussed further below. For the moment it is sufficient to note that in the period between 1964 and 1979 the Labour and Industrial Group, through its connections with union leaderships, represented an important source of industrial and labour information for the political elite. There were few rewards for labour and industrial correspondents at the end of the 1984 Coal Dispute.

Of course, good relationships with the Group were likely to be of value to senior politicians for more familiar reasons, as well. Barbara Castle was advised by Harold Wilson, as soon as her predecessor as Minister of Labour, Ray Gunter, resigned that she should immediately speak to the Labour Group in order to counter-brief against any possible comments he might make (Castle,1984: 475). Similarly, in 1968 when the government began to face mounting press criticism of its handling of a rail dispute, Castle launched a public relations offensive in which she lunched with pairs of labour correspondents every day for a week in an attempt to ensure that a more favourable perspective emerged in the news coverage (1984 : 478-483). The British Rail Board had conceded a generous settlement to the rail unions and press comment had suggested that this was a consequence of Government encouragement for the Board to break the Government's own incomes policy. Significantly, Barbara Castle was told by a leader writer on the *Financial Times* that this story had emerged from an off-record briefing from within the Treasury. Inter-departmental rivalry as an important source for the Labour Group will be discussed further below. Not only was the Group likely to be targeted by politicians interested in promoting a favourable account of the Government's record on industrial relations. For senior figures in the Labour Party, the support of leading trade unionists was very important for their personal careers and knowledge of which trade union leaders might be favourably or unfavourably disposed towards them was most valuable (for example, Crossman 1979: 316). Members of the Group were ideally placed, enjoying contact with both elites, to mark an ambitious Labour M.P.'s card in terms of union support and career prospects.

Wilson's administrations were notorious for the amount of leaking motivated by rivalry of one form or another. Whilst Wilson suspected all within his Cabinet as potential leakers and denounced the practice in Cabinet meetings, Crossman believed on more than one occasion that he was a victim of non-attributable briefings which could only have emerged from the Prime Minister's own press office (Crossman 1979:79). Crossman was convinced that Wilson was providing off-record briefings to undermine the position of George Brown at the Department of Economic Affairs in the mid-60s (Crossman 1979: 103). He also believed that Wilson was briefing against the enemies of 'In Place of Strife' within the Cabinet in 1969 (Crossman 1979:559) In his own account of office, however, Wilson claims that he was compelled to leak information to the press on one exceptional occasion only (Wilson 1979: 143). Crossman both used the practice ruthlessly against others and frequently devotes space in his dairies to identifying other perpetrators, most frequent suspects being Tony Benn (suspected of leaking proposals before being submitted to Cabinet, 1979:109), George Brown (1979:81), Callaghan and Castle (1979:220), and Wilson himself (1979:198). The Political Lobby were likely to be the most frequent beneficiaries of such political jostling but the proximity of the Labour Group to particular Ministers meant that they were likely to receive a share of the non-attributable information flowing outwards from the political elite as a consequence of political rivalry. Thus, Crossman turns to Peter Jenkins, then still a labour correspondent, to spread rumours hostile to Wilson in 1969 (1979:609).

Given the degree of proximity between the political elite and Group in this period, it is little wonder that considerable professional rivalry was generated with the Westminster Lobby. As one former labour correspondent recalls:

> ...there had always been intense jealousy between the Labour and Industrial Group and the Lobby. They hated the fact that we came to prominence in the 60s and 70s because of the sheer volume of stories and disputes which generated copy. The Lobby jealously guarded its access...they have far greater self-esteem than us. We have a fairly robust view about ourselves and the job that we do. We're not as highfalutin and prima donna-ish...They are an immensely self-esteeming group. We enjoy ourselves and we also take a more realistic view of our position in society and our position in the paper.[31]

However, the Labour Group never supplanted the position of the Westminster Lobby. In reading the diaries of Crossman, Castle and Benn or the memoirs of, for example, Wilson, Callaghan (1987), Brown (1971) or Ted Short (1989), one is struck by the relatively greater frequency with which the political elite communicated with political rather than labour correspondents. In Benn's diaries only the most senior labour correspondents, the labour editors or 'number ones', such as Geoffrey Goodman or Paul Routledge, appear as dinner guests or regular contacts. In contrast, a large number of political correspondents and senior editors are wined and dined by the Benns, including Hugo Young, Harold Evans, Alan Watkins, Adam Raphael, a number of energy correspondents, and even Bill Deedes of the *Telegraph*. This point is confirmed in the memoirs of Joe Haines (1977) who acted as press officer at Number Ten for most of the Wilson era. Only Geoffrey Goodman, once again, from the Labour Group appears to be a significant player in Haines' universe. In the main, Haines spent his time dealing with the Westminster Lobby rather than the Labour Group. This was also confirmed by former labour correspondents who noted that despite the overlap in the political and labour beats, labour correspondents rarely approached Joe Haines as a source on their beat and never contacted the press office at Number Ten. Although Geoffrey Goodman was drafted into government at the Counter Inflation Policy Unit in 1976 to take responsibility for the presentation of the government's anti-inflation strategy, it was to Alistair Hetherington (*Guardian* editor) that the political elite turned to advise on the handling of Wilson's land deal scandal (Haines 1977: 194), and to Bill Grieg (*Mirror* political editor) to work under George Brown as public relations advisor to the Department of Economic Affairs (Brown 1971: 194). Terence Lancaster, who succeeded Bill Grieg as political editor at the *Mirror*, was also very close to Wilson and Marcia Williams, providing them with advice regarding the negative publicity generated by their relationship and the land deal controversy (Haines 1977: 204). Crossman drafted in John Beavan and Alan Fairclough, both on the political staff of the *Mirror*, as policy advisors and both Crossman and Wilson approached the *Mirror's* editor, Hugh Cudlipp on several occasions (Crossman 1979:550). Under Labour administrations, then, as well as Conservative, close relationships evolved between the political elite and established figures within political journalism. Senior Labour politicians recognised the strategic importance of the few left of centre papers in Fleet Street and the potential political resource which sympathetic political correspondents, working for such papers, represented. In this sense, political correspondents and the

Westminster Lobby always had the edge over the Labour and Industrial Group.

News Flows and Tensions Within the State

Nevertheless, given the nature of the state under both Labour and Conservative regimes, and the departmental structure which reflected the inclination of the state to actively intervene in economic and industrial policy, it was inevitable that journalists within the Group would begin to move in circles close to senior ministers. It was also inevitable, then, that they would benefit from the flows of information generated through tensions and rivalries, not only involving individual politicians but also at an inter-departmental level. Perhaps, the sharpest of these and the most fruitful for members of the Group involved the Treasury and the Department of Economic Affairs which had been originally established by Wilson in 1964 in order to develop a strategic economic perspective, within which the Treasury would be obliged to work on more immediate micro-economic issues. With the new department enthusiastic for policies of economic expansion but the Treasury traditionally more cautious and inclined to policies of retrenchment (Wilson 1971:710), serious political tensions were inevitable, as each department sought to challenge the authority of the other. George Brown was suspected of using the press to undermine the political authority of the Treasury as early as 1965 and Wilson addressed an appeal to the whole Cabinet in an effort to suppress the growing volume of illicit information which the inter-departmental conflict appeared to be producing (Crossman 1979:81). Nevertheless, such tensions continued and were actually exacerbated by Wilson's decision to break up and decentralise the Government's Office of Information, which he regarded as a 'Tory propaganda machine'. The result was that each department began to organise its own information services, advertising campaigns and briefings for journalists, on and off record (Crossman 1979:242). Naturally, the nature of each set of departmental briefings was likely to reflect the departmental perspective on policy and the performance of other departments. Thus, leaks and counter leaks between the Treasury under Jim Callaghan and the DEA under George Brown, continued throughout the early years of the administration (Crossman 1979:220).

The Treasury continued to be at the centre of a number of departmental feuds which grew, on occasion, into three way departmental propaganda battles. Barbara Castle was tipped off by a member of the Group that the

Treasury was suggesting to journalists, off the record, that she had been responsible, as Minister for Labour, for encouraging employers to settle above the government's pay norm (Castle,1984: 481). However, Castle also found herself embroiled in an of the record briefing battle with Crossman, who opposed 'In Place of Strife' , the main policy proposal for the regulation of industrial relations developed by her ministry (Crossman,1979: 564). Significantly, battles between the Treasury and other departments concerned with economic and industrial policy have continued through the 1970s and into the 1980s. Michael Heseltine reports conflicts between the Treasury, with an orientation towards the City, and the Department of Trade and Industry which sought 'a separate dialogue' with managers, companies and other government departments (Heseltine,1987: 124). However, in the different circumstances of the 1980s, such tensions did not produce the copious flows of information to the Labour and Industrial Correspondents Group which characterised previous decades.

Summary

Perhaps the period between 1964 and 1979 represents the pinnacle in the Group's development, although it failed to supplant the elite position of the Westminster Lobby. Nevertheless, it did represent a unique period for labour and industrial journalism. The state under both Conservative and Labour administrations continued to expand a departmental structure which extended the boundaries of the labour and industrial beats, a process which began during the Second World War but accelerated through the 1960s and 1970s. Under Labour administrations, however, particular members of the Labour Party elite who were familiar with leading members of the Group and often had a common sympathy for labourist and social democratic perspectives, occupied key positions within the State's departmental structure. This meant that not only the departmental structure but the relationships and administrative culture associated with these departments frequently offered favourable terrain for labour journalism. The interconnections between Labour politicians and labour journalists allowed the latter to benefit from the flows of information both on and off the record which began to spring from the centre of the government. The strength of such interconnections was also reflected in the recognition of the authority of the Group which the Labour administrations offered through the co-option of labour journalists to key positions within the state and the extent to which the advice of members of the Group was sought. Beyond the personal interconnections between labour correspondents and the political elite, the interventionist orientation of both Labour and Tory administrations and the continuing 'hegemony' of the values of the post-war settlement associated with these forms of government, ensured that the editorial perspectives of most news organisations continued to prioritise labour news. This, of course, was to significantly change in the next decade.

Notes

1. Interviews were conducted with a specific focus upon the history of labour and industrial journalism, with Henry Clover (former labour number three on the *Sun* between 1965 and 1970 and subsequently press officer for the NUT), Paul Routledge (former labour editor of the *Times* between 1969 and 1987 and subsequently political correspondent for the *Observer*), Geoffrey Goodman (former industrial editor for the *Sun* and the *Daily Mirror* from the 1960s to the early 1980s), Jim Fookes (former labour number two at the Press Association in the 1960s and 1970s and later one of the team within the NALGO Publicity Department), Terry Pattinson (former number two and labour editor of the *Daily Mirror* during the 1970s and 1980s), and Clare Dover (formerly science and then health correspondent on the *Daily Telegraph* and *Daily Express* during the 1970s and 1980s). In addition, material drawn from the interviews conducted for the analysis of contemporary patterns with Phillip Bassett (former *Financial Times* labour editor now with the *Times*) and David Norris (then labour editor for the *Daily Mail*) has been included.
2. The papers include minutes of some but not all Group meetings, draft programmes of events, letters written by officers of the Group, bills and receipts for expenses. These are not kept in any systematic order and have been handed down from secretary to secretary over the years. It is assumed that the papers relating to the period before 1982 have been destroyed, as systematic archival practice is not one of the Group's strong points.
3. Evans (1953) confirms the formal establishment of the Labour and Industrial Correspondents Group in 1937. A new constitution was introduced in 1965 which may be the source of the confusion.
4. NALGO introduced a press bureau in the 1930s as did the TUC. Civil Service and white collar staff associations appear to have attached more importance to public relations than manual unions for a number of years before and after the Second World War.
5. Evans (1953).
6. A reluctance to enforce the law allowed over one thousand illegal disputes to have occured by 1941. The number accelerated through the War. Bevin insisted that conciliation rather than legal coercion was likely to offer the best solution (Barnes and Reid, 1982:159).
7. Author's interviews with former number two and three correspondents during June and July 1993. This is confirmed in the accounts of contemporary correspondents, too.
8. Only one of the interviewees disputed the chronological framework employed

here. One correspondent insisted that decline set in during the early 1960s rather than at the end of the 1970s.

9.   See Jones (1988) for an example of this kind of explanation.
10. A former number three in conversation with the author, summer 1993.
11. MORI surveys of Industrial and Labour Correspondents, conducted on behalf of British Gas and later British Rail (1982 to 1993), regularly showed journalists rating nationalised industries like British Rail, the National Coal Board, and the Electricity Boards, as amongst the best sources and most efficient organisations in responding to media enquiries. This was in marked contrast to most private sector companies.
12. Author's interview with industrial correspondents including those who also had Lobby experience during June and September 1992 and August 1993.
13. Papers of the Labour and Industrial Correspondents' Group.
14. Membership secretaries interviewed included Terry Pattinson, Kevin McGuire, and Paul Routledge. Thier terms of office covered the period between 1971 and 1993. Their estimates for previous decades may be based upon the 'folklore' of the Group but no official membership records appear to have been retained for the period before 1982.
15. Interviews conducted with a former labour editor and a number two, summer 1993.
16. Copy of the constitution produced for the 1968 AGM no in the possession of the author.
17. Ibid.
18. Interviews with former labour correspondents, summer 1993.
19. Details confirmed by former labour correspondents. Ibid.
20. Interview conducted during the summer 1993.
21. Ibid.
22. Ibid.
23. Ibid.
24. Ibid.
25. Ibid.
26. Ibid.
27. Interview with former labour and political correspondent, summer 1993.
28. Ibid.
29. Interview with former number three, summer 1993.
30. Ibid.
31. Interview with former labour and political correspondent, summer 1993.

6 Decline in the Fortunes of Labour Journalism

As we have seen, the state through the political orientation of the government of the day, plays an important part in shaping the political environment in which labour journalism is undertaken. The political and ideological climates which are fostered by particular governments with distinctive political projects have a powerful influence in shaping the editorial perspectives of news organisations. The departmental arrangements of particular governments will order the boundaries of some of the most important news beats and the orientation of government ministers and their civil servants towards the news media will determine the degree of access to the political elite which specialist correspondents enjoy. While some journalists remain convinced that the decline in the fortunes of labour and industrial journalism is the product of a temporary cyclical down-turn, a 'natural' process connected to the internal rhythm of professional journalism, and others blame the Miners Strike ('every labour story after that was inevitably an anti-climax'), more fundamental causes of decline are strongly associated with the arrival of a new government in 1979 with a very distinctive political project.

It is not suggested that governments exercising control over the state have the power to order the marginalisation of those branches of journalism which are out of favour. Rather, the policies adopted and the political climate fostered around those policies will slowly, over a period of time (particularly if one party remains in office for more than one term), begin to affect the priorities of editorial teams and the decisions they make concerning the use of resources within their news organisations. If Thatcher had not been successful in emasculating much of the trade union movement and if trade unions had sufficient political power to insist upon the retention of their position close to the centre of government, then the fortunes of labour journalism may have remained more buoyant in the 1980s.

There is, of course, considerable debate concerning the degree to which Thatcherism should be understood in terms of the political effectivity of the administration or the 'inevitable' political articulation of deeper economic forces at work in the re-structuring of British capitalism.[1] The decline in labour journalism is not a process unique to Britain. Tunstall noted this process occurring in the USA in the 1960s (1971:95) where unionisation was already below 20% of the active labour force. In fact, in the USA evidence of decline in labour journalism can be found even in the early 1950s (Hoyt, 1984). However, it is too simplistic to equate the fortunes of labour and industrial correspondents only with the vitality of trade unionism. As we have seen, trade unions represented an important source but by no means the only source of information for labour correspondents. The departments of state were probably more significant in the supply of routine information on a more regular basis, even if the 'bigger' stories often concerned trade unions. Beyond this, however, it is important to note the power of the state in framing news and offering political criteria with which to assess the importance of events. If trade unions were permitted by the state to enjoy permanent 'insider status', it is likely that even with a low membership base they would be regarded by editorial teams as 'significant' in terms of decisions over the allocation of staff and resources within news organisations.

It is not hard to find evidence of decline in the papers of the Labour and Industrial Correspondents' Group which have been retained since 1982. Tunstall found 33 correspondents working a specific labour beat (excluding an industrial beat) in the mid 60s and estimates for membership of the Group in the 1970s suggest a minimum of at least seventy (according to former officers of the Group) and a maximum of possibly one hundred if Seaton's estimate is correct (Seaton,1982). At the beginning of each year the Group would publish a list of accredited members and the news organisations they worked for. This provides a good measure of the importance news organisations attached to labour and industrial journalism because the rules governing membership of the Group required journalists to be formally identified by news organisations staffing their labour and industrial desks.[2] Thus, Group membership lists provide a good measure not just of professional interest amongst individual journalists but the importance attached to labour and industrial journalism by national and provincial newspapers, broadcasting newsrooms, and the news agencies.[3] Nevertheless, the records of the Group reveal the following pattern of membership in the 1980s (table 6.1).

Table 6.1 Membership of the Labour and Industrial Correspondents' Group,1983-1989

Year	Membership Total
1983	58
1984	65
1985	65
1986	no record
1987	62
1988	57
1989	55

Source: Papers of the Group.

Membership records for subsequent years are less complete, itself an indication of the degree of organisational decline which the Group began to experience during this period. In 1993 the Group Secretary, Kevin McGuire (then at the *Daily Telegraph*), estimated membership at 'just below fifty'.[4] It is possible that even this figure is an over-estimate. If a calculation is made on the basis of known labour or industrial staff attached to desks in the main news organisations, an accurate current figure may be below forty. There has been a decline in the number of staff attached to every industrial desk. We can safely say, then, that during the period since 1979 membership has dropped by anything between 25% and 55% depending upon estimates of peak membership in the 1970s. In 1984, the Group's Chair reported 'for the first time in several years membership was increasing',[5] which resulted from the sudden increase in activity associated with the 1984/85 Coal Strike. However, after this period in the mid-1980s, the long term pattern of decline in membership continued. It is important to note that this decline in membership could be detected before the Coal Strike and before the decrease in strike rates became most pronounced. After all, in the early 1980s there were a number of major disputes before the combined impact of mass unemployment and legislative constraints began to severely restrain union resistance.

In terms of the national dailies by 1994, the *Financial Times* had cut its labour and industrial team from six in 1985 to three, the *Guardian* had moved from five to two, the *Telegraph* from four to one, the *Mirror* from four to two, the *Sun* from two to one, the *Express* from two to half (the industrial correspondent at the time of writing also covered the education beat), and the *Daily Star* scrapped its labour and industrial desk in 1987.[6]

> The first national I worked on as an industrial correspondent was the Sun and before that I worked on the P.A. [Press Association]. There were three industrial corespondents at the P.A. and when I joined the *Sun* I was number one out of three. I think they're down to one now. Same at the Standard [*London Evening Standard*], there used to be two, myself and other dealing purely with industrial stories and we'd both be writing trade union stories a lot of the time. Now there are fewer staff, they've all been thinned out. The *Morning Star* and, perhaps, the *FT* are only ones retaining staff levels.[7]

Not only have news organisations reduced the numbers on the industrial and labour desks but journalists have found it increasingly necessary to embrace much wider briefs. Few can now specialise exclusively in labour news and many are keen to broaden their perspectives to include employment, personnel, industrial and economic issues in order to preserve their marketablity. Nicholas Jones estimated that in 1988 the balance within the Group had moved away from labour towards industrial specialists for the first time (1988) and more recently the *F.T.*, renowned for its labour news, has abandoned the labour page in favour of an 'employment section' (Hill, 1993).

The papers of the Group reveal a growing concern not only about the decline in absolute numbers but also about the loss of vitality and energy within the Group as the 1980s unfold. In 1982, the tone of the minutes of A.G.M. are still up-beat, with regrets being expressed about the failure of the officers of the Group to find ways of spending surplus monies on a 'really good thrash'.[8] In 1983, however, fears concerning redundancy were already so significant that the rules of the constitution were amended at the A.G.M. to allow journalists who had suffered redundancy and were no longer accredited through a news organisation to retain membership. The records of meetings in 1983 also reveal growing tensions and conflicts between officers and members. At a meeting in September, there were formal calls for the resignation of all officers. Minutes record a row breaking out over the planning of a social event using Group funds to subsidise the bar, 'the original idea was for a piss up, it seems to have grown out of all proportion'. More significantly, urgent complaints were registered about the failure of the Group to work effectively through the year to fulfil the functions for which it was originally formed to perform. The lunch time and evening events at which union leaders, ministers, representatives of employers and nationalised industries were invited to meet the Group had not been successful and had petered out through the year. Officers defended their record by pointing to the low attendances at the early events, 'only nine people for the director of the NEDC, only 14 people for the Chancellor of the Exchequer'. Speakers from the floor pointed to the failure of the officers to collect subscriptions or keep accurate membership records. As the meeting grew more chaotic, one speaker moved that the meeting should be abandoned because up to 25% of those present were probably not members.[9]

Records in subsequent years suggest a continuing problem of low morale, low attendance and inactivity, although not amidst such chaotic meetings. In 1984, the Group Secretary had to write to the AUEW to apologise for the low number of Group members who turned up for a social and briefing event organised around a trip down the river to the new Thames Barrier, paid for by the union. In 1985, the Treasurer, in his annual report, noted that the explanation for the depletion in funds was to be found in the low attendance at Group functions resulting in losses. The Treasurer signed off by 'wishing everyone all the best for a redundant future once the Miners Strike is over'. By the late 1980s, the records suggest a picture which will be familiar to anyone who has had experience of a moribund local branch of a political party, with evidence of a rapid turn-over in officerships, low attendance at meetings and by the beginning of the next decade, incomplete records of meetings in each year. There are far fewer papers dealing with the most recent years than the first half of the 1980s. In 1988, a letter sent by the Secretary to all members asking for suggestions regarding the future of the Group and how best to revitalise it, had itself 'received only a dismal response'. In 1991, the Secretary reported that 'the absence of the Chair on business overseas for most of the year resulted in 1991 being a wee bit quieter than usual' but the Secretary added in an attempt to remain upbeat in tone, 'plans are underway to arrange a series of newsmaking and enjoyable events'. By 1992 the Secretary found himself writing to the *Guardian* in an attempt to persuade one journalist on the industrial desk to actually join the Group.[10]

Twice in 1983 the Group attempted to secure the same rights of access in the Palace of Westminster as the Political Lobby.[11] On both occasions requests for passes were denied by the Sergeant at Arms. It might be supposed that these requests might have reflected the confidence of the Group in seeking to make further advances upon the traditional territory of political correspondents. However, the records suggest that such attempts were prompted more by desperation than confidence. The decisions to request access at Westminster were made in the context of a search for a strategy to bolster the perceived decline in the standing of the Group.

In 1985 the Group Secretary intervened to complain to the Directorate of Public Affairs at British Rail about 'the growing tendency to hold selective briefings. And it is understood there was a briefing for the Lobby'.[12] The complaint is significant not only because it suggests that by the mid-1980s the Westminister Lobby was beginning to threaten the traditional territory of industrial correspondents but also because the practice of selective briefing infringed norms concerning the collective identity of the Group. The Group existed to benefit all accredited industrial correspondents, not a select few and certainly not the Westminster Lobby. Earlier, in 1983 for example, the Group wrote to Lord McCarthy to protest 'in the strongest possible terms' about the restrictions on numbers of correspondents permitted to attend the Rail Staff National Tribunal'.[13]

In 1988 officers of the Group undertook, 'a review of membership following the gradual decline from a peak of about 75 to the current total of around 50 ...income has dropped accordingly'. A proposal arising from this review was 'to broaden the membership base to include energy, political, and financial correspondents who have a link with or interest in industrial and labour affairs'. This proposal partly reflected the blurring of traditional specialist boundaries which had been caused by the changing news priorities of editorial staff and the drive to increase the productivity of journalists by demanding greater flexibility and less specialisation. However, the proposal also suggested a degree of desperation in contemplating a survival strategy which would announce for the Group a movement away from the distinctive field of labour journalism - the Group's original raison d'être. The 'dismal response' from Group members to this and other suggestions, meant that officers felt they could not claim a mandate for such radical changes. The rule requiring membership to be restricted to journalists working full time on the industrial and labour desk was not amended but officers decided to examine 'borderline cases' more carefully.[14] In practice, it seems clear that the membership rules have been relaxed as indicated by acceptance in 1991 of an application from a journalist working for 'Personnel Today'. Very few of the current membership work exclusively upon labour news and many devote a majority of their time to a wide industrial brief which may take in employment and personnel issues, economic and industrial developments, European or international labour markets, energy and technological stories, not to mention financial journalism. This is in contrast to 1983 when an application from a journalist on '*The Engineer*' was rejected.[15]

We've all had to change, otherwise you lose the job. There was a bit of time after the Miners' defeat when there was a move to switch to employment issues and we all trundled off to the Institute of Personnel Management and wrote worthy pieces about human resources and skill shortages. That seems to have gone away and people are looking at consumer type stuff. A lot of industrial correspondents, particularly on the tabloids, will go into the regulator stuff like OFTEL, OFWAT, OFGAS. Those are covered by industrial correspondents although they are actually consumer stories. British Telecom are a good example... it's not what you expect to do, so yes the role has changed and is constantly evolving, a bit like the English language.[16]

Political marginalisation

Several factors are bound together in contributing to the decline in the fortunes of the Group. The decline in the numbers of journalists staffing the industrial and labour desks certainly contributed to the sapping of morale. However, this in itself could not explain the decline not only in numbers but vitality and dynamism. After all, the decline in numbers was being countered to a degree through the relaxation in membership rules. Clearly, the emasculation of trade unions through the 1980s was a process crucial in explaining the waning influence of the Group. However, here it is necessary to consider precisely why the decline in fortunes of the labour movement brought with it decline for the Group as well. It was not simply that union membership began to dramatically fall. Many relatively small unions had been regarded as highly newsworthy in the past (ASTMS or the NUS for example). More fundamental than the declining numbers of members was the loss of political potency and political significance which were associated with declining membership but not caused by it alone. Here, of course, the orientation of the state and ideological climate generated by a new government with a distinctive political project was important in conjunction with the broader economic processes through which labour markets were re-structured and many strongly unionised employment sectors severely weakened. A weakened union movement, increasingly bound by legislative constraints, was unable to effectively counter the propaganda emerging from government which repeatedly reinforced the message that unions had little relevance in the contemporary industrial environment and no longer could claim a legitimate place at the centre of government.

In focusing upon the power of the state and the political project of a new government three crucial and inter-related processes can be identified in determining the declining fortunes of the Group:

(a) the erosion of the hegemony of the values of the post-war settlement amongst opinion leaders and senior editorial staff within news organisations,

(b) the gradual dismantling of the departmental structure of state which underpinned the post-war settlement and defined the labour beat,

and

(c) the growing political marginalisation of the Group which became a more and more pronounced feature of the 1980s.

What unites all these processes is the power of the state both in influencing the dominant ideological and political perspectives and in granting or denying 'insider status' to particular groups of journalists.

One former labour correspondent remembers that in the final eighteen months of the Callaghan administration, as tensions between the government and unions increased, the Group sensed a 'cooling' in its own relationship with the political elite. There were fewer briefings and less informal contact because the political perspective within Cabinet was already shifting away from the values of the post-war settlement and partnership with organised labour. With the arrival of Thatcher in office, however, the Group's world was suddenly turned upside down.

Interviewer:

Some journalists believe that the decline of the Group started with the defeat of the miners in 1984-85 but it sounds as if it started a bit earlier?

Interviewee:

It started long before that with the end of the Labour government. Obviously we were closer to a Labour Government because our chief contacts were with the unions. Thatcher hated the Group [Labour and Industrial Correspondents' Group]. She saw us once, didn't like us and never saw us again. That's when she was leading the Opposition. Then all access to the roots of power were cut off and in the same way as the unions were thrown out of Downing Street so were we thrown out. Our power diminished sharply over night. It wasn't the Miners' strike, that was just the culmination of a process which had began in the last days of the Labour Government.[17]

This journalist worked as a labour correspondent throughout the 1970s and the first half of the 1980s to the end of the Coal Strike. For much of this period he was the labour editor of a leading quality newspaper. He recalls a growing reluctance on the part of Labour Party sources to maintain the traditional degree of proximity to the Group. The Labour Government, he believes, had already begun the process of pushing the trade union elite away from the centre of government and 'just as the unions were being told to take the medicine, so were we.' He continues:

That process was intensified as soon as the Tories took office. We were marginalised, just as the unions were marginalised because they [the Government] didn't want to know about unions and they didn't want to know about us.[18]

This process of political marginalisation is confirmed in the papers of the Group. The records for the year 1982 (the earliest records still retained) indicate that the Group had written to the Labour Party leadership seeking to *re-establish* pre-Conference briefings. The records for 1983 formally note the 'shock' felt by members at the refusal of the Labour Party leader, Michael Foot, to accept an invitation to meet them. Perhaps even more significantly, the papers for 1983, report that the Secretary had written to Bernard Ingham, seeking to re-establish briefing sessions with the Prime Minister and had been refused. In his annual report for 1984, the Chair commented upon the 'need to re-build the authority of the Group' but a year earlier speakers from the floor, at a meeting in September 1983, expressed this sentiment in even stronger terms. The minutes record one member, the labour editor of a left of centre broadsheet, commenting,

...it was quite obvious that the Group was going down...at a time the trade union movement was in retreat and the Government was here for a long time, as a serious organisation the Group was treated with derision by government departments. As serious journalists, something had to be done about it very quickly.[19]

One must be careful not to overstate the degree of change. The papers of the Group in the early 1980s suggest that at a formal level, the Group were not cast entirely into the political wilderness. In 1983, the Group Secretary wrote to a number of the institutions on the labour and industrial beat, including the Department of Employment, the Treasury, the Department of Trade and Industry, and the Labour Party, suggesting formal meetings. The papers do not record how many invitations were accepted but it is clear that the Group anticipated continuing routine formal contact with departments of state. Neil Kinnock, the new leader of the Labour Party, agreed to re-establish contact with the Group but on a far less regular basis than in the Wilson era (one or two briefings each year compared to the weekly meetings at Number Ten in the 1960s). The political in-fighting between left and right inside Cabinet which characterised the early years of the Thatcher administration also generated some useful copy for the Group when particular ministers were involved. Jim Prior, for example, at the Department of Employment fought back against a campaign of hostile selective briefings to the Westminster Lobby by going off-record with the Labour and Industrial Correspondents' Group (Prior,1986:163). For a time, presumably, the Labour Group represented an attractive alternative point of contact with the news media for members of the Conservative administration who felt threatened by the very close relationship which formed between the Bernard Ingham, the Number Ten press secretary, and political correspondents on right-of-centre dailies. However, as Mrs Thatcher secured the balance of power within her Cabinet, such conflicts subsided. While political correspondents sometimes appear in the memoirs of Conservative ministers who occupied positions formerly of importance on the labour and industrial beat in previous decades, these accounts suggest very little interaction with the Labour and Industrial Group (Parkinson,1992; Heseltine,1987) by the mid-1980s.

Annual invitations to speak at Group functions certainly continue to be accepted by ministers. Gillian Sheppard, the current Employment Minister, was a guest speaker in 1992. Before her, Kenneth Clarke, during his spell at the Department of Trade and Industry, Tom King (Employment), Leon Brittan (D.T.I.), and Norman Fowler (Employment) have all attended formal functions as members of Conservative Cabinets. Tony Blair, Gordon Brown and John Smith have similarly represented the Labour Party front bench team in recent years. However, it is clear that the organic link which the Group enjoyed with Labour administrations in the 1960s and 1970s is no longer in existence. Since 1990, when the TUC- Labour Party Liaison Committee was abandoned (Harper,1990), the Labour Party has continued to distance itself in organisational terms from the unions and with each subtle movement, so the political position of the Group has further been undermined.

Rather than weekly briefings and daily informal contacts, the Group can anticipate an annual ministerial appearance at a 'Group do' and the routine service provided by the press offices within ministerial departments. Ministers may still want to talk to industrial correspondents when they have something to sell and the willingness of a number of former labour correspondents to accept a wider brief is sometimes rewarded in these circumstances. Phillip Bassett, for example, recently got an 'exclusive' interview with Micheal Heseltine on the re-structuring of the DTI and the re-introduction of departments dedicated to the sponsorship of key business sectors, which appeared on the business section of the *Times* (Bassett, 1993). However, the regular and routine flows of information and exchanges of 'intelligence' between the political elite and the Group have disappeared. Significantly, as the Labour Party seeks to re-fashion its relationship with the trade unions to allow a greater public distance between the two wings of the labour movement, so relations with the Group have also become more formal and distant.

The coal strike and the destruction of the post-war settlement

The arrival of Thatcher in Government meant far more than the severing of the organic relationship between the political elite in Westminster and the Group. Thatcher's political project concerned the destruction of the framework of the post-war settlement, an end to 'corporatism', and the eradication of the political values and ideology which legitimated these arrangements. As we have seen, the importance of the post-war settlement for the Group lay not merely in the position of legitimate proximity to government it allocated to the trade unions but in the entire framework of institutions which were established to regulate industry, industrial relations and the planning of the economy. The Thatcherite project was directed not only towards the emasculation of trade unions but the dismantling of this entire edifice. It represented, therefore, a political project which would inevitably break up and re-cast the labour and industrial beat.

We can see this most clearly in the case of the nationalised industries. Many senior managers employed within the nationalised industries at the beginning of the Thatcher years had spent most, sometimes all, their working lives in the public sector. Through the experience of working in only one industry, located within the public sector, many such senior figures had acquired a set of organisational and social values which were at least compatible with the social democratic or labourist perspectives characteristic not only of trade union officials but many within the Labour and Industrial Group, as well. As the strains placed upon the post-war settlement increased through the 1970s, it is clear that the State began to contemplate the need for a change of management culture within the public sector. The appointment of Michael Edwardes at the head of British Leyland under a Labour Government is one illustration of this. However, under Thatcher the destruction of the traditional managerial culture within the nationalised industries and its replacement with a corporate culture familiar to executives in the private sector notably quickened. This was achieved in a variety of ways. In some instances, as in the case of gas, water, and telephone services, wholesale privatisation was achieved in a way which was likely to ensure that senior executives had sufficient incentives to divest themselves of any commitment to public service values. In other cases, the government not yet in a position to fully privatise, sought to replace senior personnel with executives with 'robust' track records in the corporate world. Hence, for example, the appointment of Ian MacGregor, first at the head of British Steel and then British Coal.

This process profoundly affected the workings of the Group. Firstly, industrial correspondents began to lose valuable contacts within the management of nationalised industries. In some cases, strong friendships had developed between journalists and senior executives who had been promoted from within. New appointments arriving from the private sector, familiar with a very different approach to media relations, proved far less accessible. Secondly, the concept of partnership with organised labour was re-cast. The new breed of senior executives talked of partnerships with employees but implied that such relationships would be structured in terms of corporate values. In the past, the concept of public ownership had been employed to reconcile the interests of management and labour in terms of a consensual framework to manage industrial relations. This framework provided a number of stable landmarks on the journalists' industrial beat and, to a degree, encouraged a shared culture which allowed correspondents access to both managers and union leaders. The 'partnership' between Derek Ezra, as head of the Coal Board, and Joe Gormley, as President of the NUM, in seeking to represent the interests of the industry to government was widely recognised and immediately identified as a 'problem' by the in-coming Thatcher government. For journalists on the labour and industrial beats, stable relationships between managements and unions, involving routine dialogue, regular negotiation and occasional eruptions of open conflict represented very good news gathering terrain. Another consequence of the arrival of Thatcher was the breaking up of these relations.

However, the crumbling of the post-war settlement was not merely caused by the arrival of a new government in office. Significant sections within the labour movement also began to move further from the values of social democracy which underpinned the post-war settlement. Thus, with the election of Arthur Scargill the leadership of the NUM moved leftwards, further undermining the traditional frameworks upon which labour journalists relied. The papers of the Group suggest growing difficulties experienced by labour correspondents in gaining access to contacts within the NUM headquarters. The move from London to Sheffield, in itself appeared to announce a down-grading in the priority attached to relations with the news media. It was no longer 'open house', as one journalist described the headquarters of the NUM under Gormley.

The Coal Strike in 1984-1985 brought these processes to crisis point. The dispute threw into sharp relief the changes which the Government was promoting in the organisation and culture of management within the National Coal Board, and the changing role which the state was defining for coal as an industry. Most importantly, the strike highlighted how far the politics of industrial relations could be fractured and polarised once the state dispensed with the values of the post-war settlement. Such a polarisation led to sharper, much more visible conflicts between organised labour and the state itself. It meant that the conflict manifested itself not only within the conventional arenas of industrial relations but in a much wider range of contexts including public spaces, streets, motorways, and so on, and arenas where political ideas were debated and disseminated including television studios and newspaper news rooms.

The paradox for industrial correspondents and members of the Group was that in 1984-85 they faced, perhaps, the biggest labour story of the post-war era but also the most severe crisis in terms of their practice and orientation as journalists. Much of the 'story' no longer centred around the familiar points of the labour beat, the structure of routine sources and contacts was de-stabilised and, perhaps most importantly, the political marginalisation of the Group was made highly visible. In contrast, a number of political correspondents and senior editorial staff enjoyed regular access to key sources within government and the National Coal Board, as a deliberate news management strategy evolved during the strike. One industrial correspondent recalls finally appreciating the extent to which the Group had been sidelined when his editor made it clear that he had been given

MacGregor's home telephone number and enjoyed regular access inside the National Coal Board at the highest level. This was a highly sought after contact number which had been denied to industrial correspondents throughout the strike. 'That's when I knew the game for us was up'.[20]

The movement of the NUM headquarters from London to Sheffield under the new presidency of Arthur Scargill had already created problems for the Group before the start of the strike. The minutes of Group meetings in 1984 note the difficulties journalists were already experiencing because the new facilities were inadequate and a plea was made to revert back to the 'old Euston Road arrangements'.[21] The NUM at this time was still an important point on the labour beat and fortnightly national executive meetings would be covered as a matter of routine. In London delegates from around the country would stay in two hotels known to labour journalists, the left of the executive in the County Hotel, Upper Woburn Street and the right in the Cora Hotel, opposite. Labour correspondents would meet contacts in both hotels and the Marquis of Cornwall, the NUM executive's normal London pub round the back of the Euston Road headquarters. This part of the labour beat was destroyed with the change of headquarters. Now journalists had to travel to Sheffield and while the left of the executive from coal fields in Scotland, Kent and Wales might stay in hotels which journalists could target, much of the executive right travelled from nearby fields in Derbyshire and Nottingham and were consequently less accessible, as they travelled home immediately after meetings (Wilsher,1985:56). And, of course, in the post-Gormley era journalists no longer enjoyed 'open house' at the union headquarters on a daily or weekly basis.

While Arthur Scargill was often regarded as a 'good media performer', he attached much less importance to developing a sense of rapport with labour correspondents than his predecessor. Gormley not only had a very close personal friendship with Barry Devney (*Daily Express*) but enjoyed good relations with most of the Group. He would sometimes good humouredly threaten to throw out younger reporters who had spent too long talking to Arthur Scargill downstairs and were late for the official executive press conference during the 1970s but he had 'too many friends among labour and industrial correspondents to want to erect any serious obstacles for the news media' (Jones,1986:56). Arthur Scargill by contrast, insisted upon a much more centralised and disciplined approach to the flow of information to the news media. Only the President or the President's personal assistant, Nell Myers, took responsibility for dealing with media enquiries. No one else within the union enjoyed such authority. The flow of information was tightly controlled and channelled through just one individual which meant that even Maurice Jones, the editor of *The Miner*, was not able to speak for the union in the absence of the President (Adeney and Lloyd,1986:242).

While Gormley adopted a critical but relaxed attitude to the ideological nature of newspaper journalism (Gormley,1982:156), Arthur Scargill's political analysis which prompted a movement away from social democratic consensual values, also inspired a deeper suspicion regarding established patterns of interaction between union officials and labour correspondents. As positions became more polarised during the course of the strike and the nature of media coverage itself became a major political issue, tensions between the union and the Group grew increasingly severe. The records of the Group include reports of members finding the atmosphere inside the headquarters of the NUM intimidating, press conferences were often crowded with members of the union and were routinely videoed, an experience journalists found disquieting.[22] Some members reported suffering physical attacks on picket lines and even at the union's headquarters in Sheffield.[23] Significantly, the papers indicate that officers of the Group took a decision to play down the reports of physical intimidation in the light of a greater concern about the general deterioration in the relationship between the Group and the officials of the union and the failure of the Group to maintain channels of information. At least one meeting took place between representatives of the Group and Peter Heathfield, NUM General Secretary, in June 1984 in an effort to improve relations.[24] In a letter dated 13th June 1984, the Group Secretary wrote to Peter Heathfield with a fifteen point action plan to help improve the union's public relations and media coverage. More press officers and spokespersons were needed and work done on developing a union position which could be presented at branch and local level as well as nationally. The Government and NCB twice daily release of statistics should be matched with counter information, and information could be circulated more effectively by using the Press Association or UNS. Tellingly, the list also included a plea for more on or off record briefings for accredited labour correspondents. Clearly, the Group sought to distinguish itself in the eyes of the union from the vast numbers of non-specialist and political correspondents who had been allocated to cover the strike. Policy and research documents could be launched more effectively if press conferences were planned carefully and material packaged appropriately.

All the evidence confirms a period of crisis for labour journalism. The traditional patterns of interaction between industrial correspondents and trade unions were shattered by the polarised conflict of the strike. It became increasingly difficult as the strike wore on for labour correspondents to maintain a 'balanced' position within an industrial consensus which embraced the two sides of industry. And this was not simply because the NUM viewed the practice of the news media through a much sharper political perspective. The Group itself became the focus of political attack from the right. Suspicions regarding the political sympathies of industrial journalists had always existed arising from their daily proximity to union elites. Now some newspapers, and MacGregor as Chairman of the NCB, raised this as a public issue. Paul Routledge, industrial editor of the *Times*, was accused by the *Daily Express* of being one of 'Scargill's seven shadows'. Routledge later sued and won. Paul Johnson launched a series attacks aimed at the political bias of labour correspondents and 'their dependence upon the union machine' in the Spectator (Johnson,1984; Jones,1986:117). MacGregor denounced the whole Labour and Industrial Correspondents' Group, arguing that many members were sympathetic to the NUM and those who were not remained dependent upon the union for copy (MacGregor,1986:313). John Lloyd of the *FT* was identified in particular as a target by MacGregor. Peter Walker, Secretary of State for Energy, also identified the Labour and Industrial Group as biased to the political left (Jones,1986:115). These themes were developed further by Andrew Neil in a feature article on the editorial pages of the *Sunday Times* (Jones,1986:116). For perhaps the first time in the post-war period the social democratic and labourist values of the Group were being highlighted in the public domain and identified as a political issue by those on the political right.

The position of labour correspondents became increasingly problematic as some of their own news organisations made more frequent political interventions during the course of the strike. The *Mail on Sunday* announced to its readers that it would sponsor 'Silver Birch', one of the leaders of the rebel 'working miners', the *Daily Express* also donated funds to support legal action against the NUM and newspapers, such as the *Sunday Times*, adopted overtly ideological stances in declaring that because the NUM represented a threat to democracy, 'Scargill and his forces had to be defeated and would be' (Neil,1985). Bailiffs were supplied with a security pass normally used by a *Sunday Express* photographer to gain entry to the Labour Party conference to serve a writ upon Arthur Scargill (Wilsher,1985:123). Inevitably, these overtly political interventions in the course of the strike made it extremely difficult for labour and industrial correspondents to maintain routine relations not only with the NUM but with all the trade union contacts on their regular beats. Joe Gormley's old friend Barry Devney, the *Express* labour correspondent but also a Labour Party activist, simply gave up attending union press conferences because of the hostile reception he received (Jones,1986:117). As the political polarisation of the strike made visible the erosion of post-war consensual values, so the traditional normative framework which patterned interaction between the unions and the Group was also eroded.

The crisis which afflicted labour journalism in this period not only affected relations with the labour movement. The Group found that its professional authority was undermined by the changes in the orientation of the State to media elites. Where as in the 1960s and 1970s the Group had enjoyed an 'organic' relationship with the political elite, sustained through the 'corporate bias' (Middlemas,1986) of government and the presence of trade unions at the political centre, now it found that it was no longer able to produce the most informed 'intelligence' and that its traditional sources within the National Coal Board were no longer, themselves, in control of events. The Group's authority was undermined by the ability of political correspondents and even editors, themselves, to establish contacts with key members of the political elite who were concerned to by-pass the traditional channels of labour reporting. After a very hesitant start (Adeney and Lloyd,1986:194), the National Coal Board and Government developed a much slicker public relations machine. Tim Bell, former chairman of Saatchi and Saatchi and responsible for the 1979 Tory election campaign, was drafted in by MacGregor in response to pressure from the Government, to handle public relations (Jones 1986:99). Bell was assisted by David Hart, a journalist and public relations consultant with connections to Downing Street and the senior editorial team at the *Times* (Goodman,1985:121) and who was heavily involved in supporting 'working miners groups' with resources and advice. He was able to supply Fleet Street editors with detailed information on these developments. Increasingly, MacGregor allowed this team to supplant the senior management team with formal responsibility for industrial relations (Ned Smith) and public relations (Geoff Kirk) within the NCB. Smith and Kirk were both very experienced managers who had spent most of their careers within the NCB. Over the years they had developed a strong rapport with the Group. Kirk, in particular, was regarded by industrial correspondents as a highly reliable and accessible source (Jones,1986: 99). To mark the retirement of Geoff Kirk, the Group organised a special dinner in his honour. Both Kirk and Smith were strongly committed to the traditional culture of nationalised industries. Both were alienated by the new corporate culture introduced by MacGregor (Goodman,1985: 60) and both left the NCB in the wake of the dispute. Kirk had commented in his speech at his retirement dinner with the Group that it was a matter of 'great regret that the NCB and NUM were no longer able to work in partnership together'.[25] Smith also expressed public doubts about the wisdom of open confrontation between management and unions in a Radio Four interview during the strike (Jones,1986:81). Smith was ordered to stop giving broadcast interviews (Adeney and Lloyd,1986:194) and members of the Group were astonished to witness Kirk being removed from his responsibility for press work in the course of a briefing to industrial correspondents (Wilsher et al., 1985:195). Both Kirk and Smith were manoeuvred out of their positions of responsibility during the strike because of their reluctance to abandon the traditional normative framework for industrial relations and their unwillingness to engage in the kind of full-blooded ideological onslaught against the NUM which both MacGregor and Peter Walker were demanding (Adeney and Lloyd,1986: 194-197).

Peter Walker exploited his own extensive contacts with political correspondents to try to marginalise the Labour and Industrial Group. He targeted Sunday papers over dailies and ensured that political correspondents were supplied with superior copy, denied to labour reporters (Adeney and Lloyd,1986:245) The BBC Radio's industrial correspondent describes the frustration of the group:

> Specialist correspondents were often exasperated to find that their editors had been given a fuller briefing by Mr Walker than they themselves had been able to obtain in a whole days work...(Jones,1986:115).

Another former labour editor working for a broadsheet during the strike provides the following analysis:

> The Thatcher government concentrated upon the centres of power in newspapers, not the centres of reporting...the *Daily Express*, the Conservative Party, the working miners' groups,...the Government plugged into the right contacts, the centres of authority, so editors were genuinely in a better position to assess what was going on. Somehow Andrew Neil was getting the minutes of NUM executive meetings, that was a bit of a facer for labour correspondents! These were things which industrial correspondents should have been getting...essential for assessing where we were. We were outpaced by our editors.[26]

Inevitably, the authority of industrial and labour correspondents was undermined by this process of marginalisaton. Journalists' power and influence within news organisations largely depends upon the value and range of their contacts, and the quality of the 'intelligence' which these produce. As members of the Group were 'outpaced' by their own editors, so their authority was diminished inside the news rooms and they were less able to resist the frequent re-writing, subbing and substitution of alternative copy under their by-lines which occurred during the dispute (Jones,1986:115-115; Goodman,1985:121; Adeney and Lloyd,1986:245). This, in turn, further undermined their positions in relation to trade unions and the framework of the old labour beat.

The Coal Strike did not in itself produce the decline in the fortunes of industrial and labour correspondents but it did accelerate and accentuate the political forces which were determining this process. The rise of Thatcherism and the successful attack upon the values of social democracy and post war consensual politics were inevitably going to wash away the foundations of the structures which supported the labour beat in the first three decades after the war. Sooner or later the political values and assumptions of the Group were likely to be spotlighted as an issue in the public domain. The change in the composition of the political elite which Thatcherism produced and the erosion of the organisational cultures which had characterised nationalised industries in the post-war period, were already leading towards the political marginalisation of the Group before the strike began. Nevertheless, this period in the mid 1980s remains significant because it is at this time that these processes became visible and were explicitly acknowledged by the participants.

The relationship between the Group and trade unions: 1979 to 1994

The traumatic impact of the Coal Strike was intensified by the eruption of further polarised conflict during the dispute between print unions and News International at Wapping. Once again, industrial correspondents were placed in the centre of an industrial conflict in a way which made it impossible to avoid making visible a political commitment. All three journalists on the labour desk at the *Times* resigned rather than cross print union picket lines. Others were compelled to reconcile membership of the NUJ and the Labour and Industrial Correspondents' Group with the fact of being employed by an organisation determined to break the power of trade unions in the newspaper industry. The *Sun* resolved this dilemma for its staff by temporarily abolishing the labour desk . The minutes of a meeting of the Group in 1987 record the passing of a resolution barring 'News International employees from attending Group functions if their presence was likely to prevent the attendance of a guest speaker'.[27] Clearly, the bitterness generated at Wapping had further undermined relations between labour correspondents and the labour movement. Similarly, in 1987 the Secretary wrote to TASS to complain about the treatment a particular member had received at the hands of pickets during the Hanger dispute. A letter in reply from the strike committee admitted that what had happened to Mr Burns was 'unfortunate' but insisted that it had to be placed in the context of the general bias in media coverage which had provoked members to the point where they felt compelled 'to storm the *Daily Express* building'. Mr Burns had apparently escaped relatively mildly in comparison.[28] Several other instances are recorded through the 1980s. A series of resignations, applications and re-applications in the same period appear also to be the result of Wapping inspired splits within the Group, itself.[29]

According to some industrial correspondents including Philip Bassett, formerly on the *FT* and now industrial editor of the Times,[30] in the aftermath of the Coal Strike, news values in industrial journalism began to change. As annual strike rates declined and pickets were no longer to be seen outside factory gates, so labour correspondents sought to identify new themes and wider briefs. This is only part of a more complex explanation. Firstly, research has long suggested that the frequency of strikes or disputes does not determine their newsworthiness (GUMG, 1976 and 1980). Rather, it is the political context in which disputes occur that makes them newsworthy. And this, in turn, points to the importance of the values and ideological perspectives of the political elite and senior editorial staff within news organisations. The greater the success of the political elite in marginalising trade unions at the political level, the more likely it is that they will decline in the news value hierarchy, irrespective of how may disputes occur. Secondly, Bassett, himself, represented a new generation of journalists who became industrial specialists in the late 1970s and early 1980s. He and several colleagues (for example, Tom Condon ex-industrial editor on the *Sun*) were members of a new cohort of labour correspondent whose journalism was shaped by the politics of 'new realism', associated with the EETPU and AEU inside the labour movement. By 1986 Bassett had already produced a sustained defence of new realism in the work place with considerable assistance from both the electricians and the engineers (Bassett, 1986). Of course, new realism with an emphasis upon strike free deals and single union contracts, in itself, implied a different industrial news agenda, with less emphasis upon conflict stories and a greater preoccupation with employment practices, labour law, and wider issues of technological development and business strategy.

Thirdly, as we have seen, many industrial specialists actively sought to widen their briefs in order to remain marketable and, fourthly, the reason they felt compelled to do this in the second half of the 1980s was precisely because they were aware of the down grading of trade union news by senior editorial teams. Andrew Neil had already told journalists at the end of the Coal Strike that industrial journalism would soon be totally eclipsed by financial specialists (Jones, 1988). The editor of the *Times*, Charles Wilson, told his staff that both unions and union news 'was finished' (Jones, 1987). The *Guardian* replaced its labour section with a new section on employment opportunities called 'Frontiers', while the *Independent* began a 'Workplace' feature, which the editor specified should not 'preoccupy itself with the institutional troubles of the trade union movement' (Jones,1987). Even the *F.T.* revamped its labour reporting by the late 1980s and placed coverage of trade unions in a much broader context.

The papers of the Group suggest that formal contacts continued with trade union leaders but less frequently. The lists of guest speakers for Group functions also reflect the broadening of industrial briefs and the increasing preoccupation with non-union stories. In 1983, the Group sent formal invitations to eight trade unions to send speakers for lunch or evening events at the Cheshire Cheese or The Clarence in Whitehall, including the TGWU, the GMB, NUPE, ASTMS, NGA and POEU. According to the minutes of the 1988 and 1989 AGMs, only three union speakers were invited in 1987 and only one in 1988 (Eric Hammond). In their place invitations were extended to the Industrial Society, the Institute of Personnel Management, British Steel, and the Post Office. Of course, the records of formal events organised by the Group does not provide a complete picture of the Group's contact with trade unions. Indeed, by the late 1980s many of the larger unions had already appointed full-time press officers and, to a degree, their work made the formal invitation of members of the union elites to Group events unnecessary. Nevertheless, the decline in formal contacts and broadening range of alternative invitations is indicative of the changing industrial news agenda. By the late 1980s it was rare for union executive meetings to be regarded as routine points on the industrial beat and even the TUC General Council meetings were no longer routinely covered. In 1984 the Group had regularly held its own meetings before the General Council because this would guarantee a high attendance of correspondents. The cricket match between the Group and TUC, however, does still remain an annual event.

History and the present

The second, much briefer, part of this chapter will relate the history of labour journalism and the Labour and Industrial Correspondents' Group to the empirical themes developed in the discussion of the practice of contemporary journalists and trade union officers.

The Formal and Latent Functions of the Group

The formal constitution of the Group contains a number of elements which are characteristic of a professional occupation which is preoccupied with its own status. In practice, the Group sometimes drew more from the values of traditional trade unionism in managing its affairs. The constitution declares that the 'object of the Group shall be to represent the interests of all Labour and Industrial Correspondents, to improve facilities and amenities available for the collection of news and to stimulate informal contacts with the appropriate departments and organisations'. However, rules regarding membership were exclusive. Only three labour and three industrial correspondents per news organisation would be eligible providing that they 'were engaged mainly in reporting labour, industrial and related economic matters'. It was for the Group committee to rule in cases where applicants were 'borderline' in satisfying these criteria. Membership was 'conditional upon the strict observance of the recognised standards of professional conduct' and the Group Committee enjoyed the power to discipline members and to employ the ultimate sanction of expulsion from the Group.[31]

At a formal level the Group took the view that it was appropriate for a specialised branch of journalism to be regulated according to appropriate professional guidelines. Restrictions on membership were justified on the grounds that it was necessary to keep the size of the Group within 'workable proportions.'[32] In terms of latent functions, students of the sociology of professions will recognise a familiar pattern in which the status of a group is reinforced through a strategy which seeks to ensure exclusivity. This, of course, is the probable explanation for the ferocious rivalry between the Group and the Westminster Lobby in the period up to the 1980s. As we have seen, during the most buoyant period for labour and industrial reporting during the 1950s, 60s and 70s, membership of the Group was, indeed, much sought after. The Group provided formal and informal contact with senior figures in trade unions and the political elite. During the era of Wilson's briefings to the Group at Number Ten, membership actually afforded access to much of the same territory as that patrolled by the Westminster Lobby. Membership also ensured that one's name was automatically added to the various invitation lists for events, tours and public relations exercises organised by Government departments, companies and nationalised industries - all important points on the beat. Strong demand for membership permitted the mechanism of restriction to successfully generate a status of exclusivity. The fact that the Secretary of the Group in the early 1990s was compelled to write inviting journalists to join underlines the change in the fortunes of the Group since the late 1970s and the collapse of the strategy of membership restriction.

The Labour and Industrial Group promoted the collective interests of labour journalists in a number of ways. The most concerted effort appears to have been exerted when the Group perceived that collective access to information or sources was being restricted. It is on these occasions when the Group, in the past, has sought to exert collective pressure to maintain access to significant channels of information. 'Intelligence' is the essential commodity which confers authority for correspondents in their relations with news organisations and professional rivals. The political elite and the more sophisticated elite figures within the trade union movement have long recognised the ways in which information as a commodity can be exploited to secure an advantageous position in their dealings with correspondents. In short, access to information is inextricably bound up with the distribution of power amongst political and media elites. It is recognition of this which underlay the nature of the Group response to perceived threats to its position of privileged access and prompted a collective 'trade union' response to attempts to restrict access to press conferences and significant sources, such as pay tribunals, as described in chapter five. As we have seen, in exceptional circumstances, (the 1984 Coal Strike and the 1987 disputes at Wapping and Hangers) the Group has found itself intervening on behalf of members whose information channels were threatened by the action of pickets.

The Group also attempted to enforce an 'appropriate' normative framework to ensure that regular departmental and institutional sources complied with the expectations of correspondents. At the Group's AGM a tradition has evolved to award 'bouquets' and 'brickbats' for the best and worst press and public relations work. If representatives of the nominated organisations are not present at the 'awards ceremony', then the Group Secretary will write to explain the reasons for the award. Thus, in 1983 bouquets were sent to ACAS, the TUC, COHSE and NUPE, but brickbats were allocated to the DHSS, the Department of Employment and Arthur Scargill. In 1984, the public relations department at British Telecom was awarded a brickbat for its poor performance during the national dispute whilst the union, the POEU, was awarded a bouquet for the 'open and frank' approach and the efficiency with which press enquiries were dealt with.

Finally, as we have seen, the Group also sought to exert normative control internally, where it was feared that the behaviour of individual members might jeopardise the collective interest of the group. Hence, the protracted debate in the late 1970s and early 1980s over whether or not to admit the Newsline correspondent to membership, given the danger that his presence might de-stabilise relations with ministerial sources. Membership was granted to Newsline journalists for a brief period during the mid-1980s.

The Culture of the Group

The purpose of this section is to establish a set of historical 'bench marks' with which to establish whether or not the patterns observed in the field work for this research represent significant departures from the past. It is impossible to determine whether or not there has been a decline in group solidarity, or a shift in political orientation, or even whether labour correspondents are now more desk bound unless a historical perspective is employed.

The first point to make is that current and former labour and industrial correspondents are aware of significant generational shifts in the post war period. For one ex-industrial and labour correspondent, generational changes occurred on 'a decade pattern really', because 'in the sixties you had the senior guys with a lot respect, Mike Edwards, Trevor Evans, etc. In the seventies you had Routledge and so on. Very sharp'. In the late 1980s, according to this ex-correspondent, as the status of industrial journalism declined, news organisations began to employ younger journalists on their industrial desks who were less likely to be sympathetic to the traditions of the labour movement and often regarded the industrial desk as just another rung on the professional ladder. It is certainly the case that a number of the senior correspondents, many of whom had entered industrial journalism before or just after the war, continued to exercise considerable influence within the Group during the 1960s. Ian McKay had died at the Labour Party conference in 1953 but Trevor Evans and Hugh Chevins (the other two thirds of the original thirties triumvirate) remained in Fleet Street until the late 1960s. Labour correspondents who established their names in the 1950s, including Eric Wigham, Geoffrey Goodman and Mike Edwards, rose to positions of seniority within the Group during this period and their seniority was confirmed through their possession of knighthoods, places on Royal Commissions and positions in government departments.

By the end of the sixties, however, the 'old guard' were beginning to be replaced by a new generation of Oxbridge and redbrick university educated journalists. Paul Routledge replaced Eric Wigham at the Times in 1969. Mick Costello, Donald McIntyre, and Christian Tyler, for example, all came from such backgrounds to take up posts as number one or two's on national newspapers in the very early 1970s. The elevated status of industrial and labour journalism at this time meant that news organisations could attract the most promising graduates entering daily journalism. By the late seventies a further generational shift began to occur. Journalists such as Philip Bassett, entered the specialism, similarly university educated but without the formative experience of the political atmosphere of higher education in the sixties. It was Routledge's generation who were most affected by the disturbance and disruptions of the mid-eighties. Routledge lost his job at the Times after the Coal Strike while McIntyre found himself one of the News International 'refuseniks', sacked for not crossing the Wapping picket line. This period saw a great shake up of industrial staff. Some of the remaining correspondents from the sixties like Barrie Devney and Geoffrey Goodman retired from full-time journalism. Goodman left the Mirror following the difficulties of working for Maxwell during the Coal Strike, Barrie Devney (Joe Gormley's personal friend) retired from the *Express* in 1988, his position on the labour beat also having been undermined by the Express' political interventions during the Coal Strike. Other labour and industrial correspondents from the seventies cohort moved to other specialisms (Nicholas Jones, Donald McIntyre and Paul Routledge to politics, Christian Tyler to feature writing, David Felton to Home Affairs). Mick Costello left journalism to become the industrial organiser for the Communist Party.

Changes in generation brought changes in the political perspective of the Group. As we have seen a majority of the earlier generations of industrial correspondents were positioned in the mainstream of Labour politics. Most were broadly sympathetic to Fabian or social democratic traditions in the Party which , in many ways provided the seed bed for the 'hegemony' of the post war settlement.[33] Themes stressing the legitimate role of trade unions in representing labour, balancing the power of capital and extending citizenship rights to the work place can be found in the published work of leading industrial journalists from the 1960s but also evident is an antipathy to rank and file militant politics, outside the social democratic consensus (Mason, 1981; Eric Wigham 1961 and 1969). In short, a majority of labour correspondents reflected in the 'inferential structures' which shaped their journalism, a commitment to the corporatist values of the post-war settlement. Their perspectives reflected the institutional structures which organised their beat. The beat, itself, was likely to expose labour correspondents to the views and perspectives of the trade union elite and government more frequently than the voices of capital. Keith Mason (formerly on the labour desk of the *Daily Herald* and later the *Sun*) explained:

> Most union leaders knew us by our Christian names and we were on Christian name terms with them. So did many Ministers. Most leaders in industry, on the other hand, probably would not know us by sight unless a prolonged strike brought us into frequent contact. (Mason,1981:3).

However, a minority of the Group in the 1950s and 1960s were more committed left activists (Goodman organised the Fleet Street Forum of Socialist Journalists in the 1950s, Barrie Devney was a Labour Party activist throughout his career at the *Daily Express*), while only a very few belonged right of centre.[34]

In the 1970s, with the influx of a new generation, the positions of responsibility were occupied by journalists committed to more left of centre perspectives. One former labour correspondent and officer for the Group in this period recalls:

> The Labour Group was a hot bed of politics in the Seventies and early eighties. There was a left and a right. The 'ancien regime' of the late sixties was replaced by what was regarded as the hard left,- people like me , Glyn Allen [London based correspondent for the *Yorkshire Evening Post*] and Mick Costello and we ran the show for the best part of a decade until we were ousted by the Labour right wingers from the Midlands, Tom Condon, Charles Rae and Richard Littlejohn, now a *Sun* columnist. We were called the 'SPO',- the self perpetuating officers, because we would exchange jobs. I'd be the Chair and Mick would be the Secretary. Top jobs were divided amongst those who wanted to do them, who wanted to influence the direction of the Group in relation to Ministers because remember the Group was very powerful in

those days, its now just a shadow of itself, a kind of club.It did count and we were influenced by the politics of the Sixties, on the Left, from provincial universities, usually in the Labour Party but not always, some in the C.P.[Communist Party]...the fortunes of the Industrial Group reflected the fortunes of the labour movement. When the labour movement was on the up we were on the up, when it was down we were down. When it was racked by divisions, we were racked by divisions so when 'new realism' came into the labour movement, it emerged in our Group too, so people like Phil Bassett and Tom Condon mirrored the shift to the right and we [the left] were ousted because we no longer represented the majority view in the Group.[35]

Similarly, a member of the generation who entered industrial journalism in the early 1980s recalls :

...I think one of the most important things is that there was when I started Barry Devney, Routledge, the man from the *Telegraph*... John Boyd and so on... a lot of them were quite political in ways and tied into unions... there was a whole network of them who had been covering unions for years, knew general secretaries, knew executives, knew the routine of sitting in pubs and that was how a lot of business seems to have been done talking to people in pubs. By the time I came along, there was still a bit of that...there was the monthly trip to Sheffield for the NUM executive and we used to try to grab people afterwards before they caught their trains and sit in this pub trying to weedle out of them what happened. That was the end of that kind of culture really. Since then, everything has changed, so more work is done by fax and so on.[36]

It is clear, then, that the politics of the Group have undergone a series of significant changes, linked to generational shifts and changes in the external political environment. What about the other empirical 'bench mark' questions, posed by the field work? To what extent does the history of the Group suggest that journalists are more desk bound now or that the Group has lost a close social network of contacts which bound labour correspondents to contacts within the labour movement? Was there a pub culture and has it disappeared?

Out and About: the Labour Beat and Social Networks

Intelligence and information upon which industrial correspondents can form judgements and even make predictions has always been regarded as the crucial commodity on the labour beat. This will be discussed further below.

The reputation of individual correspondents and their status within their own news organisations crucially depended upon the quality of their contacts and their record in judging 'which way it was going to go', whether this was a dispute, a union election or a tribunal judgement. In turn, the history of the development of labour and industrial reporting suggests that social networks involving correspondents and contacts within unions and nationalised industries were, indeed, an integral part of the job and that the pub often represented the appropriate arena for the fostering of such networks. Significantly, as we have seen, even the geographical distribution of pubs on the beat reflected the departmental architecture of the post-war settlement with the most popular being located close to Westminster, Whitehall, ACAS and the headquarters of the leading unions.

The pub served a dual purpose. Through the 'doorstepping' routine labour and industrial correspondents gathered together and working relationships and friendships developed. The pub next to the doorstep provided a focal point for these processes (the interaction between 'competitor colleagues' will be discussed further below). Secondly, the pub often represented a very important information gathering arena as union executive committee members or officials relaxed off-record. Thus, as we have seen labour correspondents knew in which pub to find the 'left' or the 'right' of the executive committees of, for example, the NUM or the AEU, and in which pub to meet, themselves, in order to put the pieces of the story together. It was for these reasons, presumably, that Tunstall found that only crime correspondents could match labour correspondents as 'heaviest drinkers' amongst specialist journalists (Tunstall,1971:197).

Two pubs, in particular, became central meeting points for labour journalists. If before the War the Cheshire Cheese, in Fleet Street, had become a daily 'watering hole' for the Group, after the war the Clarence in Whitehall, where the civil service unions enjoyed a special arrangement with the landlord, also became a regular venue for both formal events and informal gatherings. Most of the correspondents interviewed for this research could produce at least one tale of outrageous behaviour at these two venues, particularly at the 'socials' which followed Annual General Meetings, or 'the Group yearly freak out' as the Secretary described the fixture in 1985.[37] It is clear that such social events helped to reinforce the sense of solidarity which, as we have seen, was an important characteristic of the Group before the late 80s. Although a very small number of women have developed careers in labour journalism,[38] the dominant culture inside the Group appears to have reflected traditional male preoccupations with beer and pub humour. The rituals involved in the Group's social events, including the annual award of 'the Golden Bollock' for the worst published copy of the year, reinforce this impression of a culture of male solidarity.

The papers of the Group recording the most recent years in the late eighties and early nineties clearly confirm that older social ties and networks which bound labour and industrial correspondents together are now fragmenting. The Group is less active in organising formal events, these are now badly attended and few correspondents report contact with other labour or industrial correspondents on a daily or even weekly basis. Some contacts are maintained by telephone, the bigger annual events such as big union conferences and the TUC Conference will draw correspondents together. The annual cricket match, first introduced by Geoffrey Goodman in 1961, against a TUC eleven still takes place. Nevertheless, there appears no longer to be a very strong sense of group identity. This probably reflects both the declining importance of the Group for journalists seeking useful copy and the changing priorities of correspondents as they address the agendas of their news organisations. It also, of course, reflects the impact of 'Wappingisation', the removal of newspapers from Fleet Street, and the destruction of the journalistic networks around the nearby bars and clubs which represented 'a delicately balanced, intricate social system' (Waterhouse,1991). There is a danger of constructing a 'golden age mythology' around the end of Fleet Street but Waterhouse points to the value of the 'casual friendships' which permitted the exchange of professional advice, information and news of job opportunities in the pubs along the street. This may only have been a minor factor in the decline of the Industrial and Labour Group compared to the deeper processes at work at the level of the state and the political elite but it played a part. As one former labour correspondent recalls:

> In the old days we were all within half a mile of each other and we would all drink in the same pub, - the upstairs bar of the Cheshire Cheese. And we did drink, - on a good day there could be ten or fifteen industrial hacks in there swapping stories till around 3.00 and then they might well go off to the clubs around Fleet Street. After Wapping everything was destroyed...you're tied to a screen. A new generation don't know what it was like, what they've lost.[39]

Labour correspondents maintain links with trade unions but the nature of the social relationships has changed, the telephone and the fax machine now sustaining such relationships as a frequent substitute for the personal contacts of the beat, - a 'telephonic culture', as one former industrial correspondent describes the current situation.[40] While the telephone represents an efficient means of seeking 'factual' information rapidly and with minimum of effort, it is doubtful whether it is possible to establish a telephonic intimacy which allows the gathering of contextual and background 'intelligence' in quite the same way as the traditional social networks, involving journalist-union official and journalist-journalist intercourse.

Significant changes, then, have occurred in the social nature and culture of the Group. Is it the case that industrial and labour journalists are now more desk bound? As we have seen, correspondents have been placed under pressure to accept wider briefs covering industrial, employment, personnel and even technological fields. One or two now double up with a specialism such as education. Journalists from all areas report increasing pressure which derives from earlier deadlines for copy because new production technology allows newspapers to run more editions. The impression amongst many journalists is that they are more firmly stuck behind their desks and that there are fewer opportunities to engage in intelligence gathering exercises outside the office. Ventures outside the office are more closely 'policed' by senior management in the news organisation.[41] As one former health specialist comments:

> Twenty or thirty years ago one could make a lot of visits to places on 'spec'. Now to get out, the story has to be better than anything which could be written from the office. More questions are asked by managers, 'Do you really need to go out? That could be done by phone'. As you do one story, another is plonked on your desk and then another so schizophrenia reigns. You don't get the stories you just tripped over like in the old days. You rely more and more on people trying to flog you a story.[42]

The 'desk bound thesis' has to be placed in context. Tunstall found that 59% of labour, aviation and education correspondents spent between 50% and 75% of their time in the office (1971:126) and that even in the 1960s, telephone calls often out-numbered face to face contacts (1971:152). Nevertheless, Tunstall also found that most news organisations were willing to recognise the need to invest time in the cultivation of sources and contacts (1971:116) and evidence from the thirties (Evans ,1953) and the sixties[43] indicates a pattern whereby labour correspondents spent a considerable time away from Fleet Street during the conference season. One former correspondent recalls being sent by his 'number one' in the early weeks of his appointment to cover the union conferences simply in order to generate the contacts which would become essential for the job. According to MORI surveys of labour and industrial journalists, the number of correspondents mentioning the telephone as 'most useful source' has slightly increased between 1982 and 1993 as has the numbers identifying press releases (56% to 66%), - another possible indicator of deskboundness. However, there are problems in using this data longitudinally and the data continues to underline journalists' commitment to 'unofficial sources' and 'personal interviews' (three quarters of journalists sampled continued to identify these sources throughout).[44]

In terms of subjective experience older correspondents remain convinced that something is lost when face to face contact is limited:

> You take a union official to a pub, you buy him a drink and he'll tell you a story. You get to know them as people and they get to trust you. That personal contact gives you stories. You can get stories down the phone, especially when someone's pushing something but I'm always deeply suspicious of something being pushed. Stories are usually found out, not given to you on a plate. We should be talking to union officials directly not through intermediaries... I'm always suspicious of news management of any kind, union or other and that is why I always preferred direct contact with the official in charge. A good labour correspondent should know the General Secretary and President on first names terms and should see them regularly in their offices, at conferences, and should always be at briefings so that they know who you are. I still ring officials not press officers. We still need an independent existence outside the machine.[45]

This view is probably not typical of most contemporary labour or industrial correspondents. The appointment of press officers has generally been welcomed because it helps to alleviate the old perennial problem for journalists of being unable to easily contact officials who are in a position to answer routine press enquiries. However, there must be a danger that a combination of growing pressures within the news room combined with the increasing priority given to public relations by unions is leading to a more routinised form of news management which stifles more investigative and analytic labour journalism. The view of the older, senior labour correspondent quoted above almost certainly underestimates the extent to which journalists have always depended upon routine sources but it does illustrate the traditional professional values of labour journalism and the importance industrial correspondents used to attach to sources, contacts and 'intelligence'. Many still retain these value commitments but a combination of generational change and intensification in the work process for those journalists attached to the industrial desk is likely to lead to an erosion of such value commitments in the future.

'Intelligence': the Essential Commodity of Labour Journalism

Every year since the late sixties, the Labour and Industrial Group have held an award ceremony which usually follows the Group's AGM at the end of the TUC conference week. Attendance for this particular event continues to be high. Indeed, at the time of writing it was sponsored by the Electricity Council. The chairman in 1984, for example, invited 'nominations ...for the prize coveted by every self respecting labour and industrial journalist...your suggestions in a plain brown wrapper if necessary'.[46] Correspondents are nominated for writing what is judged to be the worst labour or industrial copy published each year and the winner receives the 'Golden Bollock'. In 1985, the Group Secretary warned that, 'there is an amazingly long list of entrants, reflecting the unerring instinct of everyone to miss-forecast the course of the miners' strike.'[47]

In other years, correspondents have been nominated for predicting that a rail strike would begin in two days, 'on the basis of a ring round briefing which everyone else checked and found to be untrue'; forecasting that the executive of the CPSA would remain in the hands of the right, 'four days before a landslide to the left was announced'; suggesting that talks between the NUM and the NCB would flounder following the arrest of Arthur Scargill on a picket line when, in fact, they continued, and confirming that water union leaders would settle for a 4.6% pay rise when 'at the end of the day the unions recommended to members an offer in excess of 5%'.[48]

The award of the 'Golden Bollock' is, in the first instance, an amusing exercise in self mockery which helps to strengthen group solidarity. Members of the Group are quick to contrast this exercise with the, perhaps, more pompous annual dinner at Westminster organised by the Lobby. However, the ritual of the award also serves to underline particular professional norms by publicly applying a symbolic sanction to a member who transgresses. In almost every case awards have been accepted with great good humour. Only one journalist, the labour editor of a broadsheet, has refused to accept with the additional threat of legal action.

In each of the above cases, the nomination refers to a failure to use information to make an accurate assessment or forecast of likely developments. In terms of the professional norms of the Group, good labour and industrial journalism involves the exercise of shrewd judgement in assessing the quality of information combined with extensive background knowledge in order to make informed assessments of developing stories. The ultimate professional goal is the story which includes an accurate forecast of how events unfold. As the nominations above illustrate, journalists are quick to spot mistakes made by colleagues in failing to follow 'professional rules' about checking the reliability of contacts against alternative sources and in drawing the wrong inferences from information supplied because of a lack of 'contextual' knowledge. Knowledge of 'context', for example, allowed one journalist in the sixties to avoid predicting the outbreak of a rail strike because he knew that 'when ASLEF threatened a strike, the NUR often withdrew from the brink'. It is 'contextual information',[49] corespondents believe, which allows judgements to be made about the veracity and accuracy of the information which is gathered. One former Press Association labour correspondent remembers that following a press conference, an immediate summary would be written up and sent to the agency for rapid circulation. The next step would be to head to the pub, - 'where the real stuff was done' - to meet sources who 'would provide the other side of the story', so that eventually a re-written item would be submitted which reflected background context. One former labour correspondent made the distinction between routine news gathering and work with sources:

You could send a basic reporter down to do that kind of stuff [press conferences and writing stories on the basis of press releases]. No, its what something really meant, the significance of an event, what it really means rather than what they would like you to think it meant...you need to know what to avoid as well, what information is unreliable. It's all right if you are forecasting something three weeks away,-by the time the event comes around the story is forgotten,- but if you forecast two days before and get it wrong then... the job was also to know when a story was going to break. It was like court reporting. At the Old Bailey you needed to know the barristers and court officials in order to judge when a trial was going to produce a good story, so one could go away for three or four days and then return to it. Not dissimilar with industrial journalism, - you wanted to know how long pay talks were going to go on for, they may go on for a month or more and finally, the union says it will have to go back to its members. That was when the story needed to be written. In that era you started thinking about whether the railways were going to run or the mines stop.[50]

These professional perspectives in part must be viewed as examples of the 'professional gloss' or ideology which is likely to develop as a response to the organisational controls which newspapers seek to exert upon journalists (Golding ,1974:65; Elliott, 1977:167-168). However, the degree to which this professional perspective is at odds with the reality of the daily grind of deadlines and production routines is not the immediate question. The point is that this occupational perspective shapes the practice of labour and industrial correspondents and directs them to prioritise the cultivation of sources, in unions, government departments, within the management of nationalised industries and so on. It is only through the acquisition of 'good contacts', it is believed, that journalists will gain access to the inside information which provides a 'contextual' perspective and allows 'forecasting' to be undertaken. In the labour and industrial specialism, it was the development of union contacts and the acquisition of inside political knowledge of the labour movement which provided the measure of the professional competence and status. Older, more senior industrial correspondents often share the view that today it is much harder for new entrants to the specialism to develop such 'intelligence' sources and that 'standards' in copy have deteriorated accordingly.

This may mean one of two things for union press officers. As we have seen one or two experienced labour correspondents condemn the hiring of press officers by trade unions because such appointments interfere with the capacity of labour correspondents to develop relations with senior union officials. All press enquiries are channelled through the 'intermediaries'. The fear is that labour and industrial copy will become standardised and tame, with the main substance derived from the press release or official briefing. However, others point to the part a skilful press officer may play in meeting the need correspondents have for 'contextual information'.

> It is the job of the press officer to make the material available as interesting as possible, and one of the ways of doing that is to provide for people who are reporting this area over a period of time a degree of contextual information...We need to know enough about an organisation to tell if a development is significant or whether something is being dressed up.[51]

In other words, press officers should be capable of supplying background material which is not designed for immediate publication but which represents 'intelligence' or information which provides context and the ability to predict. There are numerous reasons why the balance of power between union source and labour specialist is tipped firmly in favour of the latter. Nevertheless, the need for 'intelligence' which creates a dependency upon sources, does provide some counter-balance. This is all the more the case because, in the past at least, the professional standing of individual correspondents and the judgement of their peers was contingent upon such contacts. Further, their political standing within their own news rooms and in relation to senior editorial staff was shaped by the same factors.

Competition and Co-operation

As we have seen, in previous decades, the sense of solidarity amongst members of the Group was high. And yet the need for 'intelligence' or information to provide context and allow accurate assessment was likely to generate competition between rival colleagues and news organisations. Organisational pressures to meet the cyclical demand for fresh news copy were likely to encourage the search for ways of managing the tension between the values of the competitive market place of national news journalism and the collective values of the specialist group. Tunstall has already described these tensions, which have characterised most specialist groups of journalists, using the concept of the 'competitor-colleague' (1971: 222). Tunstall rejected the concept of the 'syndicate' because he found little evidence of such formalised arrangements of co-operation in existence in Fleet Street. However, he did find a less rigidly structured normative framework which often guided the behaviour of journalists within their specialist groups. Most specialists, for example, recognised a group obligation to engage in 'general exchange activity' (1971:229) or gossip. In most specialist groups, it was a common practice to 'help out' colleagues in serious difficulty (for example, journalists new to the specialism). In most groups, tensions between competitive and collective values were managed by drawing a distinction between routine and exceptional news. Routine news would be pooled, exceptional news regarded as 'exclusive'. These pressures and the group responses of journalists are, of course, now familiar in the literature on news production and journalists' cultures.[52]

Nevertheless, the history of the Labour and Industrial Correspondents' Group does confirm the degree to which such arrangements were embedded in the traditional culture of news journalism and were recognised as such by those involved. From the earliest period of labour journalism, during the thirties, it is clear that strong group norms evolved which prompted but also regulated the offering of support and advice to colleagues (Evans 1953: 16-18). One former labour correspondent who first joined a labour desk in the early sixties can remember attending his first ministry briefing and being gently taken through what a set of Government statistics actually meant by Trevor Evans, who by that stage was one of the most senior correspondents in the Group, a knight and a director of his news organisation. It is also clear that a number of 'partnerships' evolved at the same time. The 'triumvirate' of Evans (*Daily Express*), McKay (*News Chronicle*) and Chevins (*Daily Telegraph*) was just one example but it illustrated a familiar pattern whereby journalists working for news organisations located in different sections of the market, either in terms of politics or audience type, would combine (Tunstall 1971:229). It was rarer for colleagues working for news organisations working in direct competition to combine and while some 'partnerships' were unofficially tolerated by editorial staff, arrangements involving direct competitors would not be (Evans, 1953:25). Partnerships, of course, made the job easier because they relieved pressure in news gathering and provided additional help in producing an appropriate assessment. Given the demands of the job many specialists would consult colleagues, rather than employ other more time consuming reference and search strategies for information. As Evans comments the 'triumvirate' of the thirties,'...ensured a sound news service, and yet gave time for all three of us to relax without anxiety' (1953: 25).

However, all partnerships were likely to distinguish between information to be pooled and 'exclusives'. As Evans notes, there was always a 'contracting out clause for exclusive stories in which our respective offices had a distinct interest' (1953:25). Throughout the post-war period, such arrangements or partnerships continued. A former labour editor of a quality newspaper in the seventies and early eighties notes the normative framework which encouraged Group wide co-operation at a routine level but partnerships to facilitate not only more detailed information gathering but to combat rival 'rings':

> There was co-operation at the basic level of, if you couldn't go to a news conference or you had to go somewhere else someone would cover for you or swap information. In the old days without screens ... the information gathering process was a lot more laborious and there was so much to cover. Therefore, we would contact each other by phone to exchange 'basic information'. But exclusives you kept to yourself, except there were 'rings'. The *Guardian* and the *FT* operated together. The *Telegraph*, the *Mail* and the old *Sketch* operated together. When I took over as labour correspondent in 1971, there were only three of us facing the *FT-Guardian* axis. The *FT* had five correspondents so were out-numbered three to one. The first thing I did was to approach the *FT* and say 'I can't seek to undermine your arrangement but I think it's wrong... [they] didn't actually de-couple from the

Guardian but they did seek a greater degree of independence...I formed my own link with the *Morning Star* on the grounds that they weren't competitors and they didn't deal with anybody else. But it wasn't on a total swap basis. I'd talk to them, they had access to the stewards and it was very difficult for me as a newcomer...to make contacts with unions like the AEU, - the CP had a vast network of contacts and information through the shop stewards movement. It was never a formal deal like the *FT-Guardian* but the [...] had no allies at this time and I had to find some... .[53]

As noted above, correspondents working for the *Morning Star* enjoyed a particular position within the Group precisely because of the extensive contacts the CP had developed with the labour movement away from the elites of London. One 'partnership' which formed in the early 1960s involved two correspondents, one from the *Morning Star* and the other from the *Times*. As both correspondents achieved positions of prominence within the Group this arrangement was widely known about and confirmed by several former correspondents independently.[54] Stories abound of the similarity in subject matter and, even occasionally, language between items in the two papers during this period. There is even some degree of support for these stories in one piece of research on the coverage of industrial relations in national newspapers during this period, though it would be unwise to regard this as definitive evidence.[55]

The general impression amongst former labour corespondents is that there are far fewer 'partnerships' within the specialism now. This conclusion also emerges from the present field work where no evidence emerged of co-operation on the scale which used to occur when the Group was a more formidable force. By contrast, interviews with some health and education correspondents suggested that lines of co-operation were established and in some cases growing more elaborate as these specialisms were required to expand their volume of copy.[56]

The decline of labour journalism: summary and conclusion

What bearing does this history have upon the overall theme of the book which seeks to understand the relationship between trade unions as sources of news and labour journalists, and to assess the scope union officers have to make favourable interventions into the news encoding process? The short answer is that it illustrates some of the most important ways in which changes in the political-economic environment shape and constrain the practice of labour journalists and, therefore, also the opportunities for trade unions as non-official news sources.

Labour journalists clearly experienced a period of severe trauma in the years after the 1979 General Election. The process of political marginalisation which began in the final months of the Callaghan Government, accelerated as both union elites and labour correspondents found themselves pushed from the centre of Government. The bitterest disputes involving the miners in 1984-85 and the print unions at Wapping in 1987 placed the Group under the most acute strains but this was because both disputes rendered visible and obvious, processes of erosion and emasculation which were already set in motion.

The underlying causes of this process are complex and cannot be described in terms of a single determining concept. The labour movement was grievously weakened by the accelerating levels of unemployment, during the early years of the Thatcher administration, which undermined a sustained opposition to the Government. The new Government set about employing the state to develop its political project with an almost unprecedented combination of astute political skill and ideological zeal. At the same time, however, both the Labour Party and the trade union movement placed themselves on the political defensive as they engaged for a period in an introspective and debilitating internal post-mortem. And broader processes of economic change, some of them global in dimension, all played a part in weakening and re-positioning trade unions during this decade. It would be a mistake, therefore, to resurrect a version of the structural determinism which prioritised the role of state, above other forces, in the reproduction of political and ideological formations, characteristic of much critical theory a decade ago.

These processes through which capital has sought to re-cast and rationalise the organisation of production have not left news journalism untouched. Changes in the nature of the news production process and the ways in which news organisations seek to utilise the labour of journalists, have also had profound consequences for labour journalsm and the fortunes of the Group. Although by no means all the evidence confirms the view that journalists are more desk bound and under more intense pressure to deliver copy to meet a faster cycle of deadlines, many journalists believe this to be so. The re-location of news organisations away from Fleet Street, 'Wappingisation', has also accelerated the forces which were already re-casting relationships between journalists and altering their day to day occupational practice. Networks of 'telephonic' rather than personal contacts between journalists and between journalists and sources are now more characteristic of the news gathering process.

Putting all these factors into the 'mix', the Labour and Industrial Correspondents' Group now finds itself in a situation where many of the patterns which characterised its role in the period before 1979 have now been broken up or weakened. The Group no longer has the 'political clout' to represent the collective interests of members in the way it used to do. It no longer has the authority to intervene to counter threats to established channels of information. The experience of journalists during the Coal Strike demonstrated that it was possible for political and media elites to by-pass the traditional intelligence gathering processes established by industrial correspondents. All this, in turn, has had a debilitating effect upon the culture and solidarity of the Group.

From the perspective of trade unions these developments are all the more worrying. Industrial correspondents now acknowledge the decline in occupational status. A former chair of the Group (Kevin McGuire) commented that we, 'used to be up there with the Lobby...we're now below city [financial] correspondents and about on par with home affairs'.[57] Younger, ambitious journalists now see industrial journalism as 'way down the pack' (Patrick Hennesey). Hennesey made it clear that he regarded his time on the labour beat as merely a stepping stone; labour corespondents were 'a dying breed', particularly after the 1992 defeat of the Labour Party. Only three years into the job, he had already added education to his brief, 'I still cover industry but education is much more the string to my bow'.[58] As an occupational specialism, labour and industrial journalism no longer offers the rewards and prospects which are likely to retain ambitious correspondents. The 'turn-over' within the specialism is likely to increase and this will make life all the more difficult for trade union press officers, seeking to establish stable 'exchange relationships'. Such relationships are dependent upon both sides sharing not only a recognition of the implicit normative framework but also a stock of common knowledge and both of these, in turn, depend upon a degree of stability in the staffing of the labour and industrial beat.

The Political-Economic Environment and the Dilemma of Incorporation

The government of the day exercises considerable influence over the routines and intelligence gathering practices of specialist correspondents. Firstly, through the exercise of political power members of the political elite in

Westminster can allocate or deny 'insider status', thereby fostering or stifling the cultivation of political contacts. Of course, such decisions are likely to take into account the strategic value of particular types of correspondent. The Lobby are unlikely to experience the degree of political marginalisation experienced by the Group, though even political correspondents found the relationships and channels they had established with Government fairly brutally re-fashioned during early years of the Thatcher-Ingham era (Cockerell et al,1985).

Secondly, it is in the power of the government to confer status and authority upon particular individuals within news organisations. This is, in part, a function of the process whereby informal access is permitted to the higher levels of the political elite, but it is also likely to include a variety of ways in which formal recognition is announced. During the Thatcher years it was the turn of particular individual political columnists and senior editorial staff in favoured news organisations to recieve, through a combination of honours and political symbolism, the recognition of prestige and occupational authority. In the sixties and seventies, as we have seen, it was often the turn of labour and industrial specialists to receive such rewards. Such recognition opened doors and provided access to information flows which might, otherwise, have remained closed.

Thirdly, every new administration will re-structure the departments of state to reflect its particular political agendas and ideological concerns. This took a dramatic turn during the years in which Mrs Thatcher set about dismantling the institutional arrangements of the post-war settlement. As the departments of state were re-organised, so too were the news beats for specialist correspondents and Mrs Thatcher's re-fashioned departmental geography further helped to push labour and industrial journalism to the margins.

Fourthly, and perhaps most importantly, the Thatcher administration demonstrated the power of a determined administration to re-work the 'political common sense' of elite opinion leaders, including the senior editorial staff of news organisations. Just at the point at which the other changes identified above began to threaten the Group's access to the channels and information flows which provided 'good copy' and 'good intelligence', which in itself was likely to undermine the standing of labour and industrial specialists within the news room, so the view that in the wake of the collapse of the post-war settlement, trade unions would experience irreversible decline towards news insignificance, was gaining ground amongst editors. It was this which partly produced the devaluation in standing and resource allocation which the Group experienced. The network which connected key sections of the parliamentary Conservative Party, policy makers and researchers at Conservative Central Office, and the new right pressure groups, was able to generate a vision of the past and a set of prescriptions for the future which appealed powerfully to many of the senior editorial staff in national news organisations.

A circular process of decline, already primed to unfold in the final years of the Callaghan administration, was sharply accelerated by the new Conservative administration. Thatcherism weakened trade unions and eroded their political power. The political profile of unions declined and as they became less visible, so they became less newsworthy in the eyes of editorial staff. An apparant decline in the newsworthyness of unions complimented the political and ideological perspectives of a number of senior editorial staff within news organisations who believed that in the new post-1979 era, unions had 'had their day'. With such editorial judgements informing the strategic planning of news organisations and their decisions regarding the distribution of resources and staff, so the profile of unions declined even further. Each step in this descent further politically marginalised unions and rendered them even less newsworthy.

However, one must be careful not to exaggerate the effectivity of Thatcherism and the role of government, alone. The decline in labour journalism in the period since the late 1970s is the product of the intersection of a number of factors within the political-economic environment. The decline in trade union strength and vitality reflects a longer terms process of economic structural change as well as the political project of a hostile government. The decline in labour journalism must be placed against this backdrop. Secondly, the forces producing the editorial re-appraisal of the position of labour journalism were simultaneously responsible for the rise in the prospects of other 'rival' specialisms. Where as bright graduates entering journalism might select the labour beat as a 'fast track' route to seniority during the 1960s and 1970s, their counterparts today are more likely to consider financial and business journalism. This, too, is in part a reflection of the editorial perspectives of news organisations and, in part, a reflection of 'real' changes in the political-economic environment including the huge expansion in financial activity and city institutions since the mid-80s and the rise in personal investment (Parsons 1989; Negrine 1993).

What are the implications of this analysis for trade union press officers? Firstly, it is clear that as the fortunes of the Labour and Industrial Group have declined and news organisations' appetites for labour news have diminished, so the environment in which union press officers work has become harsher. The history of labour and industrial journalism also demonstrates, however, the extent to which the effectivity of the various communication strategies employed by unions is limited by broader processes quite removed from the control of particular union organisations. Chapter two traced the ways in which unions have responded to the events of the 1980s by re-assessing the importance of communication and belatedly investing more in media work. The irony, however, is that it is the conditions inducing this response from trade unions which also make the difficulties for effective union news work all the greater.

This is not to suggest that a good union press officer makes no difference. Most journalists welcome the more frequent use of press officers and publicity departments in union organisations. The case of the NUM during the Coal Strike provides an extreme illustration of the dangers which arise if media work is not prioritised. The media work of the NUM then and now is almost universally condemned by former and present labour correspondents, including those whose politics are very much to the left. The failure to provide daily briefings, ensure effective arrangements for handling press enquiries, and the mistakes made in launching key media campaigns during the Coal Strike, have been documented in a number of places (Jones,1986; Adeney and Lloyd,1986; Winterton and Winterton,1989). In other words, the NUM refused to work within the normative framework which regulates most interaction between journalists and union sources. By default the initiative in terms of the news agenda was frequently handed to the NCB and the Government. And yet there are two reasons to suspect that even the most sophisticated communication strategy would not have altered the broad contours of coverage of the Coal Strike.

Firstly, as we have seen particular departments of state were active in seeking to by-pass the normal process of labour news gathering. The state directed its media work towards editors and political correspondents, not the labour and industrial beat. Secondly, chapters three and four have demonstrated that in seeking to develop regular and stable relationships with specialist correspondents, unions must accept the normative framework, 'the rules of the game', which regulate union - source interaction but also place limitations on the themes and agendas which can be presented. The more union press officers are willing to accept the news values and selection criteria of news organisations the more highly they will be rated by labour correspondents. 'Good' union press officers are also willing to provide the 'intelligence' and 'contextual information' sought after by correspondents but it is not always in the interests of the union to divulge. The fact that 'rings' involving labour correspondents from the *Times* and the *Morning Star* would seek the same information and employ the same selection criteria underlines just how powerfully the common news sense and 'inferential structures' of labour journalists can shape the ways in which they 'construct' labour news.

Similarly, the 'rules' which regulate on and off record briefings have to be embraced by both sides and here, once again, the imprint of the state can be found. The on/off record briefing system is the primary mechanism through which the state releases information to journalists. It is significant that where as *Morning Star* correspondents had always played a prominent role in the Group, anxieties arose over the application from Newsline, precisely because of the danger that correspondents from this news organisation would destabilise the delicate normative framework regulating interaction between the state and labour correspondents. In short, the fostering of 'effective' working relationships with labour and industrial correspondents involves degrees of 'incorporation' into a normative system, in part reinforced by the workings of the state, which limits and shapes the kind of news agenda which can be presented.

Notes

1. Riddell (1983 and 1989), for example, develops a volunteeristic account which emphasises the political authority of Thatcher. Gamble (1988) and Jessop et al (1988) also focus upon the political and ideological projects developed by Thatcher 'on behalf' of British Capitalism. Writers, however, such as Coates (1989), stress much more, the fundamental aim of Thatcherism to break the power of organised labour above all else, in order to renew opportunities for Capital to maximise profit and deploy labour 'flexibly'.
2. With the exceptions of life-members who are nominated at AGM's and freelance journalists who are recognised as labour or industrial specialists.
3. As staffing on the labour and industrial desks oten changed with the departures, appointments and movements of staff to other desks, the annual membership lists required frequent amendment. As by no means all news organisations were prompt in informing the Group of changes in personnel, the annual list of members provides, at best, a 'snapshot' impression of membership levels.
4. Interview with Secretary to the Group, Summer 1992.
5. Secretary's Report to the 1984 AGM.
6. Sources include the papers of the Group (Ibid), interviews with contemporary labour and industrial journalists (Ibid), and Hill (1993).
7. Interview with labour editor and former number two on the *Sun*, Summer 1992.
8. All references to the papers of the Group refer to the papers and records retained by the Secretary of the Group (Ibid). Photostat copies of the most

important papers have been retained by the author.

9.   Papers of the Group, ibid.
10. Papers of the Group, ibid.
11. Papers of the Group, ibid.
12. Papers of the Group, ibid.
13. Papers of the Group, ibid.
14. Papers of the Group, ibid.
15. Papers of the Group, ibid.
16. Interview with current labour editor and former number two on the *Sun*, Summer 1992.
17. Interview with the author, Summer 1993.
18. Ibid.
19. Papers of the Group, ibid.
20. Interview with the author.Ibid.
21. Chairman's Report to the 1983/84 AGM of the Group, 23.2.84.
22. Ibid.
23. Ibid.
24. Original documents in the papers of the Group. Ibid.
     Copies of the notes made at the meeting and the letters exchanged are held by the author.
25. Records of the Group, 1984. Ibid.
26. Interview conducted with former labour editor and political correspondent, 4th August 1993.
27. Records of the Group, 1987. Ibid.
28. Records of the Group, 1987. Ibid.
29. Records of the Group, 1987. Ibid.
30. Interview with the author, 10th June 1993.
31. The Constitution of the Labour and Industrial Correspondents' Group. Original in the possession of the Secretary. Copy held by author.
32. Ibid.
33. Interviews with former correspondents who staffed labour desks in the 1960s suggest the overall dominance of Labour Party sympathies. This is also confirmed by Tunstall (1971:171).
34. Interviews with the author, 15th June 1992, 10th June 1993, 15th July 1993 and 28th July 1993. See also Benn (1990:230). Though sometimes regarded as a 'moderate', Goodman was active in helping to form the Fleet Street Forum of Socialist Writers in the 1950s and still in the late 1970s represented the dissident voice within the 1977 Royal Commission on the Press calling for significant state intervention into the newspaper industry, (Basnett and Goodman,1977).
35. Interview with author, August 1993.
36. Interview with former industrial correspondent on the *Financial Times*, Summer 1992.
37. Papers of the Group, 1985. Ibid.
38. Mary Stewart replaced Ian McKay as number one on the *News Chronicle* in 1953, after having worked as numbertwo during the War. Julia Somerville, Julie Copley (*Labour Weekly*), Helen Hague (*Independent*), and Jill Hartley (*Sunday Times*) all worked as labour correspondents in the 1980s. There are currently two women working as labour or industrial correspondents (Celia Weston on the *Guardian*,

Mary Fagan on the *Independent*). Otherwise, the world of labour and industrial reporting remains exclusively male.

39. Interview with former industrial and political correspondent, Summer 1993.
40. Interview with former industrial correspondent on the Financial Times, Summer 1992.
41. Interviews conducted with industrial, health and education correspondents, May, June and July 1993.
42. Interview with health corespondent, June 1993.
43. Interview with former industrial correspondent, June 1993.
44. MORI has conducted surveys with labour and industrial correspondents since 1975, though only those conducted since 1983 are available at MORI headquarters in London. Unfortunately, because these surveys have not been conducted with a longitudinal perspective in consideration and, indeed, were conducted for different clients (first British Gas and then British Rail), question design and format vary considerably from year to year and direct comparisons over time are impossible. Approximately 29 journalists were successfully contacted in most years which means that half to two-thirds of the Group responded. There are quite wide variations in responses to particular questions from year to year which is almost certainly the product of the failure to retain a stable panel across years, rather than a reflection of 'real' changes of opinion within the Group.
45. Interview with former industrial correspondent, Summer 1993.
46. Papers of the Group, ibid.
47. Papers of the Group, ibid.
48. Quotes taken from the papers of the Group for the years 1987 and 1985 respectively. Ibid. The event continues annually and is usually held now at the end of the TUC Conference week.
49. Phrase used by Phillip Bassett, labour editor on the *Times*, in interview with the author, Summer 1993.
50. Interview conducted with former labour and industrial correspondent, Summer 1993.
51. Ibid.
52. Ericson, R et al. (1989:ch 3), Schlesinger (1978:ch 4), and Chibnall (1977:ch2), for example.
53. Interview conducted by the author, Summer 1993.
54. Confirmation of the existence of this 'partnership' was provided independently by three different former labour correspondents in interviews with the author. Reference is also found in Jones (1986).
55. Hartmann, P (1976) 'The Media and Industrial Relations', unpublished report, funded by the Leverhulme Trust and produced at the Centre for Mass Communication Research, University of Leicester. Hartmann found some surprising similarities in the nature and range of coverage between the *Morning Star* and other daily papers. While there were predictable differences in rhetoric and editorial evaluation, it was possible to detect some evidence of a shared framework of news values.
56. Interviews with several current industrial, health and education correspondents during May and June and July 1993.
57. Interview conducted in Summer 1991.
58. Interview conducted in the Summer 1991.

7 Union News and Communication Work: the Journalists' Perspective

The intention now is to concentrate upon the current position of labour and industrial correspondents and, in particular, their perception of the media work of trade unions. The focus will remain almost exclusively upon the day to day practice of labour and industrial journalists, and other specialists in contact with trade union press officers, drawing mainly upon material collected through a set of interviews conducted between 1991 and 1993.[1] It will deal with the news values and working assumptions which shape the daily work of labour correspondents; their expectations of trade union press officers, and the ways in which they recognise and describe the 'exchanges' which occur when trade union officers encounter the news media.

Labour and industrial correspondents are keenly aware of the changing fortunes of their specialism. The forces at work impinge most directly, perhaps, in terms of the greater demands for flexibility and wider briefs which most labour correspondents now have to accept. As chapters five and six have described, the number of staff attached to the labour and industrial desks have been reduced and some news organisations even do without a labour correspondent all together. The occupational status of industrial correspondents has declined within the hierarchy of national news journalism and those journalists remaining at the labour desk have either had to re-invent their own broader beats as survival strategies or their news organisations have done this for them. Rather than work exclusively upon labour relations, most correspondents now contemplate a much more broadly defined canvas which includes general employment and workplace issues and even, perhaps, consumer affairs and news of the privatised utilities.

> I've become a labour editor on this paper but my job has become multi-skilled. As unions have declined I've had to look at what else I can write

about and basically I see my role as writing about people at work, which does not necessarily involve the trade unions but I'm no longer an industrial correspondent, I'm an industry wide correspondent writing about issues as they occur, privatisation, coal, railways - a big story that will keep running for two years - privatisation and how it affects people at work, and what the trade unions are saying about it, but it's a far wider brief. We don't cover the TUC like we used to. Why should we? The debates aren't so important. The industrial unions are still important but not the debates. So, of course, there has been a re-appraisal of the job we do and on the *Guardian* we're looking at the European labour scene, at the single market, the problems for British firms which will occur in Europe, the development of European works councils, its a big story for us. There's still a role for us but it's more diverse.[2]

Unlike the labour editor of the *Guardian*, working for a broadsheet paper still with a commitment to detailed coverage at least of workplace issues, the labour editor of a daily tabloid was compelled to become a 'jack of all trades', covering a story about the collapse of a holiday firm, on the day he was interviewed for the present study. Another tabloid labour editor, described himself as 'doing a bit of industry, a bit of commerce, a bit of David Mellor' (the Mellor ministerial resignation story broke during the week of the interview).[3] Some correspondents now even find themselves combining the industry brief with another specialism, such as education.[4] Geoffrey Goodman, former labour editor at the *Daily Mirror*, believed that pressures to raise the 'productivity' of staff within news organisations, combined with the trend towards the 'tabloidisation' of news values, even amongst broadsheet newspapers, were now significantly constraining opportunities for specialised work.[5]

The geographical dispersal of news organisations away from Fleet Street, in the wake of the News International move to Wapping in 1987, has disrupted and broken up the social networks which used to support the culture in which labour correspondents were immersed, - a culture which often reinforced an understanding of, if not a sympathy for, the values and perspectives of the labour movement. As described in chapters five and six, labour and industrial correspondents would meet on a daily basis at the Cheshire Cheese pub, off Fleet Street, or the Clarence in Whitehall; they would foster contacts with trade union officials and national executive members in well known pubs adjacent to union headquarters, usually located quite near to Fleet Street in London, and would meet again, as they 'door stepped' outside the offices of ACAS, or the venue for important national negotiations. Now newspapers offices are located along a ten mile 'corridor' from Kensington to Canary Wharf, and the opportunities for casual meetings amongst labour correspondents, meetings in which 'themes' could be 'floated' and 'intelligence' assessed, are far more limited.

A number of the correspondents interviewed believed that they were now more 'desk-bound'. The introduction of new print technology has allowed newspapers to produce more editions but this means earlier deadlines. Several correspondents felt that the new regimes within the newsroom implied more stringent 'policing' of time outside the office. The result is that more of the information gathering work undertaken by labour correspondents is conducted via the telephone and the fax machine.

> I'm sure its fair to say that a lot more time was spent out and about meeting people in the old days. Nowadays, a lot more, eighty or ninety percent, is done over the telephone and a lot of this is because it's very easy to gather news electronically...there's a lot more reliance upon electronic media. We can sit in front of a screen and receive statements, P.A. reports, freelance people, and get FAXes and write a very complete story without getting off your bum...that's sad in a way but it's the way of the world.[6]

This view underestimates the extent to which news gathering remains a *social* process. The social relationships between journalists and news sources have not been replaced by electronic information gathering systems but it is true that in the case of labour and industrial journalism, at least, such social relationships have been re-cast. The exchanges between union sources and journalists are now much more likely to be conducted by telephone than over a pub table but, nonetheless, they remain based upon an implicit understanding of 'exchange relationships', essentially social in nature. As discussed in chapters three and four, a growing number of union press officers are reviewing their investment in the more expensive means of electronic information dissemination and this is because it is recognised that, essentially, it is not the sophistication of the technology but the nature of the social relationships which is of the greater importance.

As this chapter will explore further below, from the perspective of labour and industrial correspondents, there remains a process whereby sources and journalists enter into implicit 'bargains' governed by a loose normative framework. However, the rise of a 'telephonic culture', as one union press officer describes it, has made a difference. While relationships between journalists and union sources remain essentially social in nature, it is possible to detect a distancing between the two when the present situation is contrasted to earlier decades. As we have seen, the geography of the old labour beat encouraged a proximity between journalists and union officials which, in turn, fostered a degree of sympathy and understanding, at least, on the part of many labour correspondents. Two decades ago even the labour correspondent of the *Sun* could write:

> Often such men [union activists] were Communists and other left wingers. I recall with a liking and respect, such men as Jack Dash of the London dockers and George Wake and Charles Doyle of the power workers. Communists are often portrayed as villains of the piece in newspapers...But as people Communists are often remarkably likeable.(Mason,1981:3).

Telephonic communication is unlikely to foster such an intimacy for a new generation of labour and industrial correspondents, most a decade further removed from the post-war settlement, and the agendas of the 1960s and 1970s. Geographical dispersal also means that the sense of community and common culture amongst labour correspondents is waning:

> The propping up the bar bit has gone away, not so much because of staffing levels but because of the way the newspaper industry has changed...the industry has spread from 800 yards around Fleet Street to eight miles from Kensington, here, down to the Isle of Dogs with Max in his little tower, so we're not in the same little puddle anymore. One of the great traditions used to be that industrial correspondents used to get together in the cellar of the Cheshire Cheese in Fleet Street because you could guarantee to get ten or twelve union press officers staggering around looking for a drink. That doesn't happen anymore, the Group [Labour and Industrial Correspondents' Group] is still going but it's different now.[7]

Paradoxically, the decision of more unions to invest in press and media work, may have encouraged a distancing and formalisation of relations. Journalists' attitudes regarding the appointment of more union press officers was ambivalent. On the one hand, there were numerous complaints about the difficulties experienced by journalists in previous years in gaining access to union staff:

> Ironically, twenty years ago when they were really needed no union had one [a press officer]. Hugh Scanlon was never available. The second biggest union but no comment. Scanlon was a bit of a Stalinist. When he gave a press conference when he had finished that was the end of it. You either had

to get Scanlon at the press conference or not at all. Similarly, the T and G didn't have one in those days but the GMB did.[8]

In the past, the large unions relied upon the presence and profile of their general secretaries and leading officials, Hugh Scanlon at the old AEU, Jack Jones at the TGWU, Joe Gormley at the NUM or Frank Chapple at the EETPU. While a dependence upon the willingness of a general secretary or senior official to provide information frequently caused journalists difficulties, it also produced two benefits. It encouraged labour correspondents to invest considerable resources in developing a rapport with such senior officials and it also encouraged them to exploit the inherent 'porosity' (Ericson et al,1989:214) of unions by searching out sets of informal sources.

While journalists welcome the improved efficiency in the release of 'official' information which has been achieved through the appointment of more union press officers, they are sometimes suspicious that the formalisation of union-media relations in such a way, has provided unions with a better mechanism for defending their 'back regions' (Ericson et al, 1989:9). The job of the union press officer is to police the 'front region' and regulate journalists' access beyond this arena. Several labour correspondents commented that, wherever possible, they still tried to by-pass the union press officer and get through to a senior official or informal source. And, as we shall see, the press officers rated most highly by journalists were those who they believed were 'on the inside track', close to the thinking of their general secretaries and the political undercurrents of their union executives. Though in some ways the ready availability of a union press officer on the end of a telephone has made life easier for labour correspondents, it may not have made the 'contextual information',[9] or intelligence, valued by labour correspondents more readily available. With the development of a 'telephonic culture' shared by journalists and union sources, the process of gathering such 'higher grade' information may be more difficult. Given the earlier deadlines and tougher drives for productivity associated with the post-Wapping regimes within news rooms, it is possible that journalists will be compelled to rely more upon routinised and bureaucratic sources. This, in turn, might provide non-official sources with more opportunities to successfully 'present' their own copy. There is some support for this view derived from studies of journalists working for news organisations where staffing levels have been reduced (Fishman,1980: ch 6; Franklin,1986; Anderson,1993). However, the present study found that in the case of labour news, few journalists were likely to digest raw, 'untreated' union copy, despite the earlier deadlines and broader briefs of recent years.

Reporting trade unions: news values and journalists' perspectives

In their understanding of what makes 'a good story', the labour and industrial correspondents interviewed in this study largely revealed a commitment to the conventional news values of mainstream journalism, documented in numerous studies (Tunstall,1971: 15-21; Galtung and Ruge,1973; Elliott and Golding,1979: ch 5; Ericson et al,1987: ch 5; Cottle,1993: ch 2; etc.). A search for the dramatic, the immediate and the personal characterised the majority of approaches, with the exception of the *Financial Times*.

> Quite often we like to personalise things, there's no such thing as Virgin Airways but there is Richard Branson's Virgin Airways, there's Arthur's barmy army...Arthur Scargill's miners union, so that the individual becomes synonymous with the organisation...like John Major's government.[10]

Union officials 'with a natural charisma of their own'[11] were more likely to generate 'useful' news stories. Jimmy Knapp (NUR), Eric Hammond (EETPU), Bill Jordan (AEU) and, of course, Arthur Scargill were most frequently cited as high profile, newsworthy personalities. An orientation towards the 'personalities' of industrial and labour news was matched by an 'individualisation' of events, whereby public issues were transmuted into private troubles (Cottle,1993:79). As we shall see in chapter eight, the health unions were able to exploit this news value in the early phase of the 1989 Ambulance Dispute to good effect. It was noticeable that some correspondents actually characterised the history of the most recent decade of industrial relations in terms of the personalities involved. Thus, for both Tony McGuire (*Evening Standard*) and Patrick Hennesey (*Daily Express*), the decisive moment of the 1980s was the 'defeat' of Arthur Scargill and the 'triumph' of Mrs Thatcher.

Strikes, of course, have obvious appeal in terms of conflict, drama and immediacy. When John Monks, general secretary of the TUC, asked how the TUC could make life easier for labour correspondents, he was told by Roy Jones of the *Morning Star*, "What you need, John, is a bloody big strike" (Hill, 1993). But not every strike will offer the ingredients of a 'good story'. The work of the Glasgow University Media Group demonstrated that coverage of strikes and industrial conflict was highly selective, with large sectors of strike-prone employment ignored and other areas 'over-represented' (Glasgow University Media Group,1976). To score heavily in terms of labour news values, industrial conflict must contain at least one of two possible features. Conflict which involves party political implications, and especially the likelihood of conflict with government, will certainly be defined as newsworthy by labour correspondents (Harper,1991). To argue that labour and industrial news has declined in salience for news editors because there are now fewer strikes, is to over-simplify. Many unions remain involved in industrial conflict of a routine nature. The essential point is that there are fewer conflicts which are of immediate significance to the mainstream political process. Industrial conflict offered the most in terms of labour journalism's news values, when 'industrial matters dominated decision making at Number Ten' (Harper,1991:33). At root, the news value of unions is intimately associated with perceptions of power. As the labour editor at the *Daily Mirror* commented:

> ...legislation makes unions impotent, they can no longer protect their members, and if they become impotent, they are no longer newsworthy.[12]

Secondly, for industrial conflict to offer maximum salience in terms of industrial news values, it must affect, in one way or another, a broader constituency than merely the immediate participants. National disputes, disputes which disrupt the daily lives of the general public, or local disputes which generate exceptional and 'publicly visible' conflict are most likely to attract the attention of labour correspondents. However, the potential capacity to intervene in the daily lives of the public cannot guarantee news media interest. As one labour editor pointed out, despite the dwindling membership of the NUM, under 30,000 members and falling fast at the time of the field work, the union retained a salience in the eyes of the news media, not justified either by its size or its capacity to influence the daily lives of the public at large. The Inland Revenue Staff Association, on the other hand, with a capacity to cripple the workings of government, directly intervene in the lives of most adults, and with a membership roughly three times greater than that of the NUM, rarely attracted the attention of journalists.[13] In labour journalism, as in other branches of journalism, news values are determined not only by 'rational criteria' but also by the deposits left by the ebb and flow of earlier ideological constructions and news media representations. It was for precisely this reason that the health unions were determined, in their dispute strategy, to minimise the opportunities given to the news media to invoke the imagery of the 1979 Winter of Discontent, during the 1989 Ambulance Dispute (see chapter eight).

Beyond the conflict of the workshop and the factory gate, political and organisational conflicts across the industrial stage are still likely to interest labour journalists. The tensions within the TUC over the question of 'new realism', no-strike and single union deals, in the late 1980s provided considerable copy.[14] The notorious walk out by EETPU delegates from the 1989 TUC Conference, led by Eric Hammond, accommodated almost all the news values a labour journalist might desire, including conflict and drama, a high profile personality, and a significance for the wider party political process at Westminster,[15] all occurring within neatly defined spatial and temporal parameters to satisfy the demand of 'event orientation'.

Not all labour journalism is preoccupied with industrial conflict and not all opportunities for unions to gain publicity are derived from industrial disputes. The power of the familiar in determining news selection, - the appetite news editors have for previously established themes and imagery (Galtung and Ruge,1973) - produces a labour and industrial news agenda which is shaped as much by the interplay between the preoccupations of news journalism and popular discourse, as by 'external' criteria, such as union size or economic significance.

> The size of an industrial organisation is quite important,- if the GMB calls a press conference, then we'll tend to go. But it doesn't always follow, the amount of attention focused upon the NUM given its size is quite ludicrous and given its position in the economy...It's not just Arthur, it's partly Scargill because he's by far the most well-known trade unionist in the country and one of these people who makes news editors hear the name and look up and the story automatically goes in the paper. People often don't understand this...Scargill will always go in, anything to do with Ford will go in, Habitat, Vauxhall, Marks and Spencer. Oddly enough the NUM still has that quality.[16]

'Consonance' (Galtung and Ruge,1973:64), the extent to which a news item conforms to the previously established expectations of journalists, sometimes combined with journalists' search for 'currency' or immediacy, may provide some finite opportunities for union sources to score useful political points. According to one health correspondent, the 'horror stories' which began to emerge after the implementation of Conservative government reforms in the National Health Service, enabled public sector unions to interest journalists in a series of stories, all highlighting resource issues.[17] However, as novelty diminished, so news salience, in the eyes of journalists declined and the health unions eventually found it much harder to attract interest in 'run of the mill' under-funding stories.[18] As far as labour journalists are concerned, there is nothing more frustrating than contacting a union for a response regarding a topical or sudden development, to find that the press officers have not been informed by local branches. One labour editor remembered finding that union press officers were dependent upon journalists for information regarding a sudden crisis in the Scottish oil industry, local union branches not having communicated vital information to headquarters.

Given this emphasis upon immediacy and topicality, and the essentially routine nature of much of the information union press officers have as their 'raw material', one strategy is to acknowledge the fact that labour journalism is sensitised to the political and to infuse even the routine with a political inflection. This is what the EETPU used to be so good at doing, according to several labour correspondents. It was possible because of the political ground which the union had chosen to occupy.

> For a newspaper, glossy stuff produced with Desk Top Publishing just goes in the bin, unless there's a story in it. The thing about the electricians was that they produced the glossy stuff but there was a story in it, which was, 'we're doing this and we don't give a shit what other people think about it. This is our new financial package, this is our new insurance package'. There was a story in it. A lot of other people started putting glossy stuff out, thinking there was a story in it but there wasn't on its own, or the story ran out...you know, union launches new cheap travel package or cheap mortgage and so on. For a couple of years, we were all writing stories along these lines but then they ran into the ground.[19]

Indeed, the labour correspondents interviewed for this study believed that it was now much harder to place routine industrial copy in their papers. As the political importance of unions declined, so a higher value in terms of selection criteria was demanded of labour and industrial copy by news editors. Kevin McGuire (*Daily Telegraph*) noted that stories which represented the bread and butter of industrial journalism a decade ago, concerning industrial tribunals and cases of discrimination, pay awards, or job losses, etc, were now much less likely to be accepted. A story now had to have a 'quirky, off-beat' element to interest the editorial team.[20] Even on the Financial Times, usually regarded as operating with distinct, 'specialist' news values, the appetite for routine union material has diminished:

When I first came [1986], one of my first stories was about an AEU executive meeting and whether or not they were likely to support a minimum wage at conference. That got about three hundred words and now that wouldn't get in the paper.[21]

Broadsheets, Tabloids, and the FT

According to several labour correspondents, the same news values guide the selection criteria of most newspapers, left or right of centre, broadsheet or tabloid. 'Under the skin, they're all the same', was a typical view.[22] In terms of the values discussed above, this is probably true. Certainly, labour correspondents appeared to be able to cross both the political and market divides between papers without undue difficulty.[23]

The exception to this rule was widely regarded to be the *Financial Times*, which was still held to operate with more specialised news values, comparable to the employment coverage to be found in the Wall Street Journal and Business Week, in the USA (Puette,1992:126). This was despite its abandonment of a daily page for union and industrial relations news. In comparison to the '*FT*', news on the *Daily Telegraph*, for example, 'had to be racier and punchier, with more relevance to the general public.'[24] The *FT* was likely to carry 'more big gun stories...interviews with the chairman of ICI, business stories that would never get in the *Standard*.[25]

And yet, beyond the common news values discussed above, there are good grounds for believing that the differences between labour journalism for tabloid and quality newspapers ran deeper than merely the number of words permitted in copy. Cottle distinguishes between 'serious' and 'popular' journalism, partly in terms of the former's emphasis upon the deployment of 'expertise' in the assessment of information and the 'rationality' of the explanatory accounts (Cottle,1993:7-8). From the accounts provided by journalists in this study, it is possible to detect a drift 'down market', a process of progressive tabloidisation amongst popular papers. Both the *Daily Star* and the *Sun*, for example, only maintained an intermittent commitment to a labour desk, at all. Journalists working for tabloid papers have always had to acknowledge the driving force of 'revenue goals' (Tunstall,1971; Elliott,1977). However, Geoffrey Goodman believed 'tabloidisation' was blighting not only all the populars but, also, some of the broadsheet papers.[26] It is possible that the 'non-revenue goals' of labour and industrial correspondents, - the acquisition and deployment of expertise in the analysis of 'intelligence' and the provision of information beyond the description of immediate events, are being eroded as competition between rival newspapers increases and labour news slips down the news hierarchy.

At the *Daily Mirror*, for example, until the 1984-85 Coal Strike, the labour editor had always been allocated a weekly slot for a discursive feature article dealing with contemporary issues in industrial and labour affairs. Under Maxwell's proprietorship this disappeared. The current labour editor, at the time the field work was conducted, appeared not to mourn the lost opportunity for more analytic journalism. He believed that popular papers had to concentrate upon the immediate story, with a 'sharp sense for news', rather than indulge in more contemplative journalism and he recounted a story to illustrate the way in which the *Mirror's* labour desk had sometimes missed the essential, popular story. The weekly feature article was once based around an interview with Michael Edwards, then in charge at British Leyland. The article contained a comment made by Edwards regarding his salary but focused mainly upon the prospects for the car industry. However, the following day the headline on the front page of the *Sun* screamed, 'Edwards - Why I'm worth £100,000', with similar leads in the other populars, all re-working the material drawn from the *Mirror*.[27]

While broadsheet and tabloid correspondents may share most of the news values identified above, the appetite for information and contextual knowledge is likely to be greater for broadsheet correspondents and this may influence their perception of sources. For example, in assessing the performance of various news sources on the medical and health beat, there were some notable differences between the views of health correspondents. The British Medical Association was rated highly by broadsheet correspondents because of its capacity to supply information and answer detailed inquiries. However, one health correspondent working for a tabloid, when asked if the resources at the disposal of the BMA made a difference, replied, 'No way! They [the BMA] are awful. The health unions are much more effective.' In contrast, broadsheet health correspondents, while recognising the importance of the unions on the health beat, were nonetheless critical of their 'axe grinding'.[28] While these correspondents acknowledged the political position of the BMA, they nevertheless had a tendency to cast it in the role of 'arbiter' rather than 'advocate' (Deacon and Golding,1994:15-17).

> The BMA are very authoritative and always available. They have more press officers and invest more resources. They have lost some credibility under the chairmanship of Lee-Potter because they were seen to be steering a line

which was more visibly concerned with self-interest. Therefore, they are more vulnerable to the 'greedy consultant stereotype' and the government has begun to use this against them. But the BMA will also produce materials and reports on a wide range of issues and provide information for journalists on a range of issues and they campaign on certain issues where they can't be accused of self-interest, like tobacco advertising.[29]

The capacity of the health unions to provide information which satisfied Cottle's criteria for popular journalism,- sentimental and empathetic material drawn from 'first hand testimony' (Cottle,1993:7-8) - may explain why some tabloid health correspondents, at least, valued their media work more highly. Though popular news values repeatedly determine selection criteria in broadsheet journalism, in their dealings with unions, broadsheet correspondents applied, in addition, a set of more cerebral news values. Certainly, union press officers believed that more opportunities existed for placing detailed information, summaries of reports, synopsies of topical data analysis produced by their research departments, and so on, in the broadsheet papers. Charlie Whelan's strategy, for example, in commissioning independent research around which an AEU theme could be 'wrapped', was welcomed by most broadsheet correspondents. In contrast, tabloid labour editors were less enthusiastic, questioning the extent to which such statistical material ever 'contained a story'.

The Art of Using an Exclusive

All journalists welcome exclusives and this aspect of the competitive nature of journalism can sometimes provide news sources with some additional leverage for securing coverage. However, a great deal depends upon the kind of 'exclusive' material which sources can offer and the news values of the organisation to which it is offered. While, for example, the health unions could sometimes offer NHS 'horror stories' as exclusives to the tabloid newspapers, for trade unions in the main, the scope for offering exclusive material to secure coverage was restricted to the broadsheet papers precisely because broadsheet corespondents had a larger appetite for political and contextual information, in addition to the personalised and dramatic. If a news source can offer an 'exclusive' this, in turn, enables a correspondent to make a stronger case for a story within the news organisation:

> I need to be able to say to my news editor that this is an exclusive - that other papers won't be running it.[30]

...an exclusive is a powerful mechanism which we can use to persuade news editors to support a story... .[31]

Offering exclusivity can inflate the news value of an otherwise uninteresting item. For example, one education correspondent remembers the National Union of Students offering their views upon the proposed Student Charter as 'exclusive' to the *Times*, a paper the union had 'targeted' as being read by Conservative Ministers and back bench MPs. In itself, he regarded it as 'not particularly interesting' but as an 'exclusive' the news editor accepted the story.[32] The calculation from the news sources' point of view is a fine one, however, because once a story appears as an exclusive in one newspaper, it often loses value to others.

Industrial, health and education correspondents frequently expressed surprise that unions used the mechanism of exclusivity so infrequently. One health correspondent suggested that this was because unions suffered from being located by journalists lower down the 'hierarchy of credibility' (a point to be discussed further below). As 'axe grinders', or 'advocates' their 'exclusive' material lacked authority. However, there may be two further reasons. To exploit the mechanism of exclusivity, a news source must enjoy extensive internal control over the flow of information in order to both time the release of information and direct its communication. As discussed in chapters three and four, unions are inherently leaky or porous; little information is likely to remain in a union's 'back region' (Ericson et al, 1989:9-10) for long if it has a political or contextual salience which would interest correspondents. Secondly, for many union press officers, working in a hostile ideological climate, their preferred strategy was to cultivate 'good relationships' with a number of correspondents, particularly broadsheet journalists, by offering them a place on 'the inside track'. The dissemination of too much material on an 'exclusive' basis to just one or two correspondents would undermine this.

Underlying assumptions and inferential structures

The political perspectives to be found within labour and industrial journalism varied in a way which was associated with generational change. Many of the older labour correspondents who had cut their professional teeth in the 1960s and 1970s, appeared still committed to a 'corporatist' agenda. As chapters six and seven described in more detail, the fortunes of labour journalism prospered in the era of the post-war settlement and the labour beat grew around its organisational and departmental architecture; the Ministry of Labour, the Department of Economic Affairs, ACAS, the TUC and the headquarters of the leading unions. An intimate political relationship between the state and the main 'actors' in the industrial arena was taken for granted by journalists, as well as by the political elite. Generational change has brought a fragmenting of political perspectives. The 1970s, as we have seen, saw the arrival in labour journalism of a new generation of ambitious graduates, influenced by the political debates occurring within university departments during this era, and who were attracted to the specialism because of its occupational standing, second only perhaps to the Lobby. In the 1980s and 1990s, the political perspectives appear to have grown even more diverse. While some journalists, including Philip Bassett have developed views sympathetic to the 'new unionism' (Bassett,1986), others have embraced the politics of the 'New Times' debate, associated with *Marxism Today,* (Leadbeater,1989). However, some of the youngest correspondents who entered labour journalism in the 1990s, appear to have moved a very long way from corporatist values and the politics of the post-war settlement. For one new entrant to labour journalism, most trade unions were out of touch and 'still dominated by old style socialist thought...modern newspapers, especially the tabloids, have a completely different agenda.'[33] The latter view is still not typical of all labour correspondents. The underlying sympathy for the values and objectives of the labour movement which Tunstall found amongst labour correspondents twenty five years ago (1971:124) can be still be detected, at least in conversation with the correspondents whose experience pre-dates the 1990s.

An examination of the underlying assumptions which direct labour and industrial correspondents in their work identifies two 'epistemological' guiding principles concerning appropriate practice for journalists in gathering and processing information ((i) and (ii) below), and two fundamental assumptions or 'inferential structures' (Lang and Lang,1955) about the character of the industrial and labour world they are seeking to describe ((iii) and (iv) below).

(i) *Empiricism and Objectivity*

In common with many journalists, one of the common operational assumptions which guides the daily work of labour correspondents, is the assumption that it is possible, through journalistic investigation, experience and shrewd judgement, to 'uncover the facts'. Allied to this view is the assumption that the raison d'être of labour journalism, at least for broadsheet correspondents, is to provide accurate, impartial information and to make forecasts regarding future events, which command authority. For most of the journalists interviewed, their conceptual understanding of the relationship between the knowledge they gathered and the world 'out there', could be described as 'objectivist', in that an unproblematic, one to one correspondence was assumed between 'real events out there' and journalists' accounts. A decline in the news value of labour news was explained as the result of a *real* decline in the significance of trade unionism. Few journalists in the interviews for this study began to explore the implications of what might be described as a 'constructivist' model, - the view that a decline in the news value of trade unions might be associated with the way in which news values are, themselves, constructed. Few were receptive to the argument that the politics of the workplace *could* be regarded as inherently newsworthy given that the experience of the workplace plays a fundamentally important part in the lives of so many newspaper readers. As Hoyt asks in the context of the decline of American labour journalism, 'how can a hundred million people be boring?'(1984:36).

(ii) *Intelligence and 'contextual information'*

All the journalists interviewed for this study regarded as an essential attribute for labour journalists, the ability to gather 'intelligence' or 'contextual information'[34] which would allow informed assessments to be produced. The skill of a 'professional' lay in acquiring the network of contacts or sources who could supply such information and in the degree of shrewd judgement, combined with experience, exercised in making the best use of this 'contextual information'. This is despite the point that, as Tuchman notes, there is always likely to be a tension between the emphasis upon interpretation as a professional skill and objectivity as a professional norm (Tuchman,1972:672). Nonetheless, most of the journalists interviewed for this study continued to adhere to the doctrine of the fact/value split; it was their job to present the facts, not side with either unions or their opponents.

(iii) *An 'individualised' view of the world*

Some correspondents interviewed for this study employed explanatory frameworks for making sense of the world which did draw upon variants of social theory and did attempt to relate immediate events to underlying structures and social processes. Charlie Leadbeater's contributions to the 'New Times' debate on the nature of late capitalism provide one example, Philip Bassett's work on the energies driving the 'new unionism' another. One or two of the older correspondents reflected, in their comments about the changing position of trade unionism and the future of labour journalism, an understanding of structure and power which drew upon the analysis of the traditional left. However, a majority of correspondents in their approach to labour and industrial news, at least, employed analytic frameworks which attended to the impact of individual effectivity and experience, rather than structure or history. In the main, the assumption appeared to be that 'news' was about the here and now, the immediate, and not the charting of unfolding historical processes or the tracing of structural connections, even though the impact of such phenomena upon the daily lives of employees and trade unionists has rarely been more visible.

(iv) *Power*

A final assumption concerns the nature of industrial news. For all correspondents, industrial and labour news gained in salience and value in proportion to the extent to which it was associated with and had significance for the powerful in society. This was implicit in the practice of correspondents but not always made explicit in their reflections upon the nature of their work. As we have seen, many labour correspondents are likely to offer lowering strike rates as an explanation for the decline of their specialism. However, it is not lowering strike rates, as such, which has led to a waning of newsroom interest. Nor is it the declining size of unions because, as discussed above, size or economic significance were never, in themselves, guarantees of news interest.[35] Rather, it is the declining frequency of the type of conflict which had immediate implications for the polity. Trade unions were high on the news agenda when their policy and practice made a difference at Westminster, in the short term or 'here and now'. When union news occasionally rises to the top of the news agenda, once again, it is usually because journalists identify a political context. Much the same point can be made about 'welfare and social services' journalism (Golding and Middleton,1982:114) and the reporting of health and medicine.[36] In not making assumptions about the intimate relationships between labour news values and power explicit, labour correspondents tend to take existing social arrangements for the exercise of power, as given. As in trade union news, there is very little consideration of alternatives to the workplace status quo.

In common with many other journalists, labour and industrial correspondents were prone to 'mythologise'. The idea of an instinct for news, inherited genetically or acquired through experience, was a concept frequently invoked to explain routine practice. Indeed, Terry Pattinson (*Daily Mirror*) claimed that a combination of experience and instinct determined whether or not he even attended press conferences ,- 'I'll ask myself is it a *really* good story?'(my emphasis)- while Kevin McGuire (*Daily Telegraph*) believed that his 'instinct' was able to detect whether a dispute was likely to escalate to a strike worthy of coverage.[37] Accordingly, in the eyes of most industrial correspondents a good trade union press officer was one who shared such a news instinct, a common orientation towards what made a 'good story', and was 'switched on to what we need', as David Norris described it.[38] In addition, the expectation of 'good press officers' was that they could frame material according to common news values and encode it using an accessible 'popular discourse'. For some labour journalists, particularly those with long track records at the popular end of the market, the use of 'tabloid discourse' was habitual in their own conversation, which was characterised by a bewildering continuous 'code switching' between tabloid and more complex forms of language. Language and modes of explanation are, of course, bound together (Elliott,1977:151) and in the case of some labour correspondents, alternation between tabloid and more complex discourses, also implied an alternation in levels of explanation. Thus, one labour editor who had demonstrated a sophisticated understanding of the underlying, structural causes of the 1984/85 Coal Strike and was sympathetic to the case of the NUM, nevertheless continued to refer to 'barmy Arthur' throughout the interview and described the crucial technical debate over energy sources as, 'barmy Arthur speak'. Even the very direct impact of institutional power and structural forces upon his own profession, was personalised and 'individualised', using tabloid discourse, as 'Rupert Murdock's audacious moonlight flit to Wapping.'[39]

The Hierarchy of Credibility

Inextricably bound up with the concept of 'objectivity' and the commitment to 'intelligence' gathering, is a scepticism towards news sources, which correspondents regard as one of the attributes of 'professionalism'. A capacity to assess the credibility of information gathered; to distinguish the 'sound' sources from 'axe grinders', by separating 'facts' from 'values', was seen as central to a correspondent's work. However, news sources tend to be evaluated and ranked, not only according to the perceived veracity of the information they supply but in measures of political authority and significance. Information supplied by pressure groups, for example, may be assessed not only in its own terms but according to the size and political influence of the group concerned (Schlesinger, 1978:51).

For the correspondents dealing with union news sources, it was clear that 'a hierarchy of credibility' existed. And yet, many correspondents appeared to work with a curious 'double think' in their orientation towards union press officers. On the one hand, it was quite clear that the political nature of press and media work was widely recognised; all the journalists interviewed for this study, acknowledged that union press officers were bound by the nature of their work to present a particular account or 'line'. And yet, labour and industrial correspondents still sought to distinguish between union officers regarded as 'honest' or 'reliable' and those whose political position within their union and associated value commitments intruded too much in their work. Thus, some union press officers were 'wrapped in the leadership' and their information 'parti-pris';[40] another was too strongly 'locked into the two guys who run the union'.[41] Too close an intimacy between press officer and leadership was regarded as undermining the credibility of a press officer and yet, at the same time, the 'best' officers were those who were 'on the inside track' and who could reliably brief journalists on thinking at the highest levels. This was a conundrum which press officers often found difficult to solve. However, as discussed further below, some of the most highly regarded union press officers were those who were able to combine a proximity to the leadership, 'on the inside track', with sufficient autonomy to release a range of information, not merely the 'official line', but also some contextual material which did not always reinforce the 'leadership position'.

Much the same approach was applied to union officials. Those most highly regarded by labour and industrial correspondents were those who either spoke for non-factionalised unions or who were able to detach themselves from the pressures of the political conflicts within certain unions. On the other hand, for example, some general secretaries were located by correspondents at the bottom of the hierarchy of credibility because they were regarded as either representing their own personal ambitions through the news media or 'belonging' to one political faction. One civil service union general secretary was widely criticised because, 'all you ever get is the view from the right'. Another leader of an education union was treated with scepticism because 'the media limelight has gone to his head'.[42]

What is clear is that trade unions are never in a position to claim status as 'arbiters', rather than 'advocates'. Labour and industrial correspondents are prepared to distinguish degrees of reliability; some union sources are trusted, others less so, but none are granted the authority to 'evaluate assertions and interpretations made by [other] advocates' (Deacon and Golding,1994:15). Correspondents from other specialisms, who have dealings with unions, are likely to be even more severe. The health and education correspondents interviewed for this study all regarded unions as producer interest groups and were less likely to make finer distinctions in terms of reliability, either between unions or particular sources within unions. The association between several unions and the Labour Party, in contrast to the other consumer interests and professional associations in the health and education arenas, reinforced this view:

> Health unions suffer because they are below doctors organisations and nurses' organisations in the hierarchy of credibility. They tend to be seen as 'axe grinders' and are too closely associated with the Labour Party. Journalists may feel that the information health unions provide is tainted with a particular aim. It is very important for a journalist to feel that a press officer is providing facts,- the BMA [British Medical Association] are good at supplying facts, where as the health unions are seen as more propagandistic...'.[43]

Although some health correspondents acknowledged that the role of the BMA as a producer interest group had become more visible in recent years, since the under the chairmanship of Lee-Potter it had entered into open confrontation with the government, nonetheless, it was still possible for it to deploy considerable 'authority' and to achieve a position as 'arbiter', at least in relation to some issues. Education correspondents applied a similarly sceptical approach to the teaching unions, although the more 'militant' NUT was placed lower in the hierarchy of credibility, than the NAHT which, for some correspondents, still spoke with authority because it was seen to retain political standing and influence at Westminster.[44]

Media bias: an astructural explanation

As discussed above, many labour correspondents, particularly more senior journalists, identified with the values of the mainstream of the labour movement and acknowledged that unions often had a difficult job in presenting their cases to the public. However, structural forms of explanation rarely surfaced when correspondents were asked to consider the reasons for these difficulties. Modes of explanation tended to be constructed around 'individualised' accounts or 'technical' accounts which pointed to a failure in understanding the mechanics of public relations. Kevin McGuire (*Daily Telegraph*), a graduate and relatively new entree familiar with 'media studies debates' (his phrase), specifically ruled out 'conspiracy' or the impact of political forces. He had never been required to alter or re-write a story on the basis of political rather than professional criteria.[45] None of the journalists interviewed in this study acknowledged any such direct political pressures. Indeed, in his book Keith Mason claims that in working throughout the transformation of the *Daily Herald* from TUC sponsored left of centre paper to its final incarnation as the *Sun* within the *News International* empire, his job was quite free of political pressures and 'changed very little' (Mason,1981:1).

For Kevin Mcguire, part of the problem for trade unions lay in the failure of many unions to fully understand how the national press actually worked. Kevin Mcguire recognised that some trade unions, such as the Transport and General Workers Union, were likely to experience more intense media scrutiny because of their close connections with the Labour Party. This might lead to more critical coverage from tabloid papers committed to the cause of the Conservative Party. Nevertheless, he believed that most union general secretaries were more interested in the 'qualities rather than the tabloids' and would get 'a fair crack of the whip with the locals and the P.A. [Press Association]'.[46] So difficulties for unions in presenting an agenda, if experienced, were largely the result of either unions' own failings or the consciously constructed political projects of particular tabloid newspapers strongly identified with the Conservative Party. Possible pressures arising from the structural location of newspaper production within specific capitalist markets and framed by particular ideological and political formations were not considered. Hardly surprising but important none the less.

For one of the newer industrial correspondents, 'society's values had moved on and newspapers simply reflected that...'. Trade unions, unreconstructed, were a thing of the past as demonstrated by the Labour Party's fourth electoral defeat. The absence of a union agenda in the press simply mirrored a public's lack of interest.[47] At the same time, however, there was a common recognition that coverage of some industrial relations issues had failed to fully articulate the merits of the union case. The 1984-85 coal dispute was frequently cited as an example. Several labour correspondents acknowledged that the NUM 'had a largely valid case'[48] but had simply failed to put its message across effectively. Once more illustrating the salience of the concept of professionalism for industrial correspondents, they argued that the NUM's response to the news media has been impaired by its ideological orientation. The suspicion and hostility directed towards sections of the news media and a failure to meet the needs of journalists in terms of availability and the flow of information were primarily responsible for the one sided coverage. The ideological stance of the NUM was contrasted with Charlie Whelan, the AEU Press Officer, who could 'ride' with the politically partisan nature of the press,

> ...because he's professional and recognises where we are, [journalists] what the politics of the paper are and understands that we have a job to do. He takes the view that as long as his union gets the best possible, effective message across, he's done his job.[49]

However, in the case of some press officers including Nell Myers of the NUM, problems arose from a lack of professionalism...

> ...because they allowed their own political views or their own judgements of a newspaper's political stance to cloud their relationships with journalists. You mentioned Nell Myers...she did say that along with broadcasting journalists working for the tabloids were 'our enemies front-line troops', so its a class struggle thing which is why she works for Arthur. She shares the same fundamentalist beliefs which is fine but it doesn't help in my job and, therefore, I would argue it doesn't ultimately help the union case, and doesn't ultimately help the miners of Wales and Geordieland and Yorkshire.[50]

Other correspondents complained about accessibility, 'always too busy, no working journalists ever get to speak to Mr Scargill on the telephone'[51] and the apparent low priority attached to press work.

According to these accounts, if unions experience a hostile ideological climate this is not the consequence of the location of the news media within particular social, political and economic structures but the result of the adoption of inappropriate strategies in dealing with journalists. In an area of academic study strongly influenced by an understanding of the ways in which such structures do shape the production of meaning and constrain the possibilities which are presented to actors, it is tempting to regard the astructural explanations provided by journalists as superficial. However, as the field work with union press officers suggested, personal relationships *are* important in shaping the nature of the regular encounters between trade unions and the news media. Of course, these encounters are, themselves, constrained and patterned by structural determinants but, nevertheless, the nature of press officer-journalist interaction is important in opening up or closing particular possibilities for news communication. In this sense, the importance attached by many journalists to such inter-personal interaction is not naive.

> Yes, he's very good [Charlie Whelan AEU Press Officer]. You get the other extreme like Nell Myers. She disseminates quotes from the President. She's never been known to put out a story. She gives these quotes to the P.A.[Press Association]. I don't think she has a relationship with any journalists except may be the Morning Star. No-one else.[52]

Again, on the question of whether the possession of wealth or resources allocated greater access to the news media, labour journalists were likely to employ astructural perspectives. Was it the case, for example, that the NUM suffered during the 1984/85 dispute because it lacked command over the kind of very significant public relations resources at the disposal of British Coal? The scepticism of Keith Harper (Industrial Editor on the Guardian), in relation to this argument, was typical of the journalists in this study.

> I think it's true looking back on the Coal Strike that the National Coal Board had umpteen press officers all over the country who were able to push British Coal's view point very effectively. However, the NUM was very effective through its President, Mr Scargill, who was on every television programme in the country. There were at least twenty members of the National Executive who spoke very volubly in different ways about the progress of the dispute. I think that despite the fact that a trade union begins with an initial disadvantage over public relations, the NUM case was put very well during the dispute by different men in the union and I don't think you can argue that the NUM lost the dispute because they suffered in comparison with the statements and coverage which British Coal and the Government were making. Why they lost the dispute was because it was badly handled by the leadership. I was on the phone constantly to NUM people as well as B.C. people at different times of the day and night, not necessarily to Nell Myers who was a conduit for official stuff from the NUM but no no no...there were always sections of the NUM, different regions, who would speak not only with the local press but the national as well.[53]

This comment illustrates the importance of 'porosity' for correspondents but also illustrates the way in which journalists often conflate interpretation and evaluation (Deacon and Golding,1994:19). For Keith Harper, honour was satisfied and balance achieved providing an NUM voice was heard; the union complaints about the interpretative framework within which 'evaluative' material (comments from sources, etc) was located are not addressed. Most labour and industrial correspondents acknowledged that unions faced a set of ideological hurdles but did not regard them as insurmountable; they were not rooted in unyielding social, political or economic structures. Effective media handling strategies could be devised providing unions understood how journalists worked and applied appropriate news values.

Journalists and union press officers: the journalists' perspective

In talking to journalists about their dealings with union press officers it is not difficult to develop a clear view of what they regard as effective media work, - there was a remarkable area of common agreement amongst the journalists in this study over what attributes made a good union press officer. While the opinions of journalists differed more widely on the performance of particular unions, it was still possible to identify one or two unions which enjoyed a high reputation amongst most labour and industrial correspondents. Conversely, there were several who were commonly regarded as poor in terms of press and media work.[54]

There appeared to be a common understanding of 'professionalism', shared by both parties. Thus, many union press officers, as well as journalists, acknowledged the importance of disseminating information speedily, recognising the salience of dominant news values, and subordinating political values to the 'priorities of the job'. Attempts by some union press officers to distinguish between newspapers according to political criteria were regarded as highly 'unprofessional'. For journalists, the 'basic assumptions' or 'inferential structures' which guided their practice, should operate for 'professional' press officers, as well. Hence, the belief that it was possible for union press officers to separate 'facts' from political values.

A frequent comment made by correspondents was that an effective press officer was able to speak with 'authority', and was 'trusted' to work independently without being required to refer upwards continuously. As noted in chapters three and four, a frequent practice in some unions was to construct an official comment or quotation from a leading official first, issue it to the news media, and then confirm it with the official concerned, subsequently. Journalists recognised this as a legitimate technique which helped them in their work, providing the relationship between press officer and senior union official was, in their eyes, credible. If they believed that the press officer had the confidence of the official concerned then industrial correspondents were unlikely to question a 'constructed' quotation.

On the basis of the interviews with journalists conducted for this study a journalist's list of ideal press officer qualities would include the following:

- the ability to speak with 'authority' (enjoying the trust and confidence of the powerful within a particular union).

- availability (taking the practical steps necessary to ensure that journalists could easily contact a press officer at work or home on a 24 hours a day basis).

- a position on the 'inside track', with access to decision making processes at the highest levels and with an understanding of the political currents at work within a union.

- 'honesty' and 'reliability' (in practice a willingness to provide more accurate information than just the leadership 'line' on particular issues, but not necessarily *all* the information).

- an awareness of current news values and the ingredients of a 'good story'.

- efficiency and the capacity to respond quickly to enquiries.

- the absence of political favour, hostility or defensiveness (as discussed above in the context of professionalism).

Very nearly every journalist I spoke to, from right wing tabloid papers to the *Financial Times*, nominated without prompting Charlie Whelan, then of the AEU, as one of the best union press officers at the time the field work was conducted:

> Charlie's brilliant...he's switched on to what we need and most of the time he can provide an immediate answer. Bill Jordan and Gavin Laird trust him and so there's no time wasting.[55]

Essentially it's all about relationships. When you work on a national newspaper, you've got to have people you can rely upon, that you can get hold of, so communication is the key, instant access, someone who knows and can speak with authority, who doesn't tell lies. Someone like Charlie Whelan you can leave a message on his 'poser phone' or answer machine at home, he has direct lines at work, you can always get hold of him.[56]

A background in journalism is not essential, as a baseline, enthusiasm and just working hard will get you a long way...For example, this week I was at the GMB annual conference watching the news at six o'clock on TV. There was a piece about John Smith (Labour Party Leader) on. At 6.10 the GMB's bleeper went off, a message from Charlie Whelan of the AEU with an idea for a story to promote. He's always enthusiastic and on the look out for an opportunity.[57]

It obviously helps if they [press officers] have a background in journalism but I'm thinking of one guy, Charlie Whelan at the AEU, who is in many ways the ideal P.O. You can ring him up and have a chat about anything from the price of potatoes to the Chelsea game and write a particular story.[58]

Efficiency and reliability, an understanding of news values as applied to labour journalism, and above all, a good working relationship with senior officials within the union, made Charlie Whelan an extremely good press officer, as measured by the labour correspondents' yardstick. In contrast Charlie Whelan's predecessor was 'an old union worthy'[59] who was often unavailable and never in a position to comment without referring upwards. As one labour correspondent put it, Charlie Whelan is 'more like a colleague.'[60] The 'best' press officers, then, were those who could be regarded as colleagues or fellow professionals; who shared a common understanding of the practices and imperatives of the news process and who acknowledged the necessity of employing mainstream news values as a template for producing descriptions of the world.

Some unions, Kevin McGuire (formerly *Daily Telegraph*, currently industrial editor at the *Daily Mirror*) says, 'just belt on a press officer' but keep them 'permanently in the dark'.[61] To be effective press officers must, 'know what's going on and speak with authority...and have the confidence to actually say what's going on'. Laurie Harris (NUR), also, was highly rated by Kevin McGuire. All the claims made by other unions to be pioneering new media strategies were, 'bollocks...Laurie was doing it first, - just one man on his own', mainly through being 'straight and honest', always being available, and being very close to General Secretary, Jimmy Knapp. Kevin McGuire pointed to the rail disputes in the late 1980s as examples of highly successful media campaigns. 'Many of the printed quotes were actually Laurie but Jimmy Knapp was quite happy, it worked very well...'. Thus, Laurie Harris was able to respond quickly to enquiries from the press with a comment 'from' the leadership of the union, even in the absence of the leadership. Charlie Leadbeater *(Financial Times)* confirms the principle, suggesting that the best press officers were 'those trusted to do the job by those they work for'.[62]

Intelligence and what happens when it is missing

'Good' union press officers, then, are privy to the thoughts of their leaderships, have access to the highest decision making forums, and are sensitive to the diverse political currents moving within their organisations. This allows a 'good' press officer to provide the 'contextual information' or intelligence sought by correspondents. That the occupational standing and self-esteem of specialist correspondents largely depends upon the range of their sources, and not merely the quality but also the exclusivity of the information obtained from them, has already been noted by researchers (Tuchman,1978:68; Schudson,1989:272). As described in chapters three and four, union press officers working in a hostile ideological climate, have relatively few bargaining chips in their dealings with journalists but they do possess some which are derived from their ability to supply 'contextual information'. As the *Times* industrial correspondent explains:

> It's the job of the press officer to make the material as interesting as possible and one of the ways of doing that is to provide the people who are reporting this area [industry], over a period of time, a degree of contextual information. Obviously it is important that if the *Financial Times* reports Concorde, it knows more about it than just that it goes up and down. We need to know enough about an organisation to tell if a development is important or significant or whether something is just being dressed up in a particular way... .[63]

The same correspondent recalled a story in which he knew that the information he had received from one source was untrue. 'I just knew that... because of the background knowledge I'd acquired'.[64] As part of the service a newspaper provides for its readership, this correspondent believed that it was important that the comments from this source be reported. At the same time, it was equally important that their doubtful veracity also be made clear. However, professional norms and political considerations constrained the correspondent from including a bald statement asserting that such information was untrue. The solution was to include additional 'contextual information' which allowed the reader to make an informed judgement. So, according to correspondents, intelligence allows correspondents to evaluate information and to empower readers, in the sense that they are equipped to make informed assessments.

Further to this, although perhaps less significant as labour news descends the news hierarchy, intelligence allows labour correspondents to 'play weather forecaster'. According to one former labour correspondent, forecasting the outcome of events, - industrial disputes, union elections, negotiating sessions at ACAS, etc,- provided labour correspondents with opportunities to demonstrate the value of their contacts and their skill in deploying 'contextual information' to interpret developments.[65] And with the decline in the number of labour correspondents employed by the main news organisations, remaining journalists on the labour beat are quick to point to what they regard as evidence of things going wrong, mistakes being made and forecasts proving wildly inaccurate, as a result of the loss of expertise and the resulting absence of good 'intelligence'. Thus, according to Philip Bassett, both the *Sunday Times* and the *Observer* were 'caught short' by the wave of public sector strikes in 1988 (Bassett,1988). Ill-informed predictions of a new 'winter of discontent' were unfounded but, according to Philip Bassett, arose from both papers' decision not to retain experienced labour correspondents.

Several other labour correspondents pointed to the difficulties news organisations now experienced in covering major strikes, having assumed that industrial disputes were a feature of a previous era and re-organised their staffing accordingly.[66] Difficulties can extend beyond coverage of disputes. The absence of expertise on the labour and industrial beat can mean, as Hugo Young pointed out in the *Guardian*, a complete failure of news reporters to pick up the significant 'news' in recent employment legislation, such as the 1993 Trade Union Reform and Employment Rights Bill, which legalised discrimination in pay against trade unionists (Young,1993). In reducing the number of correspondents or in abolishing labour desks entirely, news organisations lose both expertise in a specialised and complex field but, just as importantly, networks of contacts within the bureaucracies and the political elites of the labour movement.[67]

Tunstall first pointed to the importance of 'intelligence' in securing the position of a specialist correspondent within a news organisation. Journalists on taking on a specialism, such as labour and industry, have to become 'instant experts'; it is unusual for a journalists to have formal qualifications in a chosen area (Tunstall,1971:116). However, correspondents can consolidate their positions in relation to their news organisations by fostering an extensive range of contacts and sources, and by the judicious deployment of information. Providing a journalist can accomplish this, a 'news organisation's scope for exercising arbitrary control over him is already limited' (Tunstall,1971:116).

Negrine (1993:19) has applied a sceptical eye to the claims of correspondents to command specialist expertise, arguing that it is the needs of the news organisation, rather than the intrinsic nature of the subject matter which underpins the specialist division of labour. Journalists have 'mythologised' their expertise. The problem with this critique is that it fails to distinguish between types of expertise. In terms of 'knowledge', it may be correct to question the extent to which most journalists have the opportunity to acquire substantial expertise, although a number of labour and industrial correspondents have contributed comprehensive books on various aspects of industrial relations and labour journalism (for example, Wigham,1961 and 1969; Mason,1981; Jones,1986; Bassett,1986;). However, a meaningful definition of expertise in relation to specialist journalism should also include the acquisition of sources, contacts, and the ability to make sense of the 'contextual information' they supply. This ability is enhanced by experience on the labour and industrial beat and an understanding of the politics within the labour movement. In this sense, it is a mistake to underestimate the 'expertise' of experienced labour and industrial correspondents, as the recent examples of gaps and mistakes in labour coverage, discussed above, illustrate.

News rhythms and news routines

An understanding of the imperatives of the news production process; the pressure of deadlines (steadily advancing towards lunch time as new print technology allows more editions to be published) and the importance of news values, were mentioned by all correspondents as essential attributes in a press officer. As Terry Pattinson points out if there are 'fifteen journalists working on a story, ten from national newspapers, ITV, BBC, BBC Radio, the Sundays, commercial radio, regionals, weeklies, all chasing a general secretary in a day...in an hour(!)', then a press officer has a vital role to play in dealing with enquiries quickly and efficiently. However, a bad press officer is one who does no more than this:

> Some are very defensive. They see their role as simply disseminating information given to them by their general secretaries or national executives, and they do no more than that. They spend the rest of their lives parrying questions, purely defensively.[68]

This was a frequent complaint voiced by journalists; that some union press officers were unwilling to recognise the salience of news values, were unable to depart from an approved brief and were, thus, incapable of furnishing journalists with any of the 'inside' information required to make a 'good story'. This, in turn, relates to the different roles adopted by various press officers (discussed in chapter four). Union press officers who conformed more strictly to the 'civil service' model appeared to fall into this trap. Several journalists in this study pointed to the civil service unions and USDAW as being 'ineffective' for this reason. One senior ex-correspondent commented that, 'they're just churning stuff out, they're not taking any active initiative, they're not bringing you in, and this was what the AEU was like at one point in the old days, they are like civil servants, just servants of the executive or president.'[69]

Timing the release of information to maximise its value to news organisations was a skill recognised by journalists:

> ...but who is very good at this [timing the release of information] is Charlie Whelan. He was excellent at it when he was working for the AEU at Ford...I mean Charlie is one of the best...he really understands when to let things out, when not to, what has a certain value and how you can control it and that the point is not to try and stop everything but that the point is to use it.[70]

Similarly, in terms of awareness of timing and news values, Charlie Leadbeater points to the performance of the EETPU:

> ...they [the EETPU] were absolutely brilliant at the game of briefing journalists, getting close to them, feeding information to them, briefing behind the scenes on deals or what they were doing at the TUC or what they thought of this union or that...Hammond and co really understood the press... .[71]

So according to Charlie Leadbeater, a journalist likely to be more critical of conventional professional wisdom than most, the application of specific encoding practices, - timing, an awareness of news values, and an understanding that the judicious release of 'inside' information to oil the wheels of exchange between press officers and journalists, - does make a difference. It is questionable whether the effectivity of these encoding practices holds in all cases,- the particular political and ideological positions of both the AEU and the EETPU were likely to provoke less critical coverage from certain sections of the news media, anyway. In the case of a union, such as the NUM, it is difficult to 'weight' for the relative effect several distinct variables; the politics of the union and its historic position within the labour movement which was likely to provoke the critical fire of newspapers closely associated with the Conservative government, the ideological legacy of earlier news media representations of miner militancy, and the refusal of the union's leadership to make many concessions to the practice of labour correspondents.

Exchange relationships: conflict and co-operation

As discussed above, it is possible that the growing pressures upon journalists, with fewer staff and earlier deadlines, will lead to a greater dependence upon official, bureaucratic sources. If this is the case, then, press officers will be able to exert greater control over the information flows within their organisations, as less time is available for journalists to cultivate alternative sources and contacts. However, at the time of this study, journalists were still inclined to search for a variety of sources within union organisations. A number of journalists still adhered to the view that 'real stories don't come from press officers'.[72] If the best labour stories are ultimately about power, powerful individuals and the implications of their actions for the polity, then the most useful information would be found at a level above the union press officer. This has important implications for the relationship between correspondent and press officer.

The idea of describing interaction between correspondents and news sources in terms of 'exchange relationships' is hardly new (Goldenberg,1975;Chibnall,1977). Indeed, Seaton has applied the concept specifically to labour correspondents and union sources, though without pursuing the implications of the idea at length (1982:278). Several important points are implied by the concept of 'exchange'. Firstly, that the relationship is governed by a more less stable normative framework,- there are implicit rules to the game. Secondly, that such relationships are regulated by the capacity of both parties to exercise sanctions if they are dissatisfied with the outcome of an exchange or the performance of the other side. And thirdly, that such relationships have the potential for conflict, as well as co-operation. In this sense, they are inherently unstable. In the case of exchanges between news sources and journalists, a great deal depends upon the capacity of each side to exercise control over the flow of information.

What are the terms of the exchange between union press officers and correspondents? Only some correspondents formally acknowledged that their relationships with union sources involved a concept of 'bargaining'. Nevertheless, it was clear that both parties worked within an implicit normative framework. In return for information which satisfied correspondents' needs in terms of news value and 'contextual information'; an expectation that a union perspective should be accurately represented in the news copy produced, was acknowledged. There is also, however, an important element of tension in the relationship between press officer and industrial correspondent arising from a fundamental conflict of interest. Press officers must seek to regulate and control information flows. They will try to ensure that their unions 'speak with one voice' to the news media and this requires them to exercise effective control over the information which is disseminated. There is also a professional consideration because their own authority will be undermined if significant channels of communication open up between unions and journalists, over which they exercise no control. On the other hand, journalists will welcome 'leaky systems', unions where a number of key players, either at national or local level, supply information to the news media. Information of this kind, 'unofficial' information, often makes good copy and is more likely to satisfy the criteria defined by dominant news values.

Seaton believed that union sources had, at their disposal, at least one powerful sanction, 'they can refuse to talk to a correspondent who has offended them - and they do' (1982:278). At the time Seaton briefly reviewed the scene, labour and industrial news was still high on the news agenda and this may have leant the threat of withdrawal of co-operation a greater potency. However, Seaton's analysis ignores the inability of trade unions, as organisations, to control the number of information flows which correspondents may 'tap'. Companies often exert control over their employees dealings with the media through draconian contractual controls and the message that leaked information can hit share prices. Such powerful controls over their employees and members are not available to most trade unions. Given the factionalised nature of many unions, the springing up of alternative, unofficial information flows is almost inevitable and, in terms of exchange relationships, this will undermine the position of the press officer.

Few journalists in this study offered a formal statement of the terms of the 'bargains' which shaped relationships between themselves and union press officers. Some recognised that it was the job of the press officer 'to sell us a line' (Tony McGuire)[73] and that it was unreasonable to expect union press officers to commit themselves to a policy of full disclosure in all circumstances. Nonetheless, several journalists did specify two obligations a 'good press officer' should meet. As Tony McGuire says, a good press officer 'does not tell porkies'. In other words, whatever information is volunteered should be accurate. Selling a union line should not involve lying. Secondly, all the industrial correspondents shared a common view that a good press officer recognised the obligation to respond in all circumstances, rather than 'stonewall' in a situation of public discomfort. However, the complexity of the 'bargain' went beyond these obligations. Charlie Leadbeater explicitly framed the relationship in the following terms:

> I mean one of the things you have to accept with press officers is that you are engaging in some kind of bargain, you have to accept that both sides understand what the bargain is...press officers go bad, - a bit like the [large general union]- when they become over-professionalised...Where they know they're spinning you a line and they know that's their job and they know you've got a certain job to do, it's best when it works in this way and there's a certain mutual recognition of what's going on. When it's taken too seriously and it becomes too squeaky clean which is what the [large general union] are like, then it becomes a bit too much.[74]

Charlie Leadbeater argued that press officers were most effective when they acknowledged that they were playing an active part in the construction of news, 'people like Eddie [Eddie Barrett T and G] know what's going on' and 'know they are playing some kind of active role in it, not just passive, they're not just reflecting, actually actively playing a role'. The active political nature of the union press role is underlined in the following example:

> ...on a Sunday I called the union's press officer who was very good, very well informed, one of the best, and she said she thought a two year deal was under discussion to settle the dispute and I then put that to the union's general secretary separately and he said, 'I think that's very interesting, where did that idea come from?' And then I put it to B.T. and they said something like that is being discussed and I wrote a story saying that a two year deal was one possibility for ending the strike and that became the context for the next days talks, everyone started talking about a two year deal. That idea came from a press officer and was cooked up inside the NCU...that's an example of how it can work together and that there's an understanding whereby it works to my advantage because I'm getting a story and it works to union's advantage because they're getting a line out.[75]

However, the 'bargain' can play a part in a number of political arenas. For example, according to several correspondents, in a number of disputes the union press officer has been involved in briefing, on behalf of the leadership of certain unions, against the union's own rank and file membership. In other circumstances, the press officer may have a political role in the context of inter-union rivalry:

> They are most useful and most informative when they are doing a political job rather than just a press job because that's when they give you information. As a result of that you have to recognise that they are working for something, that they have certain interests. Press officers are good and union media operations are good when the press officers are trusted by the people they work for to do the job...

> Often in the Ford negotiations this happens...in the Engineering Employers Federation talks over new flexibilities...people were briefing against other people all the time. You just knew where to go...MSF, AEU and in the Ford talks as well...[a former union press officer] would be part of the time speaking for the Ford unions and part of the time saying we're not taking any shit from those T and G wankers. He was the best...he gave me some excellent stories in my time because he understood that it was better that they come out than not and that it was better that they come out from the AEU than anybody else.[76]

There was considerable pressure upon press officers, particularly upon those working for unions characterised by sharp internal political conflicts, where a number of individuals or factions were likely to seek to use the news media to gain tactical advantages. Union press officers were sometimes compelled to release information, placed in the context of a particular interpretation, in order to minimise the damage that might occur if the same information was obtained by journalists from unauthorised sources and, without the official 'spin' or 'gloss' provided by the press officer. There is also an additional pressure because press officers know that if they do not respond to journalists enquiries then industrial correspondents are likely to seek out alternative sources or attempt to by-pass the press officer by going straight to the top of the union hierarchy to the general secretary.

> One of the good things about being a journalist and one of the problems for press officers is the access you get directly to officials at the top which you just don't get in companies, so in unions you can call people up because they are more open, they are more undisciplined, there are more centres of power, the structures are more visible...you can get directly to the people managing a dispute and often that's the quickest way, so press officers get by-passed. In other words, the more dispersed a union... the less power a central press officer has, and the more factions a union has, the less influence a press officer has.[77]

An education correspondent provided a very similar example:

> I mean, for example, this week I know for a fact that at NATFHE, this week, the negotiators were out-voted by the rest of the executive. I mean I must have been contacted by half the executive, leaking about the other side, - they are split down the middle. It's not a good idea to take action over a dispute you claimed you won weeks before and now the employers can claim the moral high ground.[78]

And correspondents actively sought to circumnavigate the press officer:

> A union press officer won't be giving you any information the union doesn't want you to hear so you've got to dig, you've got to use your own contacts. Information about a union comes from different sources...sometimes it comes from shop stewards, sometimes a regional official, sometimes from a national officer on an off the record basis, it means you can't identify the official but you've got your story. You could, if you were lucky, be telephoned by the general secretary but that is rare...most good stories come

from the national executive, past or present, disgruntled people, people with an axe to grind, people just saying, "this is a good story for you but it didn't come from me".[79]

Factional feuding is a particularly useful stimulus for leaks, as one labour editor noted:

>...now the General Secretary of that [a civil service union] union is a real political animal, right wing, the [Civil Service union] is the Beirut of the labour movement, it makes the NUJ look organised. It's split three ways, the young Trots, the right, and the old fashioned C.P. in the middle. The General Secretary is very much on the right, press officer, editor of the journal and now General Secretary so he's a useful contact for the right wing papers because he's always got stories about mad Trots but he's sufficiently professional to be aware of the general position of the union.[80]

From the journalists' perspective, the only sensible course of action for unions was to make the best of things. It was pointless seeking to exert centralised control over information flows because, 'we're going to get the story anyway, so it's better that the press officer is there and we go through the press officer...'.[81]

There are several ways in which unions have sought to retain control over information flows. The NUM imposed a tightly controlled regime through the authority of the leadership. Within the union headquarters only the President, General Secretary or Nell Myers, on their behalf, answered news media enquiries, in contrast to a union such as NATFHE, where press officers encouraged journalists to draw upon the expertise of researchers and officials in other departments. However, the strategy of centralised control was difficult to enforce, even for the NUM, given its federated structure and determinedly independent regional area organisations. During the Coal Dispute, as journalists experienced difficulties in reaching the union leadership, so they searched and found alternative sources. Nell Myers (NUM official responsible for media work) was 'a conduit for official stuff' but 'there were always different sections of the NUM, different regions', where 'contacts would speak not only to the local press but the national as well'.[82] As described in chapters three and four, the GMB has sought to exert central control in a rather different fashion. The development of a 'professional' communications strategy, with identified target audiences and 'techniques' for placing stories in particular news media to reach key 'opinion leaders', requires that considerable centralised control be exerted over the deployment of information. And yet, here too, journalists were sceptical of the 'over-professionalised', 'over-flash' strategy and determined to seek alternative sources to the GMB's Communication Directorate. The availability of the GMB's press and media officers was welcomed but the material they supplied was regarded as, too often, bland and mundane, reflecting official perspectives but without the 'inside' material which would have made it interesting.[83]

Several journalists (though by no means all interviewed) believed that in other ways, the 'professionalised' approach was effective. There was common agreement that the GMB 'had done a pretty good job in building a different image with limited resources'[84] but image building was distinguished from press work. In contrast, the T and G press office had a good sense for news values, performed press and news media work well, but the union was regarded as experiencing severe difficulties in trying to enhance its 'corporate image':

> ...for a corporate identity to be sold you've got to create that identity and that means having to be fairly disciplined and organised. The T and G is a far flung warring confederacy so that if Eddie Barrett (T and G Press Officer) comes on the phone and says they have a fantastic plan for doing such and such a thing you know its just some Smith Square fantasy because what really matters is what they do out there in the regions. The more fragmented, fractious diverse, a union the more difficult it is to create a corporate image...the GMB has been quite effective because it has had a sense of what you need to pull the package together and make the presentation work ...the AEU has some of the same elements of style about it. The magazine has always been good, they've always had some aspects of style but underneath it is terribly unstructured. The people who do both [press and image building work] are the EETPU.[85]

So 'slick' and 'professionalised' press and media work is unlikely to succeed if it impedes the fostering of 'exchange relationships' between union sources and journalists. There has to be a recognition of the normative framework which can govern source-correspondent interaction; there has to be an understanding of what journalists need, the 'contextual information' which enhances their 'expertise' and a certain skill is required in deploying such material as 'bargaining chips'. Working as a union press officer is to engage in the 'art of the possible'. In essence, for union sources to work with labour correspondents 'successfully', there must be a recognition of the social nature of their relationship. This is why an over-reliance upon the technology of news encoding is unlikely to succeed any more than an 'over-professionalised' approach. There was almost complete agreement amongst the journalists in this study that services such as Universal News were ineffective and inappropriate, - 'a busted flush'.[86] Relationships with press officers were 'far more important'[87] than investment in technology. The 'basic tools of the job'[88] were now the 'telephone and the fax', a conclusion which emerged strongly in talking to union press officers (chapters four and five). Rather than investing in communication technology, unions would be:

> be better off investing in a person who knows the business, and then giving them unfettered access at all levels to the decision making process.[89]

Summary

There is an implicit normative framework, with mutual obligations, which organises much of the interaction between union press officers and specialist correspondents. Implicitly, sometimes explicitly, this is recognised by journalists, as well as press officers. The union sources most highly regarded by journalists were those who most willingly and most easily embraced this normative framework. The ability of press officers to satisfy the expectations of correspondents depended, in part, upon their positions within their unions; their proximity to the leadership and their access to the main political currents. Journalists valued press officers who 'spoke with authority' and yet, were capable of providing additional 'contextual information' and intelligence. The most 'successful' unions, in their eyes, were not necessarily those who invested heavily in communication technology, or embraced the perspectives of 'corporate communications' but those where the quality of the social relationship with correspondents was prioritised, albeit more via telephonic communication than face to face contact, than in the past.

'Professionalism' in journalism and press work was a unifying concept, shared by both correspondents and many union press officers. This concept encouraged both sides to define their roles in such a way as to allow the conventional values of journalism and the widely recognised 'imperatives' of news production to strongly shape their work. Thus, both journalists *and most* union press officers took the deadlines and rhythms of news production for granted, both frequently defined 'stories' in terms of agreed news values, and there was common agreement amongst journalists and *several*, but not all, union press officers that professionalism should override political orientations, through the mutual acknowledgement that each party in the relationship was 'simply doing their job'. In a number of accounts of source-journalist interation it has been assumed that control over the flow of information has placed news sources in a position of relative advantage, and journalists at a disadvantage (Chibnall,1977; Cockerell et al, 1985; Seaton,1982, etc.). Most trade unions, however, are porous and this provides experienced correspondents with a variety of information flows. In their dealings with the news media, trade unions, consequently, face a classical 'catch-22' or double bind. Most union press officers are unable to exercise effective control over all potential news flows from within their organisation, and accordingly they are likely to often be placed at a disadvantage in their exchange relations with correspondents. As several correspondents remarked, 'they know we'll get the story some how, anyway.' In this sense 'news management' is not an option, at best such press officers can aim for 'news presentation'. On the other hand, a minority of trade unions are capable of largely controlling information flows, at least at the centre, either through a disciplined culture and historic antagonism towards the news media (NUM) or through the fostering of an organisational culture which emphasises professional, disciplined corporate communication (GMB). And yet, such strategies often mean that exchange relationships between union press officers and correspondents are impaired because in the eyes of the latter, the 'terms' of the exchange are not satisfied if the material offered for 'exchange' is too bland. This, in turn, can lead to significant difficulties in presenting a union perspective.

The problem of this double-bind presents unions with a difficult choice in terms of press and news media strategies. To acknowledge the advantages of developing exchange relationships with correspondents, is to embrace the imperatives of news values, production rhythms and, perhaps, most importantly the interpretative frameworks or underlying assumptions of labour and industrial journalism, with all the constraints over the type of message to be communicated, implied by this. Press and media work in these terms is very much the 'art of the possible'. To reject the implicit terms of the bargain is to risk marginalisation and a decreasing number of opportunities to present a union case in the public sphere.

The majority of unions in this study chose to work on the inside; to accept the normative framework of exchange relations and the degree to which this implies an 'incorporation' into the mainstream news encoding process. This is not to suggest that union press officers are either duped or bullied into submission. The union press officers in this study were mostly committed to the values of the mainstream within the labour movement and, on one level, they retained a critical view of the news media and the dominant ways in which labour news was framed and represented. And yet, just as a number of labour correspondents were sympathetic to the values of the labour movement but tended to accept the practice of the news media as 'given', so many union press officers, in adopting a 'professional' approach, accepted the political geography of the news media as the 'given' landscape or external environment in which they had to get on with the job. And for both union press officers and correspondents dealing with unions, acknowledging the limited scope for explanation, the appetite for immediacy and the emphasis upon the individualised rather than collective nature of social experience, was all part and parcel of a 'professional' approach to media work. The following chapter examines the opportunities and constraints which are implied by such a 'professional approach' through a consideration of the national newspaper coverage of the 1989 Ambulance Dispute which has been frequently identified as a 'model' for good union media work. What did the health unions achieve in terms of newspaper coverage and were there either any 'communication costs' or 'political costs'?

Notes

1. Interviews were conducted with labour and industrial correspondents representing nearly all broadsheet and quality daily newspapers. Interviews with two education and four health correspondents were also conducted. Full details are supplied in appendix one.
2. Interview with Keith Harper, Labour Editor, 22nd September 1992.
3. Interviews with Terry Pattinson, formerly Industrial Editor on the *Daily Mirror*, 24.7.92, and Tony McGuire, Industrial Editor on the *London Evening Standard*, 24.7.92.
4. Interview with Patrick Hennessey, industrial correspondent at the *Daily Express*, 24.7.92. Hennessey combined industry with education during 1992. The down grading of the industry beat was particularly significant at the Express because Hennessey's predecessor, Barrie Devney, was a distinguished labour correspondent for two decades, and a close friend of Joe Gormley, former NUM President.
5. Interview with Geoffrey Goodman, former industrial editor at the *Daily Mirror* and LBC industrial correspondent, 15.6.92.
6. Interview with tabloid labour editor, Summer 1992.
7. Ibid.
8. Phrase used by Phillip Bassett, labour correspondent of *The Times*, in interview 10.6.93.
10. Interview with Tony MacGuire, labour editor of the *London Evening Standard* 24.7.92.

11. Interview with Terry Pattinson, op cit.
12. Interview with Terry Pattinson, op cit.
13. Interview with Tony McGuire, op cit.
14. Interviews with Philip Bassett and Tony McGuire, op cit.
15. Interview with Charlie Leadbeater, former labour correspondent at the *Financial Times*, 15.7.92
16. Interview with Philip Bassett, op cit.
17. Interview with Judy Jones, health correspondent at *The Independent*, 24.5.93.
18. Interview with Charlotte Atkins, formerly press officer at COHSE.
19. Interview with a former labour correspondent at The *Financial Times*, summer 1992.
20. Interview with Kevin McGuire, formerly industrial correspondent on the *Daily Telegraph*, currently industrial editor at the *Daily Mirror*.
21. Interview with Charlie Leadbeater, op cit.
22. Interview with David Norris, industrial correspondent at the *Daily Mail*, 7.7.92.
23. For example, Barrie Clement left *The Times* for *The Independent*, Phillip Bassett, left the *Financial Times* for the *Times* and Kevin McGuire left the *Daily Telegraph* for the *Daily Mirror*, all during the course of the present study.
24. Interview with Kevin McGuire, op cit.
25. Interview with Tony McGuire, op cit.
26. Interview with Geoffrey Goodman, op cit.
27. Interview with Terry Pattinson, op cit.
28. Interviews conducted with four health and medical correspondents, summer 1993
29. Interview with a former health correspondent at *The Independent*, summer 1993.
30. Interview with Judy Jones, op cit.
31. Interview with John O'Leary, education correspondent at *The Times*, 10.6.93.
32. Ibid.
33. Interview with young industrial correspondent recently appointed to a national right of centre 'middle brow' tabloid, Summer 1992.
34. Interview with Philip Bassett, op cit.
35. Seaton (1982:281) points to the example of USDAW, a huge union with members in every high street and yet, a very low media profile.
36. Health correspondents interviewed for this study explained the rising fortunes of the specialism in terms of the growing salience of health as a political issue, in the context of the New Right's critique of public provision, the Government's reforms, and 'the electoral cycle'. Interviews with Jack O'Sullivan (14.7.93), Clare Dover (9.6.93), Jill Palmer (19.7.93) and Judy Jones, op cit.
37. Interviews with Terry Pattinson and Kevin McGuire, op cit.
38. Interview with David Norris, op cit.
39. Interview with a current labour and industrial editor, summer 1992.
40. Interview with Charlie Leadbeater, op cit.
41. Interview with Tony McGuire, op cit.
42. Phrases used by senior industrial correspondents in interviews, summer 1992.
43. Interview with Jack O'Sullivan, op cit.
44. Interview with James Meikle, education editor, The *Guardian* 28.5.93.
45. Interview with Kevin McGuire, op cit.

46.   Ibid.
47.   Interview with young industrial correspondent recently appointed to a right of centre 'middle brow' tabloid, Summer 1992.
48.   Interview with Tony McGuire, op cit.
49.   Ibid.
50.   Interview with a labour editor, summer 1992.
51.   Former tabloid labour editor, summer 1992.
52.   Ibid. This source's view of the NUM may have been 'coloured' by his experience in being placed in an inviduous position by his news organisation which demanded that he took the lead in running the 'missing Russian money' smear stories. These eventually led to the establishment of the Lichtmann enquiry into the NUM's finances and Arthur Scargill's personal conduct. These stories were later proved unfounded but generated considerable tension between this labour editor and the union.
53.   Interview with Keith Harper, op cit.
54.   It is not suggested that journalists' assessments provide an objective benchmark.
55.   David Norris, op cit.
56.   Tony McGuire, op cit.
57.   Philip Bassett, op cit.
58.   Patrick Hennessey, op cit.
59.   Industrial correspondent working for a middle brow, right wing tabloid, summer 1992.
60.   Patrick Hennessey, op cit.
61.   Interview with Kevin McGuire, op cit.
62.   Interview with Charlie Leadbeater, op cit.
63.   Interview with Philip Bassett, op cit.
64.   Ibid.
65.   Jim Foulkes, former number two at the Press Association industrial desk, now NALGO press officer, interviewed 10.6.93.
66.   Interview with Tony McGuire, op cit. See also Jones, 1988.
67.   Interview with Charlie Leadbeater, op cit.
68.   Interview with Terry Pattinson, op cit.
69.   Interview with a former senior labour correspondent, summer 92.
70.   Interview with Charlie Leadbeater, op cit.
71.   Ibid.
72.   Interview with Terry Pattinson, op cit.
73.   Interview with Tony McGuire, op cit.
74.   Interview with Charlie Leadbeater, op cit.
75.   Ibid.
76.   Former broadsheet Labour Correspondent, interviewed summer 1992.
77.   Interview with Charlie Leadbeater, op cit.
78.   Interview with education correspondent working for a right of centre broadsheet, summer 1993.
79.   Interview with Terry Pattinson, op cit.
80.   Interview conducted summer 1992.
81.   Interview with Tony McGuire, op cit.
82.   Labour editor of left of centre broadsheet, interview summer 1992.
83.   Comments made by several labour correspondents during the course of interviews,

summer 1992.
84. Former labour correspondent of *Financial Times*, summer 1992.
85. Ibid.
86. Interview with Tony McGuire, op cit.
87. Interview with David Norris, op cit.
88. Interview with Charlie Leadbeater, op cit.
89. Interview with Tony McGuire, op cit.

8   Representations of Labour

This chapter takes as a case study the national daily newspaper coverage of the 1989-90 Ambulance Dispute. There are three reasons for selecting this example. Firstly, the dispute involved four of the unions selected for the study's panel (NALGO, COHSE, GMB and the TGWU) and a fifth (NUPE), which was regularly identified by journalists and union press officers, interviewed for this study, as employing one of the best union press officers (Lynn Bryan). Secondly, the health unions' media and communication strategy during this dispute has been hailed as highly successful and an exemplar for other unions (Hutchings,1989; Woolas,1990; Hill,1993). If this view is accepted, then a case study of newspaper coverage of this campaign should provide an appropriate opportunity for the evaluation of the effectivity of co-ordinated union press work. Thirdly, the Ambulance Dispute was a landmark in the development of union communication strategies because for the first time unions co-ordinated their strategy to place media work at the centre, and to tailor industrial tactics to complement this priority.

It is not the intention to provide a fully comprehensive analysis of news media coverage of this dispute. Neither, is it the intention to formally 'test' whether the use of public relations techniques 'works' in improving the image of trade unions in newspapers. Leaving aside the issue of what counts as 'positive' coverage, the term 'testing' implies an exercise involving precise comparisons under controlled conditions, which are simply not available, - it is not possible to 'control' for the unfolding of domestic news and world events. Even the most energetic and 'proactive' trade union press officer is at the mercy of news events. Thus, a carefully planned press conference to highlight the work of ambulance crews in disasters, planned by COHSE, can be wiped off the news pages by the publication of the findings of the inquiry into a   disaster,- the railway accident at Clapham in South London. It is doubtful whether the most tightly designed research plan could effectively 'control' events such as these in a way which would allow direct and strict comparisons between union media strategies to be made.

In addition, precise 'weightings' would be required for variables such as size of union, news media profile, the personality of the general secretary, structural positioning in the economy, proximity to the Labour Party, and recent levels of dispute activity, to mention only the most obvious potentially relevant factors. Rather than attempt to compact the complexity of this process within the constraints of a quantitative design, this section has the rather less ambitious objective of tracing the imprint of the unions' press and media work upon the contours of coverage, using a qualitative approach. A qualitative approach was more likely, it was assumed, to capture the nuances and inflections in the construction of stories (Berger,1991; GUMG,1980:xv ; Burgelin,1972) which might constitute evidence of the success, or otherwise, of union strategies.

Union 'successes' in presenting their arguments and perspectives have to be assessed against the picture we have of industrial and union news coverage documented in earlier research. Briefly, then, the large body of research material on this theme will be critically summarised, in order to provide an indication of the extent to which newspaper coverage in the ambulance dispute departed from the familiar.

Still bad news?

The broad conclusion drawn from the voluminous body of research in this area is, indeed, a familiar one. Unions suffer at the hands of the news media in a number of ways. In fact, the research literature, exploring patterns of coverage in Britain and the USA, suggested six ways in which trade unions are disadvantaged in news and current affairs content, though more recently 'revisionist' (Sparks,1987) writing has challenged this interpretation.

Firstly, as measured against a variety of 'benchmarks',[1] industrial relations coverage was likely to systematically distort the 'reality' of industrial relations and industrial conflict, in a way which undermined the standing of trade unions. Coverage, overall, was likely to be highly selective, dwelling upon particular industries to the exclusion of others (GUMG,1976: ch 5; McQuail,1977:144); concentrating upon industrial disputes in certain 'high profile' sectors, rather than the most significant (as measured by official statistical data) (GUMG,1976:ch 5; Hartmann,1975; McQuail, 1977:144); producing 'an overall skewing of the picture given of disputes in industry' (GUMG,1976:169). While strikes were 'over-reported', industrial accidents were 'under-reported' (GUMG,1980:400); the reality of the impact of industrial production upon the health of workers underplayed, the damage of workers' action upon companies overplayed (Parenti, 1986:85); the complexity of official economic and industrial data ignored and over-simplified (Griffiths,1977; Edwards,1979), so that 'official figures from which a number of conclusions could have been drawn were used consistently to emphasise only one interpretation' (GUMG,1980:49), hostile to a union perspective. The most recent research suggests that these patterns continue (Hutt,1987; Puette,1992).

Secondly, a 'hierarchy of access' (GUMG,1980:162) differentially filtered and controlled the frequency with which the key actors in the industrial arena secured opportunities to present their cases. The 'definitions of the powerful' (Hall,1973) were likely to predominate in news coverage because both on television (GUMG,1980:ch 5) and in newspapers (Hartmann,1975), government and state representatives and members of the elite of the trade union movement enjoyed significantly greater access than either employers or ordinary trade unionists. The 'invisibility' of management and employers was a feature remarked upon by McQuail (1977:145)[2] and confirmed in the other main studies (this does not necessarily imply that perspectives and organising frameworks sympathetic to employers were absent, as discussed below). Rank and file trade union perspectives tended to be marginalised (Downing,1980:43-44). More recent research, again, suggests that differential access continues to disadvantage 'ordinary' trade unionists (Puette,1992:36-39), though one study of British breakfast television found an even narrower focus simply upon trade union leaders, as the principal figures in industrial conflict with relatively few appearances even for government representatives (Hutt,1987). And even within the narrow category of the 'trade union elite', news values continue to direct news media attention exclusively towards a smaller group of 'high profile' leaders (GUMG,1980:105; Jones et al,1985:23-26; Puette,1992:32-33).

Thirdly, following from this last point, the range of themes and issues developed in industrial and labour coverage reflected a narrow set of concerns. There was, both in print (Hartmann,1975; McQuail,1977; TUC,1979a) and broadcasting media (GUMG, 1976:202-4; Puette,1992:35-39), an overwhelming preoccupation with industrial conflict, particularly of the kind which inconvenienced the general public; issues where trade unions had formulated constructive policy positions (for example, on investment in new technology, health and safety, links between industries and communities, etc) were much less likely to attract media attention (Philo and Hewitt,1976; Parenti,1986:80; Puette, 1992:36). Within the coverage of industrial conflict, itself, the range of issues explored was consistently narrow in focus; the 'event-orientation' of the news media producing a concentration upon the immediate and visible effects of industrial action, rather than either the more complex causes, usually not amenable to discussion within an 'event-oriented' framework (GUMG,1976:ch 7; Hartmann,1975; Morley,1976; Downing, 1980:35-39) or the eventual resolution of disputes (TUC,1979a:26).

The concentration upon events and effects, rather than contexts and underlying explanations for industrial disputes, is a widely recognised feature of news media coverage, noted by researchers from a variety of theoretical positions. The interpretation of the significance of these features is rather more contentious. McQuail, for example, studiously eschewed the opportunity to make inferences about 'bias'. However, he did comment that 'national daily newspapers are very similar in their selection and treatment of news', and that 'the "point of balance" ...on matters of controversy...does not lie equally between the two "sides" of industry' (1977:147), unions being placed at a disadvantage. As McQuail recognised, the recurring nature of coverage and the correspondence in the themes highlighted between newspapers of divergent political orientation, - a feature noted by Hartmann (1976) too - could be interpreted in rather different ways, both as a measure of the extent to which newspaper reports are free from the imprint of editorial partiality, or as evidence of a common ideological structure (1977:146).

However, McQuail did not pursue, to any great extent, the nature of the correspondence between newspapers from different political stables or the detail of the common underlying assumptions which organised the coverage. In noting the "point of balance" being located in a position which disadvantaged unions, he was reluctant to pursue the analysis developed by the Glasgow University Media Group who argued that their evidence revealed a 'world view' in journalistic practice, a set of underlying assumptions or 'inferential frames', through which the world of industry and the workplace was represented. Such frames pre-structured news material so that only particular 'interpretations' were rendered plausible. Thus, the various causes of inflation were consistently conflated as 'wage push' inflation; problems of low productivity in the car industry were persistently associated with labour indiscipline rather than other factors, such as under-investment; problems of conflict around the workplace normally placed in the context of social order and threats to the legitimate role of the state in maintaining cohesion, rather than in terms of the sources of workplace grievance (GUMG,1976:ch 7; GUMG,1980:ch 1). Morley (1976) presented a very similar analysis of the underlying, taken for granted assumptions, organising selection and presentation. The result is that media coverage rarely makes visible the industrial status quo or the underlying relations of power which structure workplace relations; the 'logic and priorities of the social and economic order thus remain unchallenged' (GUMG,1980:112).

More recent research suggests that such underlying assumptions about the nature of the industrial world and the workplace continue to organise coverage. Puette finds much of the general coverage of industry and workplace relations constructed from a 'class biased economic perspective' (1992:44). Puette's analysis of the 1990 West Virginia Coal Strike, for example, points to a series of notable parallels with coverage of the 1984/85 Coal Strike in the United Kingdom. The underlying strike issues were quickly obscured as the news agenda shifted towards the problems of violence; important legal and tactical distinctions between forms of industrial action were rarely highlighted (an important issue for the 1989/90 Ambulance dispute, too), and 'the problems of the industry' were presented in a way which privileged the analysis of management (the threat of international competition necessitating greater labour productivity and leaner workforces), and failed to acknowledge the alternative analysis developed by the United Mineworkers of America (1992:ch 7). The practice of some U.S. newspapers in assigning their police reporters to cover labour news, represents an organisational acknowledgement of these underlying news frames (Puette,1992:64).

Fourthly, quantitative analysis can map out the broad 'contours of coverage' (GUMG;1976) which delimit the 'interpretative frames' organising news content but, in contrast to McQuail (1977) who restricted analysis to the manifest and quantifiable, a number of researchers have taken the view that in order to describe how such frames actually work as ideological mechanisms, it is necessary to explore the qualitative dimension of language, image and textual devices (headlines, boundary markers, the arrangement of material, etc). For the Glasgow team, for example, the slippery way in which 'stoppage' and 'strike' were conflated (GUMG,1980:154), the coupling of wage restraint with 'reasonable' (1980:70), or the classification of information in an opening sentence as 'good news', 'bad', or 'troubling', all illustrated the surface manifestations of the underlying 'inferential frame'. Similarly, language which juxtaposes union action against the 'normality' of routine life (Easthope,1990:110-111), or contrasts normal working with the 'chaos' of strike periods (Morley,1976), or selectively classifies behaviour between the militant and the moderate, (Hartmann,1976; Morley,1976), is identified as a key mechanism in the ideological representation of trade unionism. Headlines both in newspapers (Puette,1992:ch 4; Walsh,1988:208) and television (Easthope,1990; Hutt,1987; GUMG,1980:140-144) are regarded as offering particular frames for the understanding of events; the organisation and sequencing of material can suggest particular contexts and associations between themes whilst obscuring others (GUMG,1980:147-160). The routine use of taken for granted phrases ('the miners' strike'), assign responsibility for conflict and disruption firmly to organised labour (Jones et al,1985:23).

Fifthly, the overall consequence of the particular use of language, photographs, headlines and other symbolic elements in labour and industrial reporting, according to the critical research tradition, is to imply a 'differential legitimacy' (Hartmann,1975) between the main parties in labour and industrial reporting. A variety of symbolic cues, weaken the authority of unions in presenting their case and the 'event orientation' of news coverage limits exploration of underlying processes, which often inform the rationale of a union position. At the same time, while management and employer representatives appear less frequently both in print and broadcasting media, this is often because their perspectives and working assumptions are taken as 'starting points' for the interpretation of events (Walton and Davis,1977:129). For Easthope, a 'hierarchy of realism' is constructed, a function of journalists' commitment to 'objectivity', which distinguishes between the dominant 'impartial' news text and the inadequate, 'partial knowledge' offered by trade unionists. A variety of devices within the dominant 'mastering' discourse make it clear that the partiality of trade union perspectives renders them suspect (Easthope,1990:112-113). The identification of union sources as partial (and therefore suspect) 'advocates', rather than 'arbiters' (Deacon and Golding,1994:15-16) is made quite explicit. In contrast, sources associated with the state are much less likely to be subordinated in this hierarchy and more frequently may serve as 'the factual basis for industrial coverage' (Hutt,1988:94; Hartmann, 1975). It is for these reasons, that it is argued that while news coverage may be 'balanced' in terms of the acknowledgement of competing views, it may yet still be 'ideological' in the sense that only one account is accorded authority within the text (Puette,1992:130-132; Easthope, 1990:114; GUMG, 1980: 403-407).

For this critical research tradition, then, the final conclusion drawn, which is reflected as strongly in the recent work (Hutt,1987; Walsh,1988; and Easthope,1990) as much as in the earlier and more familiar research, is that the news coverage is constructed from a set of implicit assumptions about the nature of the industrial and political world, which confine the activity of 'legitimate' trade unionism to a limited and mainly non-adversarial role. Perspectives which describe the rationale for union organisation in terms of inherent conflicts within workplace relations only infrequently appear, and are likely to be represented as beyond the sphere of legitimate political discourse. Such underlying assumptions or 'inferential frames' accept 'uncritically narrow consensus views of the nature of strikes in particular and the realities of industrial life in our economic system' (GUMG,1980:400). Rather than being understood as a response to situations of inherent conflict, unions are portrayed as sources of conflict in otherwise 'naturally' harmonious conditions (Puette,1992:154-155; Morley,1976:250). In this way an opposition is established between reasonable, consensually bounded behaviour and the pursuit of sectional minority interests (Morley,1976), or, the 'national interest' and 'trade union action' (Easthope,1990).

It is important to note that for most of these researchers, the explanation does not lie in deliberate media bias. On the contrary, the source of these forms of representation lies in the 'routine cultural practices' (Walton and Davis,1977:133) of news media personnel. As Hartmann argues, there are good reasons why news coverage is likely to dwell upon conflict rather than the routine in industrial relations, given the nature of news values and the imperatives of the news room (Hartmann,1975:7). Given the general orientation of the national news media towards Westminister and government, it is hardly surprising if labour and industrial copy reflects a similar preoccupation (Hartmann,1976:2/54). In other words, rather than assessing evidence of bias, the search for an explanation of such patterns in content 'must go much deeper...', to consider the 'basic assumptions with which news is produced' (Philo et al,1977:4-5). These assumptions, according to the critical research tradition, produce a 'cultural skewdness' (GUMG,1980:401) in news coverage which disadvantages labour and presents a 'picture of the world which is such as to assist in the reproduction of the relations of domination existing in society' (Sparks,1987:370).

Rise of the 'Revisionists'

As is well known, the critical tradition is not without its own critics both academic and from within journalism (Skirrow,1980). During the 1980s, 'a new wave of revisionist writing' (Sparks,1987:370), developed a body of research findings which explicitly challenged the work of the Glasgow team, and by implication much of the remaining work in the critical tradition.

Some of the criticisms developed by such 'revisionist' writing are well made. However, for the purposes of this study, what is important about these approaches (Anderson and Sharrock, 1979; Hetherington, 1985; Harrison, 1985; Cumberbatch et al, 1986) is that they illustrate the extent to which the 'imperatives' and taken for granted assumptions of journalism can become entangled in debates over the nature of coverage. A further point to emerge from the engagement between the 'revisionists' and the critical tradition, is the importance of going beyond quantitative analysis in any search of news content for evidence of contested agendas or struggles around political definition and meaning.

Firstly, the problem of distortion in coverage. The difficulties in attempting to measure media representations against 'bench mark' measures of 'reality', such as official statistics, are well known.[3] In Harrison's attempt to rebut the early Glasgow work, a critique is developed which rests upon the 'legitimacy' of mainstream news values and journalistic practice. It is unreasonable to expect the news media to provide a faithful representation of the Department of Employment's statistical series; media coverage is inevitably selective and, if that is the case, then the criteria employed by journalists, - the size and impact of disputes upon the general public, their political significance, etc, - are as good as any others (1985:33-41). In these terms, some strikes are simply more newsworthy than others. Further to this, Harrison argues, media coverage has to be assessed in the context of the organisational imperatives of news production, constraints of time, limitations of format, and so on (1985:39-43). These imply the necessity of selectivity and impose 'inevitable' constraints upon the depth of explanation which can be provided. Thus, to identify 'pay' as a frequent cause of disputes is not to over-simplify but to provide a reasonable account, given the circumstances in which news coverage is produced (1985:40-42). Similarly, the tendency to dwell upon leading personalities, rather than 'ordinary' figures is explicable in terms of conventional news values and journalists' practice (Harrison, 1985:66; Hetherington,1985:182).

Indeed, the 'revisionist' approach questions whether there actually is any other way of presenting the news. One of the central thrusts of the critical position is that in being driven by events, and in failing to provide substantial consideration of underlying processes or 'causes', the activity of trade unionists is represented as irrational. Harrison, however, insists in his re-interpretation of the Glasgow evidence, that 'causes' are mentioned frequently in news reports (1985:53). A great deal depends upon the distinction between 'cause' and 'explanation' here; classifying one strike as a 'pay dispute', another as a 'dispute over conditions' is hardly to discuss 'underlying reasons', as Harrison concedes (1985:59). Nevertheless, for Harrison the 'bare bones' of labour stories were covered in the ITN coverage he re-examines (1985:67); ITN did 'what can be reasonably expected of a popular medium...' (1985:68), this represented 'a reasonable compromise' (1985:66), given the resource and format constraints. Similarly, Cumberbatch in analysing coverage of the Coal Strike, agrees that 'throughout the strike there was a tendency for the news to emphasise the conduct of the strike - the epiphenomenon of union ballots, talks and negotiations and picketing violence - rather than the causes of the dispute' (1986:135). However, for Cumberbatch, 'this is hardly surprising given the event driven nature of news' (1986:135).

The Glasgow team are taken to task for demanding the impossible. How 'thoroughly', asks Harrison, can a limited news report explore underlying causes? The Glasgow team appear to be imposing standards of thoroughness in detail and explanation which are derived from their own ideological positions, rather than from an adequate understanding of television as a news medium (1985:68). Cumberbatch, again assuming the dominant conventions of television representation as given, argues that inadequacies in depth of explanation in news reports can be compensated for in current affairs programming (1986:136). However, Anderson and Sharrock go further, suggesting that research which charts the absence of underlying analysis in news media coverage, represents no more than the complaint that journalists do not interpret the world like sociologists. To insist that deeper or more thorough accounts of events should be provided is merely 'to show that the media do not accept the same theories that are presently... fashionable within sociology' (1979:372). Underpinning this latter view is an early manifestation of a fashionable relativism which logically implies the abandonment of all bench marks against which to measure news coverage and, by implication, all efforts to hold news media accountable, - a position powerfully criticised in recent contributions (Philo,1990:194-195; Eldridge,1993).

Now the assumption underpinning this study is that research which demonstrates the absence of particular explanations in labour and industrial reporting makes a valuable contribution because it allows us to map the relative success of the various social groups seeking to secure access as sources in the arena of labour and industrial news, and to the extent that such research identifies systematic patterns of 'success' or 'failure', it provides important clues regarding the distribution of material and symbolic power. However, for Harrison, the extent to which the Glasgow teams' findings can be explained in terms of the routine practice of journalism and the constraints of the news production process, he has succeeded in refuting the view that news content is 'biased' or 'skewed'. Critics (Elliott,1981), of course, have pointed to ambiguities in the way the Glasgow team explain their findings,- either through an 'instrumental' conspiracy model or a version of the dominant ideology thesis (Goodwin,1990).[4] Harrison equates 'bias' with intent and appears to assume that in demonstrating that news format and production routine, rather than intent, can explain the contours of industrial coverage, the Glasgow critique falls.

One immediate point to make is that it is a mistake to under-estimate the determining influence of production routines and formats, in themselves, as recent research has demonstrated (Cottle,1993). An argument preoccupied only with the concept of conscious bias, misses the point that formats, production routines and news values, in themselves, may produce dominant news frames which highlight particular interpretations, rather than others. Examples of conscious bias are probably quite rare. For example, as Goodwin comments, news values routinely direct journalists towards negativity or 'bad news' rather than 'good news', which explains why not only trade unionists but government ministers complain about 'bias' (Goodwin,1990:57). And these features of news production are, in turn, related to the political and economic context in which news production occurs, including associated power relationships (Elliott and Golding,1979; Murdock,1980 and 1982). Cumberbatch and his colleagues acknowledge that 'bias' may be generated through production routine and format, as well as intent, and yet still imply that an approach 'sensitive to the vicissitudes of journalism' (Brown et al,1987:383) provides the key to understanding content rather than an approach which places the ideological nature of coverage in the foreground.

To pursue this further, it is important to explore the nature of the coverage in some depth; to ask questions about the more subtle ways in which 'differential legitimacy' between actors and social groups may be conveyed. This, in turn, is likely to require a qualitative consideration of language and imagery, which the 'revisionists' are reluctant to pursue. Instead, they consider the concept of balance which *can* be assessed in quantitative terms. If the Glasgow team and other critical research points to a systematic imbalance in the attribution of responsibility for social conflict and in the access afforded to different social actors and different perspectives, the 'revisionist' project involves seeking to demonstrate that, within *reasonable* limits (as measured by public opinion), a less partisan reading of the evidence actually confirms that balance is achieved.

Cumberbatch and colleagues consider that their quantitative analysis of television coverage during the Coal Strike demonstrates that 'balance was usually achieved' between 'the main political voices of government and opposition, NUM and NCB' (1986:135). They concede that the 'balance of ideas was less evident' but insist that inadequacies in 'internal balance', here, were compensated by the external balance achieved through current affairs coverage (1986:136). For Cumberbatch then, balance is primarily achieved internally and numerically, through the representation of the elite groups within mainstream politics and the key elite figures involved in the conflict. The criteria for a 'balance in ideas' appear to be rather looser and are given less weight.

One of the ways in which Harrison tries to refute the Glasgow thesis is by demonstrating that ITN news coverage achieved balance in reflecting the range of perspectives and types of understanding within the political mainstream (1985:63-68). For Harrison, assessment of balance can only be made with reference to the perceptions of the audience and the range of political perspectives shared by a majority of the public. This view is adopted as a methodological principle by Cumberbatch et al, who compare television coverage of the Coal Strike with data gathered from their own survey of public opinion. What other benchmark is available with which to assess balance? The range of political perspectives shared by media researchers is clearly unsatisfactory as a benchmark. And yet, assuming for one moment that such a thing exists, how can 'the shop floor view', for example, actually be gauged by journalists (Harrison,1985:63)? Cumberbatch and colleagues, in response to criticism, deny establishing a 'hierarchy of credibility' with opinions drawn from their survey of the Castleford mining village at the bottom (Brown et al,1987:383) but, nonetheless, it is clear that these perspectives are not included in the equation when the assessment of 'balance' is ultimately calculated in their research. They, too, implicitly equate balance with the range of views associated with the political elites of the main parliamentary parties.

A Critique of the Revisionist Critique

The 'revisionist' critique is on strong ground in pointing to the problematic nature of any exercise which involves assessing news content against alternative 'interpretations' of events. The critique is less convincing in implying that media researchers face a stark choice between bench marks derived from opinion poll surveys or summaries of the political agenda offered by mainstream Westminster politics, on the one hand, and a set of arbitrary and idiosyncratic perspectives held by media researchers, on the other. Though the Glasgow work could be clearer on this issue, it is important to remember that their benchmark for assessing economic coverage, for example, was not wholly arbitrary but drawn from an extensive analysis, - 'the alternative economic strategy', - which enjoyed substantial support within the labour movement and elsewhere, including Parliament (London CSE Group,1980). This may have been a partial view but it was a partial view which carried very significant political weight and it is legitimate to ask questions regarding the extent to which it was 'represented' in news reporting.

What this really points to is the importance of assessing the range of news sources and the nature of the agendas which each seeks to present in conjunction with content research. Connell (1980) is quite right to point out that the news media cannot be expected to represent every diverse viewpoint in news coverage. At the same time, it is entirely possible that the range of views and agendas, enjoying substantial political support, extends beyond the bounds of Westminster politics. As is now recognised in the work of Schlesinger et al (1991), Schlesinger and Tumber (1995), Anderson (1993), and others, a consideration of the range of social groups active in a news media arena and the agendas which they may seek to present, can inform the analysis and assessment of content. This helps to anticipate the danger of the idiosyncratic reading of the news media. A familiar criticism of the Glasgow work is their failure to supplement their analysis of content with a sustained investigation of news production   (Anderson and Sharrock, 1979:373; Elliott,1981; Cottle,1993:9) while Harrison points to their relative neglect of the 'media work' undertaken by trade unions and employers (1985:ch 4). Much the same point, however, could be applied to the 'revisionist critique', itself. Both Hetherington and Cumberbatch and colleagues' work might have been all the richer for an empirical investigation of the competing news sources' media work during the Coal Strike.

Secondly, as Sparks (1987:373) notes, there are few good grounds for assuming that a majority or consensual interpretation of events should always be privileged as 'more objective'. Thirdly, as Sparks argues, 'balance' is too often equated with 'impartiality' in the 'revisionist critique' (1987:375). And yet, of course, 'biased' accounts can be perfectly 'balanced' and this, in turn, returns the debate to the status of qualitative analysis. There are good grounds for supposing that the mechanisms which may produce an ideological construction, even within a 'balanced' text, are not always conveniently arranged in discrete and quantifiable categories on the manifest level. The ways in which language, lay out, headline, ordering, photographs and imagery, interplay to produce a 'representation' are not necessarily amenable to content analysis. Harrison and Cumberbatch are sceptical of the value of qualitative analysis. Harrison is particularly scathing about the Glasgow case study material and Cumberbatch ties his colours to the mast of 'scientific empiricism' (1986:9), which he appears to assume excludes qualitative work. Even where their own work cries out for an extended qualitative discussion (coverage of the notorious Orgreave incidents during the 84/85 Coal Strike), they step back from the brink, choosing not 'to become bogged down in semiotic analysis of individual bulletins' (1986:73). This is unfortunate because as Philo argues (1988), their almost exclusively quantitative design does demonstrate the limitations of content analysis, as well as some of its strengths. Frequency does not always measure significance; some of the key mechanisms for organising the meaning of coverage lay in the interplay of language and image, not the frequency with which particular themes, personalities or 'tendentious verbs' (Cumberbatch et al,1986: 105) occur. There is a problem in focusing upon 'the words that are used rather the meanings which are conveyed' (Philo,1990:164). Most importantly, generic categories such as 'picketing violence' or 'talks and negotiations' are efficient coding categories but tell us little about the interpretative frameworks within which such politically significant episodes during the Coal Strike, were placed (Philo,1988:517-518).

It is unlikely that categories defined for the purposes of coding and quantitative generalisation will be sufficiently sensitive to the mechanisms through which a 'differential legitimacy' (Hartmann,1975) between social groups is achieved, or one 'dominant interpretation' (Philo,1990:169) secured. This is particularly important when one considers the distinction between 'balance' and 'bias'. As Philo argues, during the Coal Strike, it was clear that journalists did try to produce balanced coverage in the representation of viewpoints, but it was also possible to describe in qualitative terms, the way in which journalists' underlying assumptions shaped reporting in such a way that particular 'preferred meanings' were privileged in the news text (1990:170-171). In the Cumberbatch et al. study, there is a frequent failure to think through the political and ideological significance of the coding categories which are employed to describe content. Thus, as Sparks shows, Cumberbatch's very own frequency counts demonstrate the dominance of 'law and order' issues in television coverage during the Coal Strike and the relative infrequency of occasions in which television dealt with 'economic and social issues' (Sparks,1987:376),   the sorts of issues which the NUM would have wished to highlight.

Summary

Critics have pointed to a number of other weaknesses in the 'revisionist' case. Harrison's failure to draw upon more than typed pre-broadcast scripts of ITN coverage rather than the video material actually used by the Glasgow team presents obvious difficulties.[5] Harrison sometimes employs a 'sleight of hand' in swapping units of enumeration to refute the Glasgow case.[6] He is guilty of several of the charges he levels at the Glasgow team in ignoring contrary evidence and selectively organising his material (Collins,1986). There are further inconsistencies between the concluding section of the Cumberbatch et al. study, and the evidence supplied in the main body of the report (Philo,1988). However, the most important conclusions to be drawn from this discussion concern the concepts of balance, bias, and the status of qualitative work.

Balance does not ensure impartiality. It is a key organising principle around which journalists plan their information gathering strategies and through which they construct their copy. In terms of day to day routine, it is a rational strategy for coping with the imperatives of news production (Tuchman,1977). At the same time, balance is not necessarily equivalent either to impartiality or ideological neutrality. As a concept it is deeply embedded in the taken for granted assumptions or inferential frameworks which underpin the practice of journalism. In organising 'balanced' copy, journalists implicitly draw distinctions between mainstream and marginal news sources; between 'commonly agreed' and 'extreme' political perspectives; between established, legitimate agendas salient to 'public opinion' and 'minority concerns'. This is why arguments preoccupied by intentional bias so often miss the mark. It is the 'bias' which occurs through the underlying and routine assumptions informing news gathering and the organisation of copy , rather than arising from intentional partiality, which is most important.

And what is clear from the present study, is the extent to which in order to be 'successful', union press officers have to embrace the same underlying assumptions and inferential frames. Union press officers frequently depend upon the organising principle of 'balance' to open up opportunities to insert a union response or encode elements of a union agenda. The exchange relationships between union officers and industrial correspondents depended upon a set of common understandings not only about what made 'good' copy but also about how it should be organised and described. Whilst often retaining quite distinct political orientations, to be regarded as 'professional' by journalists, union press officers had to acknowledge the priority of these elements in their work. In this context, Connell (1980) is quite right to insist that ideas and language are not imposed from above, as he believes the Glasgow team assume. He points out that 'ordinary' trade unionists frequently employ the language and ideas which the Glasgow team regard as 'culturally skewed'. In the case of union press officers, at least, to successfully engage with the dominant agencies of cultural reproduction, it is necessary to employ particular ways of describing and particular frameworks for understanding and, to a degree, these become 'working assumptions' for both union officers and correspondents engaged in the production of labour news. In this sense, dominant frames and perspectives are 'shared'.

The extent to which such a process of cultural incorporation occurs is likely to vary from issue to issue and will depend upon specific circumstances, - the position of the trade union, the type of news media, the disposition of public opinion and the political interests of the state, etc. What is clear is that to assess the extent to which trade unions have to make compromises in terms of language and agendas, or the extent to which they can exploit the conventions of journalism, such as 'balance', in order to secure news media 'successes' is an empirical but largely qualitative exercise. There are significant dangers in loading too great a theoretical weight upon slender qualitative foundations (Elliott, 1981) but, nevertheless, quantitative coding can only describe broad 'contours of coverage'. It is insufficiently sensitive to assess union successes in combating mechanisms conferring 'differential legitimacy' or in promoting alternative 'preferred readings'.

The health unions and the research tradition

The critical research tradition, then, points to a number of potential difficulties which were likely to confront the health unions but also underlines the point that the balance of their successes and failures will be best assessed through the qualitative dimension of news content, rather than in purely quantitative aggregates.

Clearly a protracted dispute involving ambulances and 'life saving' medical teams was likely to attract intensive media interest, given the nature of the conflict oriented news values documented in the research, and particularly if emergency services to the public were affected. Such a dispute was likely to offer 'drama', 'human interest', 'conflict' and could be constructed in terms of event-oriented news frames. The unions' case was, not unusually, a complex one involving a number of technical arguments regarding pay and the terms of the existing agreement, - detail which was crucial to their case but which failed to meet the criteria of mainstream news values or the requirements of the main news frames. Given the contours of coverage documented by the critical research tradition, it was likely that the rationale for the union case would be obscured in news material by a concentration upon the immediate and particular consequences of industrial action. This was an especially sharp danger given the tendency of the news media to 'frame' disputes in terms of previously established news themes (GUMG,1976: ch 7) and the potential parallels to be drawn with the coverage of the 1979 'Winter of Discontent' (TUC,1979a).

Another problem for the health unions was that in taking action against their employers, the regional Ambulance Services, they were also inevitably going to involve the government and the Minister of Health, Kenneth Clarke. The 'hierarchy of access' identified by the critical research tradition was likely to privilege sources representing the powerful, with the state enjoying, at least the potential capacity, to act as a primary definer, even if recent research offers some hope for subordinate groups challenging such primary definitions (Schlesinger and Tumber, 1994; Anderson,1993). Kenneth Clarke, himself, was a 'good media performer' and there was a potential, given the government's 'arms length' relationship with the Ambulance Services, for the minister to present himself as a neutral 'arbiter', rather than active player or advocate (Deacon and Golding,1994:15). It was important for the health unions to embroil the minister politically, and to place the dispute in the context of the government's tight public spending limits, as quickly as possible.

The likely challenge facing the health unions was not a matter of 'merely' correcting conscious 'bias'. Rather, if the critical research tradition is correct in emphasising the significance of underlying assumptions in shaping the practices of journalists, then the perspectives of the health unions were likely to be treated with a 'differential legitimacy', which positioned them at a disadvantage. The health unions, therefore, faced a dilemma. On the one hand, they might refuse to compromise the integrity of the messages they sought to present to the news media and, by implication, challenge some of the underlying assumptions governing journalists' practice. The danger of such 'high risk' strategies is illustrated by the experience of the NUM during the 1984/85 Coal Strike and the consequences of the widening gulf which emerged between the perspectives and expectations of Nell Myers, the union press officer, and those of labour and industrial correspondents. The NUM experienced considerable difficulty in making any in-roads into a news agenda increasingly shaped by the government and the NCB, as the strike wore on (Jones et al,1985; Jones,1986; Winterton and Winterton,1989). On the other hand, the health unions might choose to accept the dominant underlying assumptions and 'inferential frames' of the news media as given. The task would then be to find ways in which these could be harnessed to communicate important elements of the union message, albeit within the inevitable constraints imposed by conventional news values and frames.

The health unions' strategy

Following difficulties experienced in attempting to co-ordinate the media work in the 1988 multi-union nurses dispute, it was agreed by all five unions involved in the Ambulance dispute that a greater degree of central control had to be exerted. In contrast to the earlier nurses' dispute, where the autonomy of local branches had resulted in a confusion of duplicated and conflicting 'days of action' involving different branches from different unions, the character and tradition of the ambulance service helped because ambulance workers were already familiar with an organisational strategy which emphasised central control and hierarchical discipline. The Ambulance Service was smaller and 'almost militaristic in the way it worked.'[7] Integration of the efforts of each union was facilitated by the fact that three of the five were already deep in merger negotiations.

It was recognised from the outset that an open confrontation with employers and the government, involving strike action, was unlikely to succeed because by 1989, the employment laws regulating industrial action imposed very severe constraints and, in any case, the union leaderships were uncertain that their memberships had sufficient appetite for strike action given their roles as members of the emergency services (Hill,1993). The dispute, then, was one of the first to identify public opinion as the main lever with which to exert pressure, and to position this, rather than industrial action, as the cornerstone of the dispute strategy. The news media were to become the main arena for engagement. Given this plan, it was believed essential that the unions did their utmost to avoid the application of news frames drawn from the 1979 'Winter of Discontent' and for this reason, the leaderships actively discouraged calls for strike action. As Lynn Bryan, NUPE press officer commented:

Industrial coverage tends to concentrate on the effects of a dispute, rather than on the causes...so the one thing we couldn't do was go on all-out strike (Hill,1993).

This was to be a dispute without strikes and, instead, the intention was to generate maximum publicity around an overtime ban which, the unions could justifiably claim, should not affect emergency services. In this way, it was hoped, the high public standing of the Ambulance Service could be preserved. As Bob Abberly, the COHSE officer given responsibility for parliamentary lobbying during the dispute, argued, it was possible to transform the memberships' reluctance to strike into the unions' 'greatest strength', providing this theme was carefully represented to the news media (Hill, 1993).

    The five unions involved agreed a common set of objectives for media work and a division of labour for media and lobbying activity, which was designed to ensure that all five unions spoke with one public voice. The NUPE press officer, Lynn Bryan, was given responsibility for day to day work with journalists; Roger Poole, also of NUPE, was chosen to present the 'public face' of the union at press conferences and in broadcasting interviews, and two officers at COHSE, Bob Amberely and Charlotte Atkins, concentrated upon political campaigning at Westminster. Mary McGuire and staff within NALGO's press and publicity department contributed to the development of the communications strategy and provided the 'back room' support. The division of labour was widely regarded as a successful arrangement by union staff and journalists, at least in the early stages of the dispute. Lynn Bryan commanded considerable respect amongst industrial correspondents[8] and Roger Poole rapidly became an accomplished 'media performer'.

> Roger was very good...he avoided ranting. He's a new style of officer, he had the right kind of image and came over as a reasonable kind of bloke...Clarke [Secretary of State for Health] had this image of being a sort of thug, where as Roger came across as this sweet-natured trade union official.[9]

According to Bryan and McGuire, the aim was to identify a limited number of uncomplicated themes to offer to the news media at every opportunity.[10] Most importantly, these themes were to be wrapped within the image of essential reasonableness and moderation, as personified by Roger Poole, - 'all suit and selfless sincerity' (Hill,1993). In contrast to the union priorities of the 1984-85 Coal Strike, access for journalists to both Roger Poole and Lynn Bryan was prioritised above all else, particularly as other union officers were instructed not to comment and to refuse all other temptations which the broadcasting media might offer. The press officers from each union conferred on a daily basis to review media strategy and confirm a common news agenda:

> It was marvellous operation, being able to present our case with a united front. The press weren't able to put a playing card between us and this was a conscious strategy worked out by the press officers at each union.[11]

At first, the close lines of communication established between union press offices and local branches worked extremely well. Mary McGuire and Lynn Bryan were able to introduce correspondents to union members at local ambulance stations and a considerable number of reports and longer feature articles, examining the 'human angle' were generated as a result. Many of these were quite sympathetic in tone but more importantly, they allowed the unions to exercise some influence over the interpretative frameworks employed, as well as the evaluative elements (Deacon and Golding,1994:19). In other words, at the beginning at least, the health unions, partly through 'human angle' interviews with 'ordinary' ambulance workers, were able to explain and communicate some of the complexities of their case, without danger of their being obscured by other familiar interpretative frames, such as threats to the authority of the state or the 'inevitable' resource constraints of the NHS.

However, in the later stages of the dispute, three factors began to undermine the effectiveness of the health unions media work, and these will be considered more fully below. Firstly, although wrong footed at first and unable to efficiently co-ordinate media work between the Ambulance Services, the chief executive of the NHS, Mr Duncan Nichol, and the Department of Health, eventually the government began to intervene more directly and more effectively. Secondly, as with any protracted dispute, the interest of the news media began to wane and as it did so, journalists searched for new angles, often not so suited to the purposes of presenting the health union arguments. And thirdly, the health unions themselves found it much harder to maintain the discipline both at local and national levels required to make the media strategy work. More militant branches pressed for tougher action and at a national level, the will to speak with one voice began to weaken.

The union message

In summarising the union preferred agenda, this study can draw upon the interviews conducted with trade union press officers, an analysis of union journals (Manning, 1996), and a number of contemporary newspaper and magazine articles. It is useful to distinguish between the elements of the agenda which were selected by the unions to highlight in their media work, and the evaluative contexts in which the unions hoped to present these elements. In making this distinction, the study draws upon Deacon and Golding's distinction between two vectors or dimensions of communication and reception (Golding,1990:97; Deacon and Golding,1994:19). The health union task was two-fold. One objective was to promote and communicate an interpretative framework which acknowledged 'facts' and information central to their argument. Here, the concern was to establish what the dispute was *about*, - what were the central issues. A second objective was to embed this interpretative framework in a positive evaluative context through its association with particular sets of symbols and cultural themes, rather than others. More specifically, as already discussed, the health unions recognised the temptation which the imagery of the 1979 'Winter of Discontent', a piece of powerful symbolic folklore regularly recycled by Conservative politicians, offered to journalists. The role of the Ambulance Service within the NHS offered alternative sets of symbols and themes with which to weave an evaluative context, - ambulance staff as life-saving heroes, the notion of dedication to public service, etc - and it was important that journalists were encouraged to embrace these, rather than the former.

The basic elements which the unions hoped would be acknowledged as constituting the interpretative framework included the following. One aim was to emphasise the essential 'reasonableness' of the union position; to underline their willingness to settle the dispute immediately through independent arbitration which, in turn, implied a reliance upon reasoned argument, rather than industrial muscle. Secondly, the unions wanted to place the issue of comparability with other emergency services, where pay was determined by an automatic cost of living formula, in the foreground. Whether or not the Ambulance Service should be regarded as an 'emergency service' was disputed by the employers and government. Even at the beginning, the dispute actually hinged upon a number of rather complex issues revolving around the previous agreement in 1986 and subsequent changes in the pay of the emergency services relative to other health sector workers. Nevertheless, the union press officers[12] were keen to construct the union message around a limited number of simple propositions:

(1) The unions are reluctantly taking action because the health service employers have offered only a 6.5% pay increase whilst inflation is running at over 8% and other groups of public sector workers have secured higher settlements.

(2) The unions are seeking an automatic pay formula along the lines of those agreed for the fire and police services. Such formulae remove the need for conflict.

(3) The previous settlement in 1986 offered comparability with the police and fire services but inflation and subsequent police and fire service awards have subsequently eroded the relative position of ambulance workers.

(4) The unions are not proposing to take strike action or to jeopardise emergency work. Part of the 1986 agreement placed a responsibility upon the employers to ensure that emergency cover, as opposed to routine ambulance work, was provided without reliance upon overtime working. In theory, then, an overtime ban should not affect emergency work, although the unions knew full well that in practice, given the restrictions on recruitment, the delivery of ambulance services (routine and emergency) depended upon overtime being worked. In other words, the unions were seeking to exploit the employers failure to honour this aspect of the previous agreement.

As described more fully below, the union 'keep it simple' strategy worked quite well in the early phases of the dispute. Many of the news items, particularly in the broadsheet papers, contained an account of the unions' position based upon three out of the four elements set out above. However, even at this stage, labour correspondents and news editors often appeared to regard the fourth proposition as too complex for inclusion. As a result, the important point that the unions' action could only be successful because the employers had failed to honour formal agreements on staffing levels was frequently missing from the newspaper coverage.

Later as the dispute wore on, the unions found it increasingly difficult to contain the range of themes which began to interest journalists. The unions found that their capacity to control the range and complexity of the elements constituting the interpretative framework was undermined, as they became embroiled in issues relating to the way local branches organised working to rule. In the middle of the dispute, a highly complex argument erupted between management and unions over whether crews were being locked out of their stations. At this stage, the unions were forced to move away from their four element strategy but the complexity of technical detail involved in establishing evidence of lock outs, often proved impossible to compact into an appropriate news format. Towards the end of the dispute, the centralised system of control exerted by union leaderships weakened and a number of local branches began to escalate action towards full stoppages. Inevitably, at this point the unions preferred interpretative framework was obscured as news media interest became preoccupied with the prospects of an 'all out strike'.

However, at the beginning, the unions also sought to embed these interpretative elements in a particular evaluative context. The intention was, as far as possible, to avoid the traditional symbolism and imagery associated with organised labour disputes in the 1970s and early 1980s. NUPE, in particular, still suffered from the symbolic legacy of the public sector cemetery workers' action in 1979. COHSE, too, was associated with 'militancy', perhaps in the mind of the public, and certainly in the memories of some senior medical correspondents,[13] - again a legacy of the 1970s. Rather than allow these old and familiar associations to be resurrected, the unions hoped to supply symbolic materials which would encourage alternative evaluative contexts to be developed. For example, it is clear both from an analysis of the COHSE Journal (Manning, 1996) and the comments of the union press officers involved, that one objective was to 'feminise'[14] the dispute. Although, in 1984/85 women had been prominent in the Miners' Wives and Support Groups, the public memory of the Coal Strike and most other protracted disputes was of picket lines and expressions of collective masculine solidarity.

The union journals are useful, here, in providing some indication of the unions' preferred evaluative contexts for the dispute. The COHSE Journal carried very little 'agitational' material. Although the dispute lasted for over five months, there were very few items dealing with it in the COHSE Journals and there was an absence of photographs of picket lines, large crowds or images of traditional union action. Instead, what discussion of the dispute there was emphasised the continuing sympathy of the public, the absence of violence, the 'responsible' approach of the crews, and in particular the involvement of women. The Journal frequently offered a new way of understanding union action which placed individuals rather than organised groups in the foreground. Thus, union action was de-coupled from the concept of masculine, collective power. NALGO's 'Public Service', on the other hand, did give prominence to themes of traditional union activism and frequently deployed material to underline the suggestion that unions derived their strength, ultimately, from the potential to organise collectively (Manning, 1996). Nevertheless, even here there was emphasis upon the involvement of women as activists.

In addition, 'Public Service' was frequently preoccupied with government under-funding of the public sector and the damaging impact of government reforms. This provided another dimension to the evaluative context. It was in the interests of the health unions to encourage an association in the public mind between the Ambulance Dispute and wider public anxieties about funding and the future of the NHS. Furthermore, the character of Kenneth Clarke, already 'personified' government policy on the NHS, a point not missed by the union journals which had frequently 'personalised' issues around Clarke's stewardship of the health service. In written comment and a number of cartoons, Clarke had been portrayed as both a bully and a Scrouge-like slasher of public funding.

Through developing close relations with local branches, the union press officers hoped to sensitise journalists to these evaluative contexts. Interviews with local crews and visits to local stations, allowed journalists to 'individualise' (Cottle,1993:79) reports with human interest angles. In contrast to the images of massed picketing and assembled crowds, characteristic of many earlier national disputes, many news items in the ambulance dispute did, indeed, reflect a different context. Interviews with, for example, women ambulance workers struggling to bring up families on under £10,000 a year provided copy which was difficult to insert into the dominant news frames of earlier conflicts. Ambulance crews frequently made effective advocates and news angles which concentrated upon their working environments and daily routines, permitted the placing of the some of the technical detail necessary to communicate the unions' preferred interpretative frameworks, within 'human interest' articles. By encouraging 'ordinary' members, rather than, local officials to speak to journalists, the unions helped to ensure that the language employed was not bound by a union vocabulary which had sometimes rendered communication clumsy in the past. By encouraging the 'personalisation' of the dispute around the two leading figures, Kenneth Clarke and Roger Poole, the unions hoped to turn another conventional news value to their advantage. Through a continual stress in press releases and in the public statements of Roger Poole, himself, upon the ultimate responsibility of the government as 'paymaster', the unions were able to draw the Secretary of State for Health into the media arena. Kenneth Clarke's 'personality' as an 'intransigent' and 'bullying' government minister could then be opposed by the 'reasonable' Roger Poole, willing at any time to go to independent arbitration to settle the dispute.

Figure 8.1   A Chronology of the Dispute

September 1989

7th. The result of the ballot is announced with strong support in favour of an overtime ban in pursuit of the union claim for a 9% pay increase and an automatic pay formula, as already applied to fire and police services. The employers argue that other health service workers have settled for a 6.5% pay award, although inflation is currently running at over 8%.

12th to 14th   Unions visit ACAS and invite the NHS employers and Department of Health for talks. Secretary of State for Health, Kenneth Clarke, refuses on the grounds that to permit independent arbitration for one group of health service employees but not others would be divisive.

14th Overtime ban commences.

26th Ambulance Officers (station managers) vote to join overtime ban.

October

23rd-24th   London crews begin work to rule, with restrictions on the use of radio communication and other procedures. The London Ambulance Service threatens to suspend crews who refuse to work normally. A situation described as a 'shambles' by the Chief Officer of the London Service results on the 24th.

November

3rd   Fire service receives over 9% pay award on the basis of the automatic formula operating for 'emergency services'.

7th   Troops called in for the first time to support the police and St John's Brigade in providing routine and emergency cover.

14th to 30th   London work to rule begins to spread outside the capital. Crews begin to be suspended for refusing to accept 'directed' radio calls produced via new computer equipment or 'greening up' (pressing a green button on vehicle radios to signify availability after completing a job). Unions continue to insist that their action is not intended to affect emergency calls. Suspended crews continue to accept emergency calls made by GP's, hospitals and members of the public.

December

2nd First 'unofficial' one day strike in Glasgow. National union officials accuse Kenneth Clarke of seeking to provoke a strike.

22nd Rally in London.

27th Unions accused by Senior Ambulance Officer of placing a baby's life in danger in Hackney after delays in responding to emergency calls.

January 1990

2nd to 5th Controversy over Kenneth Clarke's letter replying to the daughter of a Nottinghamshire ambulance worker. Clarke comments that only a minority of ambulance workers had paramedical skills and that most were only 'professional drivers doing a worthwhile job but not exceptional one'.

12th to 24th Unofficial strikes spread in Sussex, London, and the Midlands, despite pressure from union leaders.

February

6th Inquest held following death of a London man whose treatment was delayed by the dispute and a shortage of hospital staff.

10th to 19th Ambulance Services begin to seek court orders to prevent suspended crews from using stations, vehicles or equipment to provide emergency cover.

23rd Dispute settled following talks. Unions accept 16.9% over two years but fail to secure recognition as an emergency service or an automatic pay formula. Roger Poole claims that the settlement is a triumph but a number of local crews are critical and Mersey crews threaten to continue strike action.

A qualitative assessment of coverage

It is not the intention to provide a comprehensive description of all qualitative aspects of coverage. Rather, the intention is to consider evidence which will allow the success of the unions' media strategy to be evaluated. More specifically, the focus will be upon the extent to which the unions were successful in offering to the print media their preferred interpretative frameworks and the symbolic materials which would encourage journalists to develop the favoured evaluative contexts within which to embed such frameworks.

Most of the broadsheet papers followed the dispute in considerable detail throughout its five month duration. In this assessment all the news reports, feature articles, and editorials in the *Guardian* (127 items), the Independent (116 items), *The Times* (99 items) and the *Financial Times* (32 items) concerning the dispute have been examined. At the other end of the market, the *Daily Mirror*, the *Sun* and the *Daily Express* were selected. The latter two were selected as particularly 'tough nuts' for the union press officers to crack, given their political orientation and familiar ideological perspectives on trade unions. Coverage in these papers was more erratic, being triggered by particularly sharp crises in the course of the dispute, although the *Daily Mirror* did take a consistent interest in developments throughout. The *Sun*, on the other hand, ignored the dispute throughout September, remained inattentive in October and only took a serious interest once troops had been called in to provide ambulance cover in November.

The Early Phase of the Dispute: Militants and Public Heroes

A view held widely amongst union press officers was that their most fruitful media terrain was delimited not by political affiliation but by position in the market. Broadsheet newspapers, irrespective of their political character, were more likely to carry items on union affairs than their popular counterparts. This view was largely borne out in the early phase of the Ambulance Dispute, in which broadsheet papers demonstrated a consistent interest but populars maintained only sporadic coverage.

Even in the early phase, however, it was possible to detect some potential tensions in media coverage. These were inspired by a series of thematic contradictions between the cumulative history of traditional industrial relations news frames, and alternative news frames suggested by other conventional news values and popular imagery. The earlier sections of this chapter have described the traditional industrial relations news frames which news organisations habitually reproduced; the association between union activity and 'militancy', the representation of the labour movement as a channel for the pursuit of self-interest, and so on. And yet, in relation to health care and medicine an alternative traditional media mythology (Karpf,1988) offered the opportunity to construct ambulance workers as public heroes or 'angels with blue flashing lights.'[15] In fact, it is possible to set out a series of opposing symbolisations which offered news editors and journalists alternative ways of representing the ambulance crews:

PUBLIC HEROES
OR
SELF INTERESTED PRODUCER GROUP

COMPASSIONATE CARERS
OR
UNION MILITANTS

To these two sets of ideological oppositions, which are rooted in traditional popular mythologies, can be added a third, which also partly stems from a traditional media association between health care and the power of technology but owes its appearance to an intervention by the Secretary of State for Health, during the dispute:

TECHNICALLY SKILLED PARAMEDIC EMERGENCY TEAMS
OR
SEMI-SKILLED DRIVERS

Of course, each side in the dispute had a powerful interest in encouraging the news media to embrace and reproduce one set of symbolic themes, rather than the other. As we shall see, whilst there was some evidence of national newspapers drawing upon sets of symbolic themes and imagery hostile to the union side even in some of the very earliest examples of coverage, it is surprising how readily, during the first phase of the dispute, large sections of the print media placed ambulance workers in news frames which did promote a heroic mythology. Only as the dispute grew protracted and more complex, was there an ideological shift towards the more familiar and hostile imagery of trade unionism. During the early phase of the dispute, imagery and symbolisation which associated ambulance crews with life-saving drama, compassionate caring and public service, provided the health unions with a very significant advantage in their battle to secure favourable evaluative contexts for coverage.

Most newspapers identified the implications of the dispute for emergency and '999' services as a dominant theme from the outset and in the very earliest items responsibility for such disruption was, by implication, laid at the door of the health unions. Thus, for example, *The Times* (front page 8th September 1989) led with the headline, 'Overtime Ban May Hit 999 Calls', and continued:

> Leaders of Britain's ambulance crews, who voted by a 4 to 1 majority yesterday for a national overtime ban in support of a pay claim, admitted for the first time that the 999 service could be affected.

The *Guardian* first reported the possibility of the dispute on the 5th September but selected very much the same news angle as *The Times* around which to construct its 8th September report, with the headline, 'Union Action Threatens 999 Service' (page two). Similarly, the *Financial Times* (page 13) on the same day, reported developments under the headline, 'Overtime Ban Likely to Hit Emergency Services'. The framing of events masks the complexity of the issues involved, even at this early stage, and obscures some key elements of the unions' preferred interpretative framework. The strategy of the health unions was to select a form of action which did *not* threaten the '999 Service', providing employers honoured the earlier agreement on staffing and overtime working. As we shall see, the subtlety and yet crucial importance of this point was often lost in even the more detailed broadsheet reports, let alone tabloid accounts. Only the *Guardian* referred to the three year formal agreement which precluded ambulance services from relying upon overtime working for the provision of emergency service cover.

However, while this point was frequently lost, the unions were successful in communicating a number of the other key elements in their preferred interpretative agenda. The first dispute report in the *Financial Times* (8th September page 13), for example, reported the size of the vote in favour of action, the point that parity with other emergency services had been conceded in 1986; that an offer of only 6.5% was below the inflation rate of 8% and that the union side was willing to immediately resolve the dispute through binding, independent arbitration. Items in the *Guardian* and *Times* also included these elements in the unions' interpretative frameworks, and also reproduced extracts from a press release written around a quote from Roger Poole:

> Kenneth Clarke has provoked this dispute with his high handed rejection of our repeated requests for binding independent arbitration. Such contempt for the National Health Service's emergency service reflects this government's appalling treatment of Britain's health service (*Guardian* 8th September page 2).

This statement offered an evaluative context in which the dispute is related to wider public anxieties about the future of the National Health Service and sought to exploit the news media inclination to personalise issues involving conflict. The calculation was, of course, that the placing of Kenneth Clarke's personality in the foreground would work to the advantage of the union side. For good measure, Roger Poole went on to suggest that it was 'intolerable' that Mrs Thatcher was in the habit of 'bathing herself in the glory of the emergency services' during disasters such as Hillsborough or Clapham and yet refuse to adequately reward ambulance crews. Even in this short press statement, the union side can be found encouraging symbolic associations between their cause and the 'mythology' of public heroism. Both Kenneth Clarke and Duncan Nichols, Chief Executive of the NHS, responded but only the *Guardian* reproduced their attempts to stir public memories of the alternative symbolic systems with which public sector union action has been represented. Clarke suggested that 'they should not be taking this action...It is bound to hurt the vulnerable and sick', while Nichols commented that, 'We are not prepared to give in in the face of threats of action which will damage patient care' (*Guardian* 8th September page 2).

On September 11th the union side were able to put the employers and government on the defensive by visiting ACAS for 'last minute talks', with the action due to begin two days later. This placed the government at a tactical disadvantage. By refusing to attend talks at ACAS, the government was in danger of appearing 'intransigent' but to attend would be to move towards conceding independent arbitration. The union side took full advantage, Roger Poole issuing a statement to assembled industrial correspondents on the steps of the ACAS headquarters, which called upon Kenneth Clarke to accept the ACAS invitation and re-affirmed the health unions' willingness to call off action immediately in exchange for independent arbitration. This received coverage in both *The Times* and the *Guardian* (September 12th) without any response from either government or employers.

Only the *Guardian* carried a reply from Duncan Nichol, the following day which simply reiterated the line that patients were bound to suffer and that the unions should 'think again' (September 13th page 3). At the same time, Roger Poole was able to push home the simple message that, 'we will call off the action now if the government agrees to go to independent arbitration'. Through the frequent repetition of this simple proposition, and through the persona of Roger Poole, the unions were able to present a durable image of non-militant reasonableness. This was maintained throughout the early phase of the dispute and was only undermined in the later stages as the union leaderships' influence over the tactics of local branches began to weaken.

With the commencement of the dispute, the popular papers began to show more interest. The *Sun*, perhaps because the action involved a 'low key' overtime ban rather than a full-blown strike, continued to ignore developments but the *Daily Express* carried a short report on page two (September 15th), 'Ambulance Action Sparks 999 Plans', which contained sparse detail of the union case but, predictably in the light of the volume of earlier research on labour coverage, emphasised the arrangements being put into place to cope with the *effects* of the dispute, including the hiring of taxis. In this report, the union side had singularly failed to communicate the key elements of their preferred interpretative agenda. However, within the same issue of the *Daily Express*, an inside feature appeared on page 21, under the headline, 'What Price the Life Savers?', with a strapline, '*Daily Express* Special Investigation on the Ambulance Teams Forced to Fight for Decent Pay.' The piece was written by a features journalist who had travelled with two crews on 14th September and was divided into two sections. The first described a dramatic account of one 'routine' night's work for the crews, the second was based upon an interview with one of the crew members, Jacqui Ross, 'who struggles to make ends meet, bringing up three young children on take home pay of £150 a week.' The main section allowed plenty of scope to deploy popular news values and to tap into the popular mythology of health care and medical intervention, describing two life-saving call outs, one to a heart attack victim, another to an attempted suicide where the victim lay, 'slumped on his blood-soaked bed'. Having leapt from his ambulance and raced to a high rise flat, Philip Paget, 'fought desperately to find a vein to inject a body stabilising fluid':

> ...Suddenly the needle went home and the heart monitoring machine began bleeping. Then, the patient's eyes flickered open and a broad smile spread across Philip's face as he knew another life had been saved.

The article closed around a quote from the crew member, 'Don't you think after 11 years doing this work I deserve to be given a bit more than £150 a week?'. The second section described fellow crew member, Jacqui Ross' difficulties in managing a family budget on low wages, where the children 'often have to go without the toys and treats their friends expect'.

> I don't want to be called an angel or a heroine. I just want a wage which I can live on.

This example from the *Express* is illuminating for several reasons. The purple prose of emergency intervention and life saving illustrates that even strongly right of centre papers could be seduced by the popular medical imagery of 'heroines', 'angels' and 'life savers'. However, it should also be noted that very little of the unions' interpretative agenda is communicated, either in the short news report or the feature article. The latter provides an emotive account which might assist the union side in fostering an advantageous evaluative context, but did little to explain the merit of the union case to an unenlightened *Express* reader. In arranging the visit, the health unions' press officers had pulled off something of a coup,- it was most unusual for the *Express* to treat union action with such a sympathetically emotive perspective,- but the resulting coverage represented a triumph for the health unions only in terms of the evaluative dimension, not the interpretative. The potential for the familiar hostile news frames of earlier eras to be re-imposed was demonstrated by the *Daily Mirror*. The *Mirror's* first report, a small item which appeared on page two (7th September) carried the headline, '999 Men Launch Pay War', together with a photograph of Rodney Bickerstaffe, NUPE general secretary and a familiar 'folk devil' from the 1979 Winter of Discontent. Here, within a traditional industrial relations news frame, the *men* of the unions are attributed responsibility for initiating social conflict in a familiar representation of industrial relations. However, by the 12th September, the Mirror had transformed the war-like men into much less belligerent figures under the headline, 'Mercy Men Peace Bid' and an item which reported that Kenneth Clarke, 'would be urged to go to arbitration' by union chiefs who 'would immediately call off their action if he agrees'. And yet, two days later, under the headline, '999 Men Overtime Ban Goes Ahead', traditional news frames re-surfaced in the *Mirror* once more:

Last ditch attempts to avert the ambulance overtime ban failed last night. The ban which could bring hardship to millions of old and sick people began at midnight. NHS Chief Executive, Duncan Nichol, urged ambulance workers, 'Think again and call it off. Any action will cause patients to suffer'. Union chief negotiator, Roger Poole, replied, 'We will call it off if the Health Secretary, Kenneth Clarke, agrees to arbitration (*Daily Mirror*, 14th September).

So, in the *Daily Mirror*, at least, the earliest reports are characterised by an alternation between traditional industrial relations news frames, containing within them the familiar imagery of union militancy and a sectional power exercised at the expense of a vulnerable public, on the one hand, and the alternative symbolism of 'mercy men', on the other. The ambivalence in early *Mirror* coverage is a reminder that the representation of ambulance workers as agents of 'heroic' and compassionate public service, was by no means assured. Just as the NUPE grave diggers in 1979 were portrayed as refusing to bury the dead, so the danger arose that for the health unions that NUPE ambulance crews would be portrayed as failing to save the sick and injured. A great deal depended upon the success of the union side in providing journalists with opportunities to construct 'human interest' stories, along the lines of the *Express* feature above.

Availability, according to the union press officers, was also a crucial factor at this stage.[16] The union side made sure that a fresh statement, quote, or press release was continually available and that Lynn Bryan or a colleague were at all times accessible to enquiring journalists. This sustained effort appears to be reflected in the early coverage. Almost every news item contains a union perspective, even if subordinate in position to other sources, whereas on a number of occasions government and employers either did not provide comment or failed to offer a fresh slant. In the days following the ACAS visit, for example, the unions provided a dominant interpretation of developments by default. It was during this period that the *Daily Mirror* abandoned, altogether, its application of traditional industrial relations news frames in favour of the 'public service heroes' angle.

ANGER AS CLARKE BLOCKS 999 PEACE

Health Secretary, Kenneth Clarke, again angered ambulance workers yesterday by urging health bosses not to settle their pay row at ACAS. But he added it would be wrong for him to intervene. As crews began their overtime ban Roger Poole union chief negotiator, claimed Mr Clarke was 'the

invisible hand' behind the managers' refusal to go to arbitration. And he
accused Mr Clarke of 'cynically using patients as pawns.' Taxis and buses
were called to take non-emergency cases to hospital but many non-
emergency appointments had to be cancelled. Unions claimed that local
health chiefs had paid out £80,000 in taxi fares. Roger Poole said that
'Ambulance workers are bending over backwards to ensure that all 999 calls
are answered (*Daily Mirror* 15th September 1989 page 4).

This report illustrates well the union success, at this stage, in setting the pace
and in exploiting symbolic materials to secure a favourable evaluative
context but, once again, it also illustrates the difficulties for the union side in
communicating key elements in their interpretative framework. In offering a
view and an interpretation of the situation, the unions are given a free ride in
the absence of a government or employer response. Poole is able to portray
the *reasonableness* of the union position in seeking arbitration. In this sense
the evaluative context is favourable to the union side. However, there is an
absence of discussion of key elements of the unions' preferred interpretative
framework and this makes the claim by Roger Poole that his members were
'bending over backwards' to mitigate the effects of the action apparently
inexplicable. This would only become intelligible if it was also explained that
the employers were formally committed to maintaining emergency cover
without overtime working, and that the strategy of the unions was to
highlight in the public domain, the failure of the employers to honour this
agreement.

The inclination to 'individualise' what are essentially collective problems
(Cottle,1993:79) is not confined to tabloid papers. And the union side were
able to exploit this appetite for 'human interest' angles in ways which
encouraged the highlighting of the symbolic themes of 'heroism' and
'unrewarded service', in a number of the broadsheet papers. *The Guardian*,
for example, on the 14th September devoted the top half of page four to the
dispute with three articles, one reporting on the immediate consequences of
the overtime ban and the other two concentrating in detail upon aspects of the
ambulance workers' case. Keith Harper, the *Guardian* labour editor,
provided a discussion of the union claim for parity with police and fire
services, indicating that definitions of 'emergency service' were at the heart of
the dispute, an essential element in the unions' preferred interpretative
framework. However, the remaining two articles dominated the page, each
based upon 'human interest' angles with photographs of 'ordinary' crew
members at the top of the page and interviews with three ambulance crews
based at stations in Forest Hill, south London and Park Royal in north west

London, below. The angle of these reports concentrates upon the 'human cost' involved in working for the ambulance service with one interviewee attributing the anti-social hours and low basic wages to the break up of his marriage. All three interviewees provide succinct quotations pointing to the effects of low pay, job stress and the role of the ambulance service in recent disasters such as the fire at Kings Cross and the Clapham rail crash.

> I often worked 16 hours for several days running, including my time off, because even with £39 a week London Weighting I could hardly pay my bills.

> Mr Drury told of the day his unit answered the 999 call to Clapham Junction and spent nearly three hours treating injured passengers. On the way back, they were diverted to a traffic accident. This was immediately followed by a maternity call when he had to deliver a baby at home (*Guardian* 14th September page 4.).

The *Guardian* returned to the same station the following week to produce a 'fly on the wall' account of a routine shift, which included the task for one crew of explaining to a daughter that her mother had died ('No Soft Options for Crews in Ambulance Row', September 20th page four). Similarly, The *Times*, on the 18th September, produced an account by Tim Jones, 'Employment Affairs Correspondent', of the night shift at a station in Liverpool and a fresh statement from Roger Poole. Once again, the employers case went by default, and the unions were able to inject a political assessment into the interpretative framework underpinning the item. This was an attempt to anticipate the strategy of the government if the dispute dragged on. Roger Poole predicted that the government was, 'waiting for someone to be hurt so that they can turn the tide of public opinion against our members...if this is in their minds and, God forbid, someone is hurt the public will know that it is the government to blame'.

However, it is one of the first reports in the *Independent*, which illustrates how effectively a strategy of exploiting 'individualised' news values could work for the union side. On 15th September (page two), it carried an article based upon a visit and interviews with crews stationed at St Bartholomew's Hospital in the City of London:

MIXED FEELINGS OF AMBULANCE STAFF

> For trade unionists who say that they are taking action because they cannot afford to live, the two women who crew a central London ambulance have a lot to learn about militancy. Debbie Ritchie and Jane Hullott's main hope as they wait for their next call at St Bartholomew's Hospital is that their ban on overtime and rest day working will not have an effect. 'I want the public to know that they must call out ambulances only when it is absolutely necessary', says Debbie, 'otherwise people will find that there won't be crews to go on an emergency'. Hopefully, this will be over quickly. The answer given by the two women to the inevitable question as to how they can pursue their dispute, however, justified, if it will harm the sick, shows their devotion to the service. The overtime they work explains why they are taking action and why it will hurt. Jane Hulott earns £535 a month, all of which goes on her mortgage, fuel and her travel costs. To buy clothes and food for her two children, as she is a single parent, she works about 50 hours a month overtime.

The item continued to explain that staff turnover had reached 25%, and that the basis of the claim was parity with other emergency services who faced similar dangers and possessed equivalent skills. The report ended with Jane Hulott describing the painful dilemma she faced when her son woke in the middle of the night to beg her not to go out to do more overtime.

> The way we see it, the policemen and firemen are well-paid because they save the country money by stopping crime and saving buildings. We save lives but they don't seem to think that's as important.

The representation of ambulance crews as 'compassionate carers' and poorly rewarded 'public heroes' is near enough complete in this account. In the place of the *Mirror's* early militant '999 men', we find women driven reluctantly to take action by low pay and a concern for their own children. In terms of the evaluative dimension, this article is highly favourable from the unions' point of view. However, a number of the key interpretative elements are also present; the issue of parity with other emergency services, the unions' willingness to abandon action for arbitration, and the deterioration in pay leading to an over-reliance upon overtime working, are all communicated effectively through the individualised, 'human interest' news frame.

Summary

The opening phase of the dispute can be regarded as a qualified success for the union side in terms of media strategy. The symbols and myths associated with the caring professions within the field of health care pre-dated the 1989 dispute, of course. Nevertheless, the unions' media strategy worked successfully in encouraging correspondents to draw upon this stock of symbols and myths by providing frequent opportunities to talk to 'ordinary crews.'[17] The evaluative contexts produced through this, - dedicated staff rather than union militants, mothers and fathers struggling to manage family budgets, crews facing traumatic and stressful experiences on a routine basis,- were highly significant in limiting the degree to which the old familiar news frames, documented in the earlier sections of this chapter, were imposed.

At the same time, the unions were successful in 'personalising' the dispute around a contrast between the 'reasonable' Roger Poole and the 'intransigent' Kenneth Clarke. The 'open letter' which Roger Poole sent to the Secretary of State on the 14th September, and which was released to the news media, formally reinforced this news angle. However, in industrial disputes union cases are usually constructed upon complex and subtle arguments in relation to aspects of conditions of service and formal agreements. And, of course, it is this fine detail which has the least interest for many journalists. While the union side aimed to keep their messages as simple and free from jargon as possible, nonetheless, a full exposition of their preferred interpretative framework required quite detailed reference to the 1986 agreement on overtime and emergency cover, together with information on the relative deterioration in pay between 1986 and 1989. Only a limited number of broadsheet items communicated this interpretative framework intact.

This early phase was characterised by a skilful harnessing of public events to good press officer practice, on the part of the health unions. The public visit of the unions to ACAS placed the employers and government on the defensive; a union team which repeatedly announced their willingness to settle for independent arbitration immediately appeared more 'reasonable'. Roger Poole's 'open letter' kept the pot boiling in the absence of any fresh 'hard news' development. Inevitably, the employers and government were cast in a negative role, rejecting and refusing, rather than offering and suggesting. The fostering of 'human interest' copy and the maintenance of a disciplined approach in which the unions matched their organisational rhythms to those of the news desk, with fresh material each day and a press officer available to answer enquiries at all times, allowed the health unions to seize the initiative. However, sustaining this strategy over five months proved much more problematic.

The dispute deepens: the rise of the militant mercy men

There are four reasons why it becomes increasingly difficult for a trade union to sustain the kind of media strategy employed by the health unions in the Ambulance Dispute, over an extended period of time. To begin with, 'novelty' quickly evaporates. In order for a dispute to remain front or inside page material in subsequent periods, a new or dramatic angle must emerge. It is likely that such dramatic angles will be generated through news of the 'effects' and 'consequences' of a dispute and here, of course, unions are frequently placed on the defensive in being required to 'justify' to the news media the impact of these disputes upon others. It was for this reason that the leaderships of the health unions were particularly concerned to prevent escalation towards strike action.

Secondly, while it is often difficult enough to persuade journalists to include accounts of the intricate detail of a union case in the first few days of news media interest, as a dispute becomes protracted with news media interest spanning days or weeks, even sympathetic correspondents are unlikely to wish to submit copy which simply reproduces the same detail. Thus, it is likely that a number of the key elements, essential to ensuring that the interpretative frameworks which are communicated support a coherent union case, are lost. Journalists may become preoccupied with news angles which may position unions in a less favourable light.

Thirdly, while large employers and, even governments, may be caught cold in the first phases of a dispute, over a longer period of time, it is likely that they will identify ways in which their command over, normally, greater material, symbolic and political resources, can be made to tell in a public relations battle (Jones,1986; MacGregor, 1986).[18] As the Ambulance Dispute wore on, the NHS employers and the Department of Health grew more effective in countering the unions' media strategy and were able to exploit their waning influence over the interpretative frameworks offered in the news media.

Finally, given the character of many unions as organisations, it is unlikely that they will be able to sustain the high degree of centralised control required to sustain the type of media strategy employed in the Ambulance Dispute. As Charlotte Atkins noted, ambulance crews were probably more used to centralised and hierarchical organisational relations than most groups of workers and, yet, even in the Ambulance Dispute over the course of nearly six months, tensions between union leaderships and many local branches grew more acute. A number of local branches in several regions became impatient with modest sanctions; local unofficial initiatives including single day and continuous strike action began to spring up as the dispute dragged on beyond Christmas and this, of course, weakened the central plank of the union leadership's media strategy.

Overall, then, it became increasingly difficult for the unions to shape the nature of newspaper coverage and, increasingly, journalists were presented with a number of news angles which invited less favourable coverage. The danger from the unions' perspective was that such news angles would be derived from concentrating upon the effects of the dispute and its implications for readers. The unions' preferred interpretative framework was likely to become obscured if newspapers became preoccupied with the 'immediacy' and 'drama' of a possible interruption in emergency cover. The union side needed to devise their own 'fresh angles' and in the weeks leading up to Christmas this was done with some limited success but, inevitably, the number of such possibilities was finite.

On the 24th October, *The Times* featured the dispute on its front page with the headline, 'Lives at Risk as Ambulance Crisis Worsens'. Above this a strapline read, "Clarke Says 'Unions Gamble with Patients'". The item reported the escalation of the dispute in the London area where managers had begun to suspend crews 'working to rule'. All but nine out the seventy one stations in London were affected for twenty four hours. In effect, some crews were being 'locked out' but the item placed in the foreground the collapse in emergency provision in London, rather than the significance of these developments for the politics of the dispute. Comments from Kenneth Clarke were included immediately below the first paragraph of the item which detailed developments and views of Conservative back bench MPs followed at the bottom. The item included the views of the police and St John's Brigade regarding the possibilities for providing an adequate alternative service, and a call from the Secretary of the Casualty Surgeons' Association for troops to be called in. Adjacent to this item on the front page, *The Times* included a 'human interest' item, 'To hospital... on duvets and ladders', which described the unconventional way in which heart attack victims and others had arrived at hospitals in the London area, supported by a photograph of police employing the 'duvet technique' to deliver a patient. On page two, the theme of 'coping' was explored further through a report on how doctors and police volunteered to help at the ambulance control centre in order to prioritise calls. A union perspective was only to be found submerged at the bottom of page one, in the fourteenth paragraph of the lead news item, where a union spokesman suggested that management in London sought to provoke an intensification in action. In short, *The Times* coverage at this point provided an interpretative framework which precluded a full understanding of the union position. From the union perspective, what was significant about the London developments was the London Ambulance Service was disposed to prevent crews from answering emergency calls.

While there were variations in the way other broadsheet papers interpreted the events in London, the powerful appeal to conventional news values of such elements as volunteers 'lending a hand', 'do it yourself emergency arrangements, and the prospect of 'lives at risk', were too great for most papers to ignore. The *Independent*, for example, reported on the 23rd October, 'Police Stand By in Ambulance Dispute' (page two), followed the next day by a front page splash, 'London Crews Stood Down - Police Take Over Ambulance Calls'. Similarly, the *Guardian* carried the page two headline, 'Ambulance Action Escalates in London' (October 23rd) and 'Ambulance Shambles - Crews Suspended, Police Ferrying Patients, Chaos may Spread' (front page) the following day. Unlike *The Times*, the Guardian and the *Independent* allocated more space within these items to the responses of the union side and the issue of 'lock outs'. The *Guardian* quoted Roger Poole in emphasising the unions' willingness to settle through independent arbitration and his suspicion that the hardening of management attitudes was 'politically motivated' (24th October page one) and the *Independent* report included two paragraphs (four and five) which reported the willingness of crews to provide emergency cover, unpaid if necessary:

> Mr Stuart Barber, union spokesman for London crews, said staff would have to be 'physically evicted' from stations to stop them answering 999 calls. He accused Tom Crosby [LAS Chief Officer] of 'attempting to use the unions as a scapegoat for his own inability to manage the service...Our members will continue to receive 999 calls. If they are given an instruction which conflicts with their own professional judgement they will ignore that instruction. Given a couple of days we will give the public a better 999 service by freeing crews who are continually being tied up in non-urgent work' (23rd October page two).

At first glance, the interpretative frameworks offered in the *Guardian* and *Independent* coverage, in contrast to *The Times*, allow a fuller union perspective to be communicated. However, three problems can be detected. Already, the union leaderships' control of the information flows emerging from union sources was weakening. Thus, correspondents established contact with London shop stewards, including Stuart Barber, and this was to make the presentation of a common and consistent position more difficult. Secondly, as the events in London unfolded, it became clear that the unions were to find it very difficult not to surrender the news initiative to an interpretative agenda dominated by the *effects* of the dispute. This had obvious implications for the evaluative dimension of coverage, too. While the health unions' press officers remained committed to a 'proactive' approach (a dossier 'documenting' twenty needless deaths arising from ambulance service delays in the last twelve months was publicly presented to government ministers on the 23rd October), the union side found itself more frequently on the defensive, responding to an agenda determined elsewhere.

Thirdly, as the conflict intensified in October, so the issues grew more complex and this, too, presented a problem for the union side. At the heart of the escalation of the dispute in London, was a fourteen point set of guidelines on working to rule drawn up by the health unions in conjunction with the TUC. Amongst other things, these guidelines directed crews to return to their stations after completing a task, rather than 'green up' (pressing a green button inside their cabs to signal availability for another job). Computerised calling equipment was 'blacked'. This action was directed at non-urgent routine work but in retaliation managers in a number of sectors suspended crews. Without the detail required to grasp the complexity of the London situation, the union claims that their action was not directed at emergency services appeared implausible and even in the more sympathetic papers such detail was omitted from the interpretative frameworks presented.

Only the *Financial Times* chose to attach less importance to the immediacy of events over this period selecting, instead, analytic pieces exploring the underlying issues of pay comparability, skilling and definitions of emergency service. Much of the data used by John Gapper (number one on the *FT* labour desk) for the item, 'When Heroism Confounds the Pay Logic' (25th October page 9), was supplied by the union side and Roger Poole was quoted at length in offering suggestions to resolve the dispute, including a no-strike deal in return for a pay formula. At least here, the reader was given the impression of a reasonable and constructive union approach, a willingness to compromise based upon a well documented case. The previous day, the *FT* number two, Fiona Thompson, had produced an item, 'Third Among Equals', which had once again used a visit to an ambulance station as a basis for developing a 'human interest' angle on the issue of comparability with other emergency services. Of course, this reflects the distinct news values of the *FT*, with a brief to supply its readers with more specialised information on employment issues and labour market patterns. Nevertheless, the union side were successful in recognising and exploiting the opportunities such news values afforded.

Tabloid coverage offered far fewer opportunities. The *Sun* ignored events in London, only including coverage of the dispute in the following week as the prospect of troops being called in across the whole country loomed. The *Daily Express* framed an item which reported an agreement between management and unions in London to de-escalate the dispute, in the following terms:

> Troops on ambulance alert in uneasy peace. Minister accuses the union leaders of 'sheer hypocrisy' (25th October page 4).

According to the *Express*, 'union chiefs scaled down their industrial action' as...

> the government put troops on standby to take over from idle ambulance crews. The breakthrough came when union leaders in London agreed to accept conditions laid down by health service chiefs.

Both the language and interpretative framework employed here are reminiscent of the familiar ideological patterns discussed in earlier research. Crews are 'idle' (rather than actively seeking to provide emergency cover), 'union chiefs' (by implication powerful and unaccountable) are responsible for escalating 'their' action. It is the initiative of the NHS management which is responsible for moderating developments.

In the first week of November, the problems arising from the application of the work to rule in London had spread to a number of other regions. Crews working to rule were suspended and emergency cover threatened. From the union perspective, these crews were 'locked out'. On 3rd November, an 8.6% pay rise was awarded to the Fire Service, on the basis of an automatic pay formula, and this allowed Lynn Bryan to temporarily re-focus the attention of journalists upon the issue of pay comparability and the health unions' claim for an automatic pay mechanism to operate in the same way as those employed to determine the pay of police and fire staff. Only two papers, however, actually carried this story. The *Sun* briefly reported that Ken Cameron, leader of the Fire Brigades Union, had expressed support for the ambulance workers' claim, after the fire fighters award (3rd November page 2) and the *Guardian* (3rd November page 6) included a little more contextual detail. Other papers concentrated exclusively upon the prospect of troops being called in and it was at this stage that the tabloid papers began to take a sustained interest.

TROOPS ON STANDBY AS MERCY MEN TURN THE SCREW

Troops were on standby to run the ambulance service as union bosses upped the pressure in their pay battle. The unions ordered the country's 19,000 ambulance crews to ban all duties apart from answering 999 calls. That will plunge the ambulance men into a clash with health service chief, Duncan Nichol, who warned that he will stop the pay of crews who do not work normally. He is even prepared to suspend militant ambulance men which would leave the army having to take over the running of the service. Last week police officers had to ferry patients to hospital in London after crews stopped work over suspended crews. Unions chiefs decided to step up action yesterday. They want 11.5%. The government has offered 6.5%. Chief union negotiator, Roger Poole blasted Health Secretary, Kenneth Clarke, for putting the troops on standby. 'The government knows the crews will answer every emergency call. What they are trying to do is provoke the crews.' So far the crews have banned overtime and carried out a work to rule. The new ban means they will just sit and wait for 999 calls. And they will not carry out vital paperwork needed by ambulance chiefs (The *Sun* 1st November 1989 page 2).

As we have seen, few union press officers believed that the *Sun* offered many opportunities for effective press work. However, in this item, it is possible to detect evidence of an effective 'defensive action' by Lynn Bryan and the health unions' press officers. Responsibility for the threat to emergency cover is certainly attributed to the union side, as the now rather more sinister 'mercy men' ...' turn the screw'. A claim of over eleven per cent is likely to appear excessive without additional contextual detail. The ambulance workers are now portrayed as exclusively masculine and potentially 'militant'. Union 'bosses' enjoy the power to order crews to take action. Nevertheless, Roger Poole provides an appropriate response framed with a skilled use of '*Sun* language' to highlight the continuing commitment of crews to providing emergency responses. There is, at least, the suggestion that the use of troops has a political and propaganda function. On both the interpretative and evaluative dimensions, this item contains contradictory ideological elements favourable to either side.

During the first ten days in November, the news agenda in both tabloid and broadsheet papers fixed upon the introduction of troops as the dominant theme.[19] As the 'effects' of the dispute grew ever more newsworthy, so the union side enjoyed a diminishing number of opportunities to shape the news agenda and broaden the interpretative frameworks presented by daily newspapers. One example illustrates the point. In conjunction with the TUC, the health unions organised a major press conference to publicise a potential propaganda coup, the announcement of public support for the union cause on the part of the Police Federation. The chairman of the Police Federation, Alan Eastwood, agreed to attend and explain to correspondents that the Federation would 'lend its weight' to the ambulance workers' cause by exerting pressure upon government ministers. However, this press conference took place on 6th November, two days before troops appeared on the streets. While the *Independent* did give the announcement and the highly unusual support of the Police Federation considerable coverage (7th November page 2), the remaining broadsheets submerged the news in items anticipating the arrival of troops. The *Daily Mirror* devoted a whole page to a feature article under the headline, 'Mercy men are worth a good deal just like our MP's' , which provided a detailed comparison between the salaries, holidays, perks and recent pay settlement of MP's and ambulance workers (*Mirror* 7th November page 6) and while this provided favourable coverage on both interpretative and evaluative dimensions, it, too, ignored the Police Federation intervention.

In short, from the last week of October, five weeks after the start of the dispute, it is clear that the unions experienced growing difficulty in actively harnessing conventional news values to their advantage. Similarly, while some success was still achieved in offering opportunities for journalists to construct reports around the popular mythologies associated with health care workers, efforts to lay out favourable evaluative contexts through the exploitation of these themes were undermined by the concentration upon the 'drama' and 'immediacy' of the dispute 'consequences', and the spectacle of troops manning the NHS. Both the interpretative and evaluative dimensions of news coverage began to reflect elements of the more familiar news frames associated with industrial disputes.

Union successes should not be ignored. The *Independent*, for example, carried an individualised 'human interest piece inspired by the unions' press office, which was written by the paper's health correspondent one day after troops had been called in (8th November page 2). 'Bitterness Behind the Silent Telephone', explored the feelings of suspended crews who were prevented from answering emergency calls in some depth. Similarly, the *Guardian* carried an item based upon a visit to an ambulance station in Fulham (9th November page 2):

Outside the station the union banner fluttered with the plaintive message, "We are not on Strike". Inside, crews expressed their willingness to answer 999 calls and said they wouldn't go home. Evidence of this commitment came as three emergency calls were received.

By the middle of November, however, examples such as these were exceptional.

Coverage towards the end: paramedics and semi-skilled drivers

In the closing phase of the dispute, the health unions found it extremely difficult to broaden the interpretative framework presented in newspaper reports beyond a narrow focus upon the consequences of the dispute. Even the term '999 dispute' which became a habitually used piece of shorthand in news reports, obscured the unions' preferred interpretative framework; the aim of the union action, after all, had been to mount a 'non-999 dispute' and interruptions to the emergency service were the result of 'lock outs' rather than official strike action.

However, by January 1990, the difficulties for the union side increased as rank and file pressure for an escalation of action intensified. A number of branches called for one day and, in a few cases, all out strikes. This, of course, threatened to further undermine the unions strategy in prioritising media work over the exercise of industrial strength. On 1st January, *The Times* reported that the unions' leadership was resisting pressure from 'rebel ambulance crews' who were organising a campaign for 'a tougher line' (page 2). In the same report, Lynn Bryan emphasised that this was 'an unofficial move over which the unions have no control and we are urging our members to ignore it'. The two overriding tasks for union media work now became to, firstly, minimise the damage which such stories might do to the public standing of the health unions and, secondly, to target their own memberships with a communication campaign designed to retain rank and file commitment to the leaderships' strategy.

The difficulties for the union side were temporarily alleviated when Kenneth Clarke perpetrated two 'public relations blunders'. In reply to a letter from the young daughter of a Nottinghamshire ambulance man, Clarke described the majority of ambulance crews as 'professional drivers' rather than skilled paramedics. The full-text of Clarke's letter was released by the health unions and generated considerable controversy in broadsheet and popular papers between the 3rd and 8th of January. In an editorial several weeks earlier, the Independent had criticised Clark for equating the skills of ambulance staff with those of mini-cab drivers (25th October 1989). Even the *Daily Express*, in an editorial on 2nd January, conceded:

> It may be true, as he [Clarke] suggests, that the majority of ambulance staff are more or less professional drivers with a smattering of paramedical training. But to be so dismissive of their claim for parity with other emergency services is offensive both to the crews and the thousands of people who have reason to support them.

The *Express* editorial, then, worked to filter much of the interpretative framework which supported the unions' claim for parity with emergency services but certainly, on the evaluative dimension, acknowledged the legitimacy which public sympathy lent to the union argument. This reflected the experience of the unions in terms of news reports. Few of the interpretative frameworks in news items contained elements which would allow a thorough assessment of the complexities of the union case in establishing the skill level of ambulance crews, but along the evaluative dimension such reports also reflected a reluctance to accept Clarke's dismissal of the crews as 'merely drivers'. Against this background, Clarke's reply provided the unions with a means to 'personalise' the dispute once again[20] with journalists contrasting the 'bellicose' Clarke (*Independent* editorial 18th January) with the even tempered Poole, 'who shunned abrasive rejoinders'.[21]

Nonetheless, it became an increasingly difficult task to manage the flows of information emerging from within the union organisations. The *Guardian* carried an item, 'Ambulance Strikers Snub Union 999 Plea' (13th January page 2), which reported the decision of the ambulance crews in Crawley to continue indefinite strike action, despite a plea from Roger Poole to continue providing emergency cover, 'for the sake of the public'. Of course, one danger was that such developments would invite a movement in newspaper coverage more fully towards the symbolisation of militancy and unaccountable union power associated with 1979 but associated with this was the emergence of a growing number of unofficial union sources to whom correspondents could turn for additional contextual information. In this *Guardian* item, Roger Poole is restricted to a single line quotation where as a local branch representative is quoted at length.

Unofficial union action provides a powerful stimulus for labour correspondents to seek out rank and file sources not subject to the disciplines which can be exerted at a national level within union organisations. As correspondents grew more familiar with the political geography of the unions beyond the capital in the final phase of the dispute, so the unions' strategy to exert centralised control over information flows collapsed. For four months, the unions had been surprisingly successful in ensuring that they spoke with one voice, often quite literally through the presentations of one man. In the final weeks a dozen or so different voices emerged to provide points of contact for journalists.

The point should not be over-stated. As the *Guardian* item of the 13th January illustrated, the union side were still able to develop several positive themes, including the commitment of suspended crews to providing unpaid, unofficial services and even, with the help of two local authorities, a full alternative ambulance service with volunteer crews. For example, the *Financial Times* published an item, 'Unpaid workers of the emergency services' on 9th February (page 11). At Westminster, the work of Charlotte Atkins and Bob Amberley (COHSE) in briefing opposition shadow ministers and back bench MP's of all parties, also assisted in generating some additional media coverage[22] and evidence of continuing public support for the unions[23] and a record donation of over four million pounds to their cause (*Guardian* 5th February 1990 page 4), provided further symbolic material.

And yet, the overwhelming preoccupation of journalists working for both sympathetic and more instinctively hostile papers was with the accelerating amount of unofficial strike action. On the 16th January seventeen stations in North London voted for strike action, dubbed by the *Guardian* 'official' (17th January page 2) presumably because it followed a regional ballot, although the national union leadership opposed it. Two days later unofficial action spread to Manchester and in the following weeks to Dorset, Hampshire, Surrey, the West Midlands and Merseyside. Even in the more sympathetic papers, this coverage was often damaging to the union cause. Under the headline, 'London Crews Launch Unofficial Strike' (25th January 1990 page 3), it was reported that crews were beginning indefinite strike action, 'defying the appeal made by Roger Poole' and exacerbating a 'damaging split' in the unions. A NUPE branch secretary, Eric Roberts, was quoted as saying,

We talked it through and assessed the situation and the feeling was that the ordinary worker is not being properly represented.

The item continued by detailing further unofficial action about to occur in Manchester and Cheshire. The following day the *Guardian* reported court injunctions being won against striking crews in Surrey and Oxfordshire. Similarly, in other papers headlines appeared such as,

First Crews Strike as Dispute Intensifies' (FT 12th January 1990 page 7).

Pressure for all Out 999 Strike Increases (Independent 24th January 1990 page 2).

These developments, of course, made the unions vulnerable to the imposition of the traditional news frames characteristic of coverage of industrial relations in earlier decades. Thus, despite the *Daily Express'* criticisms of Kenneth Clarke and sensitivity to the existence of public sympathy for the ambulance crews, it regarded the prospect of strike action as evidence of sinister forces at work:

999 PAY BATTLE HIJACKED

Political extremists were accused last night of trying to hijack the 19 week pay dispute last night. Union leaders said an organisation called the National Ambulance Delegates committee was trying to provoke an all out stoppage. The committee had already held a series of meetings in the Midlands which resulted in calls for strike ballots. Its organisers were denounced as 'wild eyed trots' by a senior NUPE source. But more ambulance staff look set to walk out despite pleas from union leaders. Strike ballots are to take place in Hereford and Worcester and crews in North London voted to walk out. Union leaders also failed to prevent a walk out in Tottenham (*Daily Express* 18th January 1990 page 2).

The introduction of sinister 'extremists' as an explanatory mechanism with which to reconcile the involvement of consensually approved social groups ('mercy men'), with morally condemned behaviour ('going on strike'), is a familiar feature noted in several discussions of news media coverage of social conflict (Cohen and Young,1973; Morley,1976). A novel element in this case, is the apparent active involvement of a 'senior' member of the deviant group in the construction of the ideological representation. As a 'fire fighting' line during this period, the unions sought to emphasise that strike action was not supported by the national leadership or most branches and that, secondly, responsibility for such developments lay with the Government which had deliberately provoked strike action in an effort to erode public support.[24] 'Mr Kenneth Clarke is not going to provoke a strike in Britain's ambulance service. We are not going to crack' (*Guardian* 24th January page 2) claimed Roger Poole. Poole offered 'people power' (fifteen minute lunch time demonstrations involving the public) as alternatives to strike action (*Independent* 24th January page 2). Nevertheless, the interpretative frameworks in news items shifted further and further from the unions' preferred interpretative agenda and, as a consequence, the unions' success in terms of the evaluative dimension also began to wane, as the theme of strike action dominated coverage.

As unofficial action spread across the country, so the unions' problems intensified. A report in the *Guardian*, 'Mersey Crews Back All Out Strike' (20th February 1990) illustrates their difficulties. By this stage, the union leaderships found themselves drawing from the employers repertoire in pointing to the thinness of majorities in favour of unofficial action. Roger Poole claimed that he was confident, 'after speaking to the Branch Secretary that members will not depart from the national strategy for providing emergency cover' and yet this is contradicted in the very next paragraph by a local NUPE shop steward who insists that it is for the local branch to decide what will happen next. Such cracks were enthusiastically exploited by the employers side; an area health authority official commented that it was a 'great pity that crews had decided to go against their own national leadership'.

The significance of the unions' media campaign

In considering only newspaper coverage, rather than the unions' interventions through broadcasting media, the conclusions drawn have to be qualified. Roger Poole, for example, was widely regarded as an effective 'television performer' (Woolas,1990). Nevertheless, print and broadcasting news media are inextricably and symbiotically linked; the broadcasting news media observe broadly the same rhythms and imperatives. The successes and subsequent difficulties experienced by the unions in implementing their media strategy were almost certainly reflected in broadcasting as well as newspaper output.

An assessment of the overall success of the unions media work depends, of course, upon the yardstick employed. Public sympathy for the unions appeared strong throughout with opinion polls registering around a constant eighty per cent support for the crews (Hutchings,1989; Woolas,1990). As one health correspondent interviewed for this study pointed out, NHS technicians, also in dispute at the beginning of this period, probably had a better case for significant improvements in pay on the basis of the principle of comparability, but their cause received very little news media attention. The extent to which the union media strategy contributed to the continuing levels of strong public support in the Ambulance Dispute is impossible to determine precisely. Clearly, the ambulance crews and the nature of their work in an emergency service, saving lives with blue flashing lights, and their association with popular heroic medical mythologies, were an attractive raw material for news treatments, irrespective of the strategies employed by the unions. Nevertheless, the unions were able to exploit these intrinsic advantages to secure some notable successes in terms of the evaluative dimension in news coverage. This helped to minimise the danger that the old 'Winter of Discontent' news frames might be resurrected. Luck played a part here as no incidents occurred where it could be established beyond doubt that the dispute alone contributed to patient mortality.[25]

Public support and effective media work, however, proved insufficient weapons to secure for the unions their main objectives, identified at the outset of the dispute. Indeed, Roger Poole and the union leadership had to engage in yet more media work in an effort to 'sell' the eventual agreement to members. Poole's claim that 'the staggering deal' had 'driven a coach and horses through the government's pay policy' (The *Sun* 24th February page 2) was regarded sceptically by the press and many union members (the *Sun*, for example, headlined its report as '999 Men Accuse Poole of Caving In'). Although securing a slightly higher pay award over two years, the eventual agreement conceded neither the principle of parity with other emergency services, nor an automatic pay mechanism.

However, for the purposes of this study, we need only to consider the success of the unions' media strategy in its own terms. Did the unions' relatively sophisticated media work 'make a difference' to the coverage which the health unions experienced in daily newspapers, or was the pessimism of Nell Myers regarding union media work, five years earlier, justified in the case of the Ambulance Dispute, too? Firstly, the union strategy demonstrated that broadsheet newspapers, political affiliations not withstanding, do offer opportunities or 'spaces' within which unions can insert and communicate important elements of their preferred interpretative agendas.[26] Secondly, in the early phase of the dispute, the unions scored one or two extraordinary successes in the ideologically most hostile Tory tabloids, as well as the broadsheet papers. This was achieved through a carefully constructed appeal to conventional news values and the popular mythologies of medicine.

Thirdly, it is clear that without effective union work at the beginning of the dispute, the news frames employed were likely to be have drawn from the 'stock of representations' accumulated through earlier decades of industrial relations coverage, particularly the 1979 Winter of Discontent. The very early coverage of the dispute in the *Daily Mirror* (see page 333) provides one glimpse of how this might have unfolded. Later, during the final stages of the dispute, as more crews were 'locked out' and the prospect of strike action loomed larger, not only images of the 1979 Winter of discontent but also the 1984/85 Coal Strike began to appear in some newspapers. Thus, in January and February 1990, photographs of ambulance workers huddled around braziers were featured, reminiscent of the NUM pickets,[27] and some reports began to anticipate a 'drift back to work' or more weakly a 'dribble',[28] even though the vast majority of crews had never sought to stop work in the first place. For a considerable period of time, the unions' strategy succeeded in minimising the extent to which these kinds of news frames were applied.

It seems, then, that effective media practices, or a 'professional approach' as the union press officers would describe it, did 'make a difference'. A limited and simplified preferred interpretative agenda, one which could be communicated through concise and distinct propositions, helped to ensure that the union message was tailored to the requirements of both broadsheet and tabloid correspondents. Roger Poole phrased 'sound bites' to good effect and press releases and statements were crafted in a way which drew upon the conventional news values of drama, immediacy, human interest, conflict and personalisation. In the early phase of the dispute, at least, in which the unions by default were permitted to set the pace, a range of symbolic cues were successfully highlighted to counter the danger posed by pre-existing industrial relations news frames. By encouraging journalists to draw upon the experiences and perspectives of 'ordinary crews' at local stations, the dispute for a time, at least, was both 'feminised' and 'individualised' and this undermined threatening images of masculine collective strength, allowing a much more favourable evaluative dimension to be communicated. Journalists continued to show an interest in ordinary members, particularly female staff, their families, the difficulties of managing on low incomes and the pressures of the work, for much of the dispute. The union side, aware of the need to provide 'fresh angles' to maintain media interest, managed this quite successfully through, for example, the visit to ACAS, an 'open letter' to

Kenneth Clarke, an ambulance rally in Trafalgar Square, and the fifteen minute lunch time public protest.

There were, however, some significant costs involved in developing the union media strategy, and the effectivity of the tactics employed was finite. By explicitly framing their message in terms of dominant, mainstream values the union leadership had to embrace a set of political and ideological constraints. Militant unionism had to be explicitly disavowed; the traditional values of the union movement submerged below a discourse of 'reasonableness' and 'common-sense trade unionism'. In the course of the dispute searching questions were implicitly posed regarding the nature of work place relations and hierarchical control, as ambulance crews organised their own management and control systems, and in two cases, their own alternative ambulance services. However, a media strategy based upon the utilisation of mainstream news values offered few opportunities to develop such themes. By offering opportunities for journalists to 'humanise' and 'individualise' the dispute through 'human interest' angles, the unions secured favourable evaluative coverage, at least in the early stages, but the inevitable price to be paid for this strategy was an obscuring of the institutional and structural context necessary for a comprehensive appreciation of the unions' preferred interpretative framework.

The Ambulance Dispute provided an opportunity to assess the effectivity of proactive union media work because it represented a combination of favourable conditions. If a union media strategy was to 'work' anywhere, it would be in circumstances such as those of this dispute. After ten years of the Thatcherite onslaught, the pendulum of public opinion had swung back to the point where opinion polls indicated that trade unions were no longer regarded as unaccountable, baronial power-bases. At the same time, polls also indicated growing public anxiety regarding the future of the NHS and its funding and, in the public mind, low pay awards for NHS staff were all symptoms of these deeper problems. Ambulance staff, along with nurses, were held high in public esteem and benefited from the circulation of the popular heroic mythologies regarding medicine and the provision of care. And finally, in NALGO, COHSE, NUPE and the GMB, there were four of the most 'media conscious' unions in Britain. NALGO had the largest press and publicity department amongst TUC affiliates and invested very significant resources in media work. Lynn Bryan (NUPE) enjoyed an extremely high reputation amongst labour correspondents but the press officers at the other health unions were also highly respected. And finally, the imminent merger between three of the unions to form UNISON, meant that tentative organisational links had already been established which smoothed the path towards a unified and co-operative approach.

Certainly, it might be pointed out that news media organisations were no longer pre-occupied with labour and industrial news. Labour correspondents were a declining breed and unions found it harder to interest journalists in union stories. And yet, even in this respect, the circumstances were relatively favourable as news desk appetites for 'union stories' had recently been temporarily stimulated, once more, by a series of high profile public sector disputes (Bassett,1988).

However, it is clear that the unions' media strategy was at best only a partial success. While some stunning successes in terms of the evaluative dimension were secured, particularly in the early phase, it was much more difficult for the unions to maintain such success in terms of their preferred interpretative framework. Again, particularly in the early phase, a deliberately simplified interpretative agenda was communicated quite effectively, in the absence of a sustained response from employers or government. And yet, even here, as with many industrial disputes, the strength of the union case depended upon particular historic and technical detail which the unions recognised was extremely difficult to encode in news reports. To sustain news media interest in a protracted dispute is a difficult task which requires substantial material and symbolic resources. Almost inevitably, as the union side began to exhaust their supply of 'fresh angles', journalists' attention turned towards the traditional news frames of industrial reporting, the consequences of disputes and potential impacts for the general public. Power and control over material and symbolic resources cannot be ignored as factors in any assessment of media work. The greater an organisation's command over resources (particularly staff), the greater its capacity to generate 'fresh angles' and work in imaginative or 'proactive' ways. Unlike a number of private and public sector organisations which enjoy either the formal or informal capacity to curb and police their employees contact with news media, trade unions are usually organised in ways which foster public debate and open criticism. Indeed, a number of unions have invested, over the years, significant resources in training their members to work more effectively with news media organisations. One consequence of this relative openness, is that attempts to exercise centralised control over the flow information to the outside world becomes problematic. Hence, the public evidence of discord and friction between the union leaderships and branches in the final weeks of the dispute. In short, even in relatively favourable political and ideological circumstances, trade unions are still relatively disadvantaged because of their natures as organisations, because of the nature of the messages which they typically need to communicate, and because of their relatively limited command over material, political, and symbolic resources.

Notes

1.   As is well known the early work of the Glasgow team was based upon assessing television coverage against bench marks established by official economic data,- a 'reality test' (Skirrow,1980). McQuail employs broadly the same research strategy. More recently, Cumberbatch et al, recognising the promblems implicit in using official data as measures of 'reality' opted for a survey of public opinion (1986). Most frequent criticisms of this strategy are usually developed by those writers who question whether it is possible to employ any effective 'measure' of a reality and who suggest that, in any case, audiences will construct their own readings of the 'realities' presented to them (Fiske,1987:ch 15). Clearly, there are dangers in treating official government data naively; nonetheless, if one abandons the insistence that news media coverage be submitted to the discipline of evaluation in reference to external citeria of some form (alternative data sets, eye witness accounts, alternative video material, etc), then, as Philo argues, media analysis will 'drift off into the mists of relativism' (1990:205).
2.   Though McQuail found 'ordinary workers' and ordinary members of the public apearing quite frequently, his research confirms the inclination of newspapers to priviledge union elite sources over shop stewards and 'rank and file' members (1977:139).
3.   See Hyman and Price (1979) and comments above at (1).
4.   The Glasgow team do no employ the concept of a dominant ideology but they refer to 'a cultural skewedness against one particular class' (1980:401).
5.   Philo identifies over 200 discrepancies between Harrison's scripts and the video material of actual broadcasts (Philo,1976; 1977). In examining only scripts Harrison not only ignores BBC output but also the whole dimension of visual imagery.
6.   Harrison, for example, expresses dispute items as a proportion of total industrial reports, the Glasgow team in their analysis, expressed dispute items as a proportion of bulletins broadcast. Only by 'changing the goal posts' can Harrison depress the figure for dispute coverage. The point remains that on a day to day basis, viewers of television news were supplied with a great deal of dispute orientated material.
7.   Interview with Charlotte Atkins, COHSE press officer, 16.7.91.
8.   A point confirmed both in the interviews with labour correspondents conducted for this study and in the published comments of journalists (Woolas,1990; Hill,1993).
9.   Charloote Atkins, op cit.

10. Interview with Mary McGuire (NALGO press officer) 31.7.90 and Charlotte Atkins, op cit. See also, Verzuh (1990) and Hill (1993).

11. Mary McGuire, op cit.

12. Interviews with Charlotte Atkins and Mary McGuire, op cit. Verzuh (1990) and Hill (1993).

13. Interview with former senior health correspondent, 9.6.93.

14. Charlotte Atkins, op cit.

15. Ibid.

16. Interviews with Charlotte Atkins and Mary McGuire, op cit. See also comments by Lynn Bryan in Verzuh (1990).

17. The contrast with the 1984/85 Coal Strike is notable. During this dispute, journalists had to do most of their own background work in searching out material for items with a 'human angle' on miners, their families and the implications for the mining communities. The NUM offered little 'proactive' support for journalists seeking to develop these themes (Jones,1986; Winterton and Winterton,1989).

18. During the 1984/85 Coal Strike, for example, despite a number of public relations gaffs by Ian McGreggor, NCB chairman, the sheer weight of numbers in terms of staff, and the political resources available to the management team within the NCB, meant that the NUM was simply out-gunned. The public relations effort of the government and NCB together, meant that 'new' information regarding numbers returning to work, and other developments was produced and weighting for journalists to gather, on a daily basis.

19. *The Times* carried reports on the following days of November, 1st (page 2), 6th (p5), 7th (front and p5), 8th (front and p5), 9th (p10), 10th (p24), 11th (p6), 14th (p2) and 15th (p1). The distribution of coverage in the *Guardian* and *Independent* was virtually identical to this pattern. The *Financial Times* only carried two reports during this period on the 8th and 9th (p14 and p1 respectively). Coverage in the *Daily Mirror, Daily Express* and the *Sun* was more patchy than the mainstram broadsheets but all three papers featured reports on the 8th and 9th, and on at least two other days.

20. The full text of Clarke's leter was released to the news media by the unions and generated considerable coverage in both broadsheet and tabloid papers between the 3rd and 7th of January. In an effort to repair the damage and appease Conservative MPs on the back benches, Clarke briefed the Westminster Lobby over the weekend of 6th and 7th January. However, this led to further confusion as to whether the Government was prepared to authorise a higher pay offer. Clarke had to return to the news media to deny that any additional money might be available. Union spokespersons were able to condemn 'confusing and conflicting messages coming from government' and the episode generated front page headlines such as 'Offer row isolates Clarke - ambulance unions condemn confusion over pay talks' (*Guardian* 8th January). While *The Times* report noted that Clarke still had the backing of Cabinet (8th January page1), it was clear that Clarke's political capital had been eroded. His use of the Westminster Lobby was a reminder of the suspicion with which labour correspondents were regarded by the Cabinet during Mrs Thatcher's administration. Clarke's briefings to the Lobby produced reports in *The Times* (2nd January page 2 and 8th January page 1), the *Guardian* (8th

January page 1), the *Financial Times* 8th January page 1, and the *Sun* (4th January page 4).

21. 'Tempers Cool in Clarke and Poole Duel', the *Guardian* (6th January page 3).

22. 'Clarke Attacked on Ambulance Pay Policy', *Financial Times* (4th January page 1), 'Divided Tories Anxious to End the Dispute', the *Guardian* (9th January page 2), 'Minister Condemned Over Pay Shambles', *Independent* (20th January page 3), *Guardian* parliamentary report (31st January page 6).

23. An NOP Poll conducted for BBC 2 'Newsnight' indicated that 80% of those asked and two-thirds of Tory voters supported the union side in the dispute (*The Times* 9th January 1990 page 1).

24. This was 'a fear' first publicly aired at the very beginning of the dispute and regularly repeated at intervals subsequently. For example, *The Times* (30th September 1989 page 2).

25. One incident involving the death of a patient did receive some publicity. On 6th February it was reported in several papers that an 86 year old man had died from heart failure after delays in receiving treatment. An interval of several hours had passed between an emergency call being made and a police van arriving at his house to collect him. However, his admittance to hospital coincided with the shooting of Boxing promoter, Frank Warren, resulting in a further eight hour delay before the man was allocated to a ward. The coroner indicated that it was impossible to disaggregate the various contributory factors (*Guardian* 7th February page 2). *The Times* reported a 'casualty' of the dispute, a man who died of heart failure in a police car as he was rushed to hospital (9th November page 1) and the head of the St Bartholomew's Casualty Department estimated that every casualty department in London had experienced at least one 'avoidable death' since the dispute began (*The Times* 22nd February page 2). However, surprisingly and, perhaps, becasue of the difficulty in isolating precise causes, these incidents received little news coverage.

26. Some correspondents from broadsheet papers were critical of the unions' press officers for failing to keep up the supply of detailed information as the dispute developed (interview with Charlotte Atkins op cit). Union press officers are inevitably constrained by the finite number of fresh angles which can be generated and by the ryhthm of the dispute, itself.

27. See, *The Times* (10th January page 2), 'Ambulance Staff Keep Fires of Pay Protest Burning'. Scope for such photographs and imagery was, however, limited because often crews sensibly contrived to be suspended and locked into their stations, rather than locked out.

28. *Financial Times* (6th January page 1), 'Ambulance Action Intensifies'. *Financial Times* (9th February page 11), 'Unpaid Workers of the Emergency Services'. press.

9 Conclusion

The project commenced by asking whether Nell Myers, the NUM's press officer, was right to declare in despair that the use of media strategies and public relations techniques were simply not options for the union because in dealing with journalists, including labour correspondents, it faced its 'enemies front line troops'. We have now arrived at the point at which it is possible to answer this question and consider why it was worth asking. What is the theoretical significance of exploring the changing role of trade unions in Britain as news sources?

The Nell Myers position, based as it is upon an over-simplified determinist model of media power relations, fails to grasp the complexities of the forces shaping interaction between journalists and unions. From a union perspective, therefore, it is unhelpful. Labour correspondents cannot be dismissed as 'front-line troops', even if some of the news organisations they work for are institutionally hostile to the interests of the labour movement. This research has demonstrated that the relationships which develop between journalists and unions as news sources, are far more complex than the Nell Myers position acknowledges but, by the same token, the problems for unions posed by these complex relations are actually in some ways more intractable. To dismiss union use of media strategies, out of hand, as the determinist model of news media relations does, is to underestimate the extent to which, in particular circumstances, unions can secure some tactical successes through effective press and broadcasting work. The task for unions is to understand the nature of the relationships which develop between news sources and correspondents within the spheres of industrial and political journalism, and the opportunities, as well as the constraints, which are are implied by these.

If the determinist model fails to recognise the possibilities which arise from the complexities of union-news media relations, it also fails to acknowledge the extent to which the features of news media coverage of trade unions which provoke complaint, are explicable not only through analysis of the workings and political positioning of news organisations but also from the practice and ideological positioning of trade unions, themselves. As this conclusion is being written, rumours circulate of the possible, imminent expulsion of the NUM, itself, from the TUC for consorting too intimately with the non-affiliated Offshore Industries Liaison Committee, a militant organisation disliked by the TUC as much for its insistence upon articulating a radical critique of existing workplace hierarchies and social relations of production, as for its threat as a recruitement rival.[1] This throws into sharp relief the political and ideological boundaries which delimit the radicalism of the mainstream labour movement, - boundaries which are reflected in the agendas unions present both in their own journals and in those which they seek to present through the news media. And yet, it is also the case that the conservative tendencies within the labour movement are reinforced by the practices and constraints involved in fostering 'successful' relationships with journalists and mainstream news organisations. As we have seen, for labour correspondents and other journalists, the most effective union press officers,- those for whom journalists will accord high status and invest time in listening to, - are invariably those who recognise the priority of conventional news values and news frames. For many union press officers, this is all part and parcel of the 'professionalism' which they seek to bring to their position, for others it is a concious 'price' which they choose to pay in order to implement their media strategies. Either way, the framing of their media work in terms of the requirements of mainstream news values and frames, imposes limitations upon what can be articulated as an industrial or political agenda. The integration of union agendas with mainstream news frameworks is not necessarily a process of friction,- Connell has pointed to the overlap between the ideological perspectives of those 'at the top', as represented through the mainstream news media, and those 'at the bottom', including many ordinary trade unionists (1980). Nevertheless, whether conciously or unconciously unions pay a price when they employ 'accomodative' media strategies; to seek to communicate a political agenda through mainstream news media outlets is to accept, at least in part, a process of incorporation in which the requirements and possibilities determined by the practice of exisiting news organisations, shapes what is said and how it is articulated.

As researchers have noted in the context of studying environmental groups (Cracknell,1993), the poverty lobby (Whitely and Winyard,1983) and community action groups (Goldenberg,1975), the classic insider/outsider dilemma (Grant,1990) is faced not only by groups positioned ideologically and politically on the fringes or outside the arena of the party political elites but also by those similarly positioned in relation to news media elites. The problems for those groups remaining on the outside are illustrated by the experience of the NUM, during and after the Coal Strike. In making few concessions either to the news values and formats of mainstream journalism or the routine practices of news organisations, the NUM found itself in a position equivalent to an outsider group, frequently experiencing significant difficulties in communicating key elements of its preferred interpretative agenda. And yet, to move 'inside' in relation to media elites, just as with political elites, it is often necessary to compromise political positions and trim the interpretative frameworks which are presented to the public channels of political communication. The dangers in this situation are two-fold. Firstly, 'incorporation' into the news production process may encourage unions, themselves, to limit and truncate some of the essential, albeit complex arguments and observations, in their public analysis. As a NALGO press officer put it almost twenty years ago:

> ...trade union news is likely to be covered if it is 'dressed up' in a manner which conforms to the media consensus view of what is a good story. This may involve the unions using techniques of the media in the way they are often used with the unions, for example, by learning the 'tricks' involved in interviewing, arranging news or 'newsworthy' situations. This has implications for the whole question of 'news management', some of which may be disturbing. It is disturbing, for example that producers of news and potential sources of news should come to collude in the stereotyping of information in crude news models because there are few other ways of access. This, however, may be the result of the unspoken consensus underlying the news about the established order of society (Griffiths,1977:69).

Secondly, there are dangers in becoming preoccupied with media presentation to the extent that it becomes a policy straight jacket, cramping and smothering the political and organisational work of a union. As an american labour commentator warned thirty five years ago, union leaders must be wary not to allow, 'publicity about the worth of unions to be a substitute for worthy activity' (Pomper,1959:491).

However, having acknowledged these constraints and dangers, it is still possible to conclude that union media strategies, in certain circumstances and constructed in particular ways, can demonstrate a significant effectivity. The evidence produced by this research project may help unions to think more selectively about which forms of media strategy are worth pursuing and what resources should be invested. From the present investigation we can conclude that two popular models for 'news media work' are likely to be ineffective and inappropriate for trade unions and, quite possibly, for most other 'advocate' organisations. The 'high technology, high investment' model which advocates large amounts of investment in news encoding technology and services (Universal News or other electronic news link services, media output monitoring services, etc) is likely to prove ineffective and cost-inefficient if the objective is to present a union's preferred interpretative framework to the news media. This is not to suggest that investment in media technology is not justified in relation to other communication goals, for example, enhancing communication between branch memberships and union leaderships. Secondly, the 'corporate public relations' model which employs the concepts and vocabulary of 'corporate PR' to define and organise strategic communication plans for months, perhaps years, in advance, and which present the process of 'corporate imaging' as a science, rather than an art, is equally inappropriate for trade unions.

What both models fail to recognise is the importance, in the context of news media work, of the exchange relationships between news sources and journalists. It is not through investment in the technology of news encoding but through the development of an intelligent, strategic understanding of the needs of journalists and the control of 'contextual information', that trade unions are likely to make some impact upon the way in which labour and industrial stories are constructed. This, as many press officers were acknowledging as the study progressed, is now best done through the use of a telephone and a fax machine, rather than investment in expensive equipment, however capable it might be of producing and distributing so many press releases per minute. Without effective exchange relationships and an understanding of the importance of 'contextual information', the vast majority of these press releases will end in the news room bin.[2] Equally, the 'corporate PR' model implies an overly mechanical understanding of the relationships between journalists and news sources. These relationships cannot be condensed into a set of annual communication goals and differentiated targets; the efforts of the union in this study most wedded to the corporate approach left a majority of labour correspondents unimpressed.

What matters much more than the elegance of a corporate communications plan, for the purposes of news media work, is establishing, in the eyes of labour correspondents and other journalists, firstly a reputation for possessing valuable 'contextual information'; for being 'on the inside track', close to the important arenas of decision making. And secondly, demonstrating a 'professional' understanding of the needs of news organisations, of the news values and news frames which guide the practice of journalists, and of the importance of accessibility. Hard pressed correspondents are always likely to feel well disposed towards press officers who they can contact easily and who usually 'have something to say'. The most 'successful' union press officers, identified by journalists in this study, - Charlie Whelan (AEU), Mary McGuire (NALGO), Lynn Bryan (NUPE),- did not necessarily weild large budgets or wave complex corporate plans around the press office, but they all prioritised accessibility and responsiveness, a willingness to meet journalists half way.

Now, this is not to present an idealist account of relationships between the mass media and other insitutions in society. Material resources and material relationships are absolutely crucial in structuring the nature and success of union news media work. However, these material resources are of a particular kind and they work in combination with symbolic and political resources (Goldenberg, 1975:39-47; Schlesinger,1990:77). Thus, staffing levels, for example, within a press and publicity department are important in determining the extent to which unions can initiate rather than merely respond to journalists' enquiries. At NATFHE, the two press officers were often unable to depart from routine media work simply through a lack of time, given their additional responsibilites for the production of two union journals and a range of other publicity materials. Useful contacts at organisations beyond the routine education and labour beats (at, for example, BBC Radio) could not be exploited. In contrast, corporate organisations and departments of state, can often 'out-gun' non-official news sources, as eventually illustrated during the 1984-85 Coal Strike. The capacity of union press officers to mobilise and exploit political and symbolic resources, often depends upon their concrete organisational position within a trade union. Indeed, the exchange relationships which develop between union press officers and journalists are essentially material in the sense that they are underpinned by the concrete practices involved in negotiating and exercising control over flows of information from within trade unions as organisations.

The experience of the unions involved in the 1989 Ambulance Dispute provides some indication of both the possibilities and the limitations offered to unions in developing news media strategies. By employing accomodative techniques; by selecting themes which could be harnessed to mainstream news values, and in embracing the parameters determined by conventional news frames, the health unions secured some notable successes in news coverage. This was particularly the case, in the early phases of the dispute, when the employers and government allowed the unions to set the pace in terms of unfolding 'new developments', and when the unions were able to exercise effective centralised control over information flows to the news media, including 'contextual information'. However, the Ambulance Dispute also points to the limitations of such a strategy. It suggests that unions are more likely to experience success in terms of the evaluative dimension of coverage, rather than the interpretative,[3] and that unions, even in relatively favourable circumstances, with considerable public goodwill and disenchantment with government, find it necessary to trim and considerably simplify their preferred interpretative agendas. This is a dilemma which British unions do not face alone. In the USA, Douglas describes the price paid by American unions for seeking to harness elements of their prefered agendas to wider issues in the public domain:

> It makes a good deal of sense to link labor's public relations programmes to broader issues wherever possible - both in ongoing programs and those that are developed to meet special circumstances. It must be realized, however, that when this is done, basic labor-management issues often become submerged. The problems are humanized and dramatized by the media and short term solutions satisfy a concerned public. But the overall bias in labor coverage by the media is not significantly changed (Douglas,1986:285).

Precisely the same could be said of the media coverage secured by unions in the Ambulance Dispute. Public anxieties about funding of the NHS and popular mythologies associated with nursing, health care and medicine were exploited skillfully by the health unions to secure, sometimes, highly favourable coverage in terms of the evaluative dimension but this was, frequently, at the expense of more detailed information necessary to communicate the analytic detail of the union case within the interpretative framework.

The Ambulance Dispute also suggests that if campaigns become protracted unions are placed at a growing disadvantage in battles to secure ground along both the interpretative and the evaluative dimensions. This again, is a product of the unequal distribution of material, political and symbolic resources. Ingenuity and creativity in devising 'fresh angles' and different news opportunities are not wholly determined by staffing and material resources but such factors can often tell over the distance of a protracted industrial dispute. At the end of the day, there are only so many ways in which non-official source groups can mobilise symbolic resources (public goodwill, medical mythologies of selfless sacrifice, etc) to secure access to the news media without resorting to the politics of spectacle (stunts, public demonstrations, etc) which are often futile because they secure 'coverage' but not 'access' (Ericson et al, 1989:5), publicity but not opportunities to present a reasoned case. Political and corporate power, at least when it is exercised publicly and visibly, has a news value in itself which, again, over the long term, will 'automatically' attract the interest of correspondents. And finally, the Ambulance Dispute demonstrated how difficult it is for trade unions to maintain, for a sustained period, centralised control over the information flows to which journalists can get access. Unions are inherently 'leaky' organisations, a consequence of their relatively open structures and the inevitable political currents which flow within, but also a function of their relative lack of power. As effective control over information flows weakens, so it becomes ever more difficult to maintain a coherent news media strategy. In contrast, employees in departments of state, private corporations, privatised utilities, NHS Trust hospitals and even academic institutions, will testify to the ways in which powerful, relatively closed organisations can exert control over the nature of the information which their staff place in the public domain.

Beyond these points which focus upon the immediate difficulties which unions face in developing news media strategies, this study has also pointed to the changes in the political and economic environment, - changes over which unions can exert little control, yet which have the most profound consequences for their capacity to undertake successful news media work. Chapter two described such changes; the collapse of manufacturing and traditional industry, the growth in service sector, part-time, casualised and non-unionised employment; changes in the organisation of the labour process even within 'core' employment sectors; the consequent decline in union membership and further emasculation as the Thatcherite legislative onslaught simultaneously removed workplace rights and reached within to prescribe how unions should organise their internal affairs. The history of the development of labour and industrial journalism (chapters five and six) further underlines the extent to which trade unions have always been dependent upon a media environment, the 'labour beat', over which they exercised far less influence than was commonly supposed. Ultimately, the labour beat proved to be more intimately connected to the geography of the state and the national political arena and its decline, just at the moment when unions began to perceive its importance to them, reflected both the erosion of union power in the workplace, the political marginalisation of unions resulting from the dismemberment of the corporate state, and a deliberate strategy exercised by the new Conservative administration in 1979 to exclude previously influential labour correspondents from vital information flows.

Leaving aside problems of conceptual clarity (would trade unions at the height of their political influence be included as 'primary definers'?) recent commentators are quite right to point to the ahistorical and overly mechanical ways in which the concept of 'primary definer' has been applied in the past (Schlesinger, 1990; Anderson,1993; Deacon and Golding,1994). Non-official sources do have a greater capacity to challenge and modify the definitions or interpretative frameworks which are offered to the news media by 'primary definers' than has sometimes been suggested and newspaper coverage during the Ambulance Dispute provides further confirmation of this. At the same time, in tracing the relationship between the changing geography of the state and the shape of the labor beat and in noting the impact of changes in the political complexion of the dominant political elite upon the labour beat, this study has also provided one historical account of how the mechanics of primary definition are modified but maintained. By virtue of its capacity to exercise power, the state is 'newsworthy' and this allows it an important capacity to both initiate and terminate information flows. This is not to suggest that the shrinking of the labour beat is entirely a consequence of changes in the orientation of the state since 1979; the decline of labour journalism is the result of a much more complex process in which the responses of news organisations to perceived changes in political and ideological environments are overlaid upon long term economic changes in the structural positioning of trade unions. Nevertheless, the story of the rise in the fortunes of labour and industrial journalism in the immediate post-war period, as the corporatist character of the state grew and its departmental structure expanded accordingly, and the subsequent reversal in the fortunes of this branch of journalism, with the arrival of the Thatcher administration after 1979, provides one illustration of the state's strategic power in relation to primary definition. By the same token, it further underlines the relative powerlessness of trade unions as non-official sources, and their inability to exert a comparable counter-gravitional pull upon news organisations.

One of the paradoxes of the late capitalist modern age is that trade unions should awaken to the importance of political communication and respond to the structural transformations associated with late capitalism by prioritising media work, at the very historical moment when their capacity to engage in such work is significantly weakening. And here is to be found another paradox. With the proliferation in news broadcast channels and burgeoning communication technologies, it might be assumed that entry to the public sphere might be made significantly more accessible. Trade unions in representing, still, several millions of employees, have an important role to play in the advancement of citizenship through access to the public sphere. And yet, it is also clear that the costs involved in mobilising communication resources produce a widening differential in the capacity of different social groups to secure such access (Golding,1990). The main criticisms of Habermas' concept of the public sphere are familiar and have been touched upon in chapter one. A romanticisation of the early bourgeois public sphere of the eighteenth century is matched by, perhaps, an overly pessimistic account of the impact of media conglomeration, the growth of advertising and public relations industries, rising access costs and audience subordination, upon the public sphere of the twentieth century (Curran,1991). As Garnham forcefullly argues, in order to assess the contemporary health of the public sphere, we have to consider a process ommitted in the original formulation of the concept, namely that of mediation and more specifically, the 'role and social interests associated with knowledge broking' (Garnham,1986:44).

Trade unions have an important potential role to play in the allocation of citizenship and in the associated presentation of particular forms of knowledge to the public sphere. This study has pointed to some of the ways in which, despite the conflicting interests of other powerful 'knowledge brokers', trade unions can find opportunities to make effective interventions within the contemporary public sphere. However, equally importantly, it has traced the ways in which trade unions are significantly disadvantaged in relation to other more powerful social groups or 'knowledge brokers' seeking access to the public sphere. To extend Garnham's critical point, in omitting the process of mediation from the original formulation, Habermas fails to consider the possible intimate connections between aspiring entrants to the public sphere and those, such as journalists, who can facilitate entry . As we have seen, trade union press officers are likely to have to embrace relationships with journalists which both promote opportunities for the presentation of trade union perspectives but which, simultaneously, delimit the parameters of debate within the public sphere. Beyond this, the position of trade unions in relation to the political and economic environment and their command over limited material, political and symbolic resources, constrains their participation in the public sphere. In this sense, the ability of trade unionists to claim communicative rights of citizenship within the public sphere is, at best, provisional and contingent upon a process of continual struggle in which they are significantly disadvantaged.

This point, in turn, prompts more general questions regarding the theoretical application of the concept of the public sphere. As Golding (1995:29) comments, the concept as a spacial metaphor does not immediately direct attention to the symbolic and political practices and conflicts involved in the production of public discourse. This study may serve as a corrective to some of the more static accounts of the public sphere in which participants and institutional structures are taken as 'given' and in which insufficient account is taken of the dynamic processes of conflict and change, through which the institutional structures supporting the public sphere shift and the balance of advantage between participating groups alters. In examining the contested nature of labour and industrial news; the relationships of tension and symbiotic dependence which characterise union-journalist interation, and the implications of inter and intra-union rivalry for news communication, we are reminded of the inherent conflicts which are bound up in relations between 'primary definers', non-official sources and news media.

This study also underlines the point that the institutional structures which underpin the public sphere are not static but are subject to change and transformation, in part as a consequence of political struggle. Thus, the labour and industrial beat is re-cast and compressed through changes in the geography of the state and changes in the strategic thinking of news organisations. And yet, these conflicts and dynamic processes occur within the normative framework of the modern public sphere and the price of access is acceptance of these rules as legitimate. No longer are these rules or normative obligations a reflection of the culture of the patrons of the Eighteenth century coffee shop or members of the Nineteenth century debating society. They are now primarily defined in terms of the needs and practices of the news media, on the one hand, and the ideological boundaries of the political elite, on the other. As we have seen, for trade unions the cost of access to the public sphere is a willingness to acknowledge the imperatives of daily news production and the perspectives of mainstream labourism.

Fears for the future of the public sphere are sometimes regarded as over-pessimistic (Curran, 1991:46). Nevertheless, Golding identifies a number of continuing threats to the health of the public sphere including the uncertain future of public service broadcasting, the declining diversity of the British press, the rise of the 'centripetal' public relations oriented state, and the growing inequalities in access as costs of communicative work rise (1995: 30). This study further underlines the view that the grounds for a pessimistic reading of Habermas may be justified. To begin with, it provides a further illustration of the extent to which the public sphere may be compressed, at least in relation to the claims of particular social groups and organisations. Schlesinger and Tumber found that for those non-official source groups seeking to develop public discussion of criminal justice issues, only the quality newspapers and public service broadcasting offered an arena for sustained media work (1995:271-273). Though environmental pressure groups have targeted a wider range of media including tabloid papers and popular magazines (Anderson,1993:57), in the main they, too, are preoccupied primarily with the broadsheet papers and public service broadcasting and this study confirms that trade unions are similarly positioned. At a national level, again only broadsheet papers and public service broadcasting news organisations offered even moderately fertile routine terrain for trade union press officers, although the importance for trade unions of localised or regional public spheres (Downing,1992) should not be ignored. The point, then, is that trade unions in company with many other social organisations representing important constituencies are dependent upon a relatively limited number of channels of access, some of which clearly face an uncertain future. And yet, as the costs of communicative work rise, unions and other similar groups grow ever more dependent upon such compressed channels of access.

A related point concerns a dimension missing from many accounts of the modern public sphere but which is highlighted by the present study. Non-official source groups are heavily dependent upon the existence of groups of journalists with specialised expertise and interests. While Negrine (1993) may be correct to cast a sceptical eye over claims made by correspondents regarding the depth of their subject knowledge, it remains the case that the presence of specialised journalists with, at least, some expertise, professional interest, and personal contacts with relevant individuals and organisations within the field, is a pre-requisite for the maintenance of particular sectors within the public sphere. The decline of the labour beat brings with it a further shrinking of already compressed channels of access for all those groups seeking to promote public discussion of the politics of the workplace.

There are further lessons to be learnt for other advocates, non-official news sources, and aspiring entrants to the public sphere in the experience of trade unions. We now live in a 'media saturated' environment, in which investment in communication work and media activity has never been so intense. It is tempting to regard media work and the art of presentation as a great panacea, particularly as developments in social theory over the last two decades have greatly encouraged this preoccupation. In the post-modern vision, we are encouraged to abandon attempts to distinguish reality from representation; the two are regarded as collapsing into one, as we enter the age of the simulacra (Baudrillard, 1983). In such a society, it follows that processes of symbolisation and presentation should come to be prioritised as the central political activities to which social organisations should address themselves. In this light, the experience of some trade unions represents a modern cautionary tale. In their new commitment to public relations and media work, some trade unions have accepted a post-modern prescription for their ills, as have any number of other groups ranging from charities to other organised producer and consumer groups. There is a fundamental flaw in this vision. However sophisticated is the grasp of the techniques of symbolisation and presentation, they cannot act as a substitute for an understanding of the ways in which power is exercised or material and political resources mobilised (Eldridge,1993:343-349). Trade unions have grown more sophisticated in their use of communication techniques and news media strategies but the decline in membership levels has barely been stemmed; they remain politically marginalised and while the health unions may have won the 1989 publicity campaign, their final settlement could only be *represented* as a triumph. While some recent research, particularly in relation to environmental campaigns, implies that successful media work is not essentially a product of material processes, - the deployment of wealth or the exercise of political power (Anderson,1993) - the experience of trade unions strongly suggests that skillful deployment of media techniques and public relations tricks, in the symbolic domain, will only go so far. To make an effective and *sustained* impact along both the evaluative and the interpretative dimensions of news coverage, to the mobilisation of symbolic resources, it also necessary to add material and political resources, as well. A post-modern prescription will not help trade unions to secure more effective access to the public sphere; an understanding of which material resources to deploy and how they should be combined with political and symbolic resources in an integrated media strategy will help...a bit (subject to the ebb and flow of currents and changes in the political and economic environment).

Notes

1. The *Observer*, 16th July 1995.
2. This may not be true of the local context where local papers and broadcasting organisations, run on very limited budgets and small numbers of staff, have according to some commentators, a greater appetite for 'ready made' copy. See Franklin,1986 and Franklin and Murphy, 1991.
3. This is likely to be the experience of other non-official source or advocate groups including, for example, those working in the social policy and poverty arenas and those within the environmental movement. There is evidence of significant short-term successes (Seyd,1975; Seyd,1976; Anderson,1993 for example) but these are likely to be in terms of evaluative and, perhaps, transitory impacts. Evidence of longer term impacts achieved by non-official advocate groups, upon dominant interpretative frameworks which expand public understanding of the range of relevant perspectives and anlyses in each of these policy areas, is scarcer (Golding and Middleton,1982).

Appendices

Appendix One: The Selection of Trade Unions

In constructing a typology for this project, the aim was not to capture a 'representative sample' of trade unions. Given the unprecedented rate of change in the nature and composition of unions, produced through economic re-structuring and union responses to this process, which accelerated as the study progressed, this would have been a most difficult task to achieve. Indeed, decline in traditional and manufacturing industry, the growing dominance of the service sector in the British economy, the decline in the proportion of manual to white-collar work, changes in patterns of employment with a diminishing proportion of full-time, permanent jobs, and the impact of the introduction of new forms of labour organisation and technology to the production process, meant that many of the traditional distinctions between craft, industrial and general unions, upon which typologies were conventionally constructed, were simply no longer very useful.

In 1988, when a panel of unions for this study was first considered these changes were apparent but the significance of the extent to which they would re-shape the union world through merger, adjustment and re-organisation, could hardly have been guessed at. Since the panel of unions was constructed, seven out of eleven of the selected unions have been affected by the outbreak of union 'merger mania' in the late 1980s and early 1990s. NALGO and COHSE joined with NUPE to form UNISON, which now has more members than the Transport and General Workers' Union. The biggest union in the TUC is now a largely white collar and professional union, organising in the 'public sector'. The AEU and the EETPU have merged to form one powerful union with a profile not only in engineering but also, of course, in new technology and white collar sectors. The NUHKW merged with NUFLAT to form one larger union with a strong regional base in the East Midlands textile and leather industries, and finally, NUTGW disappeared only a year after the panel was finalised, being swallowed in a 'merger' with the GMB. To make matters even more complicated, two unions re-launched themselves with new names just before and during the research period (NUCPS and IPMS).

Other changes, too, have rendered the assumptions underpinning the panel out-dated. The NUM, for example, still claimed a membership of over 100,000 in 1987, allowing it to be selected as a 'large' union. Now, of course, the total number of miners employed in the industry may be below 7,000 and the NUM has become one of the smaller unions within the TUC. Even the distinction between public and private sector has become blurred as a result of the government's determination to proceed with policies of privatisation and marketisation. Accordingly, IPMS and NUCPS can no longer be described as organising exclusively in the public sector, as civil servants and government

370

scientists now find themselves employed by agencies operating in competitive markets.

Difficulties in drawing distinctions between types of union for the purposes of typology construction are not new and have been the subject of considerable discussion, even before the present period of rapid change. For some commentators, the analytic value of distinctions between white and blue collar (Cooper and Bartlett,1976:80; Jenkins and Sherman,1979:13), or between general, craft and industrial unions (Flanders,1968:29), were declining long before the impact of Thatcherism or the most recent period of accelerated change in the organisation of the labour process.

Given that such distinctions were already recognised as problematic at the beginning of the research project, and that in any case, the focus was intended to be upon the nature of union media strategies rather than the general organisational characteristics of trade unions, it was decided to construct a panel which departed from conventional distinctions but which anticipated some of the likely determinants of variation in media strategy. It was recognised that there was not a simple relationship between size of membership and news media interest (Seaton,1982:281). Nonetheless, the size of a union was likely to influence its capacity to mobilise material and symbolic resources for media work and, at least, a negative relationship could be assumed between union size and media interest. That is to say, it could be safely assumed that the Society of Shuttlemakers (membership 92), the Sawmakers Protection Society (membership 167) or the Screw, Nut, Bolt and Rivet Trade Union (membership 1,100) were unlikely to attract sustained national news media interest (examples taken from Eaton and Gill,1983). The dimension of size was, thus, incorporated into the original panel with unions enjoying a membership above 100,000 being regarded as 'large'.

Although, even in 1988 difficulties in drawing distinctions between public and private sector unions were already apparent (the TGWU, for example, historically organised in both sectors), there was some evidence to support the view that public sector unions had a track record of greater commitment to media work (Philo and Hewitt, 1976; Jenkins and Sherman, 1979; Jones, 1986). For the purposes of illuminating a variety a approaches to media work amongst unions, the distinction between public and private sector appeared worth retaining.

To size and position in public or private sectors were added two more variables. Very little information was available regarding trade union investment in media work, other than the early and limited work undertaken by the Glasgow team in preparation for the 'Bad News' studies (GUMG,1976:ch 6; Philo and Hewitt,1976) and the more recent survey undertaken by the TUC, which described only general patterns rather than investments committed by specific unions (TUC Standing Conference, 1985). In order to gather more information, a simple telephone survey was undertaken of thirty seven trade unions, including all those with a membership of over 45,000 (based on affiliation figures at 31st

December 1986). The results of this survey now have little but a historic interest for two reasons.

Firstly, an interest in media presentation and a commitment of significant resources in media and symbolic work amongst large and medium sized unions has now become the norm rather the exception. In the telephone survey, only seven trade unions employed a full-time press officer to concentrate exclusively upon press and media work and only five had organised separate press and publicity departments. Now it is unusual for a large or medium trade union not to have a full-time press officer and most unions have established a press office , if not a 'communications directorate' . Secondly, although the costs of gaining access to the communication channels of the public sphere are usually regarded as increasing, in one particular respect the arrival of a new example of communication technology has produced an equalising effect amongst unions. A number of questions included in the questionnaire referred to the use of 'news encoding technology', such as Universal News Services. However, the arrival of the cheap fax machine as a ubiquitous feature of every news room and press office in the course of the research, meant that most unions could now afford effective encoding technology for the dissemination of press releases and other materials, thus eliminating any differential advantage which might previously have been enjoyed by investing in such relatively expensive services as Universal News. Nevertheless, at the outset, the appointment of a full time press officer was a factor which represented a significant line of differentiation between unions and, accordingly, this was included as another dimension within the panel, the relevant information being drawn from the telephone survey.

It was also recognised that exogenous factors would shape variations in media strategies and media performance amongst unions. One possibility was to incorporate variations in dispute and strike activity as a predictor of news media interest. However, two difficulties were immediately apparent. Official statistics describe dispute and strike activity using a range of measures across industries and sectors of employment but not by individual trade union. In any case, one of the established points to emerge from the older literature was the low correlation between strike activity and news media profile (GUMG,1976). Stories, it was recognised, are selected by journalists and editors, often because they possess consonance (Galtung and Ruge,1973:64) and appear to represent further instances of previously established themes. Unions with historically established high media profiles were likely, therefore, to experience media interest which was not necessarily a function of their own media enterprise. To anticipate this point, newspaper interest in the period between January 1986 and October 1987, as measured by entries in The Times Index, was incorporated as a final dimension for the panel. Again, all trade unions with memberships over 45,000 (at 31st December 1986) were included. One difficulty was in finding a 'small' union with a membership below 100,000 but a high media profile. Eventually, the IPMS were selected as a union with 88,789 members and a relatively high number of Times Index entries (17), although far fewer than the NUM (104,000 members and 199 entries). COHSE (three entries) and NUHKW (nil entries) were selected as 'low profile' unions. The panel at commencement of the first phase in the research project was thus, constructed on the basis of a random selection of unions satisfying the criteria of specified for each dimension of the panel:

Panel of Trade Unions Selected for the Initial Research Phase

	Public Sector	Private Sector	Full Time Press Officer	No Full Time Press Officer	High Times Index Entries	Low Times Index Entries
Large	NALGO	TGWU	EETPU	AEU	NUM	COHSE
Small	NUCPS	NUTGW	----------	NATFHE	IPMS	NUHKW

As described above, this panel was rapidly overtaken by events, as a majority of unions appointed full-time press officers, membership decline eroded the position of 'large' unions, distinctions between public and private sectors blurred and several unions disappeared in a wave of mergers. The panel now simply serves to provide a rationale for the initial selection of unions and to guard against the charge of arbitrary or contrived selection. The appendix has dealt at length with the process of selection to provide the reader with an indication of just how rapidly change overtook the union movement in the late 1980s and early 1990s and the implications of such change for the design and direction of this study. The great advantage was that the project was given the opportunity to study the behaviour and responses of trade unions as news sources in the middle of an unprecedented period in their history. The disadvantage, of course, was that such a rate of change made a research design which depended upon perfect consistency in panel composition longitudinally, untenable.

NUTGW were absorbed into the GMB after a content analysis of trade union journals had been completed in 1990 (Manning, 1996). As preliminary enquiries in preparation for interviewing trade union press officers had already indicated that the GMB had invested significantly in media work, it was decided to include the union in the next stage of the project which concerned the work of union press officers.

1.   NALGO merged with COHSE and NUPE to form UNISON, now the largest union affiliated to the TUC in 1993.

2. The EETPU merged with the AEU to form the Amalgamated Engineering and Electrical Union in 1992.
3. See 2 above.
4. See 1 above.
5. Formerly, the Society of Civil and Public Servants.
6. NUTGW were absorbed into the GMB after the content analysis of trade union journals had been completed in 1990.
7. Formerly the Institute of Public and Civil Servants. Re-launched as IPMS in 1989.
8. NUHK merged with the National Union of Footwear, Leather and Allied Trades to form the National Union of Knitwear, Footwear and Apparel Trades in 1992.

Appendix Two: Summary of interview and documentary data collected

Interviews

Wherever possible the source of quotes has been attributed. However, several trade union press officers indicated that sections of their interviews were 'off the record' and material drawn from these sections has not been attributed to particular individuals. In the case of correspondents and journalists, a great deal more of the material was gathered off the record and the attribution of non-controversial comments to sources would allow those with a knowledge of the social networks and working environments of the national daily papers, to quickly identify the sources of more sensitive material. For this reason, very little of the material gathered in interviews with journalists has been attributed. However, a list of all interviews, interviewees and dates is provided below.

1. Contemporary Trade Union Press Officers

Mary McGuire	(NALGO)	31.7.90
Jim Fookes	(NALGO)	10.6.93
Eddie Barratt	(T and G)	6.3.91
Andrew Murray	(T and G)	6.3.91 (follow up interview 13.7.93)
Charlotte Atkins	(COHSE)	16.3.91
Charlie Whelan	(AEU)	6.6.91 (follow up interview 12.7.93)
Laurie Harris	(NUR)	25.8.89
Charles Harvey	(IPMS)	21.6.91
Ken Jones	(NUCPS)	7.6.91 (follow up interview 9.7.93)
Nell Myers	(NUM)	20.9.91
Adrian Long	(G and M)	21.6.91

Mr. A. Lomans   (NUHKW) 15.7.91
John Lloyd   (EETPU) 24.5.91
Midge Purcell   (NATFHE) 21.6.91 (follow up interview 16.7.93)
Mike Smith   (TUC)   26.6.93

Total: 15

2. *Contemporary Journalists*

(i) Industrial Correspondents

Terry Pattinson (Labour Editor *Daily Mirror*) 24.7.92
Patrick Hennesey (Industrial/Education Correspondent *Daily Express*) 24.7.92
Tony McGuire (Industrial Editor *Evening Standard*) 24.7.92
Phillip Bassett (Employment Affairs Editor *The Times*) 10.6.93
Keith Harper (Labour Editor *The Guardian*) 22.9.92
Charlie Leadbeater (Industrial Correspondent *Financial Times*) 15.7.92
Geoffrey Goodman (ex Labour Editor *Daily Mirror and Sun*) 15.6.92
Kevin McGuire (*Daily Telegraph* Industrial Correspondent) 12.6.92
David Norris (Industrial Correspondent *Daily Mail*) 7.7.92

Total: 9

(ii) Education Correspondents

John O'Leary (Education Correspondent *The Times*) 10.6.93
James Meikle (Education correspondent *The Guardian*) 28.5.93

Total: 2

(iii) Health Correspondents

Clare Dover (Formerly *Daily Express* Health correspondent) 6.9.93
Jill Palmer (Health correspondent *Daily Mirror*) 19.7.93
Jack O'Sullivan (ex Health Correspondent *Independent*) 14.7.93
Judy Jones (Health Correspondent *Independent*) 24.5.93

Total: 4

3. *Interviews with Former and Current Journalists for Historical Dimension*

Paul Routledge (*Observer* political correspondent and formerly *F.T.* (labour correspondent). 4.8.93.

Terry Pattinson (Labour Editor *Daily Mirror* until April 93, now freelance)
15.7.93
Henry Clother   (formerly on the labour desk at the *Sun* and then press officer for
NUT during 1970s). 28.7.93
Jim Fookes   (formerly labour correspondent at Press Association and now
press officer in Press and Publicity Dept. at NALGO) 10.6.93.
Interviews with Philip Bassett and Geoffrey Goodman also relevant for historical
dimension.

Total: 4

Historical and Archive Material

(i) Archive Material

The papers of the Labour and Industrial Correspondents' Group. These are held
by the Secretary of the Group, who at the time of writing was Robert Taylor, at
The Observer.
TUC papers kept at the TUC Library, Congress House, Great Russell Street,
London WCI.

(ii) Memoirs and autobiographies of labour correspondents (full references
listed in the main bibliography)
Evans,Trevor.   *The Great Bohunkus. Tributes to Ian Mackay,*1953.
Mason, Keith.   *Front Seat,* 1981.

(iii) Books on specific themes written by labour correspondents (full references
listed in the main bibliography).
Bassett, P.   *Strike Free,* 1986.
Crick, M.   *Scargill and the Miners,* 1985.
Goodman, G.   *The Miner's Strike,* 1985.
Jones, N.   *Strikes and the Media,* 1986.
Lloyd, J. and Adeney, M.   *Loss Without Limit,* 1986.
MacIntyre, D et al. *Strike: Thatcher, Scargill, and the Miners,* 1985.
Taylor, R.   *Fifth Estate:Britain's Unions in the Modern World,* 1978.
Wigham, E.   *Trade Unions,* 1969.
Wigham, E.   *What's Wrong with Trade Unions?,* 1961.

(iv) Articles written by labour correspondents.
Bassett, P.   'Labour Reporting: alive and kicking into the 1990s, in *U.K.Press
Gazette,* 13.6.93
Harper, K.   'The Spiking of the Strike Reporters', in *British Journalism Review,*
Vol 2 No 4, Summer 1991.

Jones, N. 'Unions Quietly Languish', in *The Listener*, 1.8.1987.
Jones, N. 'Labour Pains', in *U.K. Press Gazette*, 11.1.1988.
Pattinson, T. 'Monsters Wanted', in *New Statesman and Society*, 21.5.1993.
Woolas, P. 'Television First Aid', in *New Socialist*, April 1990.

(v) Autobiographies and books written by union leaders (full references listed in the main bibliography).

Chapple, F. *Sparks Fly*, 1984.
Gormley, J. *Battered Cherub*, 1982.
Hammond, E. *Maverick: The life of a Union Rebel*, 1992.
Jones, J. *Union Man*, 1986.
Paynter, W. *My Generation*, 1972.
Paynter, W. *British Trade Unions and the Prospects for Change*, 1970.

Appendix Three: Union Resources and Media Work

Union	Member-ship.	Income (£)	Political Fund (£)
NALGO	764,062	69,755,430	3,296, 329
TGWU	1,036,586	59,834,870	2,975,531
GMB	799,101	39,136,000	3,029,000
COHSE	195,519	11,117,874	505,406
NUCPS	111,831	10,548,029	584,507
NUR	105,146	9,753,000	59,000 (i)
AEU	595,537	8,154,000	342,000
IPMS	90,008	7,935,342	62,714
NATFHE	75,582	5,533,992	285,992
EETPU	354,618	4,453,080	528,681
NUKFA*	51,636	3,150,109	81,647
NUM	93,684	1,331,943	210,486
NUTGW**			

(i) Includes £43,000 spent lobbying Parliament.

* NUHKW merged to form the National Union of Knitwear, Footwear and Allied Trades in 1992.

** NUTGW 'merged' with the GMB in 1990.

Union Spending on Media and Publicity Work.

Expenditure on following items (£)

Union	Total Adminis-tration	Publica-tions	Press and Media	Other Activities	Education
NALGO	31,104,790	2,051,753	(103,200)	22,998 (i)	1,110,687
TGWU	49,080,725				562,311
GMB	31,645,000	726,000	(85,000)	127,000(ii)	1,102,000
COHSE	8,641,917				72,740
NUCPS	10,204,867		19,384	1,216,356	141,034
NUR	8,020,000	527,000			259,000
AEU	6,898,000	(835,000)*			
IPMS	5,448,015 (iii)	(459,000)			
NATFHE	4,350,296	(400,800)			
EETPU	4,231,198				
NUKFA	2,980,816				
NUM				65,758(iv)	5,852

Source: annual returns to the Certification Office for Trade Unions and Employers Associations, year ending 1992.

Figures in brackets derived from information provided by press officers and union officials.

(i) Includes £18,183 spent on arts sponsorship and £4,815 spent on parliamentary work.
(ii) Spent on campaigning.
(iii) £15,341 spent on GCHQ Campaign, £8,386 spent on TUC Jobs and Recovery Campaign.
(iv) The Campaign Against Pit Closures.

*1992/93

The annual returns to the Certification Officer frequently fail to provide detail under specific budget headings such as 'press and media' or 'campaigning. The figure for total administration is derived from union returns to the Certification Officer. Subsumed within that heading unions sometimes provided additional information and this has been included in the relevant column. The absence of figures does not indicate that a union did not spend in this area but simply that such expenditure was not disaggregated from the figure for total administration. Where additional information was provided by union staff this has been included in brackets.

References

Adeney, M. and Lloyd, J. (1986): *The Miners' Strike: loss without limit.* London: Routledge Keegan-Paul.

Adeney, M. (1983): 'Why Can't Managers Be More Like Trade Union Leaders?'. *The Listener*, 16th June.

Aglietta, M. (1982): 'World Capitalism in the Eighties'. *New Left Review*, **136**, 1-32.

Allen,V.L. (1971): *The Sociology of Industrial Relations.* London: Longmans.

Altheide, D.L. and Johnson, J.M. (1980): *Bureaucratic Propaganda.* Massachusetts: Allyn and Bacon.

Anderson, A. (1993): 'Source-Media Relations: the production of the environmental agenda', in *The Mass Media and Environmental Issues* (ed. A. Hansen). Leicester: Leicester University Press.

Anderson, D. and Sharrock, W. (1979): 'Biassing the News: technical issues in media studies'. *Sociology 3*, vol 13, September, 369-385.

Anderson, P. (1973): 'The Limits and Possibilities of Trade Union Action' , in *The Incompatibles* (ed. R. Blackburn). Harmondsworth: Penguin.

Aslakson, A. (1940): 'Labor is News: a reporter's view'. *Journalism Quarterly*, vol 17, June, 151-158.

Bain, G.S. and Elsheikh, F.(1976): *Union Growth and the Business Cycle.* Oxford: Blackwell.

Banks, J.A. (1974): *Trade Unionism.* London: Collier Macmillan.

Barnes, D. and Reid, E. (1982): 'A New Relationship: Trade Unions in the Second World War', in *Trade Unions in British Politics* (eds. B. Pimlott and C. Cook). London: Longman.

Basnett, D. and Goodman, G. (1977): *The Press: Minority Report of the Royal Commission on the Press.* London: The Labour Party.

Bassett, P. (1993): 'Heseltine's Year of Living Dangerously'. *The Times*, 28th December.

Bassett, P. (1988): 'Labour Reporting: alive and kicking into the 1990s'. *UK Press Gazette*, 13th June, **23**.

Bassett, P. (1986): *Strike Free.* London: Macmillan.

Bassett, P. and Cave, A. (1993): 'Time to Take the Unions to Market'. *New Statesman and Society*, 3rd September, 16-17.

Batstone, E et al. (1978): *The Social Organisation of Strikes.* Oxford: Blackwell.

Baudrillard, J. (1983): *Simulations.* New York: Semiotext(e).

Becker. L.B. et al. (1975): 'The Development of Political Cognitions', in *Political Communications: Issues and Strategies for Research* (ed. S.H. Chaffee). London: Sage.

Beckett, F. (1977): 'The Press and Prejudice', in *Trade Unions and the Media* (eds. P. Beharrell and G. Philo). London: Macmillan.

Beharrell, P. and Philo, G. (eds.) (1977): *Trade Unions and the Media*.
London: Macmillan.

Benn, T. (1990): *Conflicts of Interest: Diaries 1977-1980*. London: Arrow.

Benn, T. (1989): *Against the Tide: Diaries 1973-1976*. London: Hutchinson.

Benn, T. (1988): *Office Without Power: Diaries 1968-1972*. London:
Hutchinson.

Bird, D. Stevens, M and Yates, A. (1991): 'Membership of Trade Unions'.
Employment Gazette. London: HMSO, June, 337-343.

Blackwell, R and Terry, M. (1987): 'Analysing the Political Fund Ballots',
Political Studies, **xxxv**, 623-642.

Blumler, J.G. (1980): 'Mass Communication Research in Europe: Some
Origins and Prospects'. *Media Culture Society*, **2**, 367-376.

Boyd-Barrett, O. (1980): 'The Politics of Socialization: Recruitment and
Training for Journalists', in *The Sociology of Journalism. Sociological
Review Monograph*, 29. (ed. H. Christian). Staffordshire: University of
Keele. Braverman, H. (1974): *Labor and Monopoly Capital*. New York:
Monthly   Review Press.

Brawley, E.A. (1983): *Mass Media and Human Services*. London: Sage.

Breed, W. (1960): 'Social Control in the Newsroom', in *Mass Communication*
(ed W. Schramm). London: University of Illinois Press.

Briskin, L. and McDermott, T. (eds) (1993): *Women Challenging Unions:
Feminism, Democracy and Militancy*. Toronto: University of Toronto Press.

Brown, G. (1971): *In My Way*. London: Victor Gollanz.

Brown, J. et al. (1987): 'Tilting at Windmills: an attempted murder by
misrepresentation'. *Media Culture Society*, **9**, (3).

Brown, W. (1986): 'The Changing Role of Trade Unions'. *British Journal of
Industrial Relations*, **24**, 161-168.

Brummer, A. (1993): 'Hanson the Target of Miners' War of Attrition', *The
Guardian*, 2nd October.

Bullock, A. (1967): *The Life and Times of Ernest Bevin. Volume Two*.
London: William Heinemann.

Burgelin, O.(1972): 'Structuralist Analysis and Mass Communication', in *The
Sociology of Mass Communication* (ed. D. McQuail). Harmondsworth:
Penquin.

Callaghan, J. (1987): *Time and Change*. London: Collins.

Cameron, D. (1984): 'Social Democracy, Corporatism, Labour Quiescence and
the Representation of Economic Interest in Advanced Capitalist Society',
in *Order and Conflict in Contemporary Capitalism* (ed. Goldthorpe, J.).
Oxford: Clarendon Press.

Castle, B. (1984): *The Castle Diaries 1974-1976*. London: Weidenfield and
Nicholson.

Castle, B. (1980): *The Castle Diaries 1964-1970*. London: Weidenfield and
Nicholson.

Cayford, J. (1985) *Speak Up: Trade Union Responses to New Management Communications.* London: Comedia.
Chapple, F. (1984): *Sparks Fly. A Trade Union Life.* London: Michael Joseph.
Chee, H. and Brown, R. (1990): *Marketing Trade Unions.* Bradford: Horton Publishing.
Chibnall, S. (1977): *Law and Order News.* London: Tavistock.
Christian, H. (ed.) (1980): *The Sociology of Journalism. Sociological Review Monograph,* 29. Staffordshire: University of Keele.
Clarke, S. (1988): *Monetarism and the Crisis of the State.* London: Edward Elgar.
Clement, B. and MacIntrye, D.(1987): 'Why the Unions Must Adapt to Survive', in *The Independent,* 30th January.
Coates, D. (1989): *The Crisis of Labour.* Deddington: Philip Allan.
Coates, K. and Topham, T. (1980): *Trade Unions in Britain.* Nottingham: Spokesman.
Coates, R.D. (1972): *Teacher's Unions and Interest Group Politics.* Cambridge: Cambridge University Press.
Cockerell, M. et al. (1985): *Sources Close to the Prime Minister.* London: Macmillan.
Cohen, S. and Young, J. (eds.) (1981): *The Manufacture of News.* London: Constable.
Collins,R. (1986): 'Bad News and Bad Faith: the story of a political controversy'. *Journal of Communication,* Autumn, 131-138.
Collinson, M (1994): Review, *Work Employment Society,* **8** (2), 302-303.
Connell, I. (1980): Review of 'More Bad News'. *Marxism Today,* August.
Connell, I. (1991): 'Tales of Tellyland: the popular press and television in the UK', in *Communication and Citizenship: Journalism and the Public Sphere in the New Media Age* (eds. P. Dahlgren and C. Sparks). London: Routledge.
Cooper, B.M. and Bartlett, A.F. (1976): *Industrial Relations; a study in conflict.* London: Heinemann.
Cottle, S. (1993): *TV News, Urban Conflict and the Inner City.* Leicester: Leicester University Press.
Cracknell, J. (1993): 'Issue Arenas, Pressure Groups and Environmental Agendas', in *The Mass Media and Environmental Issues* (ed. A. Hansen). Leicester: Leicester University Press.
Crenson, M.A. (1971): *The Un-politics of Air Pollution.* London: John Hopkins.
Crick, M. (1985): *Scargill and the Miners.* Harmondsworth: Penquin.
Crompton, R. (1993): *Class and Stratification: an introduction to current debates.* Cambridge: Polity Press.
Crossman, R. (1979): *The Crossman Diaries.* London: Magnum Books.
Crouch, C. (1976): 'Conservative Industrial Relations Policy: Towards Labour

Exclusion?', in *Economic Crisis, Trade Unions and the State* (eds. O. Jacobi et al.). Beckenham: Croom Helm.

Cumberbatch, G. (1986): *Television and the Miners Strike*. Mimeo. London: Broadcasting Research Unit.

Cunnison, S. and Stageman, J. (1993): *Feminising the Unions*. Aldershot: Avebury.

Curran, J. (1991): 'Rethinking the Media as a Public Sphere', in *Communication and Citizenship: Journalism and the Public Sphere in the New Media Age* (eds. Dahlgren, P. and Sparks, C.) London: Routledge.

Curran, J. (1987): 'The Boomerang Efect', in *Impacts and Influences* (eds. J. Curran et al.). London: Methuen.

Curran, J. and Seaton, J. (1985): *Power Without Responsibility*. London: Methuen.

Dahlgren, P. (1991): Introduction to *Communication and Citizenship: Journalism and the Public Sphere in the New Media Age* (eds. P. Dahlgren. and C. Sparks) London: Routledge.

Davis, H. and Walton, P. (1983): *Language Image Media*. Oxford: Basil Blackwell.

Deacon, D. and Golding, P. (1994): *Taxation and Representation: The Media, Political Communication and the Poll Tax*. London: John Libbey.

Dearlove, J. and Saunders, P. (1984): *Introduction to British Politics: analysing a capitalist democracy*. Cambridge: Polity Press.

Douglas, S. (1986): *Labor's New Voice: Unions and the Mass Media*. New Jersey: Ablex Publishing.

Downing, J. (1992): 'The alternative Public Realm: the organisation of the 1980s anti-nuclear press in West Germany and Britain' in *Culture and Power* (ed. P. Scannell et al.). London: Sage.

Downing, J. (1980): *The Media Machine*. London: Pluto.

Dunlop, J.T. (1958): *Industrial Relations Systems*. New York: Holt.

Dunwoody, S. and Griffin, R.J.(1993): 'Journalists' Strategies for Representing Long Term Environmental Issues: a Case Study of Three Superfund Sites', in *The Mass Media and Environmental Issues* (ed. A. Hansen). Leicester: Leicester University Press.

Easthope, A. (1990): 'Trade Unions in British Television News'. *The Yearbook of English Studies*. **20**. (Literature in the Modern Media).

Eaton, J. and Gill, C. (1983): *The Trade Union Directory*. London: Pluto.

Eckstein, H. (1960): *Pressure Group Politics*. London: George Allen.

Economist, The. (1989): 'Corporate Eyes, Ears and Mouths'. *The Economist*. 18th March, 105-106.

Edwards, P.(1979): 'The Awful Truth About Strikes'. *The Industrial Relations Journal*. **10** (1).

Edwards, P. et al. (1992): 'Great Britain: Still Muddling Through', in *Industrial Relations in the New Europe* (Ferner, A. and Hyman, R. eds.). Oxford:

Blackwell.

Edwards, P.K. and Bain, G.S. (1988): 'Why Are Trade Unions Becoming More Popular? Unions and Public Opinion in Britain.' *British Journal of Industrial Relations,* **26** (3), November.

Edwards, R. et al. (1986): *Unions in Crisis and Beyond.* London: Auburn House.

Eldridge, J. (1993): 'Whose Illusion? Whose Reality? Some Problems of Theory and Method in Mass Media Research', in *Getting The Message. News Truth and Power.* London: Routledge.

Eldridge, J. (1968): *Industrial Disputes: Essays in the Sociology of Industrial Relations.* London: Routledge Kegan-Paul.

Elliott, P. (1981): 'Review of More Bad News'. *Sociological Review,* **29** (1).

Elliott, P. (1980): 'Press Performance as Political Ritual', in *The Sociology of Journalism. Sociological Review Monograph,* 29 (ed. H. Christian). Staffordshire: University of Keele.

Elliott, P. (1977): 'Media Organisations and Occupations: an Overview', in *Mass Communication and Society* (Curan, J. et al. eds). London: Edward Arnold.

Elliott, P. and Golding, P. (1978): *Making the News.* London: Longman.

Ericson, R.V. (1989): 'Patrolling the Facts: Secrecy and Publicity in Police Work.' *British Journal of Sociology,* **40** (2), June.

Ericson, R.V. et al. (1989): *Negotiating Control: A Study of News Sources.* Milton Keynes: Open University Press.

Ericson, R.V. et al. (1987): *Visualising Deviance.* Milton Keynes: Open University Press.

Evans, T. (1953): *The Great Bohunkus. Tributes to Ian McKay.* London: W.H. Allen.

Ferner, A. and Hyman, R.(eds.) (1992): *Industrial Relations in the New Europe.* Oxford: Blackwell.

Field, F. (1988): 'Giving the Unions a Friendly Face'. *New Statesman,* 1st July, 34-35.

Finer, S.E. (1966): *Anonymous Empire.* 2nd Edition. London: Pall Mall Press.

Fisher, N. (1973): *Ian Macleod.* London: Andre Deutsch.

Fishman, M. (1980): *Manufacturing the News.* Austin: University of Texas.

Fiske, J. (1992): 'Popularity and the Politics of Information', in *Journalism and Popular Culture* (Dahlgren, P. and Sparks, C. eds.). London: Sage.

Flanders, A. (1968): *Trade Unions.* 7th Edition. London: Hutchinson.

Foot, P. (1984): 'The Right to Reply'. *Socialist Worker,* 20th October.

Foster, J. and Woolfson, C. (1989): 'Corporate Reconstruction and Business Unionism: the lessons of Caterpillar and Ford.' *New Left Review,* **174** March.

Franklin, B, and Murphy, D. (1991): *What News: the Market, Politics and the*

Local Press. London: Routledge.

Franklin, B. and Parton, N.(1991): 'Media Reporting of Social Work: a framework for analysis', in *Social Work, the Media and Public Relations* (B. Franklin and N. Parton eds.). London: Routledge.

Franklin, B. (1986): 'Public Relations, the Local Press and Coverage of Local Government'. *Local Government Studies,* July/August.

Galtung, J. and Ruge, M. (1973): 'Structuring and Selecting the News', in *The Manufacture of News* (eds. S. Cohen and J. Young). London: Constable.

Gamble, A. (1988): *The Free Economy and the Strong State.* London: MacMillan.

Gamble, A. (1974): *The Conservative Nation.* London: Routledge Kegan-Paul.

Gamson, W. and Modigliani, A. (1989): 'Media Discourse and Public Opinion on Nuclear Power.' *American Journal of Sociology,* **95** (1), 1-37.

Gandy, O. (1982): *Beyond Agenda Setting: Information Subsidies and Public Policy.* Norwood, New Jersey: Ablex Publishing.

Garnham, N. (1986): 'The Media and the Public Sphere', in *Communicating Politics* (eds. P. Golding. et al.). Leicester: Leicester University Press.

Gerbner, G. (1969): 'Institutional Pressures Upon the Mass Media', in *The Sociology of Mass Communicators Sociological Review Monograph 13.*(ed. P. Halmos). Staffordshire: University of Keele.

Gitlin, T. (1980): *The Whole World is Watching.* London: University of California.

Glasgow University Media Group (1980): *More Bad News.* London: Routledge Kegan-Paul.

Glasgow University Media Group (1976): *Bad News.* London: Routledge Kegan-Paul.

Goldenberg, E.N. (1975): *Making the Papers.* Lexington: D.C. Heath.

Golding, P. (1992): 'Communicating Capitalism: resisting state ideology, - the case of Thatcherism.' *Media Culture Society,* **14**, 503-521.

Golding, P. (1990): 'Political Communication and Citizenship: the Media and Democracy in an Inegalitarian Social Order', in *Public Communication: the New Imperatives* (Ferguson, M. ed.). London: Sage.

Golding, P. (1974): *The Mass Media.* Harlow: Longman.

Goldsmiths' College Media Research Group (1987): *Media Coverage of London's Councils.* Interim Report (mimeo). London: Goldsmith College.

Goldthorpe, J. (1984): 'The End of Convergence: Corporatist and Dualist Tendencies in Modern Western Societies', in *Order and Conflict in Contemporary Capitalism* (Goldthorpe, J. ed.). Oxford: Clarendon Press.

Goldthorpe, J. et al. (1968): *The Affluent Worker: Industrial Attitudes and Behaviour.* Cambridge: Cambridge University Press.

Goodman, G. (1985): *The Miners' Strike.* London: Pluto Press.

Goodwin, A. (1990): 'TV News: Striking the Right Balance' in *Understanding Television* (eds. A. Goodwin and G. Whannell). London: Routledge.

Spinning for Labour: Trade Unions and the New Media Environment

Gormley, J. (1982): *Battered Cherub*. London: Hamish Hamilton.
Grace, T. (1985): 'The Trade Union Press in Britain'. *Media Culture Society*, 7, April, 233-255.
Grant, W. (1990): *Pressure Groups, Politics and Democracy*. Hemel Hempstead: Philip Allan.
Grant, W. (1987): *Business and Politics in Britain*. Basingstoke: London.
Grant, W. (1985): 'Insiders and Outsiders'. *Social Studies Review*, 1 (1).
Grant, W. (1983): 'Representing Capital', in *Capital and Politics* (King, R. ed.). London: Routledge Kegan-Paul.
Grant, W.and Marsh, D. (1977): *The C.B.I.* London: Hodder and Stoughton.
Grant, W.and Marsh, D. (1976): 'The Representation of Retail Interest in Britain'. *Political Studies*, 22.
Greenberg, D.W. (1985): 'Staging Media Events to Achieve Legitimacy'. *Political Communication and Persuasion*, 2 (4), 347-362.
Griffiths, T. (1977): 'The Production of Trade Union News', in *Trade Unions and the Media* (Beharrell, P. and Philo, G. eds.). London: Macmillan.
Habermas, J. (1989): *The Structural Transformation of the Public Sphere: an Inquiry into a Category of Bourgeois Society*. Cambridge: Polity.
Haque, H. (1990): 'TUC Carthorse Gets Back into the Big Race'. *The Independent*, 8th April, 10-11.
Haines, J. (1977): *The Politics of Power*. London: Jonathan Cape.
Hall, S. (1988): *The Hard Road to Renewal; Thatcherism and the Crisis of the Left*. London: Verso.
Hall, S. (1973): *'The Structured Communication of Events'*. Paper for the Obstacles to Communication Symposium, Unesco Division of Philosophy. C.C.C.S. Occasional Paper, University of Birmingham.
Hall, S. (1971): *Deviancy, Politics and the Media*. C.C.C.S. Occasional Paper. Mimeo, University of Birmingham.
Hall, S. and Jacques, M. (eds.) (1989): *New Times: the Changing Face of Politics in the 1990s*. London: Lawrence and Wishart with Marxism Today.
Hall, S.and Jacques, M. (eds.) (1983): *Thatcherism*. London: Lawrence and Wishart.
Hall, S. et al. (1978): *Policing the Crisis*. London: Macmillan.
Halloran, J.D. et al. (1970): *Demonstratons and Communications: A Case Study*. Harmondsworth: Penquin.
Hammond, E. (1992): *Maverick: the Life of a Trade Union Rebel*. London: Weidenfield and Nicholson.
Harper, K. (1991): 'The Spiking of the Strike Reporters'. *The British Journalism Review*, 2 (4), Summer.
Harper, K. (1990): 'Think Tank for the Shop Floor'. *The Guardian*, 3rd September.
Harrison, M. (1985): *TV News: Whose Bias?* Berkhempstead: Policy Journals.

Hartmann, P. (1979): 'News and Public Perceptions of Industrial Relations'. *Media Culture Society*, **1**, 255-270.

Hartmann, P. (1976): *The Media and Industrial Relations*. Mimeo. Centre for Mass Communication Research, University of Leicester.

Hartmann, P. (1975): 'Industrial Relations in the News Media'. *Industrial Relations Journal*, Winter.

Heery, E. and Kelly, J. (1994): 'Professional, Participative and Managerial Unionism: An Interpretation of Change in Trade Unions'. *Work Employment Society*, **8** (1), March, 1-21.

Hennesey, P. (1985): *What the Papers Never Said*. London: Portcullis Press.

Heseltine, M. (1987): *Where There's a Will*. London: Hutchinson.

Hetherington, A. (1985): *News, Newspapers and Television*. London: Macmillan.

Hill, D. (1993): 'Parting Notes of the Labour Reporter'. *The Guardian*, 6th September.

Hill, S. (1976): *The Dockers*. London: Heinemann.

Hirsch, P.M. (1977): 'Models in Mass Media Research', in *Strategies for Communication Research* (Hirsch, P.M. et al. eds.). Sage Annual Review of Communication Research, volume 6. London: Sage.

Hirst, P. (1987): 'Retrieving Pluralism', in *Social Theory and Social Criticism. Essays for Tom Bottomore* (Outhwaite, T. and Mulkay, M eds.). Oxford: Blackwell.

Hirst, P. (1989): 'After Henry', in *New Times: the Changing Face of Politics in the 1990s* (Hall, S. and Jaques, M. eds.). London: Lawrence and Wisehart.

Howard, A. (1987): *RAB - The Life of R.A. Butler*. London: Jonathan Cape.

Howard, M. (1984): 'Getting the Union Paper Read', in *Labour Daily? The Ins and Outs of a New Labour Daily and Other Media Alternatives* (Power, M. and Sheridan, G. eds.). London: Campaign for Press and Broadcasting Freedom.

Hoyt, M. (1984): 'Downtime for Labor'. *Columbian Journalism Review*, **22**, March, 36-40.

Hoyt, M. (1983): 'Is the Labor Press Doing Its Job?'. *Columbian Journalism Review*, **22**, July, 34-38.

Hutchings, V. (1989): 'Dead on Arrival'. *The New Statesman*, 1st December.

Hutt, C. (1987): 'The Reporting of Industrial Relations on Breakfast-time Television'. *Industrial Relations Journal*, **18**, Summer, 90-99.

Hutton, W. (1993): 'Waging War with the Wrong Weapons'. *The Guardian*, 18th October.

Hyman, R. (1991): 'Plus Ca Change? The Theory of Production and the Production of Theory', in *Farewell to Flexibility?* (Pollert,A. ed.). Oxford: Blackwell.

Hyman, R. (1986): 'British Industrial Relations: the Limits of Corporatism', in

Economic Crisis, Trade Unions and the State (Jacobi, O. et al. eds.). Beckenham: Croom Helm.

Hyman, R. (1985): 'Class Struggle and the Trade Union Movement', in *A Socialist Anatomy of Britain* (Coates, D. et al. eds.). Cambridge: Polity Press.

Hyman, R. (1984): *Strikes*. 4th ed. Ayelsbury: Fontana.

Hyman, R. and Elgar, T. (1981): 'Job Controls: the Employers Offensive.' *Captial and Class*, **15**, 115-149.

Hyman, R. and Price, B. (1979): 'Labour Statistics', in *Demystifying Social Statisitcs* (Irvine, J. et al. eds.). London: Pluto Press.

Hyslop, A.G. (1988): 'Trade Unions and the State Since 1945: Corporatism and Hegemony.' *International Journal of Sociology and Social Policy*, **8** (1), 53-90.

Jenkins, C. and Sherman, B.(1979): *White Collar Unionism: The Rebellious Salariat*. London: Routledge Kegan-Paul.

Jenkins, J. (1987): 'The Green Sheep in Colonel Gaddafi Drive.' *The New Statesman*, 9th January.

Jessop, B. (1990): *State Theory: Putting Capitalist Societies in their Place*. Cambridge: Polity Press.

Jones, B. (1989): 'The Thatcher Style', in *Political Issues in Britain Today* (Jones, B. ed.). Manchester: Manchester University Press.

Jones, D. et al. (1985): *Media Hits the Pits*. London: Campaign for Press and Broadcasting Freedom.

Jones, J. (1986): *Union Man*. London: Collins.

Jones, M. (1984): *Voluntary Organisations and the Media*. London: Bedford Square Press and the National Council for Voluntary Organisations.

Jones, N. (1988): 'Labour Pains.' *UK Press Gazette*, **1133**, 11th January, 11.

Jones, N. (1987): 'Unions Quietly Languish on the Political Sidelines.' *The Listener*, 1st January, 415.

Jones, N. (1986): *Strikes and the Media*. Oxford: Basil Blackwell.

Jordan, G. (1981): 'Iron Triangles, Wooly Corporatism and Elastic Nets.' *Journal of Public Policy*, **1**.

Karpf, A. (1988): *Doctoring the Media*. London: Routledge.

Kavanagh, D. and Jones, B. (1991): British Politics Today. Manchester: Manchester University Press.

Kavanagh, D. (1990): *Thatcherism and British Politics*. Oxford: Oxford University Press.

Kelly, J. (1990): 'British Trade Unionism 1979-1989: Changes, Continuity, and Contradictions.' *Work Employment Society*, Special Issue, 29-65.

Kerr, C. and Seigel, A. (1954): 'The International Industrial Propensity to Strike', *Industrial Conflict* (Kornhauser, A. et al. eds.). New York: McGraw-Hill.

King, J. (1989): 'Polish Up Public Image'. *Community Care*. 16th March.

Kingdon, J. (1984): *Agendas, Alternatives and Public Policies.* Boston: Little Brown and Co.

Kossoff, J. (1988 a): 'Everybody Out'. *Youth in Society.* **142,** September.

Kossoff, J. (1988 b): 'Rejuvenating the Unions'. *New Socialist.* 20th May, 10-11.

Labour Research (1993): 'Unions Not Beyond All Recognition'. **82,** September.

Labour Research (1992a): 'The Union Derecognition Bandwagon.' **81,** November.

Labour Research (1992b): 'Where Union Membership is Best'. **81,** June, 11-12.

Labour Research (1992c): 'New Workers Retain the Strike Weapon'. **81,** June, 4-5.

Labour Research (1992d): 'The Union Busters Charter'. **80,** March, 19-20.

Labour Research (1991a): 'Legal Services- a Union Success'. **80,** November, 4-5.

Labour Research (1991b): 'New Times for Union Journals'. **80,** August, 9.

Labour Research (1990a): 'Are Unions Young at Heart?'. **79,** September, 7-8.

Labour Research (1990b): 'Unions: merger mania?' **79,** June, 9-11.

Labour Research (1988): 'Are Unions Outside the Woman's Realm?' **77,** August, 13-14.

Labour Research (1986): 'Political Funds: A Multiple Victory.' **74,** May, 9-10.

Laclau, E. and Mouffe, C. (1985): *Hegemony and Socialist Strategy.* London: Verso.

Landry, C. et al. (1985): *What a Way to Run a Railroad.* London: Comedia.

Lang, K. and Lang, G.E. (1955): 'The Inferential Structure of Political Communication.' *Public Opinion Quarterly,* 168-183.

Lash, S. and Urry, J. (1987): *The End of Organised Capitalism.* Oxford: Basil Blackwell..

Leadbeater, C. (1989): 'Power to the Person', in *New Times: the Changing Face of Politics in the 1990s* (eds. S. Hall and M. Jacques). London: Lawrence and Wisehart.

Lloyd, J. and Adeney, M. (1986): *Loss Without Limit.* London: Routledge Kegan-Paul.

London Conference of Socialist Economists Group (1980): *The Alternative Economic Strategy. A Labour Response to the Crisis.* London: Conference of Socialist Economists and Labour Co-ordinating Committee.

Longstreth, F. (1988): 'From Corporatism to Dualism? Thatcherism and the Climacteric of British Trade Unions'. *Political Studies,* **xxxvi,** 413-432.

McCarthy, M. (1986): *Campaigning for the Poor.* Beckenham: Croom Helm.

McCombs, M.E. (1994): 'News Influence on Our Pictures of the World', in *Media Effects. Advances in Theory and Research* (Bryant, J. and Zillmann, D. eds.). Hove: Lawrence Erlbaum Associates.

McCombs, M.E. (1977): 'Newspapers Versus Television', in *The Emergence of American Political Issues: the Agenda Setting Function of the Press.*

St Paul, Minnesota: West Publishing Company.

McIlroy, J. (1989): 'Trade Unions and the Law', in *Political Issues in Britain Today* (ed. B. Jones). Manchester: Manchester University Press.

McQuail, D. (1977): *Analysis of Newspaper Content*. Research Series 4 for the Royal Commission on the Press. London: HMSO.

MacGregor, I. (1986): *Enemies Within*. London: Collins.

Machin, F. (1953): 'Ian in the the Lobby', in *The Great Bohunkus* (ed. T. Evans). London: W.H.Allen.

MacInnes, J. (1987): 'Why Nothing Much has Changed: Recession, Economic Restructuring and Industrial Relations Since 1979.' *Employee Relations,* **9** (1), 3-9.

MacInnes, J. (1987): *Thatcherism at Work*. Milton Keynes: Open University Press.

Macmillan, H. (1973): *At the End of the Day. 1961-1963*. London: Macmillan.

Macmillan, H. (1972): *Pointing the Way*. London: Macmillan.

MacShane, D. (1983): *Using the Media*. 2nd Ed. London: Pluto Press.

Manning, P. (1996): *Trade Unions, News Media Strategies and Newspaper Journalists*, Unpublished Ph.D. thesis, University of Loughborough, Loughborough.

Manning, P. (1991): 'The Media and Pressure Politics'. *Social Studies Review,* **6** (4), March.

Manning, P.K. (1986): 'Signwork'. *Human Relations,* **39**, 283-308.

Mansfield, F.J. (1943): *Gentlemen, the Press!* London: W.H. Allen.

Marsh, D. (1983): *Pressure Politics. Interest Groups in Britain*. London: Junction.

Marshall, T. (1977): 'Trouble at Mill', in *Trade Unions and the Media* (eds. P. Beharrell and G. Philo). London: Macmillan.

Mason, B. and Bain, P. (1993): 'The Determination of Trade Union Membership in Britain: a survey of the literature.' *Industrial and Labour Relations Review,* **46** (2), 332-351.

Mason, K. (1981): *Front Seat*. Nottingham: Published by the Author.

May, T.C. (1975): *Trade Unions and Pressure Group Politics*. Farnborough: Saxon House.

Middlemas, K. (1990): *Power, Competition and the State. Volume 2.* Basingstoke: Macmillan.

Middlemas, K. (1986): *Power, Competition and the State*. Basingstoke: Macmillan.

Middlemas, K. (1979): *The Politics of Industrial Society*. London: Andre Deutsch.

Milliband, R. (1991): *Divided Societies*. Oxford: Oxford University Press.

Milliband, R. (1987): 'Class Struggle from Above', in *Social Theory and Social Criticism* (Outhwaite, T. and Mulkay, M. eds.). Oxford: Basil Blackwell.

Milliband, R. (1982): *Capitalist Democracy in Britain*. Oxford: Oxford

University Press.

Milne, S. (1994) *The Enemy Within. The Secret War Against the Miners,* Verso, London

Mitchell, N.J. (1987): 'Where Traditional Tories Fear to Tread'. *West European Politics,* **10** (1), 12-22.

Molotoch, H. and Lester, H. (1974): 'News as Purposive Behaviour'. *American Sociological Review,* **39,** February, 101-112.

Moran, M. (1983): *Politics and Society in Britain.* London: Macmillan.

Moran, M. (1981): 'Finance Capital and Pressure Group Politics'. *British Journal of Political Science,* **11,** 381-404.

Moran, M. (1974): *The Union of Post Office Workers.* London: Macmillan.

Morely, D. (1976): 'Industrial Conflict and the Mass Media'. *Sociological Review,* **24** (2).

Morely, D. (1975): 'The Mass Media and Industrial Conflict'. Mimeo. Birmingham: C.C.C.S. Occasional Paper.

MORI (1993): Survey of Britain's Industrial and Labour Reporters. Unpublished.

Morrison, D. (1987): 'Policing Knowledge: a response to the review of Television and the Miners'Strike'. *Media Culture Society,* **9,** 378-388.

Mosco, V. and Wasco, J. (eds.) (1983): *Critical Communication Review Volume One: Labor, Unions and the Media.* New Jersey: Ablex Corporation.

Murdock, G. (1993): 'Communications and the Constitution of Modernity'. *Media Culture and Society,* **15,** 521-539.

Murdock, G. (1986): 'Misrepresenting Media Sociology: a reply to Anderson and Sharrock'. *Sociology,* **14** (3), 457-468.

Murdock, G. (1982): 'Large Corporations and the Control of the Communication Industries', in *Culture, Society and the Media* (eds. M.Gurevitch et al.). London: Methuen.

Murdock, G. (1980): 'Class Power and the Press; some problems of conceptualisation and evidence', in *The Sociology of Jornalism* (Christian, H. ed.). Sociological Review Monograph, 29. University of Keele.

Myers, K. (1986): *Understains: the Sense and Sensibility of Advertising.* London: Comedia.

Negrine, R. (1993): The Organisation of British Journalism and Specialist Correspondents: A Study of Newspaper Reporting. Centre for Mass Communication Research Occasional Paper No MC9311. University of Leicester.

Neil, A. (1985): Introduction to *Strike: Thatcher, Scargill and the Miners* (Wilsher, P. et al.). London: Andre Deutsch.

Newman, K. (1984): *Financial Marketing and Communication.* London: Holt Rineheart and Winston.

Newell, D. (1989): 'Trade Union Law'. *New Law Journal,* **139,** 15th September,

1234-5.

Newton, K. (1988): 'Politics and the Mass Media'. *Political Studies,* **36**, December, 696-703.

Nichols,T. and Benyon, H. (1977): *Living With Capitalism.* London: Routledge Kegan-Paul.

Offe, C. (1985): *Disorganised Capitalism.* Cambridge: Polity Press.

Ogilvy-Webb, M. (1965): *The Government Explains: A Study of the Information Services.* London: George Allen and Unwin Ltd.

Ohri, S. and Faruqi, S. (1988): 'Racism, Employment and Unemployment', in *Britain's Black Population: A New Perspective* (Bhat, A. et al. eds.). Aldershot: Gower Press.

Paletz, D.L. and Entman, R.M. (1981): *Media Power and Politics.* New York: Free Press.

Parenti, M. (1986): *Inventing Reality: The Politics of the Mass Media.* New York: St Martin's Press.

Parker, P. (1989): *For Starters: the business of life.* London: Jonathan Cape.

Parker, S.R. et al. (1981): *The Sociology of Industry. 4th Ed.* London: George Allen and Unwin.

Parkinson, C. (1992): *Right at the Centre.* London: Weidenfield and Nicholson.

Parsons, D.W. (1989): *The Power of the Financial Press.* Aldershot: Edward Elgar.

Parton, N. (1985): *The Politics of Child Abuse.* Basingstoke: Macmillan.

Pattinson, T. (1993): 'Monsters Wanted'. *New Statesman and Society,* 21st May.

Paynter, W. (1972): *My Generation.* London: George Allen and Unwin.

Paynter, W. (1970): *British Trade Unions and the Prospect of Change. London: George Allen and Unwin.*

Peers, D. and Richards, B. (1986): *Say It With Video.* London: Comedia.

Philo, G. (1993): 'From Buerk to Band Aid: the media and the 1984 Eithopian famine', in *Getting the Message. News Truth and Power* (Eldridge, J. ed.). London: Routledge.

Philo, G. (1990): *Seeing is Believing.* London: Routledge.

Philo, G. (1988): 'Television and the Miners' Strike; A Note on Method'. *Media Culture Society,* **10**, 517-521.

Philo, G. (1987): 'Whose News?' *Media Culture Society,* **9**, 397-406.

Philo, G. (1986): 'Bias and News on T.V.'. *The NATFHE Journal,* **11**, 3rd April.

Philo, G. Beharrell, P. and Hewitt, J. (1977): 'Strategies and Policies', in *Trade Unions and the Media* (Philo, G. and Beharrell, P. eds.). London: Macmillan.

Philo, G. and Hewitt, J. (1976): 'Trade Unions and the Media.' *Industrial Relations Journal,* **7** (3), 4-19.

Pomper, G. (1959): 'The Public Relations of Labor'. *Public Opinion Quarterly,* **23**, 483-494.

Potter, A. (1961): *Organised Groups in Britain.* London: Faber.

Power, M. and Sheridan, G. (eds.) (1984): *Labour Daily ?* London: Campaign for Press and Broadcasting Freedom.

Prior, J. (1986): *A Balance of Power.* London: Hamish Hamilton.

Puette, W. (1992): *Through Jaundiced Eyes.* Ithaca, New York: I.L.R. Press.

Raelin, J.A. (1989): 'Unionisation and Deprofessionalisation: which comes first?' *Journal of Organisational Behaviour,* **10**, April, 101-15.

Richardson, J.J. and Jordan, A.G. (1985): *Governing Under Pressure.* Oxford: Basil Blackwell.

Riddell, P. (1989): *The Thatcher Decade.* Oxford: Basil Blackwell.

Riddell, P. (1983): *The Thatcher Government.* Oxford: Martin Robertson.

Riley, N. (1993): 'Communication Strategies for Trade Unions'. Paper presented to the 'Unions 93 Conference'. 22nd May, London.

Roiser, M. and Little, T. (1986): 'Public Opinion, Trade Unions and Industrial Relations'. *Journal of Occupational Psychology,* **59**, 259-272.

Rollings, J. (1983): 'Mass Communication and the American Worker', in *Labor the Working Class and the Media* (Mosco, V. and Wasco, J. eds.). Norwood, New Jersey: Ablex Corp.

Romano, C. (1987): 'The Grisly Truth About Bare Facts', in *Reading the News* (eds. R. Manoff and M. Schudson). London: Pantheon.

Rose, R. (1974): *Politics in England Today.* (2nd ed. 1989). London: Faber.

Rubery, J. (1986): 'The Trade Unions in the 1980s. The Case of the U.K.', in *Unions in Crisis and Beyond* (eds. R. Edwards et al.). Aldershot: Auburn Publishing House.

Rustin, M. (1989): 'The Trouble with New Times', in *New Times. The Changing Face of Politics in the 1990s* (eds. S. Hall and M. Jacques). London: Lawrence and Wisehart.

Sapper, A. (1983): 'Media Workers in the Front Line', in *The Critical Communication Review Volume One* (Mosco, V. and Wasko, J. eds.). New Jersey: Ablex Publishing Corporation.

Sapper, A. (1977): 'Opening the Box - The Unions Inside Television', in *Trade Unions and the Media* (Beharrell, P. and Philo, G. eds.). London: Macmillan.

Sapper, S. (1991): 'Do Membership Service Packages Influence Trade Union Recruitment?' *Industrial Relations Journal,* **22** (4), Winter.

Sayer, D. (1989): 'Post-Fordism'. *International Journal of Urban and Regional Research,* **13** (4), 666-695.

Schlesinger, P. (1990): 'Rethinking the Sociology of Journalism: source strategies and the limits of media centrism', in *Public Communication: the new imperatives* (ed. M. Ferguson). London: Sage.

Schlesinger, P.(1989): 'From Production to Propaganda?' *Media Culture Society*, **11**, 283-306.

Schlesinger, P. (1980): 'Between Sociology and Journalism', in *The Sociology of Journalism. Sociological Review Monograph 29* (ed. H. Christian). Staffordshire: University of Keele.

Schlesinger, P. (1978): *Putting Reality Together*. London: Constable.

Schlesinger, P. et al. (1991): 'The Media Politics of Crime and Criminal Justice'. *British Journal of Sociology*, **42** (3), 399-420.

Schudson, M. (1989): 'The Sociology of News Production.' *Media Culture and Society*, **11** , 263-282.

Scott, A. (1990): *The New Social Movements*. London: Routledge.

Scott, W.A. (1955): 'Reliability of Content Analysis: the Case of Nominal Scale Coding.' *Public Opinion Quarterly*, **19**, Fall, 321-325.

Seaton, J. (1982): 'Trade Unions and the Media', in *Trade Unions in British Politics* (Pimlott, B. and Cook, C. eds.). London: Longman.

Seaton, J. and Pimlott, B. (eds.) (1987): *The Media in British Politics*. Aldershot: Gower Press.

Selvin, D.F. (1963): 'Communications in Trade Unions'. *British Journal of Industrial Relations*, February, 73-93.

Seyd, P. (1976): 'The Child Poverty Action Group'. *Political Quarterly*, **47**, 189-202.

Seyd, P. (1975): 'Shelter: The National Campaign for the Homeless'. *Political Quarterly*, **46**, 418-431.

Seymour-Ure, C. (1987): 'Leaders', in *The Media in British Politics* (Seaton, J. and Pimlott, B. eds.). Aldershot: Gower Press.

Shaw, D.L. (1977): 'The Press in a Community Setting', in *The Emergence of American Political Issues: The Agenda-Setting Function* (Shaw, D.L. and McCombs, M.E. eds.). St Paul, Minnesota: West Publishing Company.

Shaw, D.L. and Clemmer,C. (1977): 'News and the Public Response', in *The Emergence of American Political Issues: the Agenda-Setting Function* (Shaw, D.L. and McCombs, M.E. eds.). St Paul, Minnesota: West Publishing.

Shaw, D.L. and McCombs, M.E. (1977): *The Emergence of American Political Issues: The Agenda-Setting Function*. St Paul, Minnesota: West Publishing Company.

Sherman, B. (1986): *The State of the Unions*. Chichester: John Wiley and Sons.

Short, E. (1989): *Whip to Wilson. The Crucial Years of Labour Government*. London: MacDonald.

Sigal, L.V. (1973): *Reporters and Officials*. Lexington, Mass.: D.C. Heath.

Skirrow, G. (1980): 'More Bad News - A Review of the Reviews'. *Screen*, **21** (2), 95-99.

Smith, M. (1993): *Pressure Power and Policy*. Hemel Hempstead: Harvester

Wheatsheaf.

Smith, P. and Morton, G. (1993): 'Union Exclusion and the Decollectivisation of Industrial Relations in Contemporary Britain'. *British Journal of Industrial Relations,* **31** (1), March.

Social Trends (1995): *Social Trends 25.* London: HMSO.

Sparks, C. (1992): 'The Popular Press and Political Democracy', in *Culture and Power* (Scannell, P. et al. eds.). London: Sage.

Sparks, C. (1987): 'Striking Results?' *Media Culture Society,* **9** (3), 369-377.

Sparks, C. (1985): 'The Working Class Press: radical and revolutionary alternatives'. *Media Culture Society,* **7**, 133-146.

Streeck, W. (1987): 'The Uncertainty of Management in the Management of Uncertaintity: employers, labour relations and industrial adjustment in the 1980s.' *Work Employment Society,* **1**, September, 281-308.

Taylor, R. (1982): 'The Trade Union Problem Since 1960', in *Trade Unions in British Politics* (Pimlott, B. and Cook, C. eds.). London: Longman.

Taylor, R. (1978): *Fifth Estate.* London: Routledge Kegan-Paul.

Torrode, J. (1985): 'Don't Blame the Organ Grinder - Try the Monkey'. *The Guardian,* 11th June.

Tracey, H. (1953): 'Merchant of Light', in *The Great Bohunkus* (ed. T. Evans). London: W.H. Allen.

Trade Union Congress (1992): *Making the Most of Local Radio.* Conference Summary. London: Trade Union Congress.

Trade Union Congress (1986a): *Guidelines on the Use of Opinion Poll Data.* London: Trade Union Congress.

Trade Union Congress (1986b): *Guidelines on the Use of Audio-visual Material.* London: Trade Union Congress.

Trade Union Congress (1985): *Guidelines on Advertising.* London: Trade Union Congress.

Trade Union Congress (1983): *The Other Side of the Story.* London: Trade Union Congress.

Trade Union Congress (1981): *Behind the Headlines.* London: Trade Union Congress.

Trade Union Congress (1980): TUC Campaign Bulletin. Using the Local Media. London: Trade Union Congress.

Trade Union Congress (1979a): *A Cause for Concern,* London: Trade Union Congress.

Trade Union Congress (1979b): *How to Handle the Media.* London: Trade Union Congress.

Trade Union Congress (1977): *Trade Councils and the Media: notes for trade councils and county associations.* London: Trade Union Congress.

Trade Union Congress Standing Conference of Principal Union Officers (1985): *TUC Strategy: Union Comunications.* Conference Paper, 24th January. Unpublished.

Tremayne, C. (1980): 'The Social Organisation of Newspaper Houses', in *The Sociology of Journalism. Sociological Review Monograph*, 29 (ed. H. Christian). Staffordshire: University of Keele.

Tuchman, G. (1978) : *Making News: a Study in the Construction of Reality*. New York: Free Press.

Tuchman, G. (1977): 'The Exception Proves the Rule', in *Strategies for Communication Research* (Hirsch, P. et al. eds.). Sage Annual Review of Communication Research volume 6. London: Sage.

Tuchman, G. (1972): 'Objectivity as a Strategic Ritual: an analysis of Newsmen's Notions of Objecitivity'. *Ameriacan Journal of Sociology*, 77 (4), 660-678.

Tunstall, J. (1971): *Journalists at Work*. London: Constable.

Van Dijk, T. (1991): *Racism and the Press*. London: Routledge.

Verzuh, R. (1990): *Changing Times: British Trade Union Communication Under Thatcher*. Ottawa: Canadian Union of Public Employees.

Walder, L. (1991): 'Public Relations and Social Services. A View From the Statutory Sector', in *Social Work, the Media and Public Relations* (Franklin, B. and Parton, N. eds.). London: Routledge.

Walker, R. (1953): 'Tribute to Ian McKay', in *The Great Bohunkus* (Evans, T. ed). London: W.H. Allen.

Walsh, G. (1988): 'Trade Unions and the Media'. *International Labour Review*, 127 (2), 205-220.

Walton, P. and Davis, H. (1977): 'Bad News for Trade Unionists', in *Trade Unions and the Media* (Beharrell, P. and Philo, G.eds.). London: Macmillan.

Wasco, J. (1983): 'Trade Unions and Broadcasting: A Case Study of the National Association of Broadcast Employees and Technicians', in *The Critical Communication Review Volume One: Labor, the Working Class and the Media* (eds. V. Mosco and J. Wasco). New Jersey: Ablex.

Weighell, S. (1983): *On the Rails*. London: Orbis Publishers .

White, D.M. (1950): 'The Gatekeeper: a Study in the Selection of News'. *Journalism Quarterly*, 27, Fall, 383-390.

Whitely, P. and Winyard, S. (1983): 'Influencing Social Policy'. *Journal of Social Policy*, 12 (1), 1-26.

Wickens, P. (1987): *The Road to Nissan*. London: Macmillan.

Wigham, E. (1969): *Trade Unions*. London: Oxford University Press.

Wigham, E. (1961): *What's Wrong With the Unions?* Harmondsworth: Penquin.

Willman, P. (1989): 'The Logic of Market Share Trade Unionism: Is Membership Decline Inevitable?' *Industrial Relations Journal*, 20, Winter, 360-370.

Wilsher, P. et al. (1985): *Thatcher, Scargill and the Miners*. London: Andre Deutsch.

Wilson, H. (1979): *The Final Term*. London: Weidenfeld and Nicholson with Michael Joseph.

Wilson, H. (1971): *The Labour Government 1964-70. A Personal Record.* London: Weidenfeld and Nicholson with Michael Joseph.

Winston, B. (1983): 'On Counting the Wrong Things', in *The Critical Communication Review Volume One* (eds. V. Mosco and J. Wasco). New Jersey: Ablex Publishing Corporation.

Winterton, J. and Winterton, R. (1989): *Coal Crisis and Conflict*. Manchester: Manchester University Press.

Wood, R.C. (1994): 'Extended Review: Post Modernism (Review of Lash, S. and Urry, J. The Economics of Signs and Space)'. *Work Employment and Society*, **8** (3), September, 459-463.

Woolas, P. (1990): 'Televisions' First aid'. *New Socialist*, April / May.

Young, H. (1993): 'Shameful Saga Shows Up a Politically Sick Society'. *The Guardian*, 27th May.

Index